Supervising the Coun
and Psychotherapist

Supervising the Counsellor and Psychotherapist considers how to meet the supervision needs of trainee and experienced counsellors, psychotherapists and other helping professionals using an integrative approach that will appeal to practitioners from a broad range of theoretical persuasions. The book charts the development of the supervisor as they make the transition from therapist to supervising the work of others and includes consideration of the advanced competencies required to supervise experienced practitioners.

This third edition brings a number of contemporary perspectives to a well-known and widely respected core text for the training and development of supervisors. The Cyclical Model at the heart of the book has established its relevance as one of the best-known frameworks for teaching and learning the steps and stages of supervision. All chapters in this new edition have been extensively updated, and key elements include:

- two brand new chapters on deepening supervision practice and moving beyond supervising counsellors and psychotherapists;
- updates on recent developments in supervision;
- creativity, play and the use of metaphor and imagery in supervision;
- developing the use of self through relational supervision.

Supervising the Counsellor and Psychotherapist is a key text for trainee and experienced supervisors of counsellors and psychotherapists, those who train supervisors and supervisees wishing to better understand the supervisory process.

Steve Page is an experienced counsellor, supervisor, trainer, consultant, manager and coach, and a member of the British Association for Counselling and Psychotherapy, the Association for Coaching and the Institute for Leadership and Management. He currently works in independent practice near York and is the author of *The Shadow and the Counsellor* (Routledge, 1999). His website can be found at www.steve-page-yorks.co.uk.

Val Wosket is a former senior lecturer in counselling at York St John University, now working in independent practice. She is a BACP Registered Senior Accredited counsellor, psychotherapist and supervisor, and is a past teaching faculty member of the International Society for the Study of Trauma and Dissociation and a visiting tutor on the supervision training programme at the University of Strathclyde. Her previous publications include *The Therapeutic Use of Self* (Routledge, 1999) and *Egan's Skilled Helper Model* (Routledge, 2006).

Supervising the Counsellor and Psychotherapist

A cyclical model

Third Edition

Steve Page and Val Wosket

Routledge
Taylor & Francis Group

LONDON AND NEW YORK

Third edition published 2015
by Routledge
27 Church Road, Hove, East Sussex, BN3 2FA

and by Routledge
711 Third Avenue, New York, NY 10017

Routledge is an imprint of the Taylor & Francis Group, an informa business

First edition published by Routledge 1994

Second edition published by Brunner-Routledge 2001

British Library Cataloguing in Publication Data
A catalogue record for this book is available from the British Library

Library of Congress Cataloging-in-Publication Data
Supervising the counsellor and psychotherapist: a cyclical model / Steve
Page and Val Wosket. – Third edition.
    page cm
    Includes bibliographical references and index.
    1. Counselors—Supervision of. 2. Psychotherapists—Supervision of.
    I. Wosket, Val, 1954– II. Title.
    RC480.5.P24 2014
    616.89'14—dc 23   2014005247

ISBN: 978–0–415–59565–0 (hbk)
ISBN: 978–0–415–59566–7 (pbk)
ISBN: 978–1–315–76130–5 (ebk)

Typeset in Times
by Keystroke, Station Road, Codsall, Wolverhampton

For Paul and Sarah

Contents

Figures

Tables

Preface

When the first and, to some extent, the second editions of *Supervising the Counsellor* were published the research and literature on clinical supervision were relatively sparse within the broader field of counselling and psychotherapy studies. Since publication of the first edition of this book in 1994 there has been an exponential growth in supervision books, articles, research and informed commentaries (Bernard 2006). The third edition of this volume aims to reflect this trend and bring a number of contemporary perspectives to the theory and practice of clinical supervision.

There is a trend amongst editors of counselling and supervision journals to encourage studies that consider how supervision research may be conducted and applied in ways that make a difference to practitioners (Borders 2006). We have followed this trend in attempting a broad review of current supervision research and literature mainly in the UK and North America that offers helpful perspectives on research-informed practice.

All chapters published in previous editions of this volume have been extensively revised and updated, drawing on contemporary published sources and our own specific interests and professional development in the supervision field. We have attempted a reasonably comprehensive (though by no means exhaustive) survey of recent literature and research studies, and have summarized and applied this to our discussion and recommendations. Several hundred new supervision studies and publications are referenced and discussed. In this sense our text is grounded in research and critical thinking that extends beyond our own subjective views (although these are clearly evident too). Above all we have tried to maintain our primary focus on the practice of supervision, seen as a key feature of previous editions (Henderson 2007), through including numerous case examples to illustrate theoretical concepts.

Additional material for this edition includes:

- new chapters on deepening supervision practice and going beyond supervising counsellors and psychotherapists;
- key research findings looking at the difference that clinical supervision makes to therapists and their clients;

- sections on the use of technology in supervision and on supervising short-term work;
- consideration of the implications of the UK Equality Act for supervisors;
- clinical responsibility and relational ethics in supervision;
- consideration of supervision as a transformative process;
- encountering the mysterious and unexpected in supervision;
- developing the use of self in supervision;
- working with embodied and dissociative processes in supervision;
- working with shame in supervision;
- extended sections on creativity, play and the use of metaphor and imagery in supervision;
- fuller consideration of the supervision needs and experiences of therapists who work with extreme trauma;
- working with supervisees' personal and life issues in supervision;
- suggestions for working creatively in group supervision;
- supervising those who are not counsellors or psychotherapists;
- consideration of overlaps and distinctions between supervision, coaching and mentoring;
- many new examples taken from our supervision practice to illustrate key points.

We have aimed to produce a text that is scholarly without being impenetrable, that is grounded in theory and research without being stultifying, and that is practical without being simplistic. We hope we have infused our consideration of the supervision literature with enough clinical examples to bring the text alive and enable readers to relate the discussion to their own supervision experience, interests and dilemmas. As in previous editions, the Cyclical Model is presented as a framework for the development of an integrative approach to supervision, rather than a prescriptive set of instructions for 'how to do' supervision.

The title of this third edition has been changed for three reasons. Firstly, to reflect the lessening distinction made by many within the profession between counselling and psychotherapy, as exemplified by the change of name, in 2000, of the 'British Association for Counselling' to the 'British Association for Counselling and Psychotherapy'. Secondly, we wish to acknowledge that some of the work we describe (especially in Chapters 12 and 13) may be particularly relevant to practitioners who identify themselves, whether by dint of their training, experience or role, as psychotherapists rather than counsellors. Thirdly, we draw on research and other literature about supervision across a wide range of helping professions, but predominantly relating to both counsellors and psychotherapists.

Where detailed examples of our supervision work are included this is done with the permission of our supervisees. All identifying features have been changed or removed to ensure confidentiality and to preserve the anonymity of supervisees and their clients.

Acknowledgements

Val

I would like to thank Sue Richardson, Morna Rutherford and Linda Garbutt for so generously sharing their research, writing and wisdom about supervision.

I am indebted to my supervisees for teaching me most of what I know about supervision. In particular I would like to thank those colleagues who gave permission for me to use material from our supervision sessions to illustrate, and thereby immeasurably enrich, this volume.

Steve

I would like to thank all my supervisees, many of whom appear in examples (with their permission), in particular most recently Fran Kissack, Lenore Klassen and John Holt. I am very grateful to Joan Wilmot, my peer supervisor, for her many insights and also the members of my co-coaching group, Felicia McCormick, Helen Savage and Alison Sherratt, with whom I shared a fascinating journey.

I am thankful to Lois Gregory for her helpful comments on the chapter on difference and diversity, and also to Jill Burns and Caroline Jesper from York St John University for sharing their reflections on some of their current challenges as supervisor trainers. I would also like to thank staff at the University of York Library and the British Library Reading Room, Boston Spa, for their help whenever I floundered whilst seeking sources.

Finally, I am immensely grateful to Sarah, my wife, for her unwavering support, practical help and patience with what turned into a lengthy and very absorbing project.

Chapter 1

An historical overview

In this first chapter we will attempt to place supervision in its historical context in order to identify the source of some aspects of the role and to capture the sense of supervision being in a process of development. We will begin by identifying a number of the roots and various influences that have affected its evolution.

We find that supervision originated in 1902 as part of the informal meetings of 'The Wednesday Night Psychological Society' held at Sigmund Freud's home. Freud's authoritative approach, consistent with classic psychoanalytical therapy, comprised the conveying of knowledge and truth 'downward to the supervisee, who, no matter how bright and creative, is to receive rather than co-construct what becomes known' (Frawley-O'Dea and Sarnat 2001:16). Fleming and Benedek ([1966] 1983) describe the development of psychoanalytic supervision from the 1920s through to the mid-1960s. Apparently, within psychoanalysis, supervision was an integral part of the training process that complemented the theoretical teaching and the analysis of the fledgling analyst (Buckley *et al.* 1982).

These three elements (supervision, teaching and personal analysis) of the training process were made a formal requirement by the International Training Commission in the 1920s (Feltham 2000). Thus what had started out in 1902 as, to quote Freud, 'a number of young doctors gathered around me with the express intention of learning, practising and spreading the knowledge of psychoanalysis' (Freud [1914] 1986:82) moved through informal apprenticeship to a training structure that provides the basic components used in many current training programmes in psychoanalysis, psychotherapy, counselling and allied fields.

It is important to note that in this precise context we are referring to *trainee supervision*; that is, supervision that is part of the process of preparing the fledging practitioner. This should not be confused with supervision of someone who has completed their formal training, which we shall term *practitioner supervision*. This is an important distinction as there are many differences between, for example, supervising a second-year trainee and supervising a therapist with 20 years' experience. A trainee therapist is likely to be concerned with issues of technique, forming effective therapeutic relationships, case conceptualization, boundary issues, understanding the material the client brings, and dealing with personal feelings of anxiety and perhaps inadequacy. The experienced practitioner is more likely to be concerned with: teasing out and working with relationship dynamics, including parallel processes (see below); containing and understanding complex processes such as attachment and dependency; choosing nuanced intervention options; dealing with strong feelings (in self and client); and, as we shall consider further in Chapter 12, exploring how their personal life issues and their professional issues overlap and intertwine.

This distinction is often not made in the literature and it is quite usual for the term 'supervision' to be used when what is being described is restricted to what we are calling 'trainee supervision'. This is particularly the case in supervision literature from the United States although there is limited evidence of attention being given to supervision for more experienced practitioners. We find Rogers (1951) encouraging this as far back as the early 1950s. Although all the specific references he makes to supervision refer to trainee supervision, he does also propose the usefulness of a resource person, someone with whom an experienced counsellor can consult. More recently we have seen North American authors such as Gold (2006) and Veach (2001) advocating ongoing supervision as essential for psychotherapists to help with skills development, the management of ethical and boundary issues, and the complexities of dynamics in therapeutic relationships, including transference and counter-transference. Borders (2006) notes that, increasingly, a requirement for ongoing supervision is linked to professional licensure in the United States and that training requirements for clinical supervisors are becoming the norm.

We can trace the requirement that all practitioner members of the British Association for Counselling and Psychotherapy (BACP) be in supervision regardless of their length of experience back to at least 1992 (BAC 1992). This created quite a sizeable demand for counsellor supervision in the United Kingdom, which increased as the proportion of practitioners with significant experience grew. The role of supervisor is one of the developments to have emerged out of the professionalization of counselling and psychotherapy, which includes the recent (voluntary) registration of BACP therapists.

Interest in the development of supervision amongst experienced therapists in Europe, America and Australasia has continued to grow (Bond 2000; Rønnestad and Skovholt 2013; Watkins 2013). In Europe there seems to be an increasing openness to supervision across professions, whereby supervisors are less restricted to working principally within their 'home' profession (Bond 2010). In Australasia and North America, as reported by Bond (2010), developments in multicultural counselling appear to be creating opportunities for supervision to play an increasingly important role in supporting therapists in acquiring culturally informed and sensitive ways of working.

The evolution of supervision models and approaches

To begin with, approaches to supervision tended to take the theory and practice of a counselling or psychotherapy model and then apply the principles and processes of that approach to the practice of supervision (Friedlander *et al.* 1989; Hart 1982). Thus a psychodynamic supervisor would be inclined to interpret the material being presented and would use an awareness of the relationship dynamics between herself and the supervisee as a means of supervising (Bradley and Gould 2001; Driver and Martin 2002, 2005; O'Shaughnessy *et al.* 2010). A client-centred supervisor would be concerned to convey the core conditions of acceptance, respect and genuineness to his supervisee (Frankland 2001; Lambers 2000, 2006; Tudor and Worrall 2004). The cognitive behavioural supervisor would use methods such as goal clarification and action planning with the therapists she supervises (Ricketts and Donohoe 2000).

As the number of counselling and psychotherapy approaches increased, an increase in the use of these approaches as a basis for supervision developed, as expounded and updated in anthologies such as Bradley (1989), Hess (1980), Ladany and Bradley (2010) and Watkins (1997). Using an approach to counselling or psychotherapy as a model for supervision has the attraction of both being familiar to the supervisor and, usually, providing the therapist with a model that also fits her own practice. There is certainly a compelling argument for trainee counsellors and psychotherapists to be supervised by a practitioner who is thoroughly experienced in using the approach in which the therapist is being trained. This offers consistency and an opportunity to examine in detail the technique of the therapist and how she is applying the approach in practice. Goodyear and Bradley (1983) however provide a cautionary note for the supervisor who is all too ready to fall back on tried and trusted counselling theory in the practice of supervision: 'As a mental road map, theory focuses supervisors' attention and guides their action, but can also blind them to phenomena that are not charted on that map' (p. 63).

A further drawback of therapy-related models of supervision, as Bernard (2006) has pointed out, is that (depending on the approach) attention may be focused on learning the microskills of an approach and diverted away from the supervisory relationship. There is also the danger of confusion where supervision is based upon a therapeutic model. Let us consider an example. During supervision of a counsellor's work with a depressed client whose marriage is breaking up the supervisee mentions that he has invited the client 'out for a pint to cheer him up'. The *supervisor* in this case has a responsibility to explore and challenge the counsellor's actions as there is the danger here of an unhelpful blurring between a therapeutic and social relationship. This is quite different to an intervention a *counsellor* might make if his client mentions having asked a depressed friend out for drink.

Unless the differences between supervision and therapy are clear, for both supervisor and therapist in the above example, there are two possible dangers. If the *supervisor* is not clear about the differences then she may simply avoid confronting the counsellor, preferring to offer, for example, empathy or inter-pretation and as such fail to discharge her responsibility to monitor client safety. Let us assume that the supervisor does act and challenges the supervisee to change his behaviour, while giving a clear ethical rationale for this. If the *supervisee* is not clear about the differences between counselling and supervision he might take the supervisor's behaviour as a model for how he should behave with clients and start to become excessively challenging or directive. It is important therefore that the supervisor ensures that her supervisees understand the distinctions between these roles so that inappropriate role modelling is discouraged. A number of key differences between therapy and supervision are outlined in Table 2.1 on page 19.

Developmental models of supervision

A new strand in the evolution of supervision emerged when Hogan (1964) published his paper on the four stages of the development of the psychotherapist. This paper stimulated something of a plethora of developmental supervision models – according to Borders (1989) an estimated 25 models had been published by 1988. Subsequently this stream of developmental models slowed to a trickle and Stoltenberg and colleagues, in their comprehensive review of supervision research (1994), could find only one major developmental model of supervision proposed between 1987 and 1994. However, a recent third edition of the seminal text on the main developmental model provides some testimony to the enduring usefulness of this approach (Stoltenberg and McNeill 2010) and there is evidence (discussed below) that contemporary, creative adaptations of developmental models are giving them a new lease of life.

Initially, developmental models were based on the rationale that supervisors need to acquire a range of styles and approaches that are adapted to the individual needs of the trainee therapist as he or she moves through a sequence of, for the most part, clearly definable developmental stages. The different stages were seen as describing a more-or-less linear process of growth in competence and awareness through which the therapist moves on his or her journey from novice to 'master' practitioner. This development was understood to follow a natural and normally predictable pattern while allowing for occasional relapses to an earlier stage.

Exponents of the developmental approach argued that the supervisor could be trained (or at least alerted) to address the supervisee's particular developmental needs through a specific set of competencies matched to: the supervisee's level of therapeutic skills; their capacity to conceptualize the counselling task and process; their personal and professional development; and their awareness of the dynamics of the counselling relationship. So, for example, in Stoltenberg and Delworth's (1987) model (later revised with McNeill in 1998 and reformulated by Stoltenberg and McNeill in 2010) 'Level 1' supervisees tended to be seen as highly motivated but anxious and largely dependent on the supervisor, who therefore needed to provide a clearly structured and supportive environment where positive feedback and encouragement could allow the supervisee to begin to lessen his or her anxiety about 'getting it right'. We have summarized the four stages of this model of counsellor development together with recommended supervisor behaviours and styles of intervention in Table 1.1.

Table 1.1 Developmental stages of counsellor supervision, adapted from Stoltenberg and McNeill (2010)

Developmental stage of counsellor	*Supervisor interventions and behaviours*
Level 1 Limited knowledge of theory and technique. Highly motivated, whilst also anxious, confused and dependent on the supervisor. Awareness of self and others may be limited, although focus on self (often negative) may be intense. Low professional self-concept. Evaluation and performance anxiety. Desire to emulate experienced therapists/ supervisors. Concern with micro skills and specific interventions and applying these prescriptively. Confidence and skills begin to increase with experience and facilitative supervision.	**Level 1** Provides clearly structured and supportive environment. Has an educative function and shares knowledge about techniques and when they should be applied. Encourages supervisee to gain experience and understanding of difference and diversity across cultures. Suggests suitable intervention strategies and helps supervisee structure clinical work. Encourages risk-taking, intentionality and integration of theory and practice. Acts as professional role model. Focuses on relationship skills. Gives guidance on the management of boundaries and professional ethics. Encourages problem solving. Supports growth of autonomy.
Level 2 Motivation fluctuates. Moves between autonomy and dependence on the supervisor. Swings between over-confidence and overwhelm in response to increased awareness of the complexity of therapy. Increasingly self-assertive. Less focus on self and more on client. Growth in empathy apparent with more attention on understanding the client (verbally and nonverbally). Beginning to develop own identity and experiment with range of interventions and techniques. Dependency–autonomy conflict reduces as sense of competency increases.	**Level 2** Needs to provide emotional containment while becoming less structured and didactic. Encourages autonomy. Tolerance of possible misdirected anger and resentment triggered by supervisee's ambivalent feelings. Encourages appropriate balance between focus on self and focus on client's perspective. Encourages growth of sensitivity to diversity of client experience. Supports reflective practice and growth of therapeutic use of self. Draws attention to process and relationship dynamics. More challenging.
Level 3 Increased autonomy, self-confidence and self-awareness. More secure sense of professional identity. Motivation more stable and greater understanding and acceptance of strengths and weaknesses. Practice becomes more efficient and effective as positive experience of casework builds. Detailed knowledge of and ability to be guided by ethical frameworks. Increased creativity, flexibility and experimentation,	**Level 3** Supervision agenda and structure mostly provided by supervisee. More collaborative approach that can accommodate confrontation while remaining supportive. Increasing attention paid to parallel processes in supervision and counselling. Focus on personal and professional integration. Supervisor respects and encourages development of supervisee's personal orientation and style of working. Prescriptive

Table 1.1 Continued

Developmental stage of counsellor	Supervisor interventions and behaviours
including more therapeutic use of self. More open to insights from other theoretical perspectives. Retains fuller clinical responsibility for own work, and supervision viewed as more equal and collegial.	interventions rarely used. Specific areas for development are addressed as they arise. Supervisor may feel more challenged by supervisee on a number of levels (including their knowledge and expertise and the supervisee's expectations of supervision).
Level 3i (Integrative) A level not achieved by all. Therapist becomes fully functioning in their chosen field and is regarded as expert by colleagues. Characterized by high levels of professional autonomy, insightful awareness, personal security, stable motivation and self-challenge. Able to monitor impact of personal life changes and integrate these into therapeutic approach and sense of professional identity. Focus on specialist area(s) of practice may develop (possibly necessitating a revisit to level 1 or 2 issues). May become a supervisor in own right.	**Level 3i (Integrative)** Supervision is regarded as beneficial but is not mandated. Often supplemented or replaced by mutual consultation with a same-level colleague when deemed necessary by the supervisee.

Developmental models are attractive because they have been specifically designed for supervision and because they clearly make sense in terms of an educational process. There have been a number of research studies concerned with evaluating the validity of developmental models (e.g. Ashby 1999; Ellis and Dell 1986; Heppner and Roehlke 1984; Leach *et al.* 1997; Rabinowitz *et al.* 1986; Stoltenberg *et al.* 1994, 1995; Tracey *et al.* 1989; Wiley and Ray 1986). In general terms these studies found some empirical evidence for a developmental process, but also revealed that there is a complex set of factors influencing that process which do not fit neatly into a simple model. A relatively recent research study into supervisees' preferences (Gazzola and Theriault 2007) found that while the structure of developmental models can reduce a trainee's anxiety, supervisees in this study (numbering ten at masters level) were found to prefer 'flexibility and reciprocity in their interactions with supervisors' over a set structure (p. 200).

In our view a developmental framework is a helpful tool for a supervisor to have at their disposal, but it should be used with discrimination and in conjunction with other tools. Such a framework is certainly a useful reminder that the therapist is in her own learning process and the supervisor's expectations of her should be

tailored accordingly. It provides a means of monitoring the supervisee's development and is a useful reminder to the supervisor of his responsibility to facilitate
the therapist's continuing growth.

On occasions, having a developmental framework in mind can be helpful in
deciding whether or not to make an intervention. For example, if a relatively
inexperienced counsellor is struggling to get a client to leave when the session time
has finished, there are a number of choices open to the supervisor. She could
encourage the counsellor to define strategies to get the client to go. She could focus
on the implications for the counsellor in terms of his own boundary management
or his reluctance to assert his needs. She could introduce questions about what this
behaviour might indicate about the client, the dynamics of the therapeutic
relationship or how the process is unfolding. The developmental level of the counsellor would be one of a number of factors that would influence the supervisor's
choice. However, other factors less central to a developmental model, such as the
counselling approach being used, what the supervisor already knows about this
counsellor or this client and what has already been tried, would also play a part in
determining how to proceed.

Used on their own, developmental models can suffer from over-simplification,
when in practice the development of a therapist is a complex process (Ellis 2010;
Reising and Daniels 1983). Another limitation of many developmental models is
that they are focused on the development of the therapist and pay insufficient
attention to the development of the supervisor (Worthington 1987). It may appear
as if the supervisor is an expert who has arrived at a plateau of understanding. This
is quite inconsistent with a developmental view that must allow that the supervisor
is also in a process of learning in parallel with the supervisee.

The third main limitation of developmental models is that they mainly focus on
the trainee therapist. As such they become decreasingly useful as the supervisee
becomes more experienced. This is a reflection of the fact that the majority of the
developmental models have originated in the United States, where supervision
remains largely focused upon trainees. For the reasons already stated there is more
of an emphasis on practitioner supervision in the United Kingdom. Revised editions
of Stoltenberg and Delworth's Developmental Model (Stoltenberg *et al.* 1998;
Stoltenberg and McNeill 2010) have addressed a number of these limitations.

Some recent adaptations of developmental models continue to attest to their
enduring relevance and popularity as frameworks for tracking the supervisory
process. Wittman and Tucker (in Smith-Adcock *et al.* 2010) have applied the
stages identified in developmental models of supervision to the use of sandplay in
supervision. Young and colleagues (2011) have developed a model of 'reflective,
developmental supervision' that draws extensively on Stoltenberg and McNeill's
(2010) developmental model. Garbutt (2009) has integrated stages identified in
developmental models within a supervision approach that uses reflective writing
and draws on the concept of the 'internal supervisor'.

Rønnestad and Skovholt (2013) have recently produced a more layered developmental model based on their own research and which they term a 'develop-

mentally sensitive approach to supervision' (p. 176). In their model they advocate an approach that prioritizes observing general principles of supervision across all levels while at the same time giving explicit recommendations for level-specific supervisory interventions. So, for example, they recommend for the novice practitioner that 'the supervisor creates a reflective culture in supervision (general specific principle) while also providing structure, direction and a skill focus' (level-specific interventions) (Rønnestad and Skovholt 2013: 176–7). In this respect Rønnestad and Skovholt see their model of supervision as being in parallel with developments that are taking place in psychotherapy to identify common factors and principles of change (see below).

Contemporary models and approaches

As developmental models of supervision began to fall somewhat out of favour they were replaced by functional models that put more of an emphasis on the tasks and roles of supervision (Rapp 1996). Holloway (1995) in the United States, and Carroll (1996), Inskipp and Proctor (2002), Hawkins and Shohet (2012), Wosket and Page (2001) and Scaife (2008, 2010) in Britain have made notable contributions to the supervision literature in this area. What these texts have in common is a movement away from therapy-bound models of supervision towards recognition that the supervisory process is a separate and distinct activity that demands a different mix of knowledge, understanding and skills. These authors have demonstrated a commitment to articulating the precise elements of the supervisory task and process as, essentially, a learning alliance designed to enhance the development of autonomy in clinical practitioners.

Thus in the development of supervision over more recent years we find an ongoing process of the incorporation of concepts and ideas taken from psychotherapy and counselling but made supervision-specific. One notable example is in refinements of the 'reflection process' (Searles 1955) or 'parallel process' (Jacobsen 2007; Wilmot and Shohet 1985). These terms describe the observed phenomenon that at times the relationship dynamics between the client and counsellor or psychotherapist in the therapy setting become 'reflected' or 'paralleled' in the relationship between the supervisee and supervisor in the supervision setting. Whilst this is an observable phenomenon that supervisors from diverse orientations may discover for themselves (Mattinson 1977), the roots for making sense of the process lie within the psychoanalytic tradition.

The reflection process can be understood using the theoretical understandings developed to describe the transference process (Jacoby 1984), these understandings having themselves been developed to make sense of observed phenomena first described by Freud well over a hundred years ago (Freud [1895] 1980). Nevertheless, in the supervision field, the notion of parallel process is often accepted by practitioners from a range of traditions who would not necessarily be as comfortable with thinking about their counselling relationships from a transference perspective.

A further notable turn of events in the recent development of supervision is the growing popularity of relational as opposed to didactic or directive approaches (Nelson *et al.* 2001; Ladany *et al.* 2005; Safran and Muran 2001; Shohet 2008, 2011b). An emphasis on facilitative, congruent relationships has always been at the heart of person-centred approaches to supervision (Lambers 2000; Tudor and Worral 2004, 2007). At the same time there is now a growing emphasis on relational supervision that extends beyond the person-centred approach into psychodynamic and integrative models. In relational supervision the process is viewed as a reciprocal one in which knowledge and meaning are co-constructed between supervisor and supervisee through both cognitive and embodied processes, rather than being handed down by the supervisor (Feindler and Padrone 2009; Frawley-O'Dea and Sarnat 2001; Gilbert and Evans 2000; Gill 2001; Herron and Teitelbaum 2001; Kron and Yerushalmi 2000; Weiner *et al.* 2003; Wosket 2009). We explore relational and embodied supervision more fully in Chapter 13.

To bring us up to date in our discussion of the history and development of supervision in the United Kingdom it is important to note that the last decade has seen a rapid rise in interest in time-limited and brief forms of counselling and therapy, spurred on in parts of the United Kingdom by the National Institute for Health and Clinical Excellence (NICE) guidelines and the Improving Access to Psychological Therapies (IAPT) programme. In this way of working, as Feltham (2012) has observed, 'early identification of crises, symptoms, key personal issues or needs is crucial' and this is likely to entail 'concentration on live problematic issues' and 'skilful neglect' of underlying issues (p. 561). Ways of supervising short-term work have emerged to take account of these differences in foci (Coren, 2001; Jeffery 2008; Knight 2004a; Koob 2003; Macnab 2004; Mander 1998; O'Connell 1998; O'Connell and Jones 1997; Selekman and Todd 1995; Stark *et al.* 2011).

By way of illustrating this trend we will consider Coren's (2001) approach in a little more detail. Although writing predominantly from a psychodynamic perspective, Coren has identified a number of features of the supervision of time-limited therapy that are applicable to all short-term work. He advises that 'the supervisory relationship needs to model the central tenets of short-term work – activity, focus, brevity and curiosity' (p. 187). He recommends that the supervisor models 'active agency and the confidence that something can be achieved in a short space of time' (Coren 2001:187) not least as a counterbalance to those times when the supervisee will understandably doubt the usefulness of brief work. Additionally Coren highlights the importance of helping supervisees prepare in detail for the next therapy session and, in this respect, suggests that didactic teaching may feature more frequently in the supervision of short-term work.

From a relational perspective Coren reminds the supervisor of short-term therapeutic work that she may need to work with repeated experiences of separation anxiety in therapists who have to cope with frequent endings and separations from clients with whom they may have experienced briefly intense and intimate relationships. From an organizational perspective the supervisor of time-limited practice will have to guard against playing the power game of 'Two against the agency' (Crook Lyon and Potkar 2010) where supervisor and supervisee collude in blaming the organization for imposing time limits rather than collaborate in devising resourceful responses to obligatory contextual constraints (Macnab 2004).

Using technology in supervision

To add a more recent note to our historical review of the development of supervision, we will briefly consider here the topic of supervision using electronic means. The use of technologies and electronic media in supervision includes telephoning, texting, emailing, chat rooms, online group meetings and video-conferencing (using, for example, Skype or FaceTime). A growing number of publications address this topic and consider the advantages and disadvantages of supervision using electronic means (see, for example, Anthony and Nagel 2010; Bernard and Goodyear 2009; Casemore and Gallant 2007; Coursol *et al.* 2010; Cummings 2002; Driscoll 2007; Evans, 2009; Groman 2010; Jencius *et al.* 2010; Jones and Stokes 2009; Olson *et al.* 2002; Robson and Whelan 2006; Rosenfield 2012; Sanders 2007; Townend and Wood 2007).

Goss *et al.* (2012) have pointed out the benefits of using technologies to provide therapy-related services to marginalized groups, including those in rural and outlying communities and those who find travelling difficult for economic reasons or because of disability. The same benefits can be true for supervisees where using technologies gives access to supervision that might otherwise be problematic (Armstrong and Schnieders 2003; Fenichel 2003). An example of this is where one of us has an arrangement to provide telephone supervision to a supervisee (a single parent) on occasions where childcare makes travelling to a session difficult (for example during school holidays). From an environmental perspective, Driscoll (2007) has pointed out that using information and communications technology in supervision is ecologically friendly and reduces transport costs.

With other supervisees we have done 'one off' telephone or email supervision with them where a car has broken down, or where health issues, bad weather or a blocked road due to a traffic accident has prevented them attending a scheduled session. One experienced counsellor who lives a distance from her supervisor had only a few clients and found that to split her one and a half hours of monthly supervision into two sessions of 45 minutes' telephone supervision per month had a number of advantages. She continued to meet the supervision requirements for accreditation as set by BACP (a minimum of 1.5 hours per month); she saved time and money by using the telephone for supervision rather that driving two hours each way for a face-to-face meeting and she felt that her two or three clients received more frequent and immediate supervision by discussing them fortnightly rather than monthly. With another supervisee, who moved to a different part of the country to change jobs, telephone supervision was provided over a few months while she settled into her new counselling post and found a new supervisor.

One of us has also undertaken an experimental piece of action research email supervision, at the request of a supervisee tasked by her employer to explore the possibility of using email supervision within an in-house coaching programme. One of the most striking observations from this piece of work was the difference between the experience of an email supervision interaction between people who have previously met each other face to face and between two people whose only contact had been by phone or electronic communication. The conclusion of the supervisor involved in this project was that they would be very open to undertaking supervision by mediums other than face to face, but would always insist upon an initial face-to-face meeting taking place, in order to 'ground' the relationship.

Robson and Whelan (2006) have used their positive experience of moving to telephone supervision when one of them moved to a different geographical area as a basis for challenging the notion that long-term supervision relationships inevitably suffer from 'stagnation and complacency' (p. 207). They argue that long-term supervisory alliances can provide the 'bedrock' (2006:207) that helps to weather personal and professional changes and transitions, even when this means moving from face-to-face supervision to one that uses technology.

Cummings (2002) has evaluated an experience of group supervision using email and text-based chat rooms. In this process, which Cummings calls 'cybervision' (p. 226), each person in a group of four took turns to present their client work for supervision by email and received in response 60 minutes of supervision from the three other group members. Participants in this study experienced the cybervision as 'immediate, intense and focused' (p. 226) and generally as 'an effective and successful form of clinical supervision' (p. 229). The absence of visible clues was seen as one disadvantage, particularly in relation to challenge, where the challenger was unable to see how their challenge impacted on the person to whom it was directed. Interestingly, parallel processes frequently emerged using this form of supervision – for example where the group found their attention drawn to the partner of a client under discussion in a way that mirrored dynamics of the counselling session where the client frequently avoided focusing on himself by talking about this partner. Cummings concludes his article with a recommendation that cybervision be considered as a useful form of peer supervision for therapists in rural areas or where travel is difficult.

Jones and Stokes (2009) discuss the merits of real-time online supervision when compared with time-delayed email supervision. They suggest that if the therapist works online with clients in real time then it can be useful to parallel this in supervision, for example using 'Messenger' or an online conference room. In either case it can be helpful for the supervisee to send an email to the supervisor before an online supervision session saying what they want from supervision, as this can help to establish a clear focus.

Email supervision can be useful for unscheduled between-session contact. This can be immediate without also feeling intrusive to the supervisor – who may feel 'caught on the hop' by an unexpected telephone call. Email contact allows the supervisor time to reflect before responding. Bernard and Goodyear (2009) conclude their discussion about the use of technologies in supervision with a cautionary note. They advise that supervisors need to feel skilled and comfortable with whatever methods they use, rather than jump onto the newest bandwagon, because the 'supervision will fall flat if the method is used poorly' (p. 242).

The recent past and the present

Increasingly, innovative supervision approaches have evolved that take account of the growth in integrative and diverse counselling approaches evident since the 1980s (Culbreth and Brown 2010). This trend is observable in current editions of key supervision anthologies such as Bernard and Goodyear (2009), Hess *et al.* (2008) and Ladany and Bradley (2010). These revised editions of seminal supervision texts give increased coverage to integrative, interpersonal and context-specific approaches to supervision while also including more on multicultural and international perspectives.

Concurrent with these developments, models of supervision are emerging that attempt to identify common change factors in supervision in a way that parallels developments within the common factors paradigm in counselling and psychotherapy (Lampropoulos 2003; Rønnestad and Skovholt 2013). Similarly the positive psychology movement in therapy has begun to generate parallels in the supervision literature in the form of competency- and strength-based approaches to supervision (Edwards 2012; Falender and Shafranske 2004; Lenz and Smith 2010; Lietz and Rounds 2009). A further notable development is the application of social constructivist principles, now considered mainstream in therapeutic approaches, to the understanding and development of supervision approaches (Chang *et al.* 2009; Deaver and Shiflett 2011; Neufeldt 1997).

From the preceding discussion we can now see that it is possible to identify two distinct groups of supervisors. The first, more traditional group, comprises the approach-oriented or 'tribal' (Henderson 2007:46) supervisors. These may be from any of the many distinct counselling and psychotherapy approaches and they supervise within that approach. Often such supervisors will be attached to a training organization or therapy institution using the same approach.

The second group of supervisors is more integrative in their supervision approach and hopefully in secure possession of a supervision model that they can use to guide themselves through the supervision process, regardless of the supervisee's therapeutic orientation. It is not necessary for such supervisors to be integrative or eclectic in their own practice of therapy. They can in fact operate from one distinct approach. However, they do need to have a clear conceptual framework for understanding and managing supervision (Wosket 2000a, 2006). Before concluding our brief review. of the history of counselling and psychotherapy supervision we will address the important topic of the expanding research base for supervision.

Does supervision make a difference?

The usefulness of career-long supervision for therapists has in the past been challenged on the basis of there being 'no known empirical support for its effectiveness' (Feltham 2002:26). In a recent review of supervision–client outcome studies, Watkins (2011:252) concluded that after 'over half a century of supervision research, we still cannot empirically answer' the question 'does psychotherapy supervision positively affect patient outcomes?', although he does see positive signs that this is changing with the recent emergence of some 'nicely done studies' (2011:252). In the United Kingdom the development of a Supervision Practitioner Research Network (SuPReNet) funded by BACP shows promise of encouraging an increase in supervision research directly related to practice (Wheeler *et al.* 2011). In the following section we will consider two key questions with which we believe supervision research is finally getting to grips, namely: (i) does supervision make a difference to supervisees; and (ii) does supervision make a difference to clients?

In 2007 Wheeler and Richards conducted a systematic review of research studies from 1980 onwards (18 in total) that set out to consider what impact clinical supervision has on therapists, their clients and their practice. This review found some evidence that supervision impacted positively on supervisees in the following areas: their self-awareness; their beliefs about their effectiveness; changes and development in theoretical orientation; skill development and their experience of support (Wheeler and Richards 2007). They concluded that supervision has an indirect impact on client outcomes through the opportunities it affords supervisees to build confidence and improve their practice, although it is important to note that none of the studies they reviewed demonstrated a direct link between supervision and improved client outcomes.

As Wheeler and Richard's review indicates, investigations into the efficacy of supervision have been far from conclusive and other studies have confirmed this to be the case. In a critical review of two decades of research into the impact of supervision on client outcomes, Freitas (2002) highlighted the difficulties and complexities involved in studying a number of diverse supervisor–supervisee and supervisee–client dyads and was unable to draw any conclusions. In 2009 Crocket *et al.* conducted a narrative enquiry into how supervision practice is informed by research and found that their review of literature and research articles 'suggest there is little research evidence to support the claim that supervision contributes to therapy outcomes for clients' (p. 101).

On the other hand, a number of individual studies have provided useful insights into the ways in which supervision can have both a productive and counter-productive impact on supervisees, their development and, either directly or by implication, their practice with clients. For example, a study by Cashwell and Dooley (2001) comparing self-efficacy ratings of therapists who received supervision (n = 22) against those who did not (n = 11) found that counsellors who received regular clinical supervision indicated higher levels of self-efficacy than those who had no supervision.

Continuing the theme of supervisee self-efficacy, Gray *et al.* (2001) investigated 13 psychotherapy trainees' experience of counterproductive events (CPEs) in supervision. CPEs were defined in this study as 'any experience that trainees identified as hindering, unhelpful, or harmful in relation to their growth as therapists' (p. 371). Examples of CPEs experienced by trainees were where the supervisor was unempathic or dismissed the supervisee's thoughts and feelings, or where a supervisor pathologized a trainee's nervousness as a psychiatric symptom. The researchers found that typically the effect of these events on the supervisee's sense of self-efficacy was negative, for example they became more guarded or hyper-vigilant in supervision, deferred more to the supervisor, disclosed less and censored themselves more or became more withdrawn.

In fewer than half the reported cases the CPE was discussed in supervision, and in only one case was that discussion initiated by a supervisor. Where supervisees felt able to disclose their experience of the CPE, they typically found their supervisor's willingness to discuss the event helpful. As Gray *et al.* comment (p. 381) this may suggest that 'a more interpersonally sensitive supervisory approach may facilitate the repair of ruptured alliances'. Somewhat paradoxically the majority of trainees in this study reported that the CPE assisted their professional development to some degree, for instance through promoting autonomy and assertiveness, helping them to recognize the importance of an effective supervisory relationship and learning to trust their own instincts more.

Gray *et al.'s* study is also informative in considering the impact of trainees' experiences of CPEs in supervision on their client work. Trainees identified negative parallel processes arising from their experiences of CPEs – for example one supervisee found herself becoming more directive with clients in the same way that her supervisor had been with her. Another began to focus more on content rather than experiences and feelings in client work – again as a reflection of how the trainee experienced supervision. One supervisee found that his experience of not growing and learning in supervision appeared to be mirrored in client work where the client appeared not to be developing or gaining awareness over the same period. Exceptionally, trainees in the study believed that the CPE had a positive effect on client work by increasing their understanding of therapy dynamics. These findings underscore the argument, often voiced, that parallel processes can become important forms of negative and positive modelling (even when unintended) by supervisors.

In other studies various links between supervision and client work have been revealed. In their study of 127 clients, Bambling and colleagues (2006) found that clients of supervised therapists: (i) rated the therapeutic alliance with their therapist higher; (ii) demonstrated a greater reduction in their symptoms of depression; and (iii) evaluated their therapy more positively than did clients in a control group of unsupervised therapists. This study also found that supervision impacted positively on client retention and led to lower drop-out rates. Worthen and Lambert's (2007) study into 'outcome oriented supervision' showed how client outcomes can be enhanced where supervisees systematically monitor client treatment response and use weekly outcome measures to discuss client progress in supervision.

Other studies have uncovered links between supervision and therapist efficacy. A study by Najavits *et al.* (2004) of 44 therapists' satisfaction with manual-based treatments with drug-dependent clients unexpectedly found that participants rated supervision as a more important influence on implementing the treatment protocol than the treatment manual itself. A study by Vallance (2005) used semi-structured interviews and questionnaires to investigate 19 qualified counsellors' experiences of how supervision impacted on their client work. Vallance found that the strongest and most direct link between client work and supervision was in the areas of congruence and confidence, namely that 'a high level of counsellor congruence and confidence in the supervisory relationship leads to increased confidence and congruence in the counselling relationship' (p. 110). Vallance also found that counsellors reported benefitting from the emotional support provided by supervision and felt that this impacted directly on their client work, for example by ensuring they were less distracted by their emotions and able to keep these more separate from the client's process. Conversely this study revealed that the counsellor's confidence in their client work could be undermined by a lack of supportive supervision. A study by Quarto (2003) also revealed that supervision that is experienced as unsupportive by supervisees has the potential to undermine practice. In this study into supervisors' and supervisees' perceptions of control and conflict in supervision, conflict was found to be negatively correlated with supervisees' ability to understand their clients.

One further piece of research that it is revealing to examine in some detail is Nelson and Friedlander's (2001) qualitative study of 13 masters- and doctoral-level trainees' experiences of supervision that were considered by participants to have had a detrimental effect on their development. In particular, participants were asked to identify an impasse or non-productive conflict with a supervisor. A typical pattern to emerge (for at least 7 out of 13 participants) of negative supervisory relationships was with supervisors who were viewed as 'remote and uncommitted to establishing a strong training relationship' (p. 387). Another frequently cited pattern causing discomfort for supervisees involved supervisors who came across initially as over-familiar or too friendly in the relationship. In three of these cases supervisees felt pressured to counsel their supervisors. Other conflicts reported by supervisees in this study were:

- power struggles (for example where supervisees found their supervisors apparently threatened by age differences or supervisees' specific areas of experience and expertise that differed from their own);
- authoritarian styles adopted by supervisors when supervisees desired a more collegial approach;
- role conflicts leading to impasse (namely where the supervisor also had a management role or separate training role);
- gender and cultural insensitivity displayed by the supervisor (for instance a male supervisor who was dismissive of a female supervisee's experience of sexual harassment by a male client).

In this research study the predominant supervisee perception of their supervisors' reactions to conflict was of 'ongoing, extensive anger' (Nelson and Friedlander 2001: p. 390). This was, on occasion, accompanied by blame and threats (for example to withhold supervisee evaluations). Typical of supervisees' feelings in response to these difficulties encountered with supervisors were powerlessness, fear and stress. In findings that mirror those uncovered by Gray *et al.* (2001), as discussed above, Nelson and Friedlander found that most of the supervisees 'lost trust in their supervisors, felt unsafe, pulled back from the relationship, and maintained a guarded stance in supervision' (p. 390). Most supervisees in this study felt able to confront the supervisor about problems encountered and to seek help and advice from other sources (such as managers, trainers and peers). Again in this study the majority of respondents reported some positive outcomes of difficulties experienced. These included a strengthened sense of self and increased resilience. Many felt they had gained useful learning about organizational dynamics and how to be (or not to be) a supervisor. Nelson and Friedlander's study highlights the importance of good supervisory relationships. In this respect they observe: 'because supervision is in part a therapeutic relationship, it requires great clinical skill to be well done' (Nelson and Friedlander 2001: 390).

These findings point to the advisability of supervisors adopting an interpersonal stance characterized by warm regard and interest that avoids the two extremes of over-personalizing or distancing in the relationship. This view is confirmed in a study carried out by Ladany *et al.* (2001) that looked at the relationship between supervisor self-perceptions of their supervisory style and keys aspects of supervisory tasks and process. The authors of this study concluded that supervisors need to understand how their choice of supervisory style, including amount of self-disclosure, is likely to affect the supervisory alliance. Specifically, they recommended that 'supervisors might opt to engage in attractive and interpersonally sensitive styles in order to strengthen the supervisor working alliance' (p. 274). We will revisit the topic of good supervisory relationships in several of the chapters that follow.

In rounding off our consideration of key elements in the history and advancement of supervision we turn to a recent report by Watkins (2013) on supervision in an international perspective. Watkins reports on competency frameworks for supervision that have lately been developed in the United Kingdom (Roth and Pilling 2008; Turpin and Wheeler 2011), in the United States and in Australia. He proposes that these competency-based supervision initiatives 'have blueprint implications globally for supervision practice' (Watkins 2013:78). These frameworks share in common six fundamental areas of competency summarized by Watkins as:

1   Knowledge about/understanding of supervision models, methods and intervention
2   Knowledge about/skill in attending to matters of ethical, legal and professional concern

3   Knowledge about/skill in managing supervision relationship processes
4   Knowledge about/skill in conducting supervisory assessment and evaluation
5   Knowledge about/skill in fostering attention to difference and diversity
6   Openness to/utilization of a self-reflective self-assessment stance in super-
     vision.

(Watkins 2013:80)

Here then is an indication that shared perspectives on what constitutes a competent
and well-informed supervisor are beginning to crystalize on the international scene
and to attract further research interest (Owen-Pugh and Symons 2013). We will
return to these competencies at points throughout the book and in Chapter 2 we set
the scene by considering how the practising counsellor or psychotherapist begins
to make the transition from therapist to supervisor.

From therapist to supervisor

What is common and different in therapy and supervision

Since the first edition of this book was published in 1994, the United Kingdom has seen a significant increase in the number of therapists taking on the role of supervisor and this is reflected by the increase in supervision training courses across Britain. Alongside the possibility of moving into training, consultancy, coaching or management, supervision is the main option through which a practising counsellor or psychotherapist might further their career. This is reflected in the current British Association for Counselling and Psychotherapy (BACP) standards for supervision accreditation. This now bestows 'senior' accredited practitioner status and requires that applicants are accredited members who have completed a minimum of 150 counselling/psychotherapy hours post-accreditation (BACP 2012).

The progression from therapist to supervisor seems a natural transition because in outward appearance counselling and supervising look remarkably similar. Two or more people come together, identify their respective roles and endeavour to assist those in the consumer role, whether clients or supervisees, with difficulties they bring to that setting. This is done using a range of therapeutic and interpersonal skills. Some of these skills are fundamental to both roles: being able to listen, empathize, reflect, form and maintain a healthy and appropriate relationship, support, challenge, explore, make connections, hold boundaries, provide containment and intervene at a level appropriate to the recipient. All this takes place within agreed boundaries of time, place, duration, frequency, confidentiality and (usually) payment. Additionally the practitioner, whether therapist or supervisor, needs to be in a state of sufficient emotional robustness to fulfil their role. Heron (2001:13) defines this as being 'able to work on their distress and suffering, and to take charge of it enough to liberate their helping from it'.

Despite the areas of commonality between therapy and supervision there are fundamental differences, which have considerable significance for the practitioner. The nature and extent of these differences call into question the assumption that an experienced and competent counsellor or psychotherapist will prove to be equally effective in the role of supervisor. A number of critics have challenged this assumption (e.g. Bernard and Goodyear 2009; Watkins 1999) while Pelling's (2008) study into the supervisory identity development of 175 supervisors has confirmed that 'counseling experience and being a competent counselor seem necessary but not sufficient to being a supervisor' (p. 244). Although training courses specific to supervisors have not in the past been widespread in America, Pelling and other American writers such as Ellis (2001) and Muratori (2001) exceptionally and explicitly recommend supervisor training and supervision of supervision to promote supervisory skill development and identity, and to reduce the occurrence of poor and harmful supervision. To further our discussion at this point we would like to tease out some of the differences between the roles and activities of therapist and supervisor.

To make this distinction we have broken down each of the roles and tasks into a number of constituent parts: aims, presentation methods, timing, relationship, expectations and responsibilities. We have then summarized key elements of each of these components in Table 2.1. In looking at counselling and psychotherapy we have used medium- to long-term therapeutic work as our norm. Under supervision we have included supervising both the trainee and the experienced practitioner. Consequently aspects of what is in Table 2.1 may not apply to a specific therapeutic or supervising approach or to short-term work.

Table 2.1 Differences between counselling/psychotherapy and supervision

Counselling and psychotherapy	Supervision
Aims	**Aims**
To enable the client to lead a more satisfying and fulfilled life.	To enable the fullest therapeutic use to be made of the counselling or psychotherapy.
For the client to increase their ability to live resourcefully by healing past hurts and developing their ability to reflect on and constructively manage their own experience.	For the supervisee to foster their capacity to practise effectively by developing skills and resources together with their ability to reflect upon and conceptualize the therapeutic process.
Presentation	**Presentation**
Material is usually presented verbally, sometimes pictorially, dramatically or in an embodied way by the client.	Material is presented in various ways: reported or live, verbally, written, audio and/or visually recorded, through embodied processes, through creative exercises and role play.
Timing	**Timing**
Counsellor may withhold and 'incubate' their reactions to the client and their understanding of what is occurring for a number of sessions. The client chooses the pace.	Supervisors will focus on and address what is happening 'in the moment' with the awareness that it may only relate to the work with this client at this time. Pace is often determined by the need to reach some resolution before the supervisee's next session with the client.

Table 2.1 Continued

Counselling and psychotherapy	Supervision
Relationship	**Relationship**
This holds the client emotionally.	This holds the supervisee in their therapeutic task and provides containment for the demands of the therapeutic work.
Therapist may work extensively with the transference relationship.	Supervisor cultivates the 'real' relationship with the supervisee whilst welcoming paralleling dynamics for their informational value.
Relationship may be reparative and transformative.	Relationship is adult to adult and may also be transformative.
A regressive component may be tolerated or indeed encouraged for its therapeutic potential.	Regressive elements are dealt with as they occur; not encouraged by the supervisor.
Therapist accepts a degree of acting out by the client: e.g. the challenging of boundaries or directing strong emotions towards the therapist, as these are welcomed for their informational value.	Supervisee is expected to respect the practical boundaries and collaborate in maintaining them.
Therapist models effective self-management.	Supervisor models effective role-management.
Expectations	**Expectations**
The client attends and endeavours to make use of the therapy; they may be encouraged to come unprepared.	The supervisee attends, prepares for supervision and provides necessary materials.
Responsibilities	**Responsibilities**
Responsibility is to the client. This may be superseded by moral or ethical responsibilities, occasionally legal ones. Therapist does not assess the client's contribution to task and process.	Responsibility to the client can claim precedence over responsibility to the supervisee. Supervision has a quality-control function and supervisor may have an evaluation or assessment role.

The differences between the components included under the headings 'Aims', 'Presentation', 'Timing' and 'Expectations' are quite concrete and readily understood. We will look in more detail at those included under the headings 'Relationship' and 'Responsibilities' as they are rather more complex.

Relationship

In principle there are quite different qualities of containment or holding required in the two types of relationship (Bramley 1996). In counselling and psychotherapy the containment is principally an emotional holding of the client. The result of this is that the therapist is generally subjected to a greater intensity of emotional demand than the supervisor. This is because the distress and pain of the client is usually a more central focus in therapy than is the distress and pain of the supervisee in supervision. Even when the supervisee's distress is present in supervision and needs to be held by the supervisor, it should be understood that it remains primarily the responsibility of the supervisee to manage their own distress. This is not necessarily the case in counselling and psychotherapy where providing the client with emotional containment may legitimately be a major component of the therapist's role (Casement 1985). Thus supervision tends to be less emotionally demanding than therapy.

The containment in supervision is that of holding the therapist to their task and providing an additional layer of containment for the client's material. This may need to be done in a variety of ways. It will certainly include providing support and emotional holding. It may include challenging the therapist to identify the areas in which they are cut off from what the client is (directly or indirectly) communicating. Containment may involve assisting the therapist to untangle their responses to the client, distinguishing those that come from their own personal material from those which are called up by the client (Jacoby 1984; Page 1999a). It may include encouraging the supervisee to be more emotionally available to the client: to allow themselves and the client to get closer to one another (Shainberg 1983; Wosket 1999).

We can think of the relationship difference from a Transactional Analysis perspective (Berne 1961/1975). The therapeutic relationship can be thought of as containing a more developed Nurturing Parent–Child component. In contrast the supervising relationship contains a more developed Adult–Adult aspect. However, the supervisory relationship is curiously paradoxical in that it is both more equal and simultaneously more authoritative than the therapy relationship. Thus in addition to the Adult–Adult part there is a Critical Parent–Child component. This difference can be seen in the different ways that we would expect boundaries to be maintained. The therapist can anticipate that some clients will test out the boundaries in the relationship and may well breach practical boundaries. Provided it remains within manageable limits such behaviour potentially provides fruitful therapeutic material and, we hope, would be tolerated and explored with the client. In contrast the supervisor will normally expect the supervisee to be adult in sharing responsibility for maintaining these boundaries. Any significant boundary-breaching behaviour is likely to be challenged with the expectation that the behaviour would change.

This difference is also reflected in the way in which relationship dynamics are, ideally, addressed. A therapist may be aware of dynamics and choose not to raise them with the client at certain junctures, judging that such an intervention would unhelpfully interrupt the flow at any given point by inviting the client to examine their process. In supervision it can reasonably be expected that either party may initiate discussion at any time about the dynamics of the supervisory relationship. This is the ideal, although a number of research studies (Gray *et al.* 2001; Lawton 2000; Mehr *et al.* 2010; Nelson and Friedlander 2001) have revealed that supervisees can experience considerable difficulties in trying to discuss relationship dynamics with their supervisors.

Responsibilities

The differences under the heading 'Responsibilities' make it clear that supervisors need to be prepared to exercise a more readily identifiable authority than therapists would typically do, which includes monitoring the practice of the supervisee. This does involve evaluation, judgement and, on occasion, rare though this might be, being prescriptive about what the other person should or should not do. Research by Cikanek and colleagues (2004) has revealed that therapists at the point of becoming supervisors may be poorly equipped to take on these responsibilities and are likely to need further training, particularly in the management of ethical issues.

One of us had a poignant example of needing to exercise our authority with a longstanding supervisee. We had to arrange an emergency session because he had just been diagnosed with cancer and could be called to hospital for treatment within the week. Although the prognosis was good he faced surgery, followed by protracted treatment with some potentially very unpleasant side effects. All the natural responses of the supervisor were to empathize with his difficult situation and give space for the powerful emotional responses he was experiencing. Nevertheless the priority task for the supervisor was to look at how the needs of the individuals he counselled and supervised would be met. This included confronting the supervisee with elements of denial evident in his desire to hold onto one or two people, either through telephone contact or occasional meetings. As Veach (2001:398) reminds us 'the supervisor's ultimate responsibility is client welfare, which at times may supercede supervisee needs or preferences'. The supervisor endeavoured to act with care and sensitivity in this case, and staying with the task that had to be completed was demanding for both people involved. At one point the supervisee said that he felt he had to prepare for death and he wasn't ready to die yet.

This is an extreme example but highlights how being an effective supervisor may require tempering one's natural concern and compassion for the supervisee when supervisory responsibilities demand a different focus. There is recognition that supervisors can be experienced as persecutory when exercising what they consider to be the responsibilities of their role (Hahn 2001; Hoffman et al. 2005; Kaberry 2000; Lidmila 1997; Mehr et al. 2010; Webb 2000). However, it is important for the novice supervisor to recognize that there is an important distinction between the responsibilities a counsellor or psychotherapist has towards a client and those a supervisor has towards a supervisee. We discuss issues of responsibility in supervision more fully in Chapter 10. In the next section we aim to highlight a number of key issues that may require consideration by the therapist who is starting to supervise.

Key themes and issues for consideration by the beginning supervisor

Client welfare

The responsibility of the supervisor to protect the interests of the client is considered to be a central component of the supervision of trainees (Feltham and Dryden 1994). Attention to client welfare is equally important but usually less central in practitioner supervision. Alongside this protective or monitoring role there is another role, arguably of equal importance, which is that of facilitator of the development of the trainee. The tension between these two roles can be difficult to contain and the supervisor is tempted to gravitate towards one pole or the other. However, such polarization can lead to the supervisor being experienced as over-controlling, as if she is trying to make the trainee act as an extension of herself. One of us was reminded of this when a supervisee, who had been practising for only a few months, reported feeling like a ventriloquist's dummy as she heard herself repeating to her client much of what had been said to her by her supervisor in the previous supervision session. The other extreme of this spectrum is the supervisor who always accepts without challenge or question whatever the trainee is doing, perhaps with the rationalization that it is a 'useful learning experience'.

Leddick and Bernard (1980:192) propose that there is a spurious assumption within the supervision literature that 'authoritative relationships and facilitative relationships are mutually exclusive'. In our view any supervisor who is not endeavouring to balance these two fundamental elements of the role is avoiding one of the central aspects of effective supervision. In this regard, Nelson and colleagues (2001) recommend that training programs for supervisors provide skills training in balancing the management of supportive and evaluative relationships with supervisees.

The boundary between supervision and therapy

Another identifiable theme is revealed by Boyd (1978) in an early chapter entitled 'The psychotherapeutic approach to supervision'. In this he mixes together, in a way that now seems muddled, a psychodynamic approach to supervision with therapy for the supervisee, making no apparent distinction between the two. He seems to imply that this mixture is a necessary consequence of the psychoanalytic tradition of requiring trainee analysts to be in personal analysis, despite the clear distinction made many years earlier between training analysis and trainee supervision (Fleming and Benedek [1966] 1983).

This illustrates another of the tensions within the supervisor's role, that of balancing attention to both the client's and the supervisee's issues. So, for instance, if we happen to be working with a supervisee who is feeling angry towards a client then we would want to examine this with the supervisee from the point of view of what it might suggest about the client. However, if we are to avoid the danger of colluding with the supervisee in seeing this entirely as the client's issue we must also ensure that we consider what part the therapist's own emotional and psychological material might be playing in this interaction (Page 1999a). Thus it is not only appropriate, but indeed necessary, to engage in what amounts to a measure of therapeutic work with the supervisee (Koltz 2008).

We believe this is legitimate within supervision, provided the purpose remains that of understanding the therapeutic process and the overall intention is to enhance the work being done with the client. It can be difficult to maintain these boundaries appropriately. There may be pressure to overstep them from the supervisee and there may also be pressure within the supervisor to do so. This can be particularly difficult for the relatively inexperienced supervisor, who may be much more familiar, and possibly therefore more comfortable, with the role of therapist than that of supervisor.

Each new supervisor has to struggle with this dilemma in much the same way that the counselling and psychotherapy tradition has had to struggle to define the boundaries between the roles of therapist and supervisor. There is no simple solution or single definition that separates therapy and supervision neatly without overlap or ambiguity; rather they are necessarily interwoven activities that only become effectively separated through the practice of the individual therapist and supervisor (Neufeldt and Nelson 1999). We will return to this theme a number of times, and in Chapter 10 some specific criteria to use in determining what degree of personal work is legitimate in supervision will be suggested. In Chapter 12 we shall come full circle and suggest that when experienced supervisors are supervising experienced therapists they may need to focus increasingly on supervisees' personal issues as these will more and more overlap with their professional issues (Wosket 1999, 2000b, 2009).

Power in the relationship

A third theme that becomes evident when considering the transition a therapist makes in becoming a supervisor is that of the balance of power within the supervision relationship (Kaberry 2000; Lawton 2000; Peyton 2004). There is necessarily an imbalance of power resulting from the difference in roles between supervisor and supervisee. In order to fulfil their respective roles the supervisee is regularly exposing his or her shortcomings and difficulties in a way that is not required of the supervisor. This difference in degree of vulnerability, along with the authority within the supervisor's role, leads to a natural imbalance of experienced power (Rogers 1978) within the relationship. Unless the supervisor and supervisee have a common understanding of the nature of these power differentials and can talk explicitly about them where necessary (for instance when the supervisor has an assessment role), the supervisee is likely to be disadvantaged, may withhold sensitive information from their supervisor and, at worst, might experience abuse of power (Ellis 2010; Hess et al. 2008; Peyton 2004). Beginning supervisors may need to extend their understanding and capacity to work with power dynamics in order to be comfortable and competent with initiating and discussing this issue with supervisees.

In the case of trainee supervision this inequity is exacerbated by a structural power imbalance (Gard and Lewis 2008). In the contracts we have to supervise trainee therapists there is always a clause requiring us to give feedback to the training institution if we have serious concerns about the trainee. This is necessary to fulfil our obligations to the trainee's clients, in this instance both his current clients and potential future clients, who are put at risk if the trainee's difficulties are not resolved. It does, however, create an imbalance because the supervisor has influence over the student's future in a form that is not reciprocal (Liddle 1986).

There are also likely to be imbalances resulting from the personal material that trainee therapists bring to the supervision relationship – for example, unresolved issues about being judged and assessed, or distress from previous relationships with an authority figure (Gilbert and Evans 2000). These power dynamics offer a rich source of material to explore how similar dynamics may be at work in the relationship between therapist and client. However in order for this to happen the supervisor and supervisee have to find a way to acknowledge the dynamics and examine them with some degree of openness and objectivity. There is research evidence (Gray *et al.* 2001; Kaberry 2000; Lawton 2000; Webb 2000) that makes it clear that this is not easy to do. We will come back to the issue of how shared power can be optimized between supervisor and supervisee at several points throughout this volume.

The three themes discussed here are all, in different ways, concerned with balance:

1   the balance of providing control and allowing freedom, which for the supervisor includes balancing their responsibilities to clients with their responsibilities to the supervisee;
2   the balance between the degree of focus upon the client and the degree of focus upon the therapist;
3   the balance of power in the supervisory relationship.

Maintaining a sense of balance is a central requirement of the supervisory role. We will develop this notion further as we go on to elucidate our model and its components in later chapters.

Resources

At the start of this chapter we focused on the differences between therapy and supervision. If a counsellor or psychotherapist has satisfied herself that she wishes to supervise then she must also consider what additional resources she requires in order to be properly equipped for the new role. Stafford (2008:39) refers to the danger that exists where a therapist is encouraged or invited by colleagues to take on the mantle of supervisor and does so merely as a result of having the 'honour bestowed' on them by peers. BACP (2010:8), on the other hand, explicitly advises that supervisors have a responsibility to 'acquire the attitudes, skills and knowledge required by their role'.

Arguably the most important piece of equipment for any supervisor to acquire is a sound conceptual understanding of an approach or model of supervision. Here we use the word 'equipment' intentionally to distinguish technique from relationship. In other chapters we discuss the fundamental importance of the supervisor acquiring the relational competencies required for effective supervision. Without acquiring a good framework for understanding and applying supervision, beginning supervisors are in danger of operating from unexplored assumptions:

> To assume that therapy skills translate automatically to supervisory skills is analogous to assuming that a good athlete inevitably will make either a good coach or perhaps a good sports announcer . . . In fact, the great players tend not to become the great coaches, and vice versa, although most coaches at least have 'played the game'.
>
> Bernard and Goodyear (2009:5)

The lack of a suitable model will lead to the supervisor having no clear sense of where she is going so that whether or not she arrives at a useful place is left in the hands of fortune. Borders (1992) has made the simple but fundamental point that in making the transition from counsellor to supervisor, the beginning supervisor needs to make a cognitive shift from thinking like a counsellor to thinking like a supervisor. This involves, primarily, a shift in focus from the client to the therapist. Borders suggests that supervisors who think like supervisors, rather than like counsellors, will be inclined to ask themselves 'How can I intervene so that this counselor will be more effective with current and future clients?' Conversely, supervisors who fail to make this shift are more likely to approach sessions 'well prepared to tell the counselor what they would do with this client'. As Borders cautions, the likely result in this case is that 'supervisees become surrogate counselors who carry out supervisors' plans for counseling' (Borders 1992:137–8). Beginning to think like a supervisor is an important prerequisite to the ability to integrate and make effective use of a model of supervision.

The second major resource available to any new supervisor is his or her own experience of being a supervisee. Shulman (2006:24) has observed that in supervision 'more is caught than taught', thereby emphasizing the extent to which supervisees learn from closely observing *how* their supervisors work – as opposed to listening to what their supervisors *say about how* to practice. Supervisees who have been active in identifying what they are seeking from supervision and instrumental in negotiating supervision contracts suitable for their needs will have a good basis for entering this new role.

There are useful guides to being a proactive and aware supervisee (Inskipp and Proctor 2002; Page 1999b), which emphasize the importance of the supervisee taking authority in this process. It is important, for example, that the 'supervisee assesses whether this supervisor has the skills, knowledge, approach and commitment to meet their supervision needs' (Page 1999b:183). A supervisee who has been a proactive partner in their own supervision will be much better prepared for the transition to the role of supervisor than one who has been a more passive recipient of whatever their supervisor has chosen to offer.

One key piece of research that throws some light on the resources needed to become an effective supervisor is that conducted by Bucky and colleagues (2010). This study considered supervisees' (n = 87) ratings of effective supervisor skills and qualities – both their strengths and perceived deficiencies. On the positive side, findings showed that participants rated the supervisors they had recently worked with as of 'above-average intelligence' and as having 'a positive attitude toward themselves, ethical integrity, and strong listening skills' (p. 159). The supervisors' interpersonal attractiveness (as perceived by supervisees) also linked to supervisees' experiences of better quality supervision. On the other hand, supervisees reported that they considered that supervisors could improve in the following areas: 'awareness of counter-transference in supervision, the ability to stay focused, the ability to meet time constraints, commitment to the supervisory alliance, and an ability to challenge the supervisee effectively' (Bucky *et al.* 2010:159). This study, then, reveals a number of supervisor competencies that practitioners making the transition from counsellor to supervisor would be well advised to cultivate and develop.

Pitfalls for the unwary supervisor

We will now proceed to identify other traps into which the inexperienced supervisor may fall. Some of the internal pressures experienced in supervision mirror those of therapy – for example, there can be a strong pressure to come up with answers for the supervisee just as a therapist might experience when with a client. However, there are other internal pressures that are unique to supervision. For instance there may well be occasions when the supervisor feels that she would do a better job if she were working with the client being discussed. Farber (2006) refers to this supervisory 'conceit' as the supervisor assuming 'a mantle of omniscience' (p. 194). If such responses are not effectively contained they are likely to lead either to attempting to take over, perhaps trying to tell the supervisee what to do, or, worse still, to counselling the client vicariously through the supervisee. Frawley-O'Dea and Sarnat (2001:78) describe this failure of judgement as the supervisor attempting to treat the client 'by remote control', and suggest that it may occur as a defence employed by the supervisor to avoid feeling or appearing stupid.

Either of these behaviours is inappropriate because they both, almost inevitably, result in the supervisee feeling demoralized and deskilled. There may of course be a grain of truth in the notion that one could do a better job than the supervisee, particularly if she is inexperienced or the client brings issues with which one has a particular degree of expertise. Nevertheless, except in the unusual circumstance where it is adjudged that the supervisee is acting in a way that is unethical, the supervisor's task is to support, encourage and affirm her in the work she is doing, rather than take over her work.

There is also the trap of setting up in competition with the supervisee. Indeed this may be what underlies the desire to change places and become the client's therapist: 'Stand aside, I'll show you how to do it properly!' The dynamics of competition can be complex, often not in conscious awareness and with roots in rivalrous sibling relationships (Jacobs 1986). Quarto's (2003) research into control and conflict in supervision found that 'novice supervisors may be motivated to place themselves in a clearly superior position in the relationship and promote their own agendas instead of following the leads of their supervisees so as not to appear on a parallel developmental level' (p. 33). In other words, a beginning supervisor may assume a superior stance as a defence against the anxiety and discomfort of finding themselves, in terms of the developmental model (see Chapter 1), back at the stage of novice practitioner, albeit as a supervisor rather than as a therapist.

Generally, self-challenge and honest reflection by the supervisor (perhaps with the help of their own supervisor) is required in order to bring such processes to awareness. It is precisely because of this kind of out-of-awareness dynamic that it is important that a supervisor has an opportunity to examine the work she is doing. We will look at this in more depth in later chapters when we come to consider supervision for the supervisor.

There is a further trap, which can be termed the 'ethical inquisitor' position (Daniels 2000). This involves examining all that is reported in supervision with a view to finding mistakes. Indeed if taken to extremes it can mean scrutinizing all aspects of the supervisee's work, thereby undermining the therapist's opportunity to take responsibility for the work he is doing and for bringing difficulties to the attention of his supervisor. It is very important that a supervisor has an awareness of the ethical issues she may meet, and has an understanding of what is involved and some idea of how to proceed (Bond 2010; Cikanek *et al.* 2004). However, it is possible to be heavy handed on occasions where there are ethical concerns, leaping to solutions or action to alleviate the anxiety such situations can generate (for both supervisee and supervisor). To do so is unproductive and often results in a larger mess than first existed. We will explore these issues in much greater depth in Chapter 10; it is sufficient at this point to recognize the danger, be aware that it is largely driven by the supervisor's own anxieties and underscore the importance of developing a lightness of touch.

At the other end of the spectrum to the 'ethical inquisitor' lies the equally dangerous 'passive optimist'. We have already made reference to this position without naming it: it is where the supervisor is faced with issues that need confronting but chooses to simply affirm and encourage the supervisee. Farber (2006:184) describes this supervisory error as being 'indiscriminately approving of all interventions based on good intent' while Gard and Lewis (2008:47) have referred to this stance as adopting a 'cheerleader' approach to supervision where 'positive reinforcement' is provided 'at every turn'. This can be as a result of not seeing the issues, or of not realizing that what is being reported or not reported should be a cause for concern, or it can be the supervisor's counter-transference response to the supervisee's positive projections onto her (see Chapter 6). For all of us this is inevitable on odd occasions, but if it happens with a degree of regularity then the supervisor's fitness to fulfil the role remains in question.

The following example may serve to make this clearer. It illustrates a number of the pitfalls given above whilst also, in this case, showing a positive learning outcome for the supervisor-in-training. It is told in the first person by the supervisor of the supervision.

> Kristen, a therapist training to be a supervisor, brought to supervision a recording of her supervision work with a trainee counsellor, Joel. Kristen brought the recording to her supervision of supervision session because she felt uncomfortable about the session with her supervisee but couldn't put her finger on why this was. We listened together to the recording for about five minutes, during which I (the supervisor of supervision) noticed:
>
> *   a lot of mutual affirmation between supervisor and supervisee (e.g. Joel comments several times on how helpful Kristen is);
> *   Kristen provides a good deal of reassurance and encouragement to Joel (who happens to be going through an unconfident patch due to difficulties in his personal life);
> *   Kristen tends to stay with the content of the client session rather than focus on her supervisee's issue (for instance, Joel expresses some uncertainty and discomfort about having offered a technique to the client that is a departure from his usual non-directive way of working and Kristen responds by asking how this went rather than inviting Joel to explore his discomfort);
> *   Joel asks for approval from his supervisor, e.g. 'Do you think that was an OK thing to do?' and Kristen replies, giving her approval, 'I think it was a brilliant idea!'
>
> At this point we stop the recording and I ask Kristen what she hears happening in the relationship with her supervisee. She says 'I can hear how I am feeling quite puffed up and pleased with myself for doing a good job. It doesn't feel right, now that I listen to it – like I was feeling quite powerful and omnipotent – which isn't at all how I want to be as a supervisor.' She begins to realize that her responses to Joel help him to feel reassured and supported, but not in any way challenged to develop or grow. She also wonders if there is a danger of this dynamic being paralleled in his counselling practice, where clients may feel soothed but not challenged.
>
> So at this point Kristen has spotted her supervisee's positive transference towards herself and her own counter-transference responses, which have

echoes of the 'cheerleader' approach. We discuss how she might begin to explore this dynamic with Joel using immediacy and without coming across as punitive. The possibilities we come up with are for Kristen to:

1 own her own part in the dynamic, e.g. by saying to Joel 'I catch myself sometimes glossing over your concerns and giving you encouragement instead';
2 give Joel some feedback that is descriptive rather than accusatory: 'Listening to the tape I notice how much reassurance and approval I give you and I'm now questioning for myself how useful that is';
3 name the dynamic without sounding disapproving: 'I notice I feel quite flattered when you tell me what a good supervisor you think I am. I think this sometimes stops me from inviting us to stay with issues that are a little more difficult for you – for instance the discomfort you experience in offering a technique that doesn't seem to fit with your exploratory approach. Instead of exploring this with you in depth I catch myself giving you approval and reassurance and then we get caught in a loop where we end up telling each other what a good job we are doing!'

The supervisory task here was to help Kristen identify the dynamic between herself and Joel, and to open this up for exploration in a way that optimized self-challenge and insight for the supervisor-in-training (Sarnat 1992). Kristen was then able to go back to her supervisee and, in turn, explore this dynamic with him in a congruent way. In this example a parallel process would have occurred if the supervisor of supervision had reassured Kristen that she was doing a great job too, rather than helping her to notice and name what was being transferred onto her by her supervisee and her own unaware responses to this.

Passive optimism can also be experienced as a conscious process. In this case it takes the form of seeing a problematic issue but hoping that affirming and encouraging the supervisee will be sufficient and that the issue will simply go away. This is a form of abdication (Hawthorne 1975) driven by the supervisor's reluctance to confront. Such reluctance may be fuelled from a number of sources such as desire to be liked, fear of hostility or lack of confidence in one's own judgements. What is clear is that the problem lies with the supervisor and it is for him or her to resolve.

Benefits of becoming a supervisor

For the practitioner who is considering taking on supervision work, what we have written so far could be read as a catalogue of reasons not to do so. Although this is not our intention it does honour the long-standing tradition of testing apparent vocation by facing the would-be practitioner with the difficulties they may expect to encounter (Hume 1977). That said, in order to redress this balance, we will now consider some of the benefits of becoming a supervisor.

Taking on the role of supervisor can, as Borders (1992) has argued, provide a pivotal experience in the development of the experienced counsellor or psychotherapist. Taking on responsibility for the work of other therapists, Borders suggests, 'propels them to higher levels of professionalism' (p. 145). Additionally, integrating the skills and functions of counselling, educating and consulting into the role of supervisor can enable the practitioner to identify more clearly their own individual style of working and 'help them solidify a new professional identity' (Borders 1992:145). In a similar vein Rønnestad and Skovholt (2013:209) have written about how becoming a supervisor provides opportunities for the practitioner to 'clarify and articulate how they conceptualize client dynamics, therapeutic attitude, technique, and therapy/counseling processes'. Indeed they go further and suggest that supervisees may even 'provide a "holding" and confirming environment for [their] supervisors' (Rønnestad and Skovholt 2013:209), thus emphasizing the reciprocal nature of the supervisory relationship.

It frequently happens, then, that the act of supervising the work of another provides the practitioner with a new opportunity to examine and revitalize one's own client work. Hawkins and Shohet (2012:51–2) put it this way: 'As a new supervisor you are impelled to stop, reflect upon and articulate the ways you have worked as a practitioner, many of which you may have begun to take for granted'. Casement (1985) uses the image of a spiral to describe how supervising others can appear to take us back to the beginning of our own practice, although in reality it takes us to a new place that has familiar elements. He goes on to suggest that it is often easier to see how another therapist could have acted more therapeutically and then apply that to our own practice than it is to see our own inadequacy in isolation:

> Just as we can generally see our own errors more clearly in others, so too can we see these in supervising other practitioners. Here there are endless opportunities for therapists to re-examine their own work, when looking closely at the work of the person being supervised. Not infrequently supervisors will see reflections of their own difficulties with technique. We do not always do as we teach others to do, but we can learn a lot by trying to do so.
>
> (Casement 1985:33)

This is not a new phenomenon; as therapists we have both heard ourselves saying things to clients and realized we could usefully say the same things to ourselves. This is common and one of the potential benefits of doing therapeutic work (Kottler and Carlson 2005). Likewise as supervisors we sometimes find ourselves offering the very perspective to the supervisee that we need to apply to a piece of our own therapeutic work. These are the times when we are conscious of the parallel. There is also a less self-conscious process at work, for in supervising the work of others we are continually developing our ability to stand back and reflect upon the counselling process as it is being reported to us.

As we become able to do this whilst we are counselling (or supervising) someone, so we are utilizing the function that Casement (1985) has termed the 'internal supervisor'. If the real depth of this function is to be understood then it must be appreciated that it does not simply mean the ability to reflect; rather, it involves the ability to reflect upon the therapeutic process as it is occurring. Essentially this means reflecting on and being involved in the therapeutic process at the same time. This can be thought of as being able to operate at two parallel levels simultaneously, or at least in sufficient proximity for the reflection to inform the involvement as it proceeds. A practising therapist may feel that they have already developed this function, but supervising others will strengthen and refine the ability.

The other major benefit of being a supervisor is that it provides a contrast to doing therapeutic work. For the practitioner who spends most of their working time doing counselling or psychotherapy this contrast can be quite significant. When we examined the differences between therapeutic and supervisory relationships it became clear that the counselling or psychotherapy relationship is generally the more emotionally demanding. It is often the case that the supervision relationship is more intellectually stimulating because there is a place for exploring what is going on at an intellectual and theoretical level with a supervisee in a manner that is seldom appropriate with a client.

Lastly we believe it is true to say that being a supervisor helps the practitioner become a better therapist. This is largely because, as a supervisor, one becomes more skilled and practised in working with process, dynamics, hunches and possibilities rather than with lots of content. The nature of the supervisory encounter, where the therapist may need to bring in a number of clients in a short time span, means that there is not a great deal of time available for the unfolding of content. In supervision we need to get beyond and beneath the story (both the client's story and the supervisee's story of their work with the client) to reach engagement with emerging themes and issues. For the supervisor this usually involves a good degree of thinking aloud. This in itself is excellent practice for the essential skill of thinking aloud in a spirit of collaboration with one's own clients.

Starting to supervise

Having decided to start supervising other therapists, there remain the questions of 'when' and 'how'. 'When' is likely to be partially dictated by circumstances: an individual may be asked to take on supervision or it may be part of an employment role as a therapist. However, it is important not to allow oneself to be rushed or pushed into supervising others. The 'when', in ideal circumstances, would always be 'when ready'.

'How' to start supervising may also be determined by the situation, but it is worth considering the options. The traditional method has been simply to jump in and get on with it: the sink-or-swim approach. The problem with this is that there are inevitably casualties, be they the supervisor, the supervisee or the client. The second method is the mentor approach, embarking on supervising under the tutelage of an experienced supervisor. This can be effective provided that the mentor has a good grounding in theory as well as practice. If not then one is likely to become proficient at technique but lack some of the awareness of process and conceptual frameworks that a sound theoretical base provides.

The third method is to do a training course in supervision. There are now a number of good-quality courses specifically in practitioner supervision available in Britain. There is also generally a supervision component in counselling and psychotherapy courses at masters level, both in the United Kingdom and North America, although such a component is unlikely to be as rigorous in the aspects of theory, technique and practice as a course specific to therapist supervision. In Chapter 14 we will look in more depth at the training and development needs of both the new supervisor and the experienced supervisor.

Supervision of supervision

It should by now be clear that supervising the therapeutic work of others is a multifaceted and demanding task. At times the dynamics can be more complex than in therapy because there are at least three people involved, each bringing their own intra- and interpersonal dynamics to bear. Indeed, in many supervision situations there are additional complications resulting from the impact of the organization within which the therapeutic work takes place or the trainee supervisee's training institution. Supervising can also raise difficult issues that may not have been met before. For example, the balancing of the authoritative and facilitative aspects of the role, which we outlined earlier under the theme of client welfare, is unlikely to come up in therapeutic work in quite the same way. The supervisor may have to decide how long she can allow the supervisee to proceed in a direction that she, the supervisor, feels has significant risk for the client. The very notion of deciding whether or not to 'allow' may never have occurred to the practitioner in the therapist role.

These are examples of the complexity of the supervisory task. Because of this complexity it is essential that every supervisor should have some arena within which they can explore the supervision work they are doing (Watkins 1999). Ideally this is a supervision forum, individual or group that is specifically arranged for this purpose. It is possible to look at supervision issues alongside therapy issues within one's counselling or psychotherapy supervision. However, this creates the danger that one or the other aspect of the work will suffer because the other is more time consuming. Dividing the time between the two may end up being determined more by the needs of crisis management than by the learning needs of the practitioner.

We feel that it is advisable for inexperienced supervisors have some form of supervision that is solely for their supervision work. This provides a place to examine their supervision work in depth and with regularity. As supervisors become more experienced they will come to know when they need to seek consultation over specific supervision issues and can develop a more flexible arrangement that reflects this maturity (Jacobs 2000a).

In this chapter we have seen that becoming a supervisor requires the acquisition of a suitable model or supervisory approach. The Cyclical Model of supervision has been recommended as a fitting and adaptable model for practitioners making the transition from therapist to supervisor (Henderson 2009a; van Ooijen 2000). We will explore this model in depth in the chapters that follow.

Chapter 3

Overview of the supervision model

A model is a framework or map intended to simplify that which is complex in order to aid understanding. It is distinct from a theory, which seeks to explain what is observed in the setting under scrutiny, and an approach, which provides a way of addressing or describes an attitude towards a subject. A model of supervision of counsellors and psychotherapists articulates what is going on and how it is done. It embraces both methodology and objectives, and enables practitioners to locate themselves in the process, by mapping out the terrain. An effective model is clearly understandable, and can be readily put into practice and adapted to the demands of the situation and the needs of its users, combining sufficient firmness of structure to offer clear reference points with the flexibility to be applied to the variety of situations a supervisor will encounter.

The model of supervision we are presenting was originally developed specifically for use in the supervision of counsellors and psychotherapists. We know from our own practice and the experiences described to us by others that it has been successfully adapted for use in a variety of other supervisory situations. We have used elements of it to good effect in the supervision of social workers, managers, health care professionals, teachers and others who routinely use counselling skills in human resource management (we explore aspects of supervising those from other professions in Chapter 15). Since it was first published the Cyclical Model has been recommended as a useful model for the supervision of clinical psychologists, nurses (Van Ooijen 2000) and other mental health professionals (Scaife 2008, 2010), and as a core training model by a number of training institutions and counselling associations in Britain and Ireland. It has also been presented to use as a framework for both mentoring (Brockbank and McGill 2006) and academic supervision (Brockbank and McGill 2007).

The scope of models of supervision

Traditionally, as we have already seen, approaches to supervision took the theory and practice of a counselling or psychotherapy model and then applied the principles and processes to the practice of supervision. This tradition led to the development of the 'approach-oriented' supervisor. Such a supervisor is well able to supervise the 'purist' therapist, exclusively practising one counselling or psychotherapy approach and drawing only upon the theory and practice of that particular orientation. However, we have heard of examples of supervisees being supervised by an approach-oriented supervisor from a therapeutic approach different to their own and being frustrated and confused by interventions superimposing a different set of constructs upon their work, rather than using the diversity between supervisor and supervisee as a creative dialogue between practitioners with different perspectives.

Before they are able to supervise practitioners from other therapeutic orientations effectively, indeed safely, a supervisor who has learned their craft within a particular tradition must develop a meta-understanding of the responsibilities, tasks and processes inherent in supervision together with the skills and competencies required to provide supervision that is not limited to offering expertise only in one specific orientation (Wosket 2000a). We believe strongly that approach-oriented supervisors should restrict themselves to supervising within their own modality unless or until they have done so and are able to respectfully and effectively work with practitioners with backgrounds different to their own. That said, we also acknowledge how important it can be for a trainee counsellor or psychotherapist to be supervised by a supervisor well versed in the orientation in which they are being trained. This should result in a high level of consistency between supervision and training and enable the trainee and supervisor together to connect theory with practice in detail.

Developmental models represent one of the major strands of supervision approaches that take the process and function of supervision as their starting point. A considerable number of such models emerged, predominantly from the United States, in the 1980s. The most fully conceptualized and enduring of these is the 'Integrated Developmental Model', which has been in development for over 25 years (Stoltenberg and McNeill 2010). A summary of this model is given in Chapter 1.

In the United Kingdom Hawkins and Shohet (2012) have further developed their earlier work (Hawkins and Shohet 1989, 2000, 2006) and now include a developmental dimension to fit alongside their well-known process model, often referred to as the 'seven-eyed' model. In summary their model articulates seven discreet yet interrelated levels where supervisory attention can be focused. The first three levels sit within the therapist–client system; the second three within the supervisor–supervisee system; and the seventh is the context within which supervision takes place. In the therapist–client matrix, attention may focus upon: (1) the content of the session with particular regard to the client's perspective; (2) consideration of interventions and strategies employed by the therapist, their impact and alternative options; (3) exploration of the dynamics of the process and the relationship through attending to the boundaries of the session, non-verbal behaviours and intangibles such as images, hunches and metaphors relating to the material presented in therapy.

In the second matrix the supervision process becomes the vehicle through which supervision issues are raised and addressed through the next three foci. These are:

(4) the therapist's counter-transference responses (unaware reactions to the client stemming from the therapist's internal processes), which the supervisor helps the therapist bring into the here and now of the supervision session; (5) parallel or mirroring processes, where shifts in the dynamics between supervisor and supervisee are considered as possible reflections of the dynamics between therapist and client; and (6) the supervisor's counter-transference, where internal responses arise in the supervisor that may have been missed by the therapist but become available for consideration in supervision when the supervisor experiences significant shifts in feeling, mood or composure (for example tiredness, boredom or embarrassment). The seventh focus, to which we shall return later in this chapter, is that of the context within which supervision takes place.

Also in the United Kingdom, Carroll (1996) and Inskipp and Proctor (2002) have sought to identify, and where possible integrate, a number of theoretical dimensions of supervision. Meanwhile Milne (2009) has developed an Evidence-Based Clinical Supervision Model, within the field of clinical psychology. In differing ways these various authors seek to provide comprehensive and systematic treatment of the entire supervision process.

When we first put forward the Cyclical Model, we perceived a need for a model that provided a clear map of the entire process of supervision and also suggested a workable methodology for accomplishing supervision objectives. The need for such an integrated model had already been acknowledged in the supervision literature, both in the United Kingdom and in America (Bartlett 1983; Bernard and Goodyear 1992; Blocher 1983; Carroll 1988; Ellis 1991; Friedlander *et al.* 1989). Hart was typical of those writers and researchers who lamented the lack of systematic training and of conceptual models for the development of competent practitioners:

> Few supervisors have received formal training and even fewer have been given a conceptual framework for organising their supervisory activities. Most supervisors begin their supervisory tasks by relying on memories of their previous supervisors and on their clinical approach to therapy as guidelines. One can imitate an outstanding supervisor, but without theory or a conceptual model one does not really understand the process of supervision.
>
> (Hart 1982:27)

Back in 1980, Leddick and Bernard commented on the fragmented state of supervision theory, saying that 'there are few formulas for the successful practice of supervision, but there are many implied directives' (p. 186). In 1983 Blocher bemoaned 'the deplorable extent' of the 'theoretical and indeed intellectual malaise' relating to the literature on counsellor supervision and added that 'supervision is something done rather casually with a "seat of our pants" approach' (p. 27). Matters appeared to have moved little by 1988 when Carroll, surveying the British scene, joined the cry for a systematic framework and theory for the understanding and practice of supervision. Acknowledging the different conceptualization of the process and function of supervision in Britain compared with how it is understood across the Atlantic, he indicated the need for a model adapted to the requirements of British counsellors: 'We need to be careful that we do not transport theories that work well in other climates to Britain without serious investigation that they will adapt well to the changing environment. Counselling supervision may not be a good traveller' (Carroll 1988:389).

In 1991 Ellis was still highlighting the void in relation to generally accepted approaches to supervision. 'Apparently, the repeated appeals for a theoretically driven, programmatic, and empirically based approach to the practice of supervision have mostly gone unheeded' (Ellis 1991:238). In our view these criticisms have largely been addressed with a range of effective models and frameworks currently available to new and experienced supervisors alike. We consider the Cyclical Model to be one such model.

A cyclical model for the supervision of counsellors and psychotherapists

The model we present here provides an overarching framework for the supervision process. It applies along the spectrum from novice to experienced practitioners and encompasses aims, process, function and methodology. Our intention has been to formulate a model that is of interest and value to supervisors from a number of persuasions and professions. The framework is integrative and designed to provide a firm yet flexible structure into which a range of different approaches can be incorporated. For example, we consider there to be a very good fit between our model and Hawkins and Shohet's (2012) seven-eyed model, with the Cyclical Model providing a sequential pathway through the work, whilst the seven-eyed model offers a set of levels that is particularly applicable to working within the central 'Space'.

The Cyclical Model of supervision has been developed from practice, and by this we mean from our practice as counsellors, trainers, consultants and supervisors. It is also imbued with the awareness that we bring from our own ongoing experience of being clients within a therapeutic relationship. The idea for the model grew particularly from our experience of running what was at the time a Certificate programme in Counsellor Supervision at the College of Ripon and York St John (now York St John University). Although we covered a wide range of theories and approaches over the 12 months of the course, we increasingly found this to be a rather fragmented way of training counsellors to become supervisors. While we did not want to lose our integrationist approach to the education and development of supervisors, we increasingly felt the need to offer a more holistic framework and methodology as our training medium. We wished to do this without reducing our coverage of a range of different models and approaches as we felt that this was a strength of the course and was something that the students themselves valued highly, since they were thereby encouraged to develop their own style and ways of working rather than being forced into a singular theoretical straitjacket.

While we were clear about what we wanted to cover on the course, an opportunity for development became apparent, as expressed in the questions that sometimes arose from students, such as:

- I'm just beginning to supervise, can you tell me how to get started?
- How do we choose which approach to use, and when?
- Can you recommend one approach over another?
- I understand the theory but how do I actually use it in my supervision work?
- Can you (the tutors) explain to us your approach to supervision?

Perhaps the real test of any learning is whether that learning can be conveyed to others in a way that is understandable and able to be duplicated in practice. Although we were comfortable with our own practice of supervision and were able to demonstrate and discuss this with students, we began to realize a need to articulate some of the principles and assumptions underlying our practice more clearly and to delineate the process and methodology in a more systematic manner. In particular we have attempted to answer four fundamental questions about the supervision process through the development of our own model:

- What are we aiming to do?
- What are we actually doing?
- What works?
- Why does it work?

Because as individuals our backgrounds and training in both therapy and supervision have areas of divergence and areas of convergence, the model that we have developed is a synthesis of those differences and similarities. We hope that this adds richness and variety to the model in so much as it is developed from a combination of our two therapeutic backgrounds, which together encompass humanistic, psychodynamic and cognitive-behavioural elements. This has enabled us to consider the subject from a variety of perspectives and to overcome some of the unseen areas and limitations unavoidably inherent in a one-person, one-school approach to the topic. In so doing our hope and intention is that we have produced a model that is synergetic and accessible rather than disjointed and incoherent.

We have called this the *Cyclical Model of Supervision*, as the notion of a circle conveys the seamless pattern and recurring rhythm of the supervision process as we see it. We conceptualize supervision as a two-way, interactive process in which the supervisor and supervisee act upon and influence one another throughout a sequence where the end (re-contracting) is also mirrored in the beginning (the contract). Good supervision, we believe, should allow for a two-way flow in which both supervisor and supervisee are responsive to each other's input. Supervision therefore becomes a dynamic learning and developmental process in which both parties learn and grow together. This is not to say that we conceptualize the relationship necessarily as one of equality (unless the process is one of consultancy rather than supervision there is normally a legitimate power imbalance in favour of the supervisor), although it is certainly one of partnership where collaborative investigation provides the basis for the work done. Inherent within this conceptualization of the supervision process as an interactive one is the notion that both supervisor and supervisee are open to challenge and feedback given in honest and constructive ways.

Stages of the supervision model

The supervision model has five main stages of Contract, Focus, Space, Bridge and Review, each of which subdivides into five further steps, as shown in Figure 3.1.

Although the stages and steps are presented here as a sequential process this is not meant to imply that the supervisor should insist on starting each supervision session at Stage 1 and have worked systematically through to Stage 5 by the end

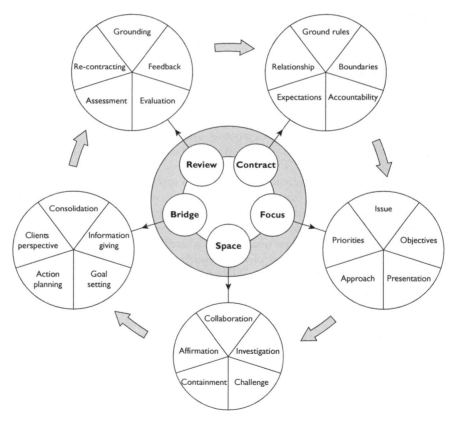

Figure 3.1 The Cyclical Model of supervision.

of the session. When a supervisor and supervisee first embark upon their work together, agreeing a working contract has to be addressed before client material can be safely explored, but beyond that the model is designed to be used with flexibility and pragmatism and can be entered at any stage. Similarly, in Figure 3.1 each stage is represented by a circle of equal size, but this is not intended to represent that the same amount of time that should be spent in each; over time we would expect that most time is spent in Stage 5: Space. The welfare of the client is always preeminent and this may well determine at which stage the model is entered, or which step of that stage is used as the access point. How this is likely to work in practice will become clearer as we move through the model stage by stage and step by step in the next five chapters.

Stage 1: Contract

Contracting in supervision, as in counselling and psychotherapy, performs a vital function in underpinning the entire process and relationship. A contract is an agreement entered into by both parties that contains, supports, gives structure, establishes informed participation by those involved, and provides direction and purpose to the work undertaken. A clear and specific contract sets the agenda for the task and process, reduces anxiety by helping to demystify the process and lays down the ground rules. Contracting should occur at the beginning of any supervisory relationship. It can also occur as re-contracting throughout the ongoing work, and the fact that re-contracting is occurring at various intervals is usually the sign of a healthy and growing relationship and a developing task.

Stage 2: Focus

The focus of a supervision session is the subject or material under consideration at that particular point or stage of the supervision process. Focusing normally starts with the supervisee presenting some aspect of their work for the supervisor and supervisee to explore together. The function of the focus is to ensure that supervision starts with a significant issue for the supervisee and is relevant to the client work. Focusing as a process develops the supervisee's responsibility for making the best use of the supervision opportunity. It encourages intentionality (direction and purpose) and reflection, and ensures that the supervisee has prepared for the supervision in advance of the meeting.

Stage 3: Space

Creating and holding a space is at the heart of the supervision process. It is the place where the therapist is held, supported, challenged and affirmed in his or her work. Space is where movement and insight can occur as a result of the exploratory work undertaken by the supervisor and supervisee. It is also the place where 'not knowing' and confusion are accepted and tolerated in the belief that time and attention given to the client and to the supervisee are beneficial to the therapeutic endeavour, even when a comfortable resolution of issues may not be achieved. It is also where most supervision time is likely to be spent, for, as Scaife (2010:83) points out in discussing the Cyclical Model:

> issues brought to supervision are sometimes given insufficient "air space", there being an apparent degree of urgency to reach a destination. This model emphasises the "space" as the part of the session that is likely to take up the most time. The space is the primary stage in which reflection can take place.

Stage 4: Bridge

The function of a bridge in supervision is to provide a way back into the work that the supervisee is undertaking with the client. It is a process that, at its best, ensures that learning and awareness from supervision are integrated and applied with caution and sensitivity in the therapeutic work. Just as the supervisee is asked to come to supervision with a focus to make sure that the supervision work is relevant to the client work, so too the supervisee is helped to go away from supervision with the recognition that the process will have made a difference, even if the difference is simply an awareness that nothing tangible needs to change.

Stage 5: Review

Review in supervision may take the form of evaluation or assessment of the supervisee's work. If this is so, it should not be the only review that is happening. Whether or not the supervisor has some formal assessment role to fulfil in relation to the supervisee's development, there should also be regular, ongoing mutual feedback taking place. At best this will happen to some extent in every session at a micro level. It should also occur at the macro level at regular intervals, where the supervisor and supervisee stand back from the immediate work to evaluate progress and the current state of their relationship and task. Building-in review as an integral part of the supervision process ensures that both partners actively reflect upon and monitor the standard and quality of their own professional practice and their mutual endeavour.

The context of supervision

It is important to give appropriate attention to the context within which supervision occurs (Copeland 2005); this is represented by the shaded area in Figure 3.1. The boundary between supervision and its context has an intrinsic degree of permeability: the context has influence upon supervision and supervision has influence upon the context in which it takes place. It is also the case that much of what takes place in supervision is rightly private, known only by the supervisor and supervisee(s) who participate.

Some contextual influences can have a direct impact upon supervision. Depending upon circumstances, these may include:

- the setting within which the supervisee works;
- the organization within which supervision takes place;
- the training institute within which the trainee supervisee is training;
- the training institute within which the trainee supervisor is training;
- requirements of professional organizations to which one or both belong;
- the impact of a professional complaint or dispute;
- the career or life stage of the supervisor or supervisee (e.g. just starting out or nearing retirement);
- the therapy that one or the other is undertaking;
- the personal matters of one or the other, such as family demands including caring commitments, medical conditions or changes in financial circumstances.

When one or more of these or similar contextual influences is having an impact it is important to acknowledge this in supervision and give some attention to any consequences, boundary issues or needs that arise as a result.

Alongside these direct influences there will be other, generally more diffuse, contextual influences that are likely to pervade the background of supervision, but occasionally make their presence felt. These may be more difficult to identify as their impact may be quite subtle, secondary or less easy to quantify. Examples of this second category might include:

- prevalent cultural, economic or political conditions;
- debates or shifts within the profession;
- media interests that overlap in some way with the work of the supervisee or supervisor.

It is important to be able to steer a course that avoids either exaggerating or minimizing the impact of such influencing factors upon supervisory work.

Assumptions underlying the model

The model is firmly grounded in a set of assumptions about supervision that govern and inform our practice. The most important of these for us are:

1   The primary purpose of supervision is to enhance the therapeutic value of the therapeutic process.
2   An important secondary function is to promote the growth of therapeutic competence in the supervisee.
3   Where the client's welfare may be at risk, addressing this should supersede any other task or function.

4 Supervision is primarily a containing and enabling process, rather than an educational or therapeutic process (although it can also be a transformative process for both supervisee and supervisor).

5 Supervision is a holistic process containing embodied, affective and cognitive elements.

6 Supervision should be supervisee-centred and take place within a relationship where the supervisor offers the core conditions of warmth, respect, genuineness and empathic understanding.

7 Good therapists do not necessarily make good supervisors, and a therapist requires training and a clear conceptualization of the practice and process of supervision in order to function effectively in the role of supervisor.

8 Supervisors require ongoing supervision of their supervision work in the same way that counsellors and psychotherapists require supervision of their client work.

In addition to these important assumptions are a number of guiding principles that govern our work as supervisors. These are:

• Both unconscious and dissociative processes can influence the process of supervision.
• We do not have to understand everything that is happening in supervision and can accept that 'not knowing' is a valuable and necessary part of the process.
• Supervision, to be effective, must be exploratory. It may also be action-oriented but this is not always necessary in order for it to be effective.
• The act of the supervisee and supervisor reflecting together upon the therapeutic process in supervision is, of itself, facilitative of that process.
• Sometimes the act of reflecting in supervision appears to move the client's process by itself – this is mysterious but observable.
• Supervision on the work with one client can free up the work with another.
• Aspects of the therapist's work with the client are often replayed in some form (normally outside of immediate awareness) in the supervision session.
• The supervisee will unconsciously both censor the material presented and also give clues as to what most needs addressing.
• Dealing with the dynamics of the relationship between supervisor and supervisee is an important aspect of the supervision process and will frequently throw light on the work with the client.
• Supervision can be experienced as more exposing for the supervisee than being a client in their own therapy.
• Supervision helps to maintain a 'field of learning' within which client, therapist and supervisor are all learning. The maintenance of this field somehow increases the potential for the client to grow. Thus the learning of the therapist can in itself facilitate growth in the client.

The assumptions and guiding principles summarized here are integrated within the model and will be explained more fully within the stages and steps to which they particularly apply. We would suggest that it is important for any supervisor to examine their core values and beliefs about supervision in order to develop their own guiding principles and make explicit those assumptions that underlie their practice. It behoves every supervisor to reflect upon their own philosophy of supervision in order that they are able, when called upon, to explain and justify their chosen style and approach to their supervisees, in the same way that counsellors and psychotherapists should be able to explain the rationale for their therapeutic conceptualization and choice of strategies to their clients. One of our prime objectives in developing and disseminating a coherent and accessible model of supervision is to take one step further the important and necessary process of demystifying the supervision process in the same way that the counselling and psychotherapy process has become more open to scrutiny over the last decades.

In summary, two criteria have been important in the development of the model. Firstly, the model needed to be sufficiently complex to encompass the realities of the supervision process and its application, and secondly, it needed to be simple to understand and use (given the existence of requisite skills in the would-be supervisor). Building on these important criteria, we have produced a model that offers a framework for the practice of supervision at two levels – both within individual sessions and also from session to session. Harris and Brockbank (2011:168) have described this feature of the Cyclical Model as 'holographic' in that 'it may represent the shape of an individual supervision session, and it may also represent the shape of an entire supervision cycle, over a year or more'.

A final word of caution needs to be added about the application of this, or any, model of supervision. A model needs to be humanized if it is to be applied with care, flexibility and sensitivity. If this does not happen the practitioner merely operates as a technician and the supervisee may well feel devalued or treated as an object. As well as internalizing a useful process model, the truly competent supervisor will possess the personal qualities and interpersonal skills to bring that model alive, so that it is used within a caring and respectful relationship (Wosket 1999).

In the following five chapters the stages of the supervision model will be described and explained in some depth. Each chapter will provide a rationalization for that particular stage with an examination of the skills and processes pertaining to its application.

Chapter 4

Stage 1: Contract

If supervisor and supervisee have sufficient tools and a framework for addressing the beginning of their supervision relationship, they are able to make an ordered and intentional start to their work together. If they lack the necessary skills and working knowledge to do this, the beginning may be ragged and confusing, with stops and starts as the participants attempt to sort out the necessary details as they go along.

Establishing a contract creates a foundation for supervision, providing a safe platform upon which client work can become the sustained focus of attention. As Hewson (1999) has argued, effective contracts work to minimize hidden agendas and create mutuality that guards against the abuse of power in supervision.

Contracting in supervision has several important aspects. These are highlighted in Figure 4.1 and will be considered in turn. It is not envisaged that every initial contract will need to take account of all aspects, although most are likely to be touched on at some point in the process of the supervision work. The parts of contracting shown in the diagram can also be viewed as separate steps to be worked through in the process of establishing a contract, or to be re-visited at any point where re-contracting is required. By contracting, we do not necessarily refer to the drawing up of a written contract read, agreed and signed by both parties, although Thomas (2007) argues for written documentation setting out the terms upon which supervision is offered in order to ensure that the supervisee makes an informed decision to undertake supervision. Contracting is often a process that occurs over a number of sessions and the supervisor should be sensitive to the needs and preferences of the supervisee in the way that the contract is constructed and implemented.

Two examples will serve to illustrate this flexible use of contracting. In the first, a new supervisee (who is an experienced counsellor) arrived for the initial session with a clear and comprehensive written account of his expectations of supervision, his preferences for ways of working and the practical issues he wished to address before discussing his client work. The first half of the session was taken up with negotiating a contract by considering each of the items on his list in turn. It subsequently emerged in a later session that the counsellor had recently had a negative experience of supervision, which he had terminated prematurely because of the supervisor's apparent inability to maintain clear boundaries around the

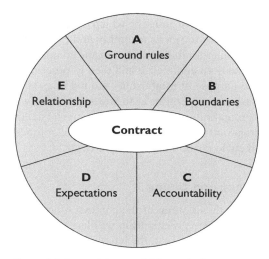

Figure 4.1 Supervision model Stage 1: Contract.

supervision relationship. Through his approach to contracting with his new supervisor, the counsellor was clearly safeguarding himself by making his expectations and requirements explicit from the outset, with the intention of preempting a repetition of his difficulties with the previous supervisor.

In the second example a new supervisee, who was relatively inexperienced and still undertaking her counselling training, was about to receive non-managerial supervision for the first time. She arrived eager to discuss her work and it was the supervisor who introduced the notion of a contract at a point where the supervisee appeared about to plunge straight into a presentation of her material. At that stage the supervisor merely highlighted the aspects of the contract that might need to be addressed during the course of the supervision work and indicated which of those he felt it was necessary to cover in the early stages. The supervisor and supervisee then agreed to spend the last ten minutes of that session covering the practical arrangements required for the work to proceed next time and negotiated to make the space for other contracting issues as, and when, they appeared relevant to the work in progress. At the end of the session the supervisee disclosed that she had felt very anxious about presenting her work, but also very needy because of her lack of supportive supervision. It had been important for her to get into the work straight away as this had felt like the best use of valuable supervision time and had helped her to overcome her 'performance' anxiety.

Both these examples demonstrate how a sensitive supervisor can respond constructively to the immediate needs of the supervisee, whilst also ensuring that the tasks necessary to create and subsequently maintain a constructive working relationship are undertaken.

Ground rules: Step I-A

By ground rules we mean the principles by which the supervision task and process are to be regulated in order to run as smoothly and efficiently as possible. The establishing of ground rules for the organization and administration of supervision is necessary for the work to commence and then to proceed in a structured and orderly fashion. The purpose of establishing ground rules is to reach agreement between the supervisor and supervisee as to how supervision will be managed and maintained. Clear ground rules help to prevent misunderstandings and unnecessary repetitive negotiations each time an administrative or procedural issue arises. Ground rules are likely to cover the following areas.

Duration, frequency and timing

Duration refers both to the duration of the contract – how long both parties are envisaging that the supervision relationship will last – and to the duration of the sessions themselves. To take the first, the length of time over which a supervisor and supervisee may choose to work together can be governed by a number of factors. In general, it is unsettling and confusing for a supervisee, particularly one in training, to switch supervisors frequently. On the other hand, a practitioner who stays with the same supervisor for many years may be in danger of falling into a comfortable, even collusive, relationship. Sometimes supervision that is unsatisfactory for the supervisee proceeds because of an assumption that the supervision will stretch ahead regardless, without opportunities ever being given to review the work or the relationship.

As a guideline, we would suggest that supervision lasting less than a year is unlikely to develop the kind of open and trusting relationship where work that is both probing and challenging becomes the norm. Newly qualified therapists and those in training are likely to benefit from the experience of being supervised by a different supervisor every two years or so. Experienced practitioners, more able to be self-challenging and self-affirming, may choose to stay longer with a supervisor who seems to 'fit' their preferred way of working and their requirements for consultative support. There is still the need to beware of complacency, and any therapist who has had the same supervisor for five years or more might do well to ask themselves whether the discomfort of losing a familiar and valued supervisor would outweigh the benefits to themselves and their clients provided by a fresh and possibly more challenging perspective on their work.

Contracting for the duration of the supervision arrangement should always, in our view, contain an agreement to review that contract after an agreed period or time, say six months, or before then if either party feels concerned about compatibility (Page 1999b). Compatibility issues may arise in terms of personality, expectations, goals, outcomes, styles or approaches used by either supervisor or supervisee. Supervision that lasts for shorter periods can still be effective and beneficial to both the supervisee and their clients, although in this case prioritizing the work and considering how to manage termination are important issues to consider from the start of the contract.

The second aspect of duration is the amount of time given to each supervision session. Different supervisors and supervisees will have differing preferences and arrangements. Whether the supervision session lasts for 50 minutes, an hour, an hour and a half or, as might happen in a group, half a day, a proportion of the time, perhaps 5 to 10 per cent of the total session time, needs to be given over to reviewing and re-contracting. The length of sessions is one of the many considerations appropriate for review and may benefit from being amended if it has become sub-optimal for one or both people involved. It is important that the supervisor and supervisee have ample time to explore issues arising from the material presented but do not continue beyond their ability to maintain a conducive level of energy and concentration. This consideration is particularly important given that lapses in concentration and energy may throw important light on the dynamics of the relationship between supervisee and client, which may be masked if concentration fatigue is occurring.

Frequency and timing give consideration to the optimum number of supervision hours undertaken in relation to number of hours of therapy undertaken and to the time of the day in which the session takes place. The British Association for Counselling and Psychotherapy (BACP) is not prescriptive about the amount of supervision required for all practitioners, but does provide some useful guidelines and recommendations (Mearns *et al.* 2008). Counsellors and psychotherapists who are accredited, or eligible for accreditation, by BACP are required to have a minimum of one and a half hours of individual supervision a month, or its equivalent[1] in group supervision (BACP 2013b), and may well need more than this to ensure that their case work, if it is substantial or challenging, is well supervised. BACP does make particular stipulations regarding the amount of supervision required by those in training, where a ratio of one hour of supervision to eight hours of client work is strongly recommended, as an absolute minimum, with every trainee having an opportunity to receive supervision on their practice at least once a fortnight (BACP 2009:9).

The timing of sessions is important in that bad timing can easily detract from the efficacy of the work. It is may seem easier for the supervisor and supervisee to arrange for a meeting to take place at the end of a busy working day, or squeeze a meeting into a lunch hour, than to make time during a hectic daily schedule. This can manifest as an overworked or exhausted supervisor struggling to give time and concentrated attention to a rushed and stressed supervisee, who perhaps has a head full of the jumble of a just-completed intensive day's work, where too many clients have been seen in a period with insufficient breaks or administration time.

Ideally, the supervisor and supervisee should arrange, in advance, to meet at regular intervals and at times where they can make the psychological space for the work. For the supervisee, particularly, this might mean giving half an hour before the meeting to a quiet time for reflection and composure. If the supervisee is in a fairly relaxed state for the supervision it is likely that this will enhance insight and awareness as he or she will be less distracted by extraneous thoughts and more open to the emergence of ideas, feelings and images generated by the material under discussion.

Location

Giving attention to the setting in which supervision takes place is also important. Heery (2008:23) puts it thus:

> I believe getting the basic setting right is fundamental in setting up a working relationship for supervision and paying attention to the details of setting it up is especially important for student supervisees, in that it acts as a model in setting up their own client work. For me, this refers to the taking care of reliability and regularity of sessions, observing time boundaries, ensuring that supervision is unlikely to be interrupted by telephone calls or other demands.

We feel that it is the responsibility of both supervisor and supervisee to ensure that they are mentally, as well as physically, as fully present as possible for the supervision work. Supervision, as much as any other activity, can suffer from the phenomenon of 'presenteeism' (Proctor and Ditton 1989:3), whereby physical attendance belies an absence of full engagement with the task in progress. Occasionally the rigours of professional practice mean that supervisor, supervisee, or both, arrive for the supervision meeting feeling rushed, drained, preoccupied or otherwise distracted. In extreme circumstances this might necessitate either party cancelling and re-scheduling the session. In our experience such a contingency is rarely necessary, as supervision normally has a remarkably re-generative effect on both participants. If this is not the case, it is usually worth considering whether fatigue or boredom are a clue to 'something else' going on in the dynamic between supervisor, supervisee and client. We have had several experiences where supervisees have arrived for supervision in, or close to, tears and yet have been determined to carry on with the task after a few minutes of talking about the immediate difficulty with a supervisor who shows herself to be sufficiently flexible and accommodating to allow that personal material can intrude into, but need not diminish, the supervision work. Such instances occur at the interface of supervision and therapy: we believe that the supervisor can legitimately listen to and acknowledge the personal distress of a supervisee without slipping into being a therapist for their supervisee.

In less extreme instances it is normally sufficient for either person to acknowledge their immediate difficulty and ask for a minute or two to 'fully arrive', perhaps taking the necessary time for themselves by describing their journey or briefly outlining the 'sort of day' they have had. The collegial nature of practitioner supervision can sometimes allow for self-disclosure of this kind to be made by the supervisor without it having a detrimental effect on the supervisee. On the contrary, one could argue that by so doing the supervisor is modelling appropriate self-management, congruence and the legitimacy of being 'good enough' without being infallible.

Fees

It is important to determine the method and level of fee payment at the contracting stage, and it is the supervisor's responsibility to make explicit the fee required and method of payment if this is to be paid directly by the supervisee. In our view it is the responsibility of the supervisor to be transparent about the costs of supervision from the outset to ensure that supervisees are able to make an informed decision about accepting the financial cost inherent in the supervisory contract. Some training providers allocate supervisors to trainees, and in such cases very particular attention should be given to how this takes place to safeguard against trainees feeling, or indeed being, exploited financially.

Where the supervisor is being paid by an organization it can be very helpful to identify a named person within the organization who can then be contacted if any problems over payment arise (Copeland 2005). This can help to separate the payment process from the supervisory work in the sense that the supervisee is not directly responsible for payment and may have no control over how quickly payment takes place. When establishing fees it is also important to be clear about the fee implications of cancelling or missing a session. Without such clarity, supervisors may find themselves in the position of not knowing whether to charge for sessions cancelled at short notice. The consideration, at an early stage, of procedures to handle such occurrences can prevent later anxiety, annoyance, uncertainty and misunderstanding.

Ethical framework

Many agencies and organizations, particularly those in the fields of health and social work, have their own codes of ethics and practice, to which counsellors and psychotherapists working for them are bound. It is therefore important for the supervisor to be aware of any such codes, as these will affect the management and direction of the supervision. Where both supervisee and supervisor are members of BACP it can be useful for them to spend some time together considering the *Ethical Framework for Good Practice in Counselling and Psychotherapy* (BACP 2013a) as this provides clear guidelines about the nature of the work, issues of responsibility, competency, confidentiality, boundaries and the management of the task.

Contact between sessions

It is very important to clarify whether and how the supervisee may contact a supervisor between sessions, otherwise the supervisee may find themselves dealing with, for example, dangerously suicidal clients not knowing whether they can contact their supervisor. We both normally contract that supervisees may make contact between sessions if they are very concerned about the safety or continued wellbeing of a client, or are faced with a difficult issue with ethical implications that will not wait until the next arranged meeting. In our experience this is not onerous, with perhaps a handful of calls each year that have generally been about serious and urgent issues we preferred to be aware of immediately, given that as supervisors we hold a degree of accountability for the actions of our supervisees.

Boundaries: Step I-B

The establishment and maintenance of clear boundaries to structure and hold the work is as important in supervision (Stokes 2009) as it is in counselling and psychotherapy. Boundaries provide safety and containment, and thereby encourage risk-taking and non-defensive engagement. While boundaries in supervision need to be clearly defined this does not also mean that they are narrowly restrictive. A boundary zone, for example, can include a transitional area where negotiation and overlap take place and such a space can be viewed as the interface between two fixed boundary points. Figure 4.2 shows the boundaries and interfaces between training, supervision and therapy.

As well as the boundaries and interfaces between training, supervision and therapy, other important boundaries to consider are those applied to confidentiality, to roles that conflict with the supervisory relationship (for example friendships, business or financial relationships and overlapping work roles) and to sexual relationships. Let us consider each of these in slightly more detail.

Training and supervision

Kadushin (1985) has given equal weight to the educative function of supervision when placed against its administrative and supportive functions. Traditionally, as we have seen, the American paradigm has conceptualized supervision as having

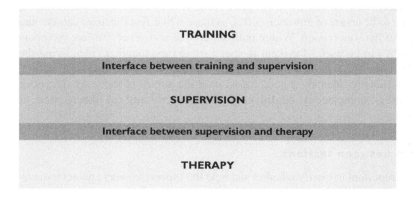

Figure 4.2 Boundaries and interfaces between training, supervision and therapy.

primarily a training function, although we note that in their most recent edition Hess *et al.* (2008:19) talk of 'the dual roles of support and instruction that beneficial supervision provides'. Our own view is that there is little place in supervision for the pupil–teacher aspects of training where the supervisee is viewed as a 'recipient' of the acquired wisdom and knowledge of the more experienced supervisor.

Supervision is not the place to initiate basic training or undertake extensive remedial training with the developing practitioner. A supervisee in need of the acquisition of basic skills, theoretical knowledge and therapeutic characteristics should be directed to a suitable training course where such needs can be addressed systematically and methodically, rather than be dealt with in an *ad hoc* way in supervision. The supervisor should expect (and respect) an amount of knowledge, skill and competence that even a novice practitioner will bring to their therapeutic work and to the supervision. The job of the supervisor is to help the therapist enhance and fully utilize these attributes as they are brought to bear on the work with particular clients. Michael Carroll expresses this elegantly when writing about supervision as a learning journey: 'All learning begins from the learner's frame of reference – teaching invites the learner into the world of the teacher. Who enters the world of the learner?' (Carroll 2011:17).

Learning that enhances the counsellor's skill in using techniques and interventions can take place in a number of ways that do not involve direct or didactic teaching – for example, through role play, feedback, coaching, and the sharing of information and experience. Supervisors may play an important part in helping to articulate the links between what a trainee is learning on their training programme and how that applies to their work with a client, but we see this as facilitating the supervisee's development of their reflective capabilities, rather than teaching. These aspects of the interface between training and supervision will be considered in Stage 4 (Bridge) of the model. There is also a place in supervision for activities intended to expand awareness of diversity and difference, which we will consider in Chapter 11.

Supervision and therapy

Although supervision is not counselling or psychotherapy, it does encompass elements and functions of both. This means that although a boundary between the two certainly exists, and should be adhered to, the boundary is not always immediately apparent until further work at the interface between the two has been undertaken. An example will make this clearer. A female supervisee may present with difficulties in relating to an older, male client. In the course of the discussion the supervisee begins to realize that part of the difficulty concerns her unresolved feelings towards her own father. The supervisor helps her to more fully articulate some of these feelings in order to bring them into awareness and to enable her to decide which emanate from her personal history and which legitimately relate to the here-and-now of her working relationship with the client. This exploration frees the therapist to use some immediacy (Egan 2013) or 'you and me talk' with her client in the next session, which results in a more positive and constructive therapeutic relationship. This supervisee can be contrasted with a second therapist who has several older male clients, all of whom remind her of her father in some disquieting way. The wise supervisor soon refrains from attempting to help the supervisee with examination of these difficulties as if they are purely client-related and indicates the need for her to explore her relationship with her father more deeply through her own personal therapy.

Our view is that personal issues arising from the material presented in a supervision session can legitimately be addressed if, by so doing, the benefit gained for the client work through increased therapeutic potential generated in the supervisee is not outweighed by the loss of focus on the client that such work necessitates. Indeed, there will be occasions when it is essential to step into the space where supervision and therapy overlap in order to safeguard the client. This is because sometimes it is only through work with particular clients that aspects of a supervisee's personal psychological material will emerge and be identifiable. At the same time we need to be aware of the risk of being drawn into collusion with a supervisee's narcissistic self (Tamborski *et al.* 2012), resulting in the locus of attention drifting onto and centring around the supervisee rather than their clients.

Teyber (2000:230) suggests a number of questions that therapists can use to reflect on this boundary territory for themselves:

1   What are my feelings and reactions towards this client?
2   How do my reactions parallel those of significant others in the client's life?
3   What is the client doing to arouse such feelings and reactions in me, and how do these behaviors tie into my conceptualization of the client's generic conflict and interpersonal coping strategies?
4   Do my feelings typify my reactions to significant others in my life and/or to other clients, or are they more confined to this particular client?

These questions support what Neufeldt and Nelson (1999:131) describe as one of the key functions of the supervision of trainee practitioners, namely 'to help novice therapists to develop into reflective practitioners'. Whilst it is more likely that previously unrecognized personal psychological material will be brought to the surface by client work when the counsellor or psychotherapist is inexperienced, development is a continual process and supervisors need to be open to the possibility of this occurring even with highly experienced supervisees.

Whilst recognizing similarities, Ekstein and Wallerstein (1972) understood the essential difference between psychotherapy and supervision as one of *purpose*. While both are helping processes, the main task of psychotherapy is the resolution of inner conflict, whereas the main task of supervision is leading the supervisee towards greater therapeutic skill with his or her clients. Villas-Boas Bowen (1986:298) differentiated between the two in terms of focus: 'In psychotherapy the client has absolute freedom to talk about any realm of experience, but in supervision there is a primary focus—the interaction between the supervisee and the client.' We find such differentiations invaluable in helping us to avoid the sometimes seductive trap of falling into therapy with our supervisees or in pulling us back from the brink when we get close to mixing the two. We agree with Blumenfield's caution, voiced from a psychodynamic perspective, that the supervisor should refrain (from respect if nothing else) from treating the supervisee as if he or she were a client:

> There are many reasons for the supervisor to resist such a temptation. The supervisee has not come as a patient. There has been no history taken, no diagnosis made, no framework for the therapy established . . . The supervisee may be completely unaware of emotional illness, or if aware, has not agreed to expose it to the supervisor. In the absence of full information, the supervisor cannot know what conflicts he or she may be stirring up in the supervisee . . . Interpretations made on such a basis must suggest (and by example, teach) 'wild analysis'.
>
> (Blumenfield 1982:7–8)

Whiston and Emerson (1989) have highlighted the particular vulnerability of the trainee counsellor when invited to enter a counselling relationship with their supervisor, who may also have an assessment role:

> Trainees consent to be supervised; they do not normally consent to be counseled. If they do consent to be counseled, the consent may not be completely voluntary . . . Trainees could feel compelled to acquiesce to counseling because of their perceptions of the consequences of refusing.
>
> (Whiston and Emerson 1989:321)

This highlights a power issue at the heart of the argument against supervisors engaging in therapy with their supervisees. Supervisees may, quite understandably, be reluctant to disclose personal material that they fear may have a negative effect on the supervisor's evaluation of them. In Whiston and Emerson's view the inequality of power in the supervision relationship is likely to transpose to the counselling relationship, in which case

> it is expected that the counseling would proceed at a slower pace and that identification of underlying issues may never occur. In attempting to counsel trainees, the supervisor may, in fact, preclude the trainees from seeking the assistance they need.
>
> (Whiston and Emerson 1989:321)

Blocher (1983) has gone a step further in expressing a viewpoint that places uninvited therapeutic interventions in supervision alongside the abuse of power: 'To assume that the supervisor has the right . . . to function purely in a self-appointed, unrequested therapy role is the epitome of egocentric insensitivity, and verges closely upon the unethical and unprofessional' (p. 29). In a study that investigated changes in supervisors' and supervisees' perceptions of the supervisory relationship over ten sessions, Kauderer and Herron (1990) discovered that while supervisors tended to have clear boundaries between supervision and therapy, supervisees did not. Supervisees were found to have 'a tendency to blur these boundaries, since they saw self-exploration as a positive characteristic of their participation' (pp. 478–9). It is therefore an important responsibility of the supervisor to monitor and maintain the boundary between supervision and therapy, as this may not always be apparent to the supervisee engrossed in their own introspective work.

Although supervision is not therapy, and should not be used by the supervisor as an occasion for covertly influencing the supervisee to disclose personal material that he or she may later regret, it can be the medium through which the supervisee makes their way into personal therapy (Sharratt Wise *et al.* 1989). In a study of 142 advanced graduate students' experiences of supervision, Allen *et al.* (1986) discovered that a quarter of their sample entered counselling or psychotherapy as a result of their involvement in supervision. Supervision can be therapeutic in the same way that it can be educational, while remaining a discipline that is separate from both training and therapy.

Confidentiality

Confidentiality is fundamental to the ethical and safe practice of supervision and it is the supervisor's responsibility to make explicit at an early stage in contracting any limits to absolute confidentiality. We believe that all counsellors and psychotherapists should inform their clients that they receive supervision, for a number of reasons. Firstly, telling our clients that we discuss our work with a supervisor makes explicit the boundaries of confidentiality. Secondly, this gives a message about the level of professional standards to which we work and lets the client know something of what they should expect from good therapeutic practice. Thirdly, we model for our clients that it is acceptable to need the help and support of another person and, fourthly, it lets our clients know that an additional level of support and containment exists for their benefit. In disclosing that we receive supervision, we recognize that the client is being asked to take an enormous leap of faith. Not only are we asking clients to entrust their innermost thoughts and feelings to their therapist, we are also expecting them to entrust their disclosures, second hand, to an unknown third person: the supervisor. It is therefore of the utmost importance that the parameters of confidentiality are watertight, and in supervision this sometimes involves introducing particular safeguards.

Supervision and therapy are fairly 'incestuous' professions due to the many interlocking networks created by a finite number of counselling and psychotherapy practitioners within a particular community, and many will not only see clients but also be involved in training and supervision. Extra precautions are therefore often required in the management of confidentiality to prevent seepage and to ensure that anonymity is maintained. This may involve not using any names or distinguishing characteristics, or not playing audio or video recordings in which participants are likely to be recognizable. It is also useful when contracting to make explicit that such overlaps may exist, unknown to both parties at the initial stages of contracting. It is therefore helpful to agree that if an overlap emerges, or appears to be possible because the supervisor thinks they may know who is being talked about, that this will be acknowledged immediately and the boundary issues considered with the intention of putting in appropriate safeguards. This may involve, for example, an agreement that certain client work will be taken to a different supervisor or indeed that it is time for the supervisee to consider moving to a supervisor in a different geographical area to that in which they work.

Role boundaries

A further dimension of the boundaries needed to contain supervision relationships effectively concerns those separating supervision from friendships, work roles, social and sexual contact, or business and other financial relationships. We are doubtful that friendships or close working relationships mix well with supervision, due to the difficulty in keeping the supervision separate and untainted by other relationship dynamics. In particular the twin dangers of collusion and avoidance are almost certain to threaten the efficacy of the work where the participants have a vested interest in maintaining a sound working, or social, alliance over and above their joint responsibilities to the supervision relationship. Where an overlap of work or social roles with a supervision relationship exists, the supervisor is responsible for making explicit the boundary between them and for ensuring, as far as is possible, that one relationship does not intrude on the other.

The damaging nature of power abuse by a therapist misusing a privileged position to obtain sexual gratification has been well charted (Gabbard 2002; Garrett 2002; Norris *et al.* 2003; Russell 1996; Sarkar 2004). Similarly, the power component in the role of supervisor can lead to the sexual exploitation of supervisees. Celenza (2007) sets out clearly one aspect of why 'sexual involvement between supervisor and supervisee constitutes a violation of the letter and intent of existing ethical principles in every mental health discipline' (p. 66) when she explains that

> the supervisory contract includes a mission to impart ethically based practice to the supervisee in various ways: direct teaching, modeling, role-play, identification, and so on. Engaging in a sexual or sexualized transgression with a supervisee is a perversion of this aspect of the supervisory contract since what is being modeled is unethical, the opposite of the purpose and desiring of the mission and context.
>
> (Celenza 2007:66–7)

The powerful and complex dynamics surrounding the use and misuse of power in supervision relationships mean that abuse can also occur in more subtle and insidious ways. One such is through overlapping financial or 'business' relationships. For example, a supervisor might invite a supervisee, who possesses an area of expertise that compliments their own experience and knowledge, to lead a training workshop with them. At first glance this may seem an attractive opportunity for the supervisee, reminiscent of the 'master–apprentice' aspect of traditional mentoring relationships. However, it is rife with pitfalls; some potential and others inevitable. Are they to act as equals in planning and delivering the workshop and, if so, how does that sit with their supervisory relationship? How is payment divided and what happens if the feedback from participants is strongly positive towards the supervisee, resulting in them being asked back to run further workshops on their own? It requires little imagination to see how this would inevitably impact very considerably on the supervisory relationship, possibly damaging it irrevocably. The issue of power in supervision is discussed more fully in Chapter 11.

Accountability: Step 1-C

In our view it is important that supervisor and supervisee explore together to whom they are each accountable, both for the supervisee's client work and what transpires in supervision. This should reduce risk of misunderstandings and can also help in identifying the stakeholders whose influence may be felt, intensely at times, during their supervisory discussions. It will also, in part, clarify the limits to the confidentiality of supervision and as such can usefully model parallel discussions the supervisee needs to have with their clients.

For this purpose accountability can be thought of as existing at a number of layers:

- The first layer, which supervisee and supervisor share, is accountability to the clients of the supervisee. The supervisee and supervisor will seldom be asked to answer for their work together by clients, except in the rare event of a complaint by a client or some form of external investigation if something has gone badly wrong. Nevertheless in our view it is to the clients of the supervisee that primary accountability is due and it is helpful to keep that in consciousness, not to generate fearful defensiveness, but rather to generate a sense of the importance of what the supervisor and supervisee are undertaking together.
- The second layer is accountability to one another: supervisor and supervisee are accountable to each other for their preparation for supervision, ensuring that they keep to agreed arrangements, offer a high quality of attention and focus during each session, and complete any task they have agreed to undertake outside of the sessions. In this respect they each must rely on the other to play their part in the collaborative endeavour of supervision: they are mutually interdependent.

- The third layer of accountability is to any direct stakeholders. These might be the college, university or institute where either the supervisor or the supervisee is undertaking a training programme or the agency where the supervisee sees clients, when that agency may have a direct stake in contracting for or paying for supervision or an indirect stake through their 'vicarious responsibility' (King 2001:12) for the clients of the supervisee. If the supervisor is undergoing training they should obtain permission from their supervisee(s) to take anything from the supervision work into the training course (for example where the supervisor-in-training receives supervision of their supervision practice within a peer- or tutor-led group).
- The fourth layer is accountability to the professions of counselling and psychotherapy: the professional body or bodies to which they each belong and the requirements for good practice as defined by that body or those bodies. In general the professional body can be thought of as representing and maintaining the good name of the profession. Specifically this layer includes consultative supervision of supervision which we believe the supervisor should tell their supervisees they receive.
- The fifth layer is accountability to the general public: the communities within which clients live and work. Members of this more diffuse group will want to be confident that they can entrust friends, family and colleagues to therapists working in their communities.

In summarizing these layers, we have intended to emphasize the interdependence between the supervisor and supervisee, in order to go some way towards addressing what Falender (2010:22) describes as the challenge of 'balancing tension between fostering a collaborative supervisory relationship and maintaining supervisory accountability'. It is also important to clarify from the outset any specific reporting procedures or evaluation processes (Karpenko and Gidycz 2012) that will need to be undertaken in the future. At the contracting stage it is helpful to establish the principles by which any necessary evaluation will take place, and this is further discussed in Chapter 8.

Expectations: Step 1-D

We will consider expectations of supervision in three categories: those of the supervisee, the supervisor, and other stakeholders. Expectations cover such fundamental issues as the aims, goals, functions and purposes of supervision, together with the preferences, anticipations and responsibilities of the parties concerned.

Given that 'supervisory effectiveness is enhanced by the presence of mutual goals and expectations' (Leddick and Dye 1987:139), it is of fundamental importance that the functions, purpose, aims and goals of supervision are commonly agreed between supervisor, supervisee and organization. Within non-managerial supervision, the agreed aim of supervision is likely to be couched in terms that emphasize the support, development and monitoring of the supervisee. Kadushin (1985) memorably named the three functions of supervision, which underpin such an aim or purpose, as *educative, supportive* and *managerial*, while Proctor (1988) usefully termed them *formative, restorative* and *normative*. By *educative* or *formative* is meant developing the skills, understanding, abilities and professional identity of the supervisee through exploration and reflection on the supervisee's work with clients. The *supportive* or *restorative* function of supervision enables the supervisee to debrief and deal with the emotional effects of intimate therapeutic work, with containment and affirmation provided by the supervisor. The *managerial* or *normative* function provides the quality-assurance aspect of supervision, where the supervisor helps the supervisee to ensure that the needs of the client are being addressed within clearly defined standards of ethical and professional practice. These functions will be considered in more depth in Stage 3 (Space) and Stage 4 (Bridge) of the model. At the contracting stage the priority is for the supervisor, supervisee and, if appropriate, the employing or training organization to reach shared understanding of the balance or emphasis that will be given to each of these functions in supervision.

It is worth looking more closely at the range of responsibilities that pertain to the supervisor and the supervisee in relation to the work undertaken in supervision sessions. If these are not made explicit the work may become untidy, lose focus or boundaries, or degenerate into a muddled and imbalanced encounter.

It is the supervisor's responsibility:

- to ensure that the needs of the client are being addressed through good standards of ethical, professional and non-discriminatory practice;
- to ensure that the time is managed, that the work starts and ends promptly and is divided according to the needs and priorities of the supervisee (or the perceived needs of the client if these appear to be different and paramount);
- to ensure that boundaries between supervisor and supervisee and between supervisee and client are maintained;
- to ensure that the work is focused and that an appropriate balance is maintained between supervision and elements of training/therapy;
- to inform the supervisee of the methods, approaches and supervision style that he or she characteristically uses;
- to address the issue of how the supervisee will prepare and bring material to supervision (e.g. case notes, audio recordings, transcripts);
- to provide a facilitative relationship and to ensure that the work is supervisee-centred by taking into account the supervisee's preferred style of learning and of being supervised;
- to provide feedback that is constructive, balanced and given at regular intervals, and to be open to receiving feedback from the supervisee;
- to provide opportunities to review the work in a formative way, regardless of any summative assessment requirements.

As well as describing his or her responsibilities to the supervisee, the supervisor should also explain clearly what he or she considers to be the supervisee's responsibilities and invite negotiation where this is needed.

Supervisee responsibilities include:

- preparing for the supervision and being clear about objectives for the session;
- being open to feedback and asking for this when it would be welcomed and is not forthcoming;
- developing a non-defensive attitude to the exploration of issues;
- being honest in bringing doubts, difficulties and concerns related to work with clients;
- opening up a dialogue with the supervisor when there are difficulties in the relationship, or in the way the supervision is conducted, which are not being addressed by the supervisor.

It is useful for the supervisor to help the supervisee articulate their expectations and preferences at the outset as such discussion can provide reassurance and confidence in the supervision process or, if it seems sufficient common ground cannot be found, lead to an early termination of the contract. As Blocher (1983) has noted, supervisees 'come with their own unique and worthwhile learning styles and past developmental histories' (p. 33) and it is expedient for the supervisor to spend time eliciting some of these from prospective supervisees as an aid to planning the supervision experience. Asking the supervisee to say something about what they found positive and negative in previous supervision or learning experiences, and how this then fits with what they want and don't want from the current supervision experience, can do this.

An early study undertaken by Allen *et al.* (1986) to evaluate comparisons 'of best and worse psychotherapy supervision' discovered that 'worst experiences are most easily characterizable by what they fail to provide rather than what actually occurs' (p. 95) and early discussion of expectations can hopefully forestall some such omissions. A therapist receiving supervision for the first time may anticipate a rather daunting process whereby their weaknesses in therapy are to be scrutinized and their deficits systematically addressed. To hear that, contrary to such beliefs, the process and relationship will be supportive and enabling can inspire confidence and openness.

Carroll and Gilbert (2005), Inskipp (1999) and Page (1999b) and are amongst those who have written about the preparation of therapists to receive supervision. This process of induction, where supervisors discuss with beginning supervisees their understanding of tasks, purpose and process, can be done through outlining a model of supervision such as the Cyclical Model and discussing how this will be used in practice.

Relationship: Step 1-E

We find it helpful to conceptualize the supervisory relationship as having two distinct aspects or layers: (i) the affective or qualitative relationship between the supervisor and the supervisee; and (ii) the working or 'functional relationship'

(Hart 1982) through the operation of which the tasks of supervision are accomplished. Here we shall consider the quality of the affective relationship while the working relationship will be examined in Stage 3 (Space) of the model.

The affective relationship or supervisory bond that forms the interpersonal foundation upon which the tasks and processes of supervision can take place and the goals achieved needs to be warm and supportive (Bordin 1983; Sloan 2005). Starr and colleagues (2013:345), in their recent research into the supervision experience of a sample (n = 19) of female psychological therapists, articulate the case for the importance of achieving a strong affective relationship based upon their findings: 'This study has found two key tensions within the supervisory experience: (1) the comfort versus the challenge and (2) the experience of knowing and not knowing'. They go on to say, 'It is suggested that it is the supervisory relationship, which is perceived as "safe" and the working alliance therein, that facilitates a supervisee to engage in these conflictual experiences' (Starr *et al.* 2013:345). They then propose that 'the safe supervisory relationship . . . is created through the processes of empowerment, support and joining' (2013:344). Thus having a safe, warm, supportive relationship is not an end in itself but rather a platform for the work to be undertaken together, without which the supervisory dialogue is likely to be restricted and risk averse rather than creative and courageous.

In a study exploring the perceptions of clinical supervision and its influence on work satisfaction and work-related stress amongst a sample of mental health counsellors (n = 71), Sterner (2009) found that the better the supervisee perceived the working alliance with their supervisor to be, the greater their work satisfaction and the lower their level of perceived work-related stress. In a comparable study of a sample of counsellors (n = 232), Gnilka and colleagues (2012) studied supervisees' perceptions of both the working alliance with clients and the supervisory working alliance, and considered how these related to both supervisee stress and coping resources. They found that as supervisees' stress levels increased, their perception of their capacity to form and maintain therapeutically beneficial working relationships with clients reduced. In addition they found that the greater the supervisees' coping resources, the better their perception of their working alliances with clients. Alongside these findings relating to client work they also found that those supervisees reporting lower levels of stress and greater ability to control their environment (one of the coping resources) also reported stronger supervisory alliances.

All of these studies add weight to the beneficial significance of a positive supervisory relationship for the supervisee. It is not possible to extrapolate from these studies that a strong supervisory working alliance has a direct positive impact on client outcomes – a research hypothesis that remains difficult to confirm (Watkins 2011). Nevertheless the findings do support the proposition that a strong supervision relationship is beneficial to the supervisee.

In an earlier study, Webb and Wheeler (1998) surveyed 96 counsellors about their experiences of disclosing sensitive material in supervision (e.g. sexual feelings towards clients, strong feelings towards their supervisors and instances of unorthodox practice). They found a positive correlation between supervisees' perceived levels of rapport with their supervisors and their ability to disclose sensitive issues in supervision. Similarly, a negative correlation was found to exist between the level of rapport with the supervisor and inhibitors of disclosure of sensitive issues. Webb and Wheeler's research indicated that the quality-assurance function of supervision may be importantly mediated by the quality of the supervision relationship if, as their findings suggest, the quality of rapport between supervisor and supervisee is a key determining factor in supervisees' willingness to disclose difficult issues and dilemmas.

A process of negotiation at the contracting stage may serve to promote the quality of the supervisory relationship from the outset and thereby increase the likelihood that the quality-assurance function of supervision will be adequately served. Thus, while it is indisputable that supervisors have a clear mandate to monitor the practice of their supervisees to ensure that client welfare is protected, how this will happen in practice can be talked through with the supervisee. A question during initial contracting, such as 'If I am concerned about your practice, how would you like me to address this with you?' can come as something of a relief to the supervisee and lead to a useful dialogue in which the concerns and expectations of each person are aired in a constructive and open manner. Being allowed to have some say in how their work will be monitored will help the supervisee feel more like an involved party in a true partnership, rather than a potential culprit waiting to be 'caught out'. Such a discussion acknowledges the power differential inherent in the supervisory relationship while seeking to minimize it. Delano and Shah (2006:36), writing in the context of residential social work, offer some insight into why the power balance can be problematic for both supervisee and supervisor:

> It is clear that the structure of power in the supervisory relationship is heavily weighted towards the supervisor. It is an enormous responsibility that can be difficult for the supervisor to accept and be able to use in a thoughtful and ethical way. The feeling of having power weighted so heavily in the supervisor's favour can also lead to much anxiety and even fear for the supervisee.

It is important that supervisors are willing and able to acknowledge the power distribution in the relationship. Bernard and Goodyear express this task well when they suggest that 'supervisors must become accustomed to seeing their power and influence through the eyes of their supervisees' (2009:148). At this early contracting stage of the relationship it is important that power imbalances are acknowledged, thereby naming what exists and putting it on the agenda for further discussion. We shall return to consideration of the power imbalances in the supervisory relationship in Chapter 11, when we examine issues of difference and diversity in supervision.

One of the key supervisory interventions that has been demonstrated to help develop the supervisory relationship, at least when used wisely, is that of self-disclosure (Farber 2006). A study by Ladany and Lehrman-Waterman (1999) revealed that the degree of supervisor self-disclosure appears to predict the strength of the supervisory working alliance. Their data showed that 'the more frequently a supervisor self-disclosed, the greater was the agreement between the supervisor and the trainee on the goals and tasks of supervision and the stronger was the emotional bond between the two' (1999:156). The authors of this study recommended that intentional self-disclosure, used with discretion, is an effective supervision intervention that can be introduced by the supervisor to significantly enhance the quality and productiveness of the supervisory encounter. In particular, their analysis of the data provided by trainees suggested that the willingness of a supervisor to share their vulnerability through disclosing their own struggles with therapeutic dilemmas was especially appreciated by supervisees and helped to correct the power imbalance in the relationship. It is important to note, however, that Ladany and Lehrman-Waterman also found that excessive or inappropriate self-disclosure by the supervisor tended to significantly undermine the supervisory process and relationship. They warned, for instance, that 'supervisor self-disclosures that emphasize the specialness of the supervisor may be a form of counter-transference whereby the supervisor attempts to satisfy her or his needs for approval and adequacy' (1999:153).

A supervision relationship that offers the Rogerian core conditions of respect, empathy and congruence (Rogers 1961) can enormously enhance the quality of the supervision work. The establishment of such a relationship builds a safe and secure framework within which the supervisee can risk exploring difficult and even painful issues, which, if worked through, can prove extremely efficacious to the supervisee's client work. Though hierarchical, the supervision relationship can be experienced as facilitative and even therapeutic. Although trust, respect, empathy and genuineness cannot be taken for granted and have to be demonstrated and earned in a relationship, it can be very reassuring for a supervisee to hear their supervisor voice the hope and intention of providing these at the start of the supervision work. If this is done at the contracting stage it begins already to imbue the work with humanity and warmth and, equally important, encourages immediacy when this might be necessary within the relationship. Such measures during contracting can go a long way towards helping to redress the inequalities inherent in a hierarchical supervision relationship, as well as providing a model for the supervisee about how to establish a facilitative and therapeutic relationship with clients.

We will conclude this chapter with a supervisee's perspective on the place and value of contracting within supervision. These are her words:

> The contracting session with a supervisor for me is vital to underpin the whole of the supervisory relationship. It is important in giving the opportunity to negotiate not only what is expected of me in terms of preparation prior

to supervision and the nitty-gritty issues of payment, frequency, etc. but also for me to say what I want and need from supervision – what I expect. This gives a real sense of mutual respect, which significantly heightens my preparedness to bring those issues that concern me the most in my counselling work – to put myself on the line. I need a supervisor who has the skills and insight to really challenge me and my work and also to support and encourage me, not only by what they do, but by who they are. If my supervisor models contracting effectively and efficiently it gives me a real sense of their competency.

Note

1   For BACP (2013b), group supervision 'hours' are calculated as follows: for groups of four supervisees or less the actual hours are divided by two. For groups of more than four supervisees hours are divided by the number of supervisees participating. For example, a three-hour group with six supervisees provides the equivalent of 30 minutes of supervision for each supervisee.

Chapter 5

Stage 2: Focus

Following the establishment of a contract, attention can shift to the material the supervisee is bringing to supervision. We call this point of entry into the central work of supervision the 'Focus'. A focus is both a locus of attention and a point of convergence and, in supervision, is the topic or issue towards which both supervisor and supervisee are directing their concentrated energy and attention. In gestalt terminology (Houston 2013) it is 'figure', while the context of the supervisee's client work constitutes the 'ground' from which the focus emerges. It is important for a focus to be established and maintained in order that the work develops systematically and purposefully, and irrelevancies are minimized.

The steps that comprise the process and task of focusing are given in Figure 5.1. Not all steps are required to be worked through in every supervision session, although sometimes this is necessary. It is, for instance, important for the supervisee to come to each session with a supervision issue. However, the approach the supervisor will use in helping the practitioner explore the issue may have been predetermined at the contracting stage, particularly if the supervisor favours one orientation or style of supervision. Supervisors who work in a more eclectic or integrated fashion may gear their approach, session by session, to what appears most useful in matching the supervisee's particular issue or issues, as they arise.

Issue: Step 2-A

It is the norm for the supervisee to bring with them one or more issues they wish to explore in supervision. Usually this will form the main focus or foci for the session and will be where the supervision starts. Only in the case of significant overriding concerns should the supervisor impose his or her own agenda at the start of a session; we shall consider circumstances when this might occur in Step 2-E.

The examples of supervisory topics below offer some indication of the range of issues that we have dealt with in supervision. Against those topics not transparently focused on work with the client we have included some indication of how the issue can be kept relevant to the client. Keeping issues relevant should not be an onerous task for the supervisor; that is they should not find themselves

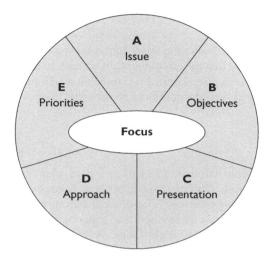

Figure 5.1 Supervision model Stage 2: Focus.

constantly dragging an unwilling supervisee back to the client. Rather, the supervisee should be a willing ally, provided a shared understanding of the tasks of supervision has been agreed at the Contract stage. Whatever the issue, a fundamental question for the supervisor to keep in mind at this step is 'Why have you chosen to bring this issue to supervision today and to present the work in this manner?'

Current clients

Work with a current client is by far the most common issue brought to supervision. This can vary from the supervisee simply wanting space to reflect upon the work with a particular client through to consideration of significant concerns about risk, appropriateness of the length or type of therapy being offered, or feeling lost or stuck in the work with the client. Supervisees with very few clients may simply come expecting to talk about the clients they have and may benefit from encouragement to sharpen their focus – to define what aspect of the work with the client they want to highlight or what they want out of time spent discussing their work with that client. Those with larger caseloads will typically have prioritized certain clients, perhaps some they have not previously brought to supervision, those for whom they have a concern, those with a presenting issue they have not previously encountered or they may simply feel time spent in supervision will help enhance the work with that client.

An experienced supervisee chose to bring a client to supervision precisely because she felt that this client was very easy to overlook. The supervisory discussion centred upon the client's current unmet needs and her behaviour patterns, which made it unlikely that her needs would be noticed. A number of questions emerged about the client's early experiences as well as strategies for bringing her current needs into the open. In the subsequent supervision session, the supervisee reported that the questions she took back to the client had revealed that she had grown up with a sister with significant health problems and that the client had recognized how she continues to subsume her needs, as she had as a child.

Skill deficits

Sometimes supervisees will want to focus on a particular skill or method about which they feel uncertain. This can happen in the early stages of training, or where a practitioner is changing their way of working or starting to work with a different client group. Provided it is understood that supervision is not a substitute for training, this can be an appropriate focus. A psychotherapist, familiar with operating open-ended contracts in private practice, had recently started a part-time post in a university counselling service, which operated an assessment plus six sessions model. He came to supervision wanting to explore his frustration about how little he felt he could achieve in the sessions available. Having given the supervisee space to express his feelings for a few minutes, the supervisor asked if he was regretting taking the university post, at which the supervisee laughed and said 'I took it because I wanted to learn about working in a time-limited way and now I know how much I have to learn!' They were then able to have a constructive discussion about a number of ways he could take that forward by attending training, by reading and by talking to colleagues in the service about how they worked. The supervisee then went on to present a student with whom he had undertaken an assessment, setting the supervisory objective of identifying an appropriate focus for time-limited work.

Emerging themes

A therapist came to supervision saying that she wanted to talk about three clients, all of whom she had identified as dealing with issues of loneliness in their therapy. The supervisor asked if loneliness was an issue for the supervisee at present and she felt it was not, so they proceeded to focus on each client in turn, drawing out some useful understandings about the work with each. As they started to discuss the third client, the supervisor asked the supervisee if she was holding back in some way and the therapist agreed that she wanted to reach out and comfort the client, whom she felt was very isolated. When they came to review their session the therapist said that the intervention about holding back had been very useful because she had realized at that moment that the common ground was not that the clients were all dealing with loneliness, but that they were all clients whom she at times felt she wanted to reach out and hug, and she did not know what to do about that. The supervisor acknowledged that hearing the supervisee name the theme of loneliness had probably guided her to wonder if the supervisee was holding back in some way. They agreed to pick up on the issue of wanting to hug clients at a future session.

Organizational issues

A counsellor working in a busy doctors' surgery explored in supervision how issues such as lack of communication between himself and doctors, insufficient breaks and administration time between sessions, pressure to move clients on to make room for new referrals from a growing waiting list and lack of information about changes in clients' medication were proving inimical to effective counselling work. These aspects were then discussed in relation to one particular client, whose anti-depressant medication had recently been increased, without the counsellor being informed, to the apparent detriment of the counselling process. As the discussion progressed, the counsellor became aware of a strong sense of frustration and of feeling undermined in his work. An outcome of the supervision was the counsellor's objective to request attendance at a meeting of the practice partners and to put some of his organizational issues on the agenda for discussion.

Stress

A therapist working for a busy voluntary agency brought the issue of management of her case-load. Several of her colleagues were absent from work for extended periods and she had felt under pressure to increase her intake of clients to cover the shortfall created by their absence. The counsellor was frequently working throughout the day and into the evening, by which time she felt drained and emotionally exhausted. The supervisor encouraged her to explore the effect that her exhaustion had on those clients seen in the evening slots. The counsellor began to recognize that distraction and edginess caused by tiredness and resentment might leave her clients feeling unheard and misunderstood. She also became aware that the pressure to increase her case-load had come, not so much from outside pressure, but from her own, possibly misguided, belief that all troubled people who approached the agency had to be seen immediately. As a result of the supervision the counsellor became open to considering other options, such as referring would-be clients to another agency or giving them an appointment for a time in the future when another counsellor would be available to see them.

Motivation

All counsellors and psychotherapists will, on occasion, question their motivation for the work. Inevitably too, they will feel lack of motivation at certain times and this can affect the therapeutic process. Such doubts and uncertainties are natural and particularly common as part of the 'learning curve' for trainee therapists, in which they are often linked to the normal and passing phase of feeling deskilled wherein trainees will doubt they have what it takes and may for a while feel quite demoralized (Watkins 2012a). It is therefore important that the supervisor has created a relationship and structure within which the supervisee can take the risk of disclosing doubts and anxieties that may go to the core of their professional sense of self (Eckler-Hart 1987). If these concerns are not allowed expression and are not accepted and tolerated by the supervisor, they are likely to seriously undermine the work with clients, for example where the counsellor attempts to overcompensate for feelings of fraudulence by trying too hard.

> Half way through a two-year diploma course, a counsellor disclosed in supervision that she was feeling as if she had nothing of any use to offer any of her clients, couldn't think of any reasons for wanting to continue her training and was wondering whether she had 'just been kidding' herself when she had started the course believing she had some kind of vocation for the work. Without minimizing these feelings, the supervisor gently encouraged and supported the counsellor to continue with her work at a level at which she felt competent, which entailed mainly listening to and supporting her clients. He disclosed that he had suffered a similar 'crisis of conscience' mid-way through his own training and that it had taken some time to resolve. The counsellor was given plenty of space in the subsequent supervision sessions to express her self-doubts and gradually regained her commitment and built up her confidence.

Having taken time to listen and respond empathically to the supervisee's doubts about motivation, it is often helpful to encourage the supervisee to discuss them in relation to how they affect the work with a particular client. The practitioner can then be affirmed and gently challenged to acknowledge what they are doing well with the client, (Knight 2004a) despite very real self-doubts. If self-doubt stems from unrealistic expectations of the therapeutic process the practitioner can be challenged to become more of a realist and less of a perfectionist. It can also help if the supervisor points out, when appropriate, that temporary questioning of motivation is a healthy and natural part of the practitioner's development.

Personal issues

Although we hope to have shown clearly in Chapter 4 that supervision is not and should not be personal therapy for the supervisee, their personal issues can, and often do, become entwined with their therapeutic work. It is therefore vital that a supervisor provides a climate in which the supervisee feels able to disclose personal material that may be affecting, or being affected by, their work. Supervisee and supervisor can then consider together the interplay between the personal material of the therapist and their therapeutic work with their client or clients in a spirit of collaboration. If the necessary work on establishing the boundaries between supervision and therapy has been well done in Stage 1-B of the model, the supervisee should feel able to risk disclosing relevant personal material without fear that they will be reprimanded, denounced as inadequate, or pushed unwillingly into stirring up issues that will leave them feeling raw and exposed.

> A supervisee disclosed early in a session that his partner had just suffered a miscarriage and that he was concerned that his feelings about this might be affecting his work with a pregnant client. The supervisor encouraged him to talk about these feelings and how they related to his client. As they talked, the supervisee realized that he had been attempting to deny his own feelings of loss in order to 'be strong' for his partner and this denial had manifested as irritation and anger towards his client who, he felt, was not caring for her unborn child as well as she should. As an upshot of this increased awareness the supervisee and supervisor were able, more objectively, to discuss how he could access space and support in dealing with his feelings of loss and consider whether he should refrain from working with his pregnant client until he had resolved more of his own distress.

Undigested feelings

It is quite common for supervisees to want to focus on a strong feeling or cluster of feelings they have when with one or more of their clients. The focus then becomes one of teasing out those feelings, identifying what the feelings may illuminate about the client or about the relationship between therapist and client, and also what may belong to the therapist. This is often fertile territory for the development of the therapeutic work with the particular client and for the personal and professional development of the supervisee. Such feelings may be introduced as a focus upon the client, a focus upon the relationship or a focus upon a personal issue for the supervisee, but the supervisory exploration is generally most productive when any judgement as to originating source is suspended and allowed to reveal itself as the discussion progresses.

Where it emerges that the feelings are linked to a personal issue of the supervisee's, then one of the tasks is to consider whether and how this can be sufficiently contained so that it does not unduly impact upon either the client or the supervisee. These can be complex, multilayered issues to address effectively in supervision and may need to be revisited over a period of time (Henderson 2009b).

Success

Supervision necessarily deals most frequently with a supervisee's difficulties, deficits and 'failures'. Facilitative supervision should, after all, provide the space where mistakes can be aired and viewed as learning opportunities. If a supervisee were never to bring such issues to supervision the supervisor would, quite rightly, have serious concerns about the practitioner's self-awareness and even probity. The importance of acknowledging and celebrating success should not, however, be lost by this concentration on reconstructive work. Valuable learning and integration also take place through highlighting strengths and achievements; indeed, this is one of the major components of the solution-focused approach, as applied in supervision (Knight, 2004a; Gray and Smith, 2009). It is important for the supervisor to instil the good but all too often infrequent habit in the supervisee of recognizing what they have done well. So, for example, where a supervisee has spent some time delineating their own deficits or exploring difficulties in relation to a client, it can be pertinent for the supervisor to ask 'And what are you doing well with this person?' Encouraging the practitioner to acknowledge what is more positive, alongside the frustrations of the work, serves to redress the balance and can lift their self-confidence. Such interventions by the supervisor also have an educative function and can provide invaluable modelling for the supervisee in how to challenge strengths and resources in their clients.

To ensure that successes are consolidated the supervisor can ask the supervisee to identify what particularly helped to achieve the success, and how the therapist can now make that a part of his or her repertoire of therapeutic competence so that it is more freely available for use with future clients. An example of this would be where a therapist has been successful in using advanced empathy (Egan 2013) with a client through 'playing a hunch' based on clues given by the client and which the supervisor has helped him or her to spot. Acknowledging the value and effectiveness of such intuitive work can enable the therapist to consider using advanced empathy at opportune moments in future therapy sessions.

Bringing no issue

On occasion the supervisee may choose, or may negotiate with their supervisor, to come 'unprepared' and free-associate when they start. If such is the case it is still, of course, important for the supervisee to prepare themselves psychologically for the supervision.

An experienced practitioner who normally came to supervision with clear issues written down negotiated with his supervisor to come to one session with nothing prepared. Although he did not work psychodynamically himself he was in therapy with a psychodynamic therapist and, having experienced the power of 'free association' in getting to the heart of his own issues, wished to try this approach in supervision. The session was recorded and an extract from the beginning of the session is presented here.

SUPERVISEE: We agreed at the last session that I would not prepare this time. That feels a bit scary. So all I've done is just look briefly through my file and it feels quite strange. In a way I'm sitting here, not terribly sure what to do, because I'm used to being very well prepared. I feel quite anxious now . . .

SUPERVISOR: . . . and a bit, sort of, adrift from it?

SUPERVISEE: Yes, because we agreed that I would do that and that we would work psychodynamically, and yet I've never done that before and so I'm thinking 'What am I supposed to be doing?' So I may need some help.

SUPERVISOR: OK, perhaps I can give us a hand in getting started.

SUPERVISEE: Please.

SUPERVISOR: You said all that you did was look through your file. Did anything come up when you did that – about any of the people you're working with? Or now, when you think about going through your file, does anything come to mind?

SUPERVISEE: I think what comes to mind is – how many people I'm seeing and the messiness of it. That's how it feels now, quite messy. And I think that's reflected in – you said 'adrift' before – and I think I feel a bit adrift in my counselling. Not in the actual process, but how I'm handling the overall counselling – the beginnings and the endings – the whole series of counselling sessions.

In this illustration it is apparent that the supervisee did have a clear issue that the supervisor helped him to bring into focus very early in the session, even though the issue had not been prepared in advance. Enabling the supervisee to clarify their supervision issue can be an important part of the supervisor's task in the focusing stage.

Objectives: Step 2-B

A significant component of the focusing stage is clarification of objectives by the supervisee, the supervisor and, where applicable, the organization or training institution. Establishing objectives encourages intentional work and provides the basis for review and evaluation (discussed in Chapter 8). By objectives we mean the desired outcomes sought from the supervision session so that purpose, direction and goal are established and can shape the work.

A supervisee's objectives for a session might, by way of example, encompass the following four goals:

1   To make sure I am fully present in the supervision by taking a few minutes at the start of the session to identify any immediate feeling or thoughts that may distract me, describe them briefly to my supervisor and then focus on the client issues I want to bring.
2   To improve my awareness of time by taking charge of time keeping, with the goal of dividing the remaining time equally between discussion of two clients.
3   Minimize presentation of background information about the clients in favour of getting straight into the supervision issues.
4   Let my supervisor know I would particularly appreciate her help with challenging my blindspots with these clients, as I feel I am missing something important with both.

The reflective and self-challenging supervisor is also likely to have formulated some specific objectives for the session. These might range across such goals as:

1   ensuring the session ends on time with the last ten minutes given over to review;
2   finding a way of sensitively challenging my supervisee to cut down on the amount of background information he normally gives about each client before we get to his issue;
3   monitoring my tendency to offer advice and suggestions early on and, instead, encouraging my supervisee to consider his own alternative strategies.

An organization's or training institution's objectives may need to be addressed in the session when, for example, a joint learning statement or report needs to be compiled or when new directives governing the practitioner's work within an agency, which may affect supervision, need to be communicated to the supervisor. Where such considerations need to be incorporated into the supervision session they should not unnecessarily cut into the time allocated for supervision of client work. A joint learning statement can, for example, be drafted between meetings and then reviewed and finalized in one session; it may be compiled during short periods allocated to it over a number of sessions, or an additional session can be arranged specifically for writing the statement.

It is usually helpful and respectful practice for objectives to be made explicit at the start of a session in order to engage the co-operation of both parties. Where the supervisee has stated how they would like to divide the time, for example, the supervisor can then support the supervisee's timekeeping and respect the supervisee's need to move on. On occasion the explicit statement of objectives might be detrimental to the work or the relationship, in which case it may be preferable that these remain private or only acknowledged in retrospect during the session review. An example would be if the supervisor has the objective of being more challenging in their style of supervision. To convey this intention to the supervisee might increase the supervisee's anxiety unnecessarily or make both individuals unhelpfully self-conscious. On the other hand, a supervisor who is working with a supervisee who has difficulty knowing how best to make use of the time, or what to bring to supervision, might decide to be more overtly proactive in encouraging the supervisee to set and state objectives at the start of each session.

Presentation: Step 2-C

Presentation covers both the *method* used by the supervisee to bring his or her issues for supervision and any *background* given to contextualize the issues. Appropriate methods for presenting issues are audio and video recordings, case-notes, sections of session transcripts, verbal reports, free association and creative approaches (Lahad 2000).

Method

A particular method of presentation may be chosen to fit the supervisee's objectives for the supervision session. A supervisee who is concerned about a tendency to be over-directive in their work may wish their supervisor to hear a section of audio recording that appears to show this happening in a session. A therapist wanting to discuss a general difficulty in ending sessions on time may wish to report verbally on several occasions where this occurred in recent sessions.

Audio or video recordings are particularly useful in the supervision of trainees, where the supervisee may request help with the evaluation of specific strategies or interventions. The advent of digital technology has made this a more flexible process. As Jencius and colleagues point out, in a chapter describing a range of innovative technologies that can be employed in supervision, 'the use of digital video recordings means that supervisors and supervisees can target specific instances of a counseling . . . session for examination' (2010:67). Recordings have the merit of giving the supervisor an immediate and true flavour of the practice being undertaken and, as Haggerty and Hilsenroth have pointed out, video recording can also illuminate aspects of non-verbal behavior during psychotherapy sessions:

> [V]ideo recordings of psychotherapy sessions in face-to-face work illustrate that both clinician and patient are moving almost all of the time, whether fidgeting or changing their sitting position, and paying attention to these patterns can reveal a valuable fund of information about changes in rapport and involvement as well as emotional intensity and quality . . . Paying close attention to these nonverbal cues, or enactments, between clinician and patient may lead to more effective psychotherapy and better outcomes.
>
> (Haggerty and Hilsenroth 2011:199)

Haggerty and Hilsenroth further suggest that 'video also allows the supervisor and the clinician to deconstruct and micro-analyse certain moments in a session that were potentially problematic or especially useful' (2011:200).

Where video or audio recordings are used it is often helpful for the supervisee to edit or set the recording at a place that gives the point from which the supervision issue arises, rather than expecting their supervisor to undertake the onerous and time-consuming task of listening to or watching the whole session. Occasionally the supervisee may wish the supervisor to gain a more holistic or qualitative perspective on their work by watching or hearing a complete session, for example, where the therapist is giving attention to the pacing of sessions or issues of boundaries and structure. Where this happens it is important for the supervisee to negotiate any extended listening time with their supervisor in advance, rather than simply arriving at a session expecting to play an hour's recording. In such instances it may be best to give the recording to the supervisor beforehand to give him or her a chance to listen or watch and reflect upon it prior to the meeting, or to negotiate a longer supervision session where viewing and discussion can take place concurrently or consecutively. The supervisee should be prepared for the supervisor requiring an additional fee if extra time is given to such an enterprise. Alternatively, the supervisee and supervisor might agree to undertake an Inter-Personal Process Recall or IPR (Kagan 1984) approach to supervision. In this approach, supervisee and supervisor listen to or watch a very recent recording (as its efficacy has been found to fall off quickly as the interval between recording and supervision increases) of a therapy session, either pausing the recording to explore what the supervisee was thinking, feeling, experiencing in their body or imagining at the selected moment.

The playing of audio or video recordings in supervision should always be done with the (preferably written) consent of the client. He or she should have been clearly briefed on the use of the recording, including who will hear or view it, in what context and what will then happen to it afterwards.

Verbal reports, normally supported by case-notes, are the preferred way for many counsellors to bring their work to supervision. In compiling pre-session notes it is helpful for the supervisee to have some focusing questions in mind:

• What is my particular difficulty or problem in working with this client?
• If I could risk telling my supervisor what really concerns me in my client work, what would that be?
• What do I need from my supervisor to help me work more effectively with this client?
• What do I need to tell or offload to my supervisor so that I can work more freely with this client?
• Is there anything I want to celebrate or feed back to my supervisor from previous supervision sessions?

Such reflections prior to supervision allow the supervisee to take a step back in order to see the overall picture or shape of their work, enabling themes, patterns and recurring issues to be highlighted and supervision needs identified. Clarity stimulated by such self-questioning can prevent the phenomenon, which we have sometimes experienced, of the supervisee introducing an important issue that they have 'just remembered' towards the end of a session, when there is insufficient time to address it.

Supervisors who have the necessary skills and experience may wish to encourage their supervisees to present and identify issues in creative ways. Approaches such as sculpting, where small objects such as coins, shells, pebbles, Russian dolls or figurines are assembled to represent aspects of, or individuals involved in, an issue, or drawing an image or metaphor relating to a client may prove particularly useful where the supervisee is uncertain about the specific issue (Deaver and Shiflett 2011; Henderson 2009b; Lahad 2000). The following example of an experience one of us underwent of using artwork as a supervisee serves as an illustration of how this might work in practice, and also highlights the power of the approach, which should always be used with sensitivity and caution:

I had a clear image of a young woman I had recently worked with sitting in a chair in the counselling room. The client normally appeared bright and animated and frequently laughed or smiled when talking. Despite my intention of drawing the client with these characteristics, I found a very different picture emerged on the paper. The final drawing showed a fragile and waif-like figure sinking back into an enormous chair, bounded by huge arm rests. The client's face appeared expressionless and cadaverous, with empty looking eye sockets. My attempt to touch up the face to make it look more lifelike, including adding a red mouth and darkening the eyes, merely served to make the face appear more desolate and lifeless.

On being invited to share my experience of drawing the picture, I became overwhelmed with feelings of great sadness. I started to sense how vulnerable the client might be behind her show of brightness and cheerfulness. I realized that I had been colluding with her determination to minimize the damaging effects of a past incident of sexual abuse and her father's current rejection of her. With the help of the tentative probing of the group supervisor I began to see that the huge chair arms that appeared to imprison the client in the chair were in some way representative of my feelings of wanting to 'hold' her in the counselling process and provide some containment for her distress, which, while previously denied by both of us, now seemed very apparent as it came to light through the picture.

This illustration shows that working in this way can evoke strong feelings for a supervisee. Clearly it is important that such a powerful approach is used only by supervisors who feel competent and confident with this method of working. Supervisors should allow themselves to be invited into an exploration of a supervisee's drawing through tentative questions and respectful observations, so that the supervisee is encouraged to identify their own meaning from the picture, rather than being subjected to the supervisor's interpretations.

A number of authors have presented creative or 'right brain' models and methods to use in supervision, using metaphor or drawings (Amundson 1988; Deaver and Shiflett 2011; Ishiyama 1988; Lahad 2000). These can provide valuable ways of opening up material otherwise inaccessible to the supervisee.

The supervision session described under 'Bringing no issue' in Step 2-A above, where the counsellor decided to focus through free-association, provides evidence of the importance of allowing the supervisee some freedom in choosing how to present their material for supervision. Even this apparently small step in focusing can be empowering for the supervisee, and the way they choose to present their work can throw important light on the issue itself. This is an aspect of what we mean when, under the guiding principles governing our supervision work outlined in Chapter 3, we say that the supervisee will both censor the material presented and also give clues as to what most needs addressing. You may recall that the supervisor here used the word 'adrift' in an empathic response to the counsellor's expressed anxiety and uncertainty about how to proceed with the supervision. The use of this word was not mere serendipity; rather, it was based on the supervisor's awareness that the counsellor was unusually anxious and uncertain in beginning to present his work. On one level this could easily be attributable to the new and different way of presenting his issue, through free association. However the supervisor was sufficiently open to the possibility that the way the supervisee was presenting might also provide a clue to his issue that the word 'adrift' was offered as it surfaced in the supervisor's awareness. In the event this word resonated with the counsellor and became the one he chose to describe his current feelings about his counselling work.

Background

The second aspect to presentation is background: the amount of information that is given about a client during presentation of the supervisee's issue. Supervisors and supervisees will have different preferences and opinions on the amount of background necessary to contextualize or frame the issue brought to supervision. Our own view is that little initial background material is normally required, as necessary information can be brought into the discussion as and when it appears relevant. For example, when a therapist is experiencing a client as needy and clinging or as angry and rebellious, it might well be important for the supervisor to ask the supervisee to talk about the client's experience of being parented.

Too much initial background can result in the locus of attention shifting to the client's 'case', with the risk of objectifying the client and the therapeutic work. Supervision (in the sense that we use the term) is not principally about casework management where the central question is the best way of handling the client (although this question may arise and require attention). Rather, the locus of attention is how the supervisee is managing herself or himself in responding to the client in terms of the interventions offered and the dynamics of the relationship.

A supervisee with a tendency to present the supervisor with a lot of detail and history about the client may find this a more comfortable area for discussion than exploring their own doubts or difficulties in working with the client. This can be a ploy (often used unconsciously) for keeping anxiety and the supervisor at bay, and it is one with which a supervisor who is anxious about their own ability to offer useful interventions can easily collude. A supervisor wishing to challenge unnecessarily protracted presentation of background material can gently stop the supervisee to ask: 'What is the nub of your issue with this client?', or 'Can you express your difficulty with the client in one sentence?' This said, a supervisor who works from a psychodynamic perspective might wish to encourage background information, particularly about a client's family, early experiences and previous relationships. These would be important antecedents to unearth in relation to current transference issues in the therapeutic relationship, when these are under discussion in supervision. Where the supervisor suddenly and uncharacteristically feels the need to ask about a client's history or background this can often be a clue to something that, if pursued, will throw light on the current issue, as in the following example.

A counsellor had discussed her work with a particular client on several occasions with her supervisor. At one point the counsellor was exploring her difficulty with getting the client to self-challenge in relation to generalizations he frequently made about the untrustworthiness of everyone he came into contact with. The supervisor suddenly felt the urge to ask the counsellor about the client's father, whom he couldn't remember having heard mentioned during any of their discussions. When he did ask, the counsellor realized that she, too, had only a vague recollection of the client having mentioned his father, although his mother was frequently referred to. Following the supervision, the counsellor took an opportunity to ask the client, at what seemed an appropriate moment, to say something about his father and learned that the father had deserted the family when the client was a small child. The counsellor was then able to consider the client's characteristic suspicion of others against the backcloth of parental abandonment, a vantage point that created far greater understanding of the client's perspective.

Approach: Step 2-D

We have included approach as part of the focusing stage as this concerns the way the supervisor responds to what the supervisee presents. It covers a number of elements, in particular the theoretical models and orientations, supervision styles, techniques and interventions employed by the supervisor. There is considerable scope for developing personal approaches to supervision, hopefully enhanced and evolved through regular feedback elicited from our supervisees during the review stage. However, every supervisor needs to ensure that their approach integrates essential professional and ethical requirements, including monitoring for evidence of behavior by the supervisee that may result in risk to the safety and wellbeing of clients, and sensitivity to issues of difference and diversity as they may affect themselves, their supervisees and the clients of their supervisees.

Even supervisors/therapists who work mainly or exclusively with same-race supervisees/clients are not exempt from rigorously examining assumptions and prejudices that fail to acknowledge and take account of aspects of intra- as well as intercultural difference and disadvantage. These may be aspects of: class, education, socio-economic status, age, sexuality, gender, religion, spirituality, mental and physical ability or appearance, urbanicity, norms relating to marriage and childbearing, and so on. Supervision is a triadic relationship and it is important to think about how complementarity and conflict between any two of the participants will impact on the supervisory and therapeutic process (Wosket 2009). The subjects of ethical practice and working with difference and diversity in supervision are covered in some detail in later chapters.

It is as important for the supervisor to develop or evolve their own characteristic approach and style. Where the supervisor has not done this they are in danger of operating in a haphazard fashion. At worst this can result in highly inconsistent supervision, ranging across a spectrum from ineffectual bumbling to wild eclecticism. This raises the question of how a particular supervisor's approach will work with a range of supervisees. Cheon and colleagues (2009) undertook a study of supervisees (n = 132) that examined quite a wide range of variables shown to have an impact upon the supervisory relationship, role conflict and supervisee satisfaction. They considered a number of contextual variables including sexual orientation, religious/spiritual preference, ethnicity, age and gender together with environmental variables such as the setting in which supervision took place, length of time in current setting, total time in supervision, training, and methodological variables of supervisory format, structure, interventions and theoretical styles.

Cheon and colleagues found no evidence of a link between supervisee satisfaction and the degree of match between supervisor and supervisee on the contextual and methodological variables. In line with other studies (Green and Dekkers 2010; Inman 2006; Starr *et al.* 2013), they found that the strongest correlation was between the working alliance and supervisee satisfaction. They also noted a significantly higher satisfaction with supervision that took place in a private practice setting (rather than agency, hospital or elsewhere). They suggest this may be linked to the higher likelihood of multiple relationships between supervisor and supervisee in these other settings, leading to dissatisfaction and role conflict. Other research (Gatmon *et al.* 2001; Green and Dekkers 2010) has found that the degree to which the supervisee perceives the supervisor to be culturally competent is a strong predictor of satisfaction. Taken together these findings suggest that supervisees' perceptions of how effectively the supervisor is seen to address cultural or contextual issues within supervision has a significant impact on supervisee satisfaction, whereas the level of match or mismatch between supervisor and supervisee on cultural or contextual variables does not. We shall consider aspects of this further in Chapter 11.

What these findings suggest is that supervisors need not be concerned that developing their own approach will restrict the range of supervisees with whom they can successfully work. These studies all support consistent findings that the quality of the supervisory relationship is the best predictor of supervisee satisfaction and successful learning.

Supervisory styles

Magnuson and colleagues (2000) interviewed 11 experienced counsellors (ten of whom were themselves clinical supervisors) about their unproductive experiences as supervisees. A category analysis of data from their interview transcripts revealed 'six aspects of supervision that were both prominent and repetitive' in respondents' comments about 'lousy' behaviours of supervisors that they had been subjected to as supervisees (Magnuson *et al.* 2000:193). We have summarized these 'lousy' supervisor traits as follows:

1   Unbalanced: the supervisor who gets hung up on detail, or focuses too much on one aspect of supervision at the expense of seeing the bigger, systemic picture or context.

2   Developmentally inappropriate: these are supervisors who are fixed and static, and who fail to acknowledge or respond to the changing needs of supervisees.
3   Intolerant of differences: characterized by the supervisor who does not encourage autonomy and individuation in supervisees and, instead, tries to persuade the supervisee to become a clone or close replica of the supervisor.
4   Poor model of professional and personal attributes: these are supervisors who fail to observe professional boundaries and are intrusive, exploitative or abusive.
5   Untrained: supervisors who enact the role without adequate preparation or professional maturity.
6   Professionally apathetic: frequently described by research participants as the 'lazy' supervisor who is not committed to the profession, their supervisees and, by inference, their supervisees' clients.

A supervisor's chosen style, as revealed in his or her responses to the supervisee, will be governed by a number of complex factors. Foremost amongst these are likely to be:

•   theoretical orientation as a counsellor or psychotherapist;
•   experience of being a supervisee;
•   previous personal and professional roles, for example teacher, parent, therapist, manager;
•   short- and longer-term goals for the supervision process (both for self and for the supervisee);
•   confidence, interest and experience in the role of supervisor;
•   level of self-awareness and personal development, including experience of being a client;
•   awareness of the supervisee's preferred learning style and feedback mode;
•   consideration of the supervisee's experience level and current developmental issues.

It can be an informative exercise for the supervisor to reflect upon the key influences governing their own supervisory style using the factors outlined here, plus any others from their individual experience. However, this does not address the question as to what supervisees want from supervision and by extension what they want from their supervisor. Starr and colleagues (2013:340) conducted interviews with 19 therapists and identified key aspects of what their sample experienced and wanted from supervision: '(1) usefulness of supervision support, (2) fear of exposure versus gaining new knowledge, (3) comfort versus challenge, (4) knowing and the use of not knowing – a safe uncertainty, and (5) supervision as space'. They proceed to analyse the theme of supervisory support further and identify three sub themes of '(1) having someone available, (2) addressing personal issues, and (3) feelings of empowerment' (Starr *et al.* 2013:340). Extrapolating from these findings, a supervisory style that is likely to be effective and welcomed by supervisees will balance support and challenge, will encourage a degree of risk-taking appropriate to the level of development of the supervisee, will safeguard a 'safe enough' reflective space within the sessions and will include sufficient empathy to demonstrate understanding of the supervisee's experience of exposing aspects of their work to scrutiny.

Supervisory interventions

The manner and type of interventions employed by the supervisor will be heavily influenced by his or her theoretical orientation as a counsellor or psycho-therapist. A supervisor with a client-centred training style is likely to engage in more reflective and empathic responses than, say, the supervisor from a behavioural or solution-focused background, who may more frequently use instructive, information giving or questioning interventions. As we have emphasized previously, it is important that supervisors do not assume that the same style and pattern of responses will work in supervision as have seemed to work in their therapeutic role.

A useful tool for the supervisor to help him or her review intervention and communication skills is that provided by Heron's (2001) model of 'Six Category Intervention Analysis'. Heron defines an intervention as 'an identifiable piece of verbal and/or nonverbal behaviour that is part of the practitioner's service to the client' (p. 3). The emphasis in the definition of each category of intervention is on intention – that is, what the intended effect, point or purpose of the intervention is when used by the practitioner in '*responding appropriately to a given situation*' (p. 4, author's italics). We would add that, in supervision, the way the supervisee receives, understands and responds to the intervention provides a good measure of whether it has been used appropriately.

Heron's six categories, with examples of each type of intervention as it might be used in supervision, are summarized below. The interventions are divided into 'Authoritative' and 'Facilitative', the former tending to be hierarchical in the sense of involving the supervisor in being directive with the supervisee while the latter are less hierarchical, encouraging supervisee autonomy, self-awareness and affirmation.

Authoritative

Prescriptive – Give advice or direct the behaviour of the supervisee. 'You need to re-establish time boundaries with your client.'

Informative – Give information or instruct the supervisee by imparting knowledge or ascribing meaning. 'If you challenge your client that fiercely so early in the process you might scare them off.'

Confronting – Give direct feedback or non-aggressively challenge in order to raise the supervisee's awareness. 'You appear to have introduced your own agenda here, possibly as a result of over-identifying with your client.'

Facilitative

Cathartic – Enable the supervisee to connect with and discharge feelings or release tension. 'How did you feel when your client dropped that bombshell?'

Catalytic – Encourage reflection and problem solving to develop self-directed learning in the supervisee. 'How have you dealt constructively with this kind of resistance before?'

Supportive – Valuing and affirming the worth of the supervisee and his or her work in an unqualified manner. 'You really stayed with your client well and helped to hold all that distress.'

No category of itself is inherently less valid, significant or important than any other as all are legitimate in any given supervision situation. However, Heron emphasizes that the six types of intervention are valid only when they are rooted in the core qualities of respect, empathy and genuineness in relation to the client or supervisee. They are invalid when used degeneratively or perversely. To be valid, an intervention needs to be appropriate to the supervisee's current stage of development and to the stage of development of the supervisor–supervisee relationship. It also needs to use appropriate language and be delivered in a relevant and timely manner. Degenerate interventions, while not normally deliberately malicious, are those that are used inappropriately through lack of sensitivity, skill, experience, self- or other awareness, or through insecurity or defensiveness. Perverted interventions, rather than being rooted in lack of awareness, experience or training, spring from the shadow side of supervision and are deliberately harmful or damaging to the supervisee. An example of such an intervention in supervision might be where the supervisor deliberately and maliciously provokes a psychological attack on a supervisee through envy or sadism. Fortunately such maliciousness is rare and not normally to be found in supervision practice.

Supervisors who wish to take a closer look at their own intervention style can use Heron's model to analyse their in-session behaviours. This can be done in a straightforward manner by using recordings or feedback from an observer and a 'supervisee' within a training situation. More will be said about the use of supervision training groups in Chapter 14.

Priorities: Step 2-E

Stating that the supervisee should be allowed to start with his or her issue is not the same as saying that the supervisor has no say in what is covered in the session. It is legitimate for, and on occasion incumbent upon, the supervisor to negotiate with the supervisee about the items potentially on the 'agenda' for the session. This may include discussing the order in which different issues will be explored and the proportion of available time that will be given to each, particularly when the supervisor needs to ensure that concerns for the welfare of clients or the wellbeing of the supervisee are addressed.

Negotiating a change to the focus requires sensitivity, good timing and assertiveness on the part of the supervisor if it is not to result in the supervisee feeling taken over, jolted out of their own track on the subject, or put down. What follows are some examples of situations where it would be legitimate for the supervisor to alter the focus of the supervision in order to deal with a more pressing priority.

Unacknowledged personal issue obtruding on the work with the client

As Wheeler puts it, '[t]he supervisor is not the therapist but must at times draw attention to unrecognized, misunderstood or resisted aspects of the counsellor as they emerge in the relationship with the client' (2007:255). Even where the supervisor does not have a direct responsibility for the therapeutic work, for example in co-supervision with a same-level colleague, we believe it is an ethical imperative for the supervisor to raise the issue and encourage exploration, bearing in mind that, as Wheeler states, '[t]he therapist's wounds are a potential conduit to a deep understanding of the client's wounds' (Wheeler 2007:255).

A therapist mentioned 'in passing' that she would have to cancel the next session with her supervisor as she would be away for a few weeks, looking after her father who had been taken ill. The therapist then began to discuss her work with a client who had recently been bereaved. The supervisor intervened to ask how the therapist felt about working with loss issues, given her father's illness, and how she planned to tell her bereaved client about the forthcoming absence. This resulted in the therapist exploring how her own feelings about her father's illness might impinge on her work and discussing in greater depth with her supervisor her decision not to disclose the specific personal reasons for her absence to her bereaved client.

Unfinished business from previous client work affecting current clients

A supervisor was aware from a previous supervision session that his supervisee had been badly shaken by her first experience of a client making a serious suicide attempt, following which the client had been referred for a psychiatric assessment. In the next supervision meeting the supervisee chose to discuss an organizational issue that was concerning her. Knowing that the supervisee worked with several clients who were at risk of harming themselves the supervisor intervened to ask how the work was going with these individuals. In response, the supervisee acknowledged her concern about one particular client who had recently threatened suicide, and mentioned her intention of phoning the client to check how he was and to ensure that he would attend his next appointment. The supervisor steered the discussion in such a way that the supervisee was able to acknowledge how her residual distress and anxiety from the previous experience might be leading her to become overprotective towards other clients. She was encouraged by the supervisor to express her feelings about the suicide attempt and then helped to decide whether she should desist from working with suicidal clients until she had resolved more of her own 'unfinished business' over the issue.

Unaddressed boundary issues

A trainee counsellor asked his supervisor to listen in advance of the supervision session to a recording of his first meeting with a new, female client. As the supervisor listened to the recording she picked up that the client was being seen in her bed-sit and appeared to be sitting on the bed during the session, while the counsellor took the only available chair. When the supervision session started, the supervisee said that he wanted to look at how he could have been more reflective and less interrogatory in order to keep the dialogue with the client going. The supervisor responded by saying that she would be pleased to look at this issue and had also become aware, from listening to the recording, that there might be some boundary issues that it would be important to consider at an early stage in the discussion. She was then able to invite him to consider any dilemmas that might arise for a counsellor seeing a client in such circumstances and with these seating arrangements.

Information the supervisor needs to give the supervisee

An example of this would be the supervisor needing to tell the supervisee that this will be the last occasion they can meet for some time, due to a personal crisis necessitating a sudden and unexpected absence by the supervisor. It would be crucial for the supervisor to bring this up early in the session, to allow time for dealing with the supervisee's responses to this forced termination and for alternative arrangements for supervision to be addressed.

During the focusing stage, both parties prepare the ground and sharpen their senses in anticipation of the exploratory work to be undertaken in the next stage, Space, which is the heart of the supervision process.

Chapter 6

Stage 3: Space

After agreeing the contract and what it is that the practitioner wishes to focus on, the supervisor and supervisee attune their attention to the space that now opens up before them. This is the heart of the supervision process, the part of supervision in which reflection, exploration, recognition, insight and understanding can all occur. Within this space new possibilities can emerge, that which is blocked can be released, the supervisee can be heard and understood – and can hear and understand themselves in new and different ways – and go forward with renewed vigour and courage. These are the aspirations, the best possibilities of supervision, and this chapter is concerned with how these hopes can be brought to fruition.

In considering the importance of reflective space in supervision, Rønnestad and Skovholt (2013) have identified the dangers inherent in supervision that places a premium on action over reflection. They suggest that if supervisor and supervisee cannot 'tolerate the discomfort associated with not immediately understanding what is happening, and "escape into" an unreflected upon action-orientation, both the supervisor and supervisee may be quite pleased with each other, but may both contribute to the other encouraging premature disclosure' (p. 185). In tune with this approach we hope in this chapter to convey a number of the benefits of viewing supervision primarily as an exploratory, rather than a problem-management, process.

The five components of Stage 3 (shown in Figure 6.1) are interrelated, each needing others in the circle in order that the supervision maintains an appropriate balance. In the microcosm of an individual session it may well be that the supervisor primarily concentrates on one or two of the areas. This might be 'investigation' and 'challenge' if, for example, the supervisee believes they have become complacent with their client and may be missing something, or it may be 'containment' and 'affirmation' if the supervisee has enabled the client to make a traumatic disclosure that has left her feeling shocked and unsure about how to proceed. Taking a longer-term view, we propose that all five elements need to be present to a significant degree over the course of supervision. If that is not the case the process will be distorted and become unbalanced as a consequence.

At this point it is helpful to consider a different way of picturing the Cyclical Model. This alternative version, which we have called 'The Cyclical Model as a

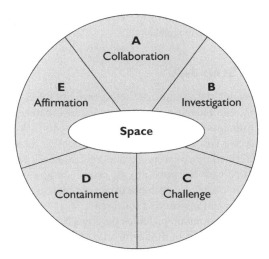

Figure 6.1 Supervision model Stage 3: Space.

Container' (Figure 6.2), emphasizes the manner in which the four other stages provide a container for the creative potential of a secure supervisory 'space'.

In a macro sense the structure of the model becomes the container for the supervisory task and process. In a micro sense the contract–review cycle provides the outer or structural layer of containment, whilst the focus–bridge cycle

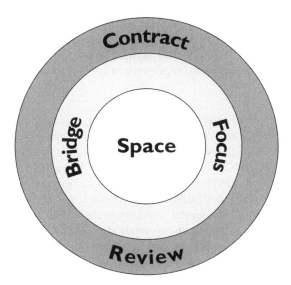

Figure 6.2 The Cyclical Model as a container.

provides the inner or application layer of containment. When these are established and functioning well supervisor and supervisee can have confidence to take risks and be experimental within the space.

Collaboration: Step 3-A

In Chapter 4 we considered the nature of the supervisory relationship and explored the affective aspect, emphasizing the importance of creating a safe and secure relationship as a foundation for the work of supervision. We were describing there something that we will now term the 'basic affective relationship'. This is a relationship characterized by empathy, respect, genuineness and concreteness. In this section we will re-visit the necessity of establishing a solid basic affective relationship in order to develop a collaborative approach to supervision and in so doing will draw on relevant research in this area.

The basic affective relationship provides the foundation upon which a working supervisory relationship can be built. Webb's (2000) research into blockages that prevent supervisees being open with their supervisors supports this view and found 'a positive correlation . . . between the supervisee's perception of the level of rapport with his supervisor and his ability to disclose sensitive issues relating to his client' (p. 64). Though small in scale (nine participants), an in-depth study conducted by Weaks (2002) throws light on this topic through exploring what constitutes 'good supervision' in the views of experienced practitioners. Weaks concludes that:

> Without exception all the participants viewed the supervisory relationship to be of paramount importance. The most striking feature of the whole study was the strength of feeling surrounding the supervisory relationship. My interviews appeared to be consistently saying to me that a good supervisory relationship holds the key to the experience of good supervision.
>
> (Weaks 2002:36)

From her analysis of in-depth interviews using grounded theory principles, Weaks extrapolated three key components of good supervisory relationships. These are *safety*, *equality* and *challenge*, which she terms the 'core conditions' of supervision (Weaks 2002:36). Safety, as described by participants in this study, includes: feeling secure and not having a need for self-protection; permission and freedom to discuss any and all aspects of client work; and acceptance and respect for the supervisee's chosen model. Equality includes the establishment of 'an equal power base in the supervisory relationship' (Weaks 2002:36). This is enhanced by appropriate supervisor self-disclosure – for instance the supervisor's own experiences of mistakes and vulnerability in their practice. Key words used by participants to express equality were 'mutuality, collegiate, collaborative [and] consultative' (p. 37).

In this study, *challenge* was found to include two aspects: firstly, where the supervisee gained new insight and awareness; and secondly, where the supervisor maintained a clearly boundaried and professional relationship. Interestingly the theoretical model of the supervisor, in contrast to their ability to form an effective supervisory alliance, appeared of little consequence to the supervisees interviewed.

Effective use of the supervision space largely depends on the supervisee's willingness to make professional and, on occasion, personal disclosures (Farber 2006). This capacity for self-disclosure rests, in turn, on the quality of the basic affective relationship between supervisor and supervisee (Walsh *et al.* 2003). Mehr and colleagues (2010) have brought some sobering statistics to the subject of the supervisory relationship in their research into trainee non-disclosure in supervision. They conducted a study of 204 therapists in training that explored their actual experiences of non-disclosure in supervision together with their willingness to disclose in one (their most recent) supervision session. The results indicated that 84.3 per cent of trainees withheld information from their supervisors within a single supervision session, with an average of 2.6 non-disclosures per session. Significantly for our discussion, non-disclosures were found to relate more to supervision-related issues, for example negative feelings towards the supervisor, than to clinical issues, for example negative feelings towards the client.

The main reasons given for non-disclosure by supervisees in this study were 'impression management' (concern that the supervisor would see them in a negative light), 'deference to supervisor' (feeling unable to disclose to an authority figure) and 'perceived negative consequences' (fear that disclosure might have adverse consequences for the supervisee) (Mehr *et al.* 2010:110). This study underscores the need for a strong interpersonal alliance in order to foster optimum levels of supervisee disclosure. Mehr and colleagues advise (2010:111) that supervisors use their 'clinical skills' of 'empathy, positive regard and reflections' to enhance the basic affective relationship. Additionally supervisors are encouraged to offer a balance of challenge and support, and to provide sufficient structure and role induction for trainee therapists, to help create an environment in which their supervisees feel safe enough to disclose.

Arising from this research, Mehr and colleagues (2010:111–12) have produced the following recommended best practice for supervisors in order to build effective, collaborative relationships with trainee supervisees. Most, if not all, of these recommendations we consider to be equally applicable to the supervision of qualified therapists.

1   'Demonstrate openness to feedback and willingness to change' (through modeling this and making it explicit).
2   'Own your own power and empower trainees' (for example by inviting them to choose and direct the focus in supervision sessions).
3   'Discuss evaluation – they're already thinking about it' (this includes inviting supervisees to collaborate in ongoing evaluation of their progress and development).

4   'Foster trainees' sense of confidence' (for instance through inviting explora-
     tion of trainees' feelings of inadequacy and their areas for development, and
     through highlighting their strengths).
5   'Sometimes silence actually is golden' (allow supervisees to choose what they
     disclose but encourage them to see supervision as a place where personal
     issues that may have an impact on client work can be spoken about).

Hess and colleagues (2008) found that supervisee non-disclosure occurred in both
good and problematic supervisory relationships although their research revealed
a significant difference between the two. Supervisees who experienced good
supervisory relationships (n = 8) tended, when they did withhold, to withhold
disclosures about 'countertransference, transference, therapeutic relationship [and]
perceived mistakes' (p. 406), i.e. mainly issues relating to perceived competence
and their personal reactions to clients. In contrast the non-disclosures of supervisees in problematic supervisory relationships (n = 6) related more to their
overall dissatisfaction with their supervisory relationships, including 'issues
related to the supervisor's theoretical orientation, the supervisor's mixed messages
or expectations' (Hess *et al.* 2008:406). One finding of concern in this study is that
supervisees who experienced satisfactory supervisory relationships felt their
supervisors might have helped them disclose more (e.g. by asking focused
questions or disclosing their own similar experience) while those supervisees in
problematic supervisory relationship felt that nothing would have helped them
disclose more or did not know what would have helped. A clear implication of
these studies is that supervisors should expect non-disclosure in supervision
and therefore be alert to ways they can manage their relationships with supervisees to maximize the possibility of disclosure of ethical, professional and
relational issues.

Through conducting a pilot study into what can be learned from listening to
supervisors' and supervisees' experiences of supervision, West and Clark (2004)
also uncovered the theme of 'what is not said' in supervision. To try to minimize
non-disclosure in supervision they suggest that in a healthy supervisory relationship it is productive for the supervisor to run a health check every so often by
asking 'Are there things about your practice you shy away from discussing in
supervision?' (p. 25). They recommend that supervisors intentionally model this
form of sensitive disclosure by sharing their own difficult moments in counselling
and supervision with their supervisees.

Research studies such as these provide the rationale for time and effort to be
given over to establishing a good basic affective relationship and they help us to
identify the key ingredients of this relationship. There follow two examples, which
will be developed further as the chapter progresses, given to show how additional
facets of the supervisory alliance can be understood and utilized providing that a
primary relationship is established which is characterized by the 'core conditions
of supervision' as described by Weaks (2002) above. In both examples there is a
good basic affective relationship between supervisor and supervisee and a sense

of mutual warmth and regard wherein both anticipate their supervision sessions with some enthusiasm.

In the first example the therapist, David, starts uncharacteristically to feel quite angry towards his supervisor, Sharmila, seemingly resenting the attention given by her to his clients. He expresses this by being increasingly perfunctory in his preparation and less engaged in the supervision sessions. Sharmila feels increasingly pushed away and finds that when she makes interventions that are focused on the experience of the clients these tend to be dismissed. This tension gradually builds over a number of sessions until David declares that he feels like changing supervisor as he feels his needs are being disregarded. Sharmila invites him to step aside from his feelings and reflect with her upon their possible source. Fortunately David is willing and able to do this.

In our second example the therapist, Joyce, is describing her work with a particular client. The supervisor, Milton, feels increasingly bored and disinterested in what Joyce is saying. He comments on this and Joyce responds by saying that she has been feeling that Milton does not really understand what she is talking about. Happily, they are then able to consider together where this misunderstanding might stem from and what it might mean. In both examples it was essential in working with this material that, firstly, supervisor and counsellor were in a good enough basic affective relationship to disclose their experience of one another to each other and, secondly, were able to step aside from the emotional component and reflect, together, on the possible meaning of their felt experience.

We will use the term 'reflective alliance' to describe this second aspect of the supervisory relationship, which comes about when supervisor and supervisee are both able to step back from their affective experience sufficiently to engage in mutual consideration of what is taking place.

As can be seen in Figure 6.3, we have divided the supervision relationship into three components. In doing so we are not suggesting that in practice a relationship can, or should, be compartmentalized in such a manner. In reality an effective supervisory relationship is likely to be experienced as seamless and moving fluidly between various dynamic stages and levels of awareness. The following is merely a device to assist in conceptualizing these dynamics.

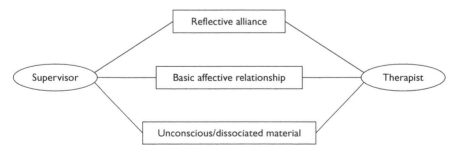

Figure 6.3 Components of the supervisory relationship.

The reflective alliance is the place from which supervisor and supervisee observe and consider. This includes not only reflecting upon the client and the therapy process but also upon the supervision process itself. This reflective place can be thought of, in the terms Sterba (1934) used, as 'an island of contemplation' – a place outside of the stream of the supervision process but from where that process remains observable. In its theoretical conception it may seem quite detached, an observing rather than experiencing place. However, in practice it is not discrete. The supervisor and supervisee need to move between experiencing and reflecting with the sense, at times, of merging these different aspects. Indeed if the supervision stays in a detached reflective mode most of the time, this should be considered as a possible defence from the affective experience and, with awareness, may need to be challenged. At best supervision is as much a feeling and embodied process (see Chapter 13) as it is a thinking activity. It is increasing the capacity to reflect upon felt experience, to move between affective experience and reflection, which assists both therapist and supervisor in the development of their internal supervisor function (Casement 1985), as already described in Chapter 2.

In addition to the basic affective relationship and the reflective alliance, the third element of the relationship is the unconscious or dissociated process. This is often experienced through its imposition upon the basic affective relationship, as illustrated in the examples above of David and Joyce. It is possible for unconscious or dissociated material to be recognized in a number of other ways. These include slips of the tongue, such as calling a client by the name of someone else with whom the therapist has acknowledged relationship issues. This may be an unconscious means of suggesting that similar issues are present with the client being discussed. Physical sensations may intrude, for example one of us had a supervisee who always started to feel hungry when in the presence of a particular client, even after having eaten immediately prior to the session. It transpired that the client was starving herself as part of a self-punishing strategy. On another occasion one of us had a supervisee who always began to burp when talking about a particular client. He seemed unaware of this until the supervisor brought it to his attention and invited him to consider whether there might be any connection (however fanciful) between his indigestion and the client. The counsellor soon found himself talking about how hard it was for the client to digest the possibility that she might be bisexual.

In addition to these examples the supervisee may behave in an untypical manner, such as 'absentmindedly' arriving an hour early for supervision, perhaps as an attempt by the supervisee to communicate how needy he was feeling on that day. Stray thoughts or images may intrude. For instance, one of us supervised a therapist who had the experience of fantasizing about the need to double glaze the window in his consulting room whenever working with a particular client. On exploring this in supervision (rather than following the first inclination to dismiss it as poor concentration) it became a means of understanding how invaded this client felt on occasions. The unconscious may even go so far as to create hallucinations: take the case of a therapist who regularly 'heard' a non-existent baby crying when working with a particular client who had been abandoned at an early age; or the supervisor who 'heard' a non-existent house alarm sounding as the supervisee calmly described his client's hobby of collecting ceremonial knives.

There are three common sources of unconscious or dissociated material in supervision: the supervisor, the supervisee and the client. Others sources are possible and not uncommon, such as the organization or wider environment in which the supervision occurs (see Chapter 3). However, for the purposes of this chapter, we will concentrate on the first three. Coming from a relational position, Frawley-O'Dea and Sarnat (2001:2) argue that contemporary approaches to supervision (even psychodynamic ones) need to expand their consideration of the organizing principles of psychic material to accommodate 'dissociation as well as repression'. Accordingly we will revisit this topic in Chapter 13, where we take a more relational approach through considering how dissociated material may be accessed through the embodied experience of supervisee and/or supervisor. At this juncture we will examine the manifestation of unconscious material using the concepts of transference, counter-transference and parallel process, looking briefly at each of these in turn.

Transference

It is worth stepping aside for a moment to clarify the use of terms being adopted here. The term 'transference' is a description of the process whereby person A acts towards person B as if person B were person C. Transference has been traditionally used to describe an unconscious process between a client and their therapist. Thus Jacobs (1986:6) suggests that 'transference' is the term used when 'in the relationship style(s) which the client adopts towards the counsellor there are signs of past relationships'. Adopting this same custom in the supervision setting means that the transference material is some historical relationship material of the supervisee's that is being transferred onto the relationship with the supervisor. This might be a negative transference whereby the supervisee would unrealistically anticipate that the supervisor would be 'hostile, critical, abandoning, negligent, stupid, or exploitative' (Horowitz 1989:57–8), or it might be positive transference in which the supervisor will be expected to be 'loving, all-providing, omnipotent, admiring, erotic' (Horowitz 1989:58).

In counselling and psychotherapy, certainly when the therapist has a psychodynamic orientation, such transference material is welcomed and viewed as potentially therapeutically valuable to the work with the client. In contrast, when such transference material has a significant impact upon a supervisory relationship this will, in all probability, interfere with the furtherance of the supervisory task, which is to facilitate the therapeutic work with the client, not to be therapeutic for the supervisee. This (as we have already identified in Table 2.1 on p. 19) is one of the areas in which therapy and supervision are fundamentally different in their respective purposes.

The supervisory relationship, like any other, is inevitably imbued with vestiges of previous relational experiences. The supervisory task in relation to transference material is to identify and name what is taking place, to find ways to contain the effect upon the supervisory relationship and for the supervisee to take this material elsewhere, most likely their own therapist, for further exploration and resolution.

Counter-transference

In therapy 'counter-transference' was the term originally coined to describe the unconscious responses of a psychoanalyst to the client. Based on their research, Ladany and colleagues (2000:111) have defined counter-transference in supervision, in a similar vein, as the supervisor's 'exaggerated, unrealistic, irrational, or distorted reaction' towards the supervisee. It can be helpful to think of counter-transference in supervision as having two possible sources. It can be either:

1   the supervisor's response to the transference material being directed towards him or her by the supervisee, or
2   the supervisor's unconscious material, arising from his or her own unresolved issues, being directed towards the supervisee.

An example of the first form of counter-transference is where a supervisee, Eugene, begins a supervisory relationship by telling his new supervisor, Fran, that he felt overcriticized and misunderstood by his previous supervisor, and that his self-confidence has taken a dive as a result. He says he is hoping things will be different with Fran as he liked what she said about 'offering collaborative supervision' on her website. Fran subsequently finds herself, in an uncharacteristic manner, giving Eugene frequent approval and being unusually cautious in challenging him.

An example of the second form of counter-transference might be where the supervisor, Stu, comes to supervision feeling that he is giving out too much to others and resenting having to give his attention to his supervisee, Lenard, particularly whenever Lenard comes seeking reassurance or direction. Stu may give off signals that he expects Lenard to find his own way forward. This response may stem more from Stu's sense of neediness than from his relationship with his supervisee. This then is a reaction stemming from the supervisor's own psychological material, and it is imperative that he learns to contain such responses during the supervision and takes them, as necessary, to his own supervision or therapy.

Parallel process

We first touched on the concept of parallel process in Chapter 1. Here we consider parallel phenomena as a particular form of unconscious material imposing upon the basic affective relationship. Often when parallel phenomena are described, what is being referred to is the reflection in the supervisory relationship of the dynamic in the therapy relationship (Mattinson 1977). Ladany *et al.* (2000:103) define parallel process as 'when a therapist interacts with a supervisor in a similar manner as a client interacts with the therapist'. Williams (1995:147) describes parallel process as the 'tendency within a system to take up matching forms', and he warns that this is a form of 'cloning' that, if not checked, can spread through the system 'like a hard-to-detect virus' (1995:147). Although deriving from psychodynamic theory and practice, parallel processes can spring forth to enrich all relational approaches to supervision (Ladany *et al.* 2000). They are, as Jacobsen (2007:32) observes, 'a powerful tool for the supervisor to use regardless of theoretical orientation'.

Williams (1995) introduces a cautionary note by suggesting that parallel process is a 'borderline' area in supervision that needs to be approached with sensitivity and some restraint in order for it to be kept in perspective. He writes:

> Focus on it too much, and supervisors and trainees begin to see it under every bed, behind every tree; after a while they cannot discuss anything without it becoming a 'parallel', and supervision becomes decadent. Ignore it altogether though, and there is a real danger of missing 'the pattern that connects'.
>
> (Williams 1995:151)

An example of parallel process would be where a therapist, working with a particularly passive client, starts to act in an atypically passive manner towards his supervisor. Thus the passivity within the client–counsellor relationship is paralleled in the counsellor–supervisor relationship. A further example is provided by the case of Joyce and Milton, which we return to below. Most supervisors welcome parallel phenomena, as the resulting dynamics provide a more direct way of experiencing the counselling process than second-hand reporting by the counsellor. Indeed parallel phenomena are often the mechanism by which transference and counter-transference material within the counselling or psychotherapy relationship becomes accessible to supervision.

It is important to recognize that in addition to the reflection of therapy dynamics in supervision, it is equally possible, if not inevitable, that supervisory dynamics will be reflected in the therapy relationship (Heuer 2009). An example of this is when the supervisor acts in a rather punitive and critical manner towards his supervisee, who in turn acts in a similar manner towards the client. This aspect of parallel process has been thoroughly studied and described by Doehrman (1976), whose work is a sobering reminder of the importance of maintaining a good quality of supervisory relationship. The clear implication of her work is that it is possible for an ineffective or contaminated supervisory relationship to have a destructive impact upon the therapy relationship. It is equally true that a healthy supervisory relationship can have a positive impact upon the relationship between therapist and client, a fact that suggests a strong argument for some supervision time being utilized for maintenance of the relationship between supervisor and supervisee.

It may well be that supervisors do not wish to explore the supervisory experience using a psychodynamic perspective in the way that we have done here in delineating this step of the model. However, if one is to be an effective supervisor it is, in our view, essential to at least be aware of the possibility of transference, counter-transference and parallel process, and to have the courage to acknowledge one's own psychological material when it emerges. Without an understanding of the potential complexity of the supervisory relationship, as we have attempted to describe above, it is difficult to see how full and effective collaboration within supervision can take place.

When a sound collaborative relationship has been established between supervisor and therapist, this lays the groundwork for the kinds of investigative work we go on to consider next.

Investigation: Step 3-B

Rice (1980) has described how inexperienced counsellors can easily fall into the habit of 'smuggling' in 'under the guise of a "reflection" ideas or connections that one thinks the client should be aware of but isn't' (p. 138). There is a similar danger in supervision wherever the supervisor tries to sneak in suggestions or interpretations in order to direct the supervisee. The key to effective investigative work in supervision, as we shall see, is for the supervisor frankly to own their own thoughts and reactions, and to offer these as invitations for consideration by the supervisee rather than (overt or covert) directives. Here we will revisit the cases of David and Joyce to carry forward our discussion.

In considering the examples given above of David (who seemed to resent his supervisor, focusing on his clients and directing attention away from himself) and Joyce (whose supervisor became bored in the session and by whom Joyce felt she was not heard or understood), we described the first part of a two-step process – the first step being to move aside from the affective experience in each case and into the reflective alliance. The second step is to investigate possible sources of the affective experience.

In the example of David it quickly becomes apparent through a simple process of thought association, which his supervisor Sharmila helps him to undertake, that there is a link between David's feelings towards his supervisor and the childhood experience of being the first of a large number of children. David is able to take this realization to his own therapy, where he fruitfully explores his hitherto unacknowledged resentment towards his mother for the attention given to his siblings, which he felt to be at his expense. Thus what occurred between David and Sharmila comes under the category of transference material: archaic feelings out of David's awareness superimposed themselves upon the basic affective supervision relationship. Having identified the material, David was also able to resume a sound basic affective relationship with his supervisor and thereby re-instate the supervision process on an adult-to-adult basis.

In the second example, of Joyce, the felt experiences of supervisor and supervisee were considered 'as if' they might be a reflection of what was going on between Joyce and her client. In the following supervision session Joyce reported that she had used the insight gained from supervision to initiate a discussion in which the client had acknowledged his belief that no one would understand or be genuinely interested in him and so did not talk about how he was really feeling. This resulted in a deepening of the therapeutic work with this client. Thus the affective experience between Joyce and her supervisor, Milton, was taken as a parallel phenomenon: they considered what they experienced 'as if' it was a reflection of what Joyce and her client were experiencing with each other. The insight gained by considering what occurred from this perspective informed and facilitated Joyce's work with her client.

Our two examples yield unconscious material from two quite different sources. There is no simple formula for discerning the source of affective responses; it requires reflection and honest self-analysis. However, these examples do provide clues that can assist in this discernment process. In David's situation the feelings towards his supervisor were pervasive, building over a number of sessions. The persistence of these feelings may well indicate that the source of the difficulty apparent in supervision lay in David's relational history. For Joyce the feelings were restricted to the point in supervision when the work with one specific client was under discussion. This may indicate a different source – in this case the relationship between Joyce and her client, which is then mirrored in the dynamic of the supervisory relationship.

We are deliberately tentative in the way we describe the processes discussed here because, as with any interpretive approach, it is important to remain aware that the understandings being reached are at the level of hypothesis. Using this 'as if' technique allows space to play with the material and to 'hold uncertainty so that creative thinking can occur' (Lidmila 1992:100). In the supervisory investigation, hunches, images, feelings, stray thoughts and passing associations are as valid as well-formulated hypotheses.

Play in supervision

A number of writers have discussed the value of adopting a playful stance in supervision. Stainsby (2009:35) reminds us that supervisors' capacity for play may rest on the fact that they share many of the traits displayed by creative people, among which she lists: 'autonomy, ability to take risks, curiosity, attraction to complexity, enjoyment of fantasy and "inner world", delight in relationships with self and others'. Smythe and colleagues (2009:24) sum up the usefulness of a playful stance in observing that supervisors who value play in supervision 'rest not in "knowing" but rather in being open to all they are yet to know'. Drisko (2000:157), meanwhile, observes that 'play liberates the spirit of growth and development', and describes the quality and potential of a play space in super- vision thus: 'In this "larger than self" play space we can creatively re-examine, re-experience and re-shape confusing, frightening or overwhelming experiences, sharing in the strength, calmness and wisdom of others' (2000:155).

From within this play space, hypotheses can emerge that are not merely the application of dry theory but arise directly from exploration of the work with clients. The validity of a hypothesis is then tested by the degree to which it is useful to the therapy process. If this is forgotten then there is a danger of supervisor and supervisee being beguiled by the elegance of the interpretation into granting it a greater degree of validity than is merited.

Playing with metaphor and imagery

We begin to see that investigation in supervision may be better served by playful wonderings and meandering than by serious analysis. In this regard Adamson (2011:92) has stated that 'accepting uncertainty, and not knowing' are two key meta skills required by both supervisors and supervisees that allow 'for fresh insights to emerge beyond our analytic minds' (2011:92). A question such as 'What do you imagine the client may be trying to communicate to you at this point?' can only elicit a fantasy or an informed guess from the supervisee but nonetheless can lead to new and more fruitful options than have hitherto been pursued. Useful playful meanderings in supervision may be generated by the supervisee or the supervisor, or emerge out of the dialogue between them (Rodgers 2011; Smythe *et al.* 2009).

Using metaphor and imagery is a valuable way to play with the material in supervision. Young and Borders' (1999) research into supervisors' intentional use of metaphor in supervision found that supervisees tended to remember their supervisor's use of metaphor as 'important supervision events' (p. 146), thus indicating their lasting impact. On this topic Meekums (2007:96) explored the use of spontaneous symbolism in supervision and suggested that a virtue of working in the realm of metaphor and imagery is that this provides 'a way of seeing things afresh . . . as if from a new position in space'. Sturm and colleagues (2012:230) have referred to metaphors used in supervision as 'evocative comparisons that illuminate'. Here is an example from our own practice to illustrate this:

> The supervisee, Meena, wished to explore her work with a young adult client who was tussling with issues about his sexuality and gender identity, and with difficulties in separating from his mother. This work had been ongoing for about a year and Meena felt as if it had stalled. She was unclear about what she wanted from supervision but was following her impulse to bring her sense that 'something is needed'. For an hour or so both the supervisor and supervisee talked back and forth about Meena's work and relationship with this client. At different points both found themselves saying such things as:
>
> > 'I've lost the thread here'
> > 'I don't know why I'm saying this'

'I don't know where I'm going with this'
'I'm not sure why I just said that'
'I'm confusing myself here'.

As they talked a few images that seemed to fit for the supervisee emerged. One was that both shared a feeling as if they were chasing wet soap around. The supervisor commented 'as soon as we hit on something it seems to slip out of our grasp and eludes us again', and Meena remarked that this paralleled her experience of being with her client, where she often felt that a focus or sense of direction eluded her. Another image elaborated by both supervisor and supervisee was the notion of the metamorphosis of a caterpillar into a butterfly.

Although this is an image that is frequently used to portray a process of change or rebirth, what particularly engaged the supervisee's and supervisor's attention in this session was the idea that the caterpillar does not know that it will emerge as a butterfly. Neither does it know that in order to do so it will need to go through a dormant phase – the chrysalis stage – before trans-formation is possible. This transformation cannot be forced or hurried along, otherwise the butterfly's delicate wings will be damaged and its flight impaired. In some way this seemed to parallel the process of therapy at this stage, where not much seemed to be happening except that the client was experiencing the relationship with his therapist (who happened to be of a similar age to the client's mother) as a secure attachment.

Supervisee and supervisor emerged from playing with these images towards the end of the session. At this point Meena became suddenly clear about something. She commented that she now had a feeling, arising from playing with the images, that it might be time to draw this phase of her work with her client to a close in order that he could experience separating from her and that (unlike his mother) she was willing to let him go. Meena also had the thought that she could suggest to the client that he might consider going on to work with a therapist who might be differently suited to help him with the next phase of his 'metamorphosis', for instance a younger, gay, male therapist.

The process described in this example illustrates that clarity can emerge from obscurity if sufficient space is afforded for play and exploration. The example also illustrates that interpretation does not need to occur for meaning to emerge. Lahad (2000:16) has expressed this well:

During the supervision session, it is possible to stay within the realm of images and metaphor, and not to concern oneself with explanations and interpretations. Staying *with* the metaphor is different from using metaphors as unconscious material to be brought into consciousness. Supervisors and supervisees who are involved can find the real counterparts and "translate" the language of images into the language of reality, when appropriate.

As we have seen then, the investigation phase may well generate hypotheses that can be applied directly to the counselling situation. In this regard Carroll (2011:27) marries together the contemplative and transformative functions of supervision when he observes that supervision 'meditates on the past in the present to prepare the future'.

In order to preserve the sense of space during this phase of supervision it is also important to remember that the reflections resulting from investigation do not, at this point, need to be directly applicable to the therapeutic work. As Jacobs and his colleagues (1995:113) have advised, working within the supervision space demands the ability 'to sustain curiosity and suspend premature closure'. The task of application comes in the fourth stage: Bridge. The task in Investigation is to generate possibilities, to re-stimulate the creative flow, which in itself can be so facilitative of the therapeutic process.

Challenge: Step 3-C

In moving into the area of challenge in supervision there is something of a shift of emphasis in that challenge is normally directed towards the supervisee, although supervisors themselves should of course invite challenge and demonstrate that they are open to this. The challenge may be the supervisee's own self-challenge or a challenge proffered by the supervisor. The purpose of any challenge or confrontation is to shed light on an area currently in the shadows, or as Heron (2001) puts it: 'A confronting intervention unequivocally tells an uncomfortable truth, but does so with love, in order that the one concerned may see it and fully acknowledge it' (p. 59). If the challenge is effective then the supervisee will learn something; they will develop as a result. The most incisive challenges are invitational rather than persecutory and are those that will 'stimulate but not overwhelm' (Wosket 2006:47) the recipient.

It is difficult to challenge effectively: to name 'what is' in a way that encourages the person to hear this rather than feel attacked and become defensive. Blocher (1983:31) gives the essence of the supervisor's dilemma here: 'When little or no challenge exists the learner will not grow. When the mismatch is too great the learner may disengage physically or psychologically because of excessive anxiety or discouragement'. Of interest to note here is that a key finding in Weak's (2002) study of good supervision is that where challenge is missing from the supervisory relationship, supervisees feel that this undermines the purpose and integrity of the relationship and becomes a reason to seek a change of supervisor. This research highlights the pivotal importance played by challenge in maintaining effective supervisory relationships.

In discussing challenge Heron (2001:62) talks about finding the balance between 'pussyfooting' on the one hand and 'clobbering' on the other. This not only refers to the manner in which a particular challenge is delivered but also includes the timing of that challenge and the overall level of challenge. If the supervisee comes to supervision fearful of the level of confrontation they anticipate, then the supervision is experienced as unbalanced in that the supervisee is receiving insufficient affirmation. There may be plenty of support intended but it must be both conveyed *and* received to be effective. In large part the effectiveness of a challenge rests with the skill of the supervisor in delivering that challenge in a clear and unthreatening manner (Freeman 1985) and at a time when the supervisee is most receptive (Hoffman *et al.* 2005).

Research conducted by Ladany and Melincoff (1999) showed that supervisors struggle with giving challenging feedback, most notably where this relates to 'negative reactions to the trainee's counseling and professional performance' (p. 168). Hoffman and colleagues' (2005) study of supervisor feedback revealed that supervisors find it easier to give feedback to supervisees about their skills and clinical concerns than about their professional behaviour, personality or how they are experienced within the supervisory relationship. This study of 15 supervisors found that the strength of the supervisory relationship was a 'major contributor to what made it easier to give feedback' (p. 11) and largely determined how supervisees received and integrated their supervisors' feedback.

Effective challenge requires sufficient ego strength in the supervisee to receive the challenge in a way that is useful. Ladany and Melincoff's (1999) study found that the most common reason for withholding challenging feedback was where supervisors believed that the supervisee was not developmentally ready to take on the challenge. This can be a problematic area when supervising inexperienced therapists, who are likely to present the supervisor with aspects of their counselling that may require challenging but who may well not be ready to make use of such challenge, needing rather to be affirmed and encouraged. Stoltenberg and McNeill (2010) consider this dilemma for the supervisor when they suggest that Level 1 supervisees (see Chapter 1) are often too anxious to make good use of confrontation, which, if used too early, 'may freeze the supervisee and halt development' (p. 68). They do, however, recommend the gradual inclusion of supportive confrontation as the means of assisting the novice therapist to move towards the next developmental stage, from Level 1 to Level 2: 'Confrontation may be necessary to move the therapist beyond what is safe and to try new interventions or work with more challenging clients' (Stoltenberg and McNeill 2010:68).

The material that is most likely to provide fertile ground for challenging interventions can be grouped into four main areas.

Challenge by confirmation

The first group consists of challenging by confirmation, where the supervisor corroborates what the supervisee already knows, or suspects. For example Emil comes to supervision to explore the possible reasons why his client has abruptly discontinued her counselling sessions. His supervisor asks him if he has a 'hunch' about why this may have happened. Emil says that he suspects that he may have missed picking up sufficiently on her reluctance to come for counselling, which she mentioned in the first session, and, instead, ploughed on regardless with trying to help her identify the changes she wished to make in her life.

A simple statement from the supervisor such as 'I agree, you seem to have overlooked her ambivalence about counselling at the start' then becomes the challenge. It is a challenge because it holds the supervisee to facing what he did and encourages him to consider what he could have done differently. The supervisor's task in this situation is to offer this holding, providing Emil with space to challenge himself. The temptation can be to rescue or collude with the supervisee in rationalizing why the choice he made was the best one.

Challenging the therapist to listen to indirect communication

The next group of challenges concerns those where the supervisor endeavours to enable the supervisee to hear, see, feel or understand what the client has been attempting to communicate. For example, a supervisee was experiencing a degree of exasperation with a client who repeatedly became quite distressed when complaining how family members did not understand the depth of his depression. When describing this in supervision the supervisee was challenged with the question 'Do *you* fully appreciate the depth of this client's depression?' This question made it possible for the therapist to recognize how she was defending herself against empathizing with this client: a daunting prospect with someone who is deeply depressed. Indeed, challenging the supervisee to be with the client as fully as possible is arguably one of the major tasks of supervision:

> It is the task of the supervisor to enable the supervisee to become more aware of what actually takes place in the session—behaviours, experiences, and transformations of himself and the patient. It has been my experience as a supervisor that many therapists drown their empathy or appreciation of the patient's struggle by worrying that they are not doing enough for the patient, or that they are doing the wrong things.
>
> (Shainberg 1983:164)

Challenging the impact of the supervisee's behaviour on the client

The third group of challenges consists of where the supervisor points out something in the behaviour of the supervisee and the likely effect of this upon the client. One of us supervised a counsellor who had a tendency to tell clients about the difficulties that she, the counsellor, used to have but had now overcome. Whilst this was apparently intended to encourage the client, the evidence suggested that this was not the actual effect.

After a number of gentle attempts to dissuade the counsellor from this behaviour, with little success, the supervisor said with a smile: 'You are now a very "together" person. How do you think your clients might feel to hear that they have such a well-sorted-out counsellor?' The counsellor was initially 'pulled up short' by this question but after some thought said: 'Maybe it could feel quite patronizing and they might feel inadequate compared to me – which would be awful and not what I'm intending at all!' This turning of the tables is a powerful form of confrontation and should be used with caution, but if done with compassion such a challenge can offer the supervisee a salutary lesson that is likely to stick.

Challenging the supervisee's expectations of the client

The fourth group of challenges concerns those that evaluate expectations or assumptions. Probably one of the most difficult areas for therapists to face is the limitation on what they, or their client, can be realistically expected to achieve. An example of this struggle was seen recently in a supervisee who was troubled that his client was accepting quite a low level of affection in her marriage. The therapist felt that the client was selling herself short in what she was prepared to accept. The supervisor reminded her supervisee that it is not their task to define the client's goals but rather to assist the client in defining their own realistic and workable goals and then to support the client in achieving those goals (Egan 2010; Wosket 2006). When the supervisee was challenged to identify the nature of the investment they had in encouraging the client to seek more affection, it transpired to be a consequence of the disappointment the therapist was currently feeling about his own daughter's unsatisfactory marriage.

The purpose of challenging is primarily to open up new areas for investigation. Challenge may also be needed in certain instances to contain behaviour by the counsellor that is deemed to be unhelpful or, in extreme circumstances, unethical. Ethical aspects of challenging are covered in Chapter 10.

Containment: Step 3-D

The supervisor's own sense of security, as a person and within their supervisory role, provides a vital means of containment for the insecurities of the supervisee in relation to their work. If those insecurities can be contained within supervision, then this provides the supervisee with a safe place in which to experience and explore their doubts and anxieties, and, it is hoped, affords a route through and beyond those insecurities so that the therapist is re-grounded sufficiently to return with steadiness and vigour to their client work. This aspect of containment is allied to the notion of holding the therapist to the task in hand, a concept that Coren (2001:188) describes as 'a major supervisory function'. Containment is not necessarily conscious or deliberate on the part of the supervisor; rather supervision is in itself the container, provided it is experienced as a safe and welcoming environment. When supervision is working well the therapist will feel reassured and strengthened to perform his task simply by the knowledge that the supervisor is concerned about his needs and committed to providing him with a sense of being 'held'.

There is nothing new in this concept of containment, which is explored extensively in the psychoanalytic literature and well described by Casement (1985). Essentially the process of containment in supervision is much the same as that which takes place within the therapeutic encounter. The basic structures around the supervision process, the boundaries of time, space, contract and shared purpose, provide one level of containment. In addition to this a more deliberate containment takes place whenever the supervisor recognizes the need to contain some aspect of the therapy, for example when the therapist moves into 'rescuer' mode, or when they help the supervisee to contain the impact of client work on themselves.

As we noted above, containment is also about the ability of the supervisor and by extension, the supervisee, to tolerate the uncertainty and confusion of not knowing, rather than seeking immediate clarification. Inappropriate haste to resolve dilemmas in supervision can encourage the therapist to be intolerant of the client's mess. Allphin (1987:239) has described how supervisors can sabotage this part of the supervision process by an early or over-emphasis on making sense of material that is perplexing or obscure:

> The supervisor needs to be able to tolerate the confusion with the therapist, just as the therapist needs to be able to tolerate it with the patient. If I become too anxious about the confusion, I may become critical of the therapist, pushing for more details or facts about the case. At such times the therapist himself is likely to become more confused and unclear because he feels criticized by pushing for clarification when he is not in conscious control of any clarifying information. The therapist, in fact, may be communicating what it is like to be with the patient and needing help managing the confused experience he has with the patient.

Additionally, supervision may provide a containing function by offering the supervisee a place in which to debrief. On occasion the therapist will be left with powerful emotional reactions to what they have heard, particularly when they work with trauma (see Chapter 12). Often supervision is the only opportunity where it is professionally appropriate to disclose what clients have divulged. If space is provided for this in supervision then it will minimize the tendency the therapist may otherwise have to 'leak' confidential material in inappropriate ways (Baker and Patterson 1990).

It is possible that on occasions a supervisor will find themselves having to contain the shadow (Jung 1951[1968]:8–10) side of their supervisee. The shadow is the unacceptable side of the self, that part of ourselves which we dismiss to 'the shadows' or recesses of our conscious awareness. From the perspective of analytic psychology one of the key tasks in the process of becoming whole is that of discovering and repossessing our shadow (Johnson 1991).

Not surprisingly the shadow side of those of us in the helping professions often includes those parts of ourselves that are antipathetic to our chosen field (Page 1999a). Thus a counsellor or psychotherapist may, for instance, have in their shadow desires to bully, inflict or witness pain, judge or exert power over others. Uncovering and facing these aspects of ourselves can be quite shattering; indeed, doing so inevitably breaks a psychological defence we have previously had in place. Thus enabling the supervisee to see their own shadow is a delicate process requiring sensitivity and empathy. However, when such aspects of the supervisee do emerge it is important that as supervisors we do not avoid naming what we see. Left uncontained and unacknowledged this same shadow material can have a highly destructive impact upon the supervisee's clients – as when a therapist consistently pushes a client into areas of distress and leaves them there without providing the space for re-grounding or processing of the emotional experience. We say more about working with the supervisee's shadow in Chapter 12.

Affirmation: Step 3-E

The need to affirm the supervisee is both a specific and a general task. It is specific in that there are occasions when it is important to recognize and acknowledge that the supervisee has done a particularly good piece of work or managed him or herself well within an unusually difficult situation. The task is general in that the therapist needs to feel in a sustained way that they are valued and considered worthwhile by the supervisor. This is part of what creates the sense of being held, as described under Containment.

Therapy is a depleting task, with counsellors and psychotherapists often giving of themselves more than they receive. Much of what is given is difficult to quantify; it is emotional and relational. Just as if one does a hard day's physical work one needs food, relaxation and sleep to restore the depleted physical reserves, so too a therapist needs relaxation and nourishment to restore their depleted reserves of emotional and relational energy. Effective supervision provides some of the nourishment for this restorative process. Indeed, a survey by Davis *et al.* (1989) of 120 randomly selected counsellors in the United States found that those counsellors who experienced dissatisfaction with their supervision more frequently experienced feelings of emotional exhaustion and burnout than those who felt they were effectively supervised. The restorative process of supervision happens both through the general quality of the relationship and also specifically by affirming the worth and value of the work the supervisee is doing.

To take an example: a supervisee arrives at supervision feeling drained and doubting the usefulness of what he is doing. This continues as he recounts the stories of two clients who both seem to be making no headway. The supervisor's first task is to hear and accept how the supervisee is feeling. She may go on to replenish the therapist in a number of ways. If there has already been progress with these particular clients it may be important to point this out. The supervisee may need help in recognizing his competencies and strengths, perhaps being encouraged to recount past successes: 'What has worked well in the past with clients presenting like this?'

The affirming task is a particularly pleasant one that should be undertaken seriously and with sincerity. It has a preventive mental health function for the supervisee: if done well it goes some way towards counteracting the despondency and sense of hopelessness that can lead to burnout (Farber and Heifetz 1982). However, this can only be achieved providing the therapist is operating in a reasonably healthy environment. It is important that supervision is not seen as an antidote to intolerable working conditions. Counsellors and psychotherapists should work a reasonable number of hours and have the resources and facilities they need to do the task. It is difficult to define what constitutes a reasonable number of client hours per working week as this varies with different therapists, their level of experience and the nature of their client group. As a rough guide between 15 and 20 therapy hours per week has been recommended (BACP 2008) as a realistic maximum for an experienced practitioner working full time. In the next chapter, we move on to consider how insights gained through exploratory work in the supervision space can be applied to the therapeutic work with clients.

Chapter 7

Stage 4: Bridge

The fourth stage is called 'Bridge' as a way of indicating that it forms a return link between supervision and the therapy being supervised. The ideas, musings and possibilities developed during the Space stage can now be sifted through and decisions reached about how, if at all, they will be taken back into the therapeutic work with the client. For ease of understanding we have again described this phase as comprising five elements, which we present in the order shown in Figure 7.1. The degree to which some of the elements are used will vary depending upon the ways of working of a particular supervisor and supervisee. For example, some supervisory pairings may use goal setting and action planning regularly, whereas others may not. Some supervisors may give a lot of information, using this as one of the opportunities to undertake the teaching aspect of supervision that Carroll has described, although he points out that while

> few would disagree with the 'teaching' task of supervision – there is wide variation in the way the teaching task is implemented by different supervisors. Some refuse to give 'information' to the supervisee and believe information-giving should take place on the training course.
>
> (Carroll 1996:50)

Thus in this Bridge stage all the elements are not essential use for every supervisor, but we feel it is important that all five are recognized as being available, to be used if appropriate.

What we do think is necessary is some identifiable form of bridging process between supervisory exploration and the subsequent counselling or psychotherapy sessions – in other words we need to think about application.

Unless attention is given to application it is quite possible that the client will experience a discontinuity as a consequence of the supervision, with the therapist having significantly shifted her perspective or intended behaviour between sessions in a way that the client, of course, is unaware. We must remember that the client is not privy to what has taken place in supervision and would normally not know that a particular supervisory discussion had occurred. Consequently if the client experiences a significant difference in their therapist, this can be quite

Figure 7.1 Supervision model Stage 4: Bridge.

disturbing. This is illustrated by the case of a client (himself a trainee counsellor) who, in discussing with a friend his experience of having counselling, said: 'I noticed how different my counsellor was in our last session and I thought "he's been talking about me in supervision!"' The friend asked 'And how did you feel about that?', and received the reply: 'I felt both *relieved* – because he was getting some help at a difficult point in our work and *betrayed* – because he hadn't told me that he was having supervision'.

Given that the reliability and predictability of the therapist are generally very important, experiences such as the one recounted above could easily become counter-therapeutic for the client (Langs 1982). Thus in our view the bare minimum of bridging that must take place is that of reflecting upon what will be taken back into the work with clients and ensuring that this is managed in a sensitive and thoughtful way.

Consolidation: Step 4-A

This is the beginning of the transition towards application. It requires a change in perspective as the reflections within 'space' are brought to an end and attention is given to the issue of how to apply any insights or learning. In the interests of shared power and working collaboratively it is important that supervisees are given as much ownership as possible of the supervisory process at the bridging stage of supervision. Doing so promotes supervisee autonomy, is likely to minimize supervisee resistance (because the therapist does not feel that a way of working is being imposed upon them) and lessens the danger of the supervisor doing therapy with the client vicariously through the supervisee.

In discussing the issue of resistance in supervision Breene (2011:171) advocates a partnership model where 'it is better if the supervisor joins in on the journey that interests the supervisee, so the supervisee mainly leads, with the supervisor following'. Borders (2009:201) uses similar phrasing in highlighting the collaborative nature of the supervisory endeavour at this juncture although she positions the supervisor rather differently in the journey, as a leader rather than as a follower: 'The supervisor's job is to set the stage, to ask the right questions, to lead supervisees subtly down the path to their discovery'. Carroll (2009) meanwhile uses an image of the supervisee taking control of supervision in the same way that a musical director takes control of an orchestra to emphasize that supervision should be supervisee- rather than supervisor-led. The spirit of collaborative enquiry suggested by these authors is what characterizes the bridging phase of the supervision model.

This transition from space to bridge may be introduced by a question that invites reflection on what has happened so far in the supervision. Examples include:

- Where are you now with what we have been exploring?
- What would you like to hold in mind from our discussion when you next see your client?
- What stands out as significant for you from what we have covered?
- Is there anything that might make a difference when you next see this client?
- Are there questions that we have to leave unanswered at this point?
- What would you like to take away from our discussion today?

Alternatively, a statement may be made that indicates to the supervisee that it is time to move from one phase to another. For example, the supervisor could suggest: 'It might be useful at this point to start to consider how you want to link our discussion back to your work with the client'.

When the discussion in Space has been particularly intense or emotional it is important that this transition into the next phase of supervision is undertaken deliberately. There needs to be sufficient time for the supervisee, and sometimes for the supervisor also, to make an internal shift. This may involve allowing strong feelings to dissipate and detaching somewhat from what has been under scrutiny. This can take a little while and if rushed is unlikely to lead into a particularly satisfactory discussion about application. The act of shifting attention and starting to think about the next time the supervisee expects to see the client under discussion will, in itself, help the therapist allow their feelings to subside.

The process of consolidating, then, involves gathering up what seems useful – any insights, new understandings and hypotheses generated – and deciding what to do with them. The process might stop there, with the new material noted and the supervisee left with the task of deciding how to apply or reflect further on what they have discovered. However, it is possible, and at least with inexperienced practitioners often preferable, to sift through the new material as part of the work of supervision.

This sifting involves deciding what to do with each possibility. Some may perhaps be abandoned as wild or unhelpful. Others, it may well be decided, will be held in awareness by the supervisee to be used should it seem appropriate – to be put on a shelf to be brought down if an opportune moment arises. For example, one of us had the experience in our therapy practice of introducing an idea that had emerged in our own supervision some months earlier. The particular insight from supervision had been that this client appeared to be very frightened of a sense of emptiness within himself, so much so that he defended against feeling this emptiness by frantically burying himself in his busy daily life. At the time of the supervision there seemed no way to introduce this notion without simply increasing the client's defensiveness. Three months later, however, the client was talking about how he experienced therapy and used the description of 'a space that I find difficult to fill'. On hearing this phrase the therapist, remembering the earlier supervision discussion, was able to tentatively suggest that this might also be a description of how he experienced himself at times. The client accepted this interpretation quite readily and was able to explore it further with good results. This is an example of how the understanding of the therapist, and supervisor, may be ahead of the client.

For some this step may be a very clear cognitive process: identifying what fits with the current aims and objectives of the therapeutic work and the stage of the client. For others it may be much more intuitive; noticing which has a sense of rightness about it or what thought or perspective lingers and seems to make everything fall into place. There is a place for both these approaches, and others that may lie alongside or between these two.

Any new insights or possibilities that are to be applied directly need to be formulated in a way that ensures that they will be introduced with appropriate caution and sensitivity. This is the work of the goal setting and action planning phases, but before moving into these areas it is possible that new or additional information is needed.

Information giving: Step 4-B

We have included this component in the Bridge stage because there are situations in which it is helpful for the supervisor to introduce some new information. This may be particularly relevant for the inexperienced practitioner, who is likely to welcome information from their supervisor in a range of areas (Stoltenberg and McNeill 2010). Such information may be introduced in a number of ways.

Direct suggestion

One way the supervisor has of introducing information is by means of direct suggestion. Ladany and Lehrman-Waterman's (1999) study into supervisor self-disclosure identified didactic mentoring as a form of self-disclosure that is infrequently used but is valued by supervisees. Overholser (2004:6) identified 'directive guidance' as especially useful 'when dealing with difficult or high-risk situations' although he also cautions the supervisor to be alert to falling into 'the trap of providing rambling lectures to pontificate on different issues' (2004:7). Let us take the example of a relatively inexperienced female therapist working with a young adult male client who is struggling to form relationships with women. In the course of the supervision a hypothesis emerged, on the basis of the therapeutic material presented, suggesting that the client was still very attached to his mother and that there had been a considerable amount of symbolic sexual contact between the client and his mother during the client's adolescence.

The supervisor made a strong suggestion that the supervisee should disclose nothing of this hypothesis but rather that careful note should be taken of the client's way of being in his relationship with her (the therapist). This suggestion was made in the knowledge that this supervisee had a tendency to blurt out what she was thinking to her client and the supervisor felt that the client would probably find the Oedipal hypothesis quite alarming at this stage and that a better understanding of the transference relationship was required before it could be decided how, if at all, to introduce this delicate material.

In this case, the supervisee was able to understand and welcome this direct suggestion. In other cases, as Borders (2009) has argued, supervisees may resist direct suggestion in order to reduce the anxiety they experience in supervision or in relation to their practice, or because they are understandably resisting taking on something that they don't understand or see as helpful. This kind of resistance can be seen as a refusal to be controlled – the supervisee's capacity to say 'stop' or 'no' – and in this sense should be respected by the supervisor as an expression of liberation and autonomy. Breene (2011) sees supervisee resistance as 'a natural path' that expresses the desire 'to avoid the impositions of others' (p. 163), experienced at its worst by the 'Here's where you screwed up' approach (2011:177).

Self-disclosure

Another type of information giving involves the supervisor sharing her or his own experience as a therapist. This has a double benefit in that not only is it a means of introducing ideas to the supervisee but it can also emphasize that the supervisor is also a practising therapist; a reminder that they share common struggles and similar processes of learning and development (Knox *et al.* 2008). An example of this would be for the supervisor to acknowledge that when she worked with a dependent client, she also found it difficult to refuse repeated requests to advise the client about how to lead his life.

A cautionary note is needed here in that supervisors should beware of suggesting, through self-disclosure about their own practice, something that the supervisee is not yet sufficiently skilled or experienced to do. This will at best confuse the supervisee, it may also leave them feeling incompetent. At worst, they may take a guess at what the supervisor means and then take a flying leap into the unknown by foisting this guesswork on the client. An example of this would be where the supervisee, a trainee, has a hunch about an unexpressed feeling the client is experiencing and has failed to elicit this through asking questions. The supervisor may think it would be useful for the supervisee to use advanced empathy (Egan 2010; Wosket 2006) with the client. If the trainee doesn't understand this concept or yet have the skill to use it, it would be better for the supervisor to encourage the supervisee to use more basic empathic reflections and to ask fewer questions as a different way of encouraging the client to connect more with her feelings.

As a further illustration of the importance of this concept, one of us recently gave a mis-attuned challenge to a recently qualified but still relatively inexperienced supervisee. The supervisee, Austin, reported that in a recent session with his client, Mira, he had suggested an imagery technique to her and in the following session asked if she had found the technique useful. The client admitted that she couldn't remember much about the technique and hadn't tried it out. Austin had then reminded his client about the technique and explained again why he thought it might be helpful to her. On hearing this recounted in supervision the supervisor suggested to Austin that he had adopted quite a self-protective stance by explaining his rationale to his client, rather than remaining open to the possibility that a more fruitful course of action might have been to further encourage Mira's expression of resistance and autonomy conveyed by her not taking on his suggestion.

The supervisee became angry with his supervisor at this point, declaring 'I don't think I was at all defensive with the client!', and the supervision stalled. Work on repairing the supervision relationship took up most of the rest of the session. In hindsight the supervisor realized that perhaps Austin did not yet have the experience or confidence to see and welcome a client's non-compliant behaviour as a possible sign of the strength and vigour of the therapeutic relationship, and viewed it instead as evidence of something having gone wrong. She realized that a better approach would have been to encourage Austin to think through for himself the usefulness of his response to Mira and what alternatives might have been better. Borders (2009:201) refers to this supervisory skill as leading supervisees 'subtly down the path to their discovery'.

New technique

Another form of information giving is to introduce a new idea or technique. An example of this was when one of us described to a supervisee the use of an intervention that could be described as deliberately 'thinking out loud'. This technique, as Borders (2009) observes, has a number of advantages: it provides modelling for the supervisee in how to approach moment-by-moment decision making in a session; it provides insight into the process of using the internal supervisor; and it also takes the onus away from the therapist as the one in charge of making the decisions and gives decision making back to the client.

In suggesting this technique, the supervisor was intending to offer a new way the supervisee might use to introduce a dilemma in her work with a particular client. The client in question seemed highly compliant – that is to say, he was eager to please his therapist. The supervisor offered an example of the way the intervention might be formulated: 'Just at this moment I find myself wondering whether we should go further into this new issue or if we should return to our original focus'. This simple device provided a means of offering the choice of direction to the client whilst giving no clues as to the therapist's preference. The client is thereby invited to make a choice either explicitly, by a direct response, or implicitly through his next statement.

Role play

A fourth way of introducing new information is by means of role play. In supervision, this typically involves the supervisee being invited to take on the role of their client in order to explore the client's experience of them, the therapist. Thus, for example, when supervising a practitioner, Noreen, who tended to ask a lot of probing questions, the supervisor, Stefan, suggested that the supervisee play their client. When Stefan then started asking Noreen a number of probing questions, she quickly recognized the degree of discomfort this created. It is also possible for the supervisor to demonstrate specific techniques through role-play, although in general it is a more powerful learning device for supervisees if they have the experience first hand of doing something differently, rather than simply being shown a new way. Role play, the theoretical underpinning of which has been examined in some detail by Yardley-Matwiejczuk (1997), offers a powerful and immediate way of exploring the therapeutic process, and is perhaps particularly useful for supervisees who learn best through direct experimentation.

Giving references and suggesting resources

We find that supervisees are often glad to be recommended an article, a book, a website or a workshop that is relevant to a particular client or an aspect of counselling or psychotherapy practice. This fifth type of informative intervention (Heron 2001) may be particularly welcomed by therapists who are not currently in training, as it provides them with a new source of stimulation. Suggesting specific reading material can also be helpful to trainee therapists, who may be baffled by the volume of professional literature on offer and welcome guidance as to where to look for ideas about specific issues or interests.

These are five ways of introducing new information at this point, after the main exploration has taken place but prior to any decisions about how to apply the new understandings to the therapeutic work. In this way the supervisee has plenty of opportunity to identify new possibilities first. If the supervisor introduces possibilities too early in the supervision process this may inhibit the creativity of the supervisee, the encouragement of which is an important supervisory task. We would also suggest that this offers an appropriate discipline for supervisors. It is all too easy to fall into the trap of shifting into teacher mode early in a supervision session and so take the attention away from the supervisee. This can be a form of collusive defence between supervisor and supervisee, who are then both relieved to avoid challenges and difficult feelings (for example, of stuckness or incompetence). If supervisors confine their didactic inputs until the Bridge phase then this danger is restricted, if not avoided entirely.

Goal setting: Step 4-C

We have written elsewhere in some detail about a goal-directed approach to supervision using an application of the Cyclical Model that draws on Egan's 'Skilled Helper' model (Wosket 2006). In this publication it is argued that the uses of a goal-directed approach to supervision include: (i) providing a case management model; (ii) becoming an orientating device to help therapist and client locate where they are in the therapeutic process and to help review progress; (iii) helping to get back on track after a therapeutic 'derailment'; (iv) enhancing intentionality (direction and purpose); and (v) providing a framework to help refocus the work where it has lost energy or momentum. In this chapter we will confine our necessarily briefer discussion to three more general aspects of goal setting: therapeutic goals for the work with the client; learning goals for the counsellor's development; and supervisory goals for the supervision process itself.

Therapeutic goals

In order to explore this aspect of goal setting we will consider the case of a client, Angela, who is seeing Edward for counselling. Angela is in her twenties and has come to counselling because she is experiencing increasingly dark moods. She is happily married, with no children, and she and her husband are both in employment. As Edward and his supervisor explored the work with Angela in supervision a number of interesting pieces of information had come to light. Angela had an unwanted pregnancy in her teens and had the pregnancy terminated. She had told no one in her family about this and it had taken place at a time when her parents were splitting up. As it transpired, within a few hours of the termination taking place her father had left the family home. Angela and her husband now want to start a family but Angela is quite frightened at this prospect. In addition Edward feels very protective towards Angela, feeling quite pained on her behalf.

Edward and his supervisor have hypothesized that Angela's dark moods may well be a consequence of the unresolved guilt about the termination, which may or may not be linked to some primitive belief that in some way she contributed to her parents' divorce. In addition it would seem likely that Angela remains angry with her father for deserting her at this point in her life, when she really needed the support of both her parents. Edward's feelings towards Angela seem rooted in a fatherly counter-transference, and exploring this in supervision leads Edward and his supervisor to the view that the frightened young girl within Angela is transferring onto Edward her desire for a protective father figure.

From exploration in supervision the following therapeutic goals are formulated:

1   to assist Angela to explore possible feelings of guilt and consider ways in which now, ten years later, she can forgive herself;
2   to explore Angela's feelings towards her father;
3   for Edward to contain his emotional responses towards Angela and note any shifts or changes in these feelings.

It would be quite appropriate for Edward to discuss the first two goals with Angela, offering some explanation of the reasoning behind them. Indeed this might be helpful for her as it will involve her in the therapeutic process and also offer an explanation of how her current moods, which she finds quite frightening, may be linked to her life history. It is less likely or advisable that Edward would discuss the third goal with his client.

It is noteworthy that in the case of Angela a distinction can be drawn between her life goals and her therapeutic goals (Ticho 1972). Angela's life goals, as far as we know them, include being free of her low moods and to have a child or children. The three therapeutic goals above are not directly related to these life goals but rather are intended to make it possible to achieve them. In this case, distinguishing between the life goals and therapeutic goals is relatively straightforward. This distinction is not always so readily apparent; nevertheless, it is important to remind the therapist that there is a distinction between the two and that their responsibility is to define and work with the therapeutic goals, leaving clients to define and work towards their life goals for themselves (Kopp 1977; Wosket 2006). Making this distinction can be a safeguard against any omnipotent desire therapists may have to run their clients' lives for them.

The example of supervising the work of Edward with Angela is based within a long-term therapeutic relationship in which there is no set time limit on achieving the therapeutic goals. However, as discussed in Chapter 1, supervisors need to adapt to the realities of what it means to supervise time-limited forms of therapy that are now the norm within many counselling settings. In short-term work there is some urgency in clarifying what therapist and client are endeavouring to achieve. As Feltham (1997:76) has advised: 'Successful time-limited work is almost always focused, even if the focus is not always on explicitly specified goals'. Thus therapists whose work is time-limited will often need to leave supervision with a clear focus for each client discussed. This may include strategies for defining priorities and goals with the client, or it may primarily be to assist the supervisee in identifying appropriate interventions (Budman and Gurman 1988; Cooper and McLeod 2011; Coren 2001; Dryden and Feltham 1992; O'Connell 1998).

Learning goals

During the course of supervision, it is not uncommon to identify an area in which the therapist feels they have learning needs (Horton and Varma 1997; Rønnestad and Skovholt 2013; Stoltenberg and McNeill 2010; Wilkins 1997); indeed, if this does not happen on occasion then the supervision is failing to meet one of its primary purposes. These learning needs may relate to skills or knowledge and indicate that further training is required, or they may be more to do with the development of the practitioner's level of self-understanding and the enhancement of their capacity to work at increasing psychological depth (Mearns and Cooper 2005; Page 1999a; Wosket 1999). The latter may involve the counsellor or psychotherapist taking up some form of therapy or self-development.

Returning to our earlier example, Edward realized from his work with Angela that he needed to understand more about working with bereavement and loss, and therefore sought out a training course specific to this area. In addition he felt that he wanted to focus on his experience of the transference relationship and in particular his own counter-transference responses. This was an area in which Edward felt reasonably comfortable, but with Angela his responses were particularly strong. This second developmental goal did not require training but rather was a learning objective, which Edward could work out himself in consultation with his supervisor.

A learning objective such as the second one set by Edward can have a beneficial effect on the therapeutic process, even though it would seem to distract attention from the client. Indeed we have both argued elsewhere (Page 1999b; Wosket 1999) that identifying such issues becomes increasingly important for any therapist and is essential to the development of an effective individual practitioner identity (Rønnestad and Skovholt 2013).

Supervisory goals

There is a third set of goals, described by Borders and Leddick (1987), who, writing from a cognitive-behavioural perspective, have suggested: 'The results of your developmental assessment [of the supervisee] then, may indicate additional, perhaps unspoken, goals, and influence how you intervene to help supervisees move towards their specified goals' (pp. 24–5). These 'perhaps unspoken' goals are those that the supervisor may have for her task in facilitating the development of the supervisee. Such goals may be discussed with the supervisee, but it is equally possible that the supervisor will not speak of them, simply using the goals as aids to her selection of supervisory interventions. An example of such a goal would be to encourage more reflection in the supervisee through open questions, minimal prompting and greater use of silence. With another supervisee a supervisory goal may be to encourage the supervisee to do more of their own research and self-education in some areas by offering references rather than providing information and answers or suggesting how to intervene.

Action planning: Step 4-D

The defined goals are the intended outcome, the desired end result of a process. The action plan is the means of achieving the desired outcome: a sequence of steps which, if successfully implemented, will lead to the goal being attained. When it comes to planning action, supervisors should take care to ensure that decisions are explicitly handed over to supervisees and owned by them. Here is an illustration of this process, taken from our own practice, which combines an embodied approach to supervision (see Chapter 13) with action planning. It is recounted in the first person.

> My supervisee, Marijke, is worried about appearing prejudiced or judgemental with her client, Rick, who is considering returning to work in the sex industry. Yet she admits to herself and to me that part of her *does* feel judgemental and therefore she experiences herself as being incongruent with her client. He has told her that he is drawn to returning to this work because he desperately needs the money and knows the work is easy to get and is well paid. In supervision I explore with Marijke her feelings of judgementalism by asking 'What happens to you in the session when he says that he is considering doing that? What is it like in your body?' Marijke says: 'I have a sinking feeling in the pit of my stomach and I want to say 'Oh no, don't do that!' I then ask her: 'What does that sensation in your stomach and the thought that goes with it connect to?'
>
> Marijke's response to this is to remember several things that Rick has previously told her. One is that he didn't want his younger brother growing up knowing his big brother was a sex worker and another is that he had told her how ashamed and dirty he had felt when doing this work. She also remembered that Rick had briefly told her that he was sexually abused as a child, but had said that he didn't want to talk about this yet in his therapy.
>
> I then ask Marijke if it is possible in any way for her to voice the reaction she has just described to her client. I ask whether her embodied experience could help here. After some reflection Marijke says she thinks she might be able to say something like: 'When you tell me you are thinking of going back into commercial sex work I have a sinking feeling in my stomach and an urge to say "Please don't do that". I think this comes from knowing you have told me that you don't want your little brother to grow up with a big brother who, to use your word, "prostitutes" himself and also remembering how ashamed and dirty you told me you felt when you were previously doing this work. I am also concerned about someone who was abused as a child feeling they need to do this kind of work. I know we haven't talked about that much yet but you have been able to let me know that happened to you and I am fearful of you suffering further abuse.'

In the next supervision session Marijke recounted that when she had said this to Rick he started to cry and said knowing that she cared about him helped him to believe he might be worth caring about.

In this example we see that action planning is certainly taking place, that the supervisor is prompting the process, and also that the precise form the action might take is decided by the supervisee and arises from her felt experience of being with her client.

In writing about action planning as part of the counselling process Egan (1986:48) has stated:

> One reason people fail to achieve goals is that they do not explore the different ways in which the goal can be reached. They choose one means or strategy without a great deal of exploration or reflection, try it, and when it fails conclude that they just can't achieve that particular goal. Coming up with as many ways of achieving a goal as possible increases the probability that one of them or a combination of several will suit the resources of a particular client.

The same argument applies in supervision so it is important that supervisor and supervisee are prepared to spend time looking at a number of possible routes to a goal. Furthermore, strategies should remain flexible and tentatively formed: 'To work at its best, implementation needs to be tactical and to allow for the unexpected. In this sense, any plans that are made are required to be open to change and adaptation' (Wosket 2006:91).

If we return to the case of Angela we can consider possible strategies for achieving the first two goals: (i) to assist Angela to explore possible feelings of guilt and consider ways in which now, ten years later, she can forgive herself; and (ii) to explore Angela's feelings towards her father. The first line of thought that Edward and his supervisor pursued was to identify the various people involved with the teenaged Angela with whom she may have unresolved issues. The list becomes quite extensive: her father, the unborn child, the father of the child, her mother and other members of her family. This raises a number of possible strategies. Angela could be invited to do this exercise for herself, perhaps on paper or simply verbally with Edward. This might provide the necessary cathartic impetus (Heron 2001) to get the emotional work under way. It could be taken further, with Angela being invited to have imaginary conversations with one or more of the characters, most probably the unborn child, the child's father, or perhaps her own father or mother.

The second set of possibilities comes out of focusing specifically on the issue of guilt, with the associated issues of damaged self-esteem and the need for a means of forgiveness. One possible strategy that emerges is to have Angela identify someone in her life now who is the age she was then and to consider what resources this person has and what it is reasonable to be able to expect them to do.

This would be done with the intention of helping Angela separate her adult self from her teenage self and thereby create the possibility of forgiving the teenager rather than imposing her adult expectations upon her younger self. There is also the option of encouraging Angela to express any suppressed anger associated with her feeling of guilt. It would also be possible to discuss with Angela the process of self-forgiveness and the necessary conditions for forgiveness to take place. We could generate further possibilities, but perhaps what we have given here is sufficient to demonstrate the range of options available.

It is important to understand that action planning is a process, not a single event that takes place in supervision and is then applied in therapy. Thus any plan needs to be reviewed and then modified in light of what transpires in the therapy. Any attempt to stick rigidly to a plan defined in supervision is doomed to strangle the creativity of the therapeutic process and limits therapy to being the application of techniques or theories to the client in a mechanistic manner. If the counselling or psychotherapy relationship is to be therapeutic it must be enabled to unfold in new and unexpected directions. Only then can therapy be said to be responding to the client, enabling this unique individual to move forward in the way best suited to him or her.

Client's perspective: Step 4-E

It is imperative that at some stage prior to the supervisee returning to the therapeutic arena any action or intervention that is being considered is evaluated from the perspective of the client. On this topic Borders (2009) has argued that it is important for supervisees to maintain consideration of the client's perspective for two reasons. The first is that in itself this is a discipline that encourages the development of the capacity for taking multiple perspectives – a key cognitive skill all therapists need to hone. Secondly, the capacity to consider the client's perspective is a key therapeutic principle to be applied directly in every counselling session in order to maintain an approach that is client-directed rather than therapist-directed. Borders (2009:204) suggests that two useful questions for the therapist to keep in mind at this stage are: 'Does the client understand my intention?' and 'What does the client need from me right now?'

If, in supervision, the supervisor consistently models attention to, and interest in, the supervisee's perspective on what is happening in the supervision process and relationship, this is likely to 'rub off' on the supervisee and encourage them to do the same with their clients. Considering the client's perspective is, of course, not possible to do directly in supervision but nevertheless can be attempted by endeavouring to imagine the effect upon the client of the planned strategy (Andersson et al. 2010). This is an empathic process, which has also been termed 'trial identification'. Casement (1985:35) describes using this technique as a therapist when trying to 'listen (as the patient might) to what it crosses my mind to say, silently trying out a possible comment or interpretation'.

In the context of supervision, trial identification may be applied in a similar way to a specific intervention or to a type of intervention or course of action. For example, the supervisor can invite the therapist to face an empty chair in which he imagines the client is sitting. The supervisee then runs through what he is considering saying to the client as a result of the supervision. The supervisor then has the supervisee switch chairs and imagine that he is the client, 'hearing' what his therapist has just said. The supervisee is then invited, in the role of the client, to voice what impact he feels that this intervention has had on him. Strategies can be reviewed in the light of any new awareness this brings.

Returning once more to the example of Angela it is possible to apply a trial identification to each of the possible action plans already proposed. When this was done in the supervision Edward felt that Angela would probably sabotage cathartic interventions. He considered this was likely because what emerged when he tried identifying with Angela was a belief that she deserved to feel bad because she had been 'bad' in having had her pregnancy terminated. As a result of this trial identification, Edward decided to tackle the possible guilt first. He felt that only when the guilt had been worked through would Angela be prepared to engage in the emotional work that also needed to be done.

Thus by checking what is being considered against the imagined impact upon the client, it is possible to make an informed decision as to how to proceed. The true test of the planned intervention or strategy will take place when the supervisee is with his or her client, and it is for the therapist to remain alert to what takes place, and if necessary change plans in the light of this.

Using the bridge as a way of focusing

As we draw this chapter to a close we wish to illustrate the flexible nature of the Cyclical Model by including an example of how the bridging phase of a supervision session may lead back into the focusing stage.

> The supervisee in this example started her session by stating that she definitely needed to discuss one client at length and might talk about another if time allowed. After exploring the work with the first client only five minutes of the session remained. The supervisor said 'Do you just want to name the issue with your second client, even though we won't have time to explore it?' The supervisee replied 'OK – I'm being too directive with my client and she gets angry with me'. The supervisor then said 'Now that you have recognized that as your issue, do you have a thought about what you might need to do differently?' The supervisee replied 'I need to stop being so directive – no, that's not right. I'm directive when I'm challenging her reckless behaviour and when I think she'll get hurt, because I care about her. She gets angry when I challenge her. What I need to do instead, I'm thinking now, is let her know that I'm following an impulse to challenge her because I care about her and I'm concerned that she'll end up in another abusive relationship.'

This vignette illustrates how bridging (the supervisor's question about what the supervisee might want to do) can lead to a useful focus and amplification (the supervisee's reflections on her directiveness) even when time is short in supervision.

Having concluded the client-focused part of supervision, there remains the task, for supervisor and supervisee, of reviewing together their own experience of the supervision session. This will be the subject of the next chapter.

Chapter 8

Stage 5: Review

Following the exploratory work of Stage 3 (Space) and the re-connective work of Stage 4 (Bridge), the final stage of the model concerns the process of reviewing and evaluating. This stage is built into the model to ensure that both supervisor and supervisee regularly reflect upon the quality of the supervisory relationship and the effectiveness of the work done in supervision.

Figure 8.1 outlines the five steps into which we have divided the review stage of supervision. As in some previous stages, the steps frequently shade imperceptibly into one another or are used selectively at appropriate points within the supervision process. Grounding, feedback and evaluation are likely to be pertinent to every session, re-contracting may occur intermittently or at fixed points in the ongoing process, while assessment may not be relevant at all, depending on the nature of the supervision alliance.

The review stage brings the collaborative nature of supervision to the foreground: it gives attention to how supervisee and supervisor each contribute to

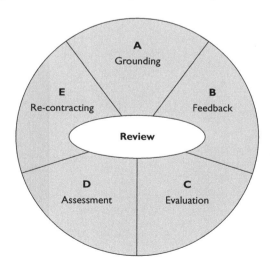

Figure 8.1 Supervision model Stage 5: Review.

their work together and therefore to the effectiveness of their working alliance. Reviewing can cause discomfort and even provoke anxiety. Nevertheless there is sufficient evidence (McIntosh *et al.* 2006; Webb and Wheeler 1998; Yourman 2003) that supervisees frequently hold back from expressing how they feel in supervision, including when they experience supervision as dysfunctional, for us to believe that regular reviewing is essential to good practice.

A supervisee who was not in the habit of systematically reviewing his progress with clients was exploring his discomfort with this aspect of the process. In response to supportive challenging from his supervisor, he was enabled to see that avoidance of reviewing his work with clients was one way that he habitually put himself down; as he put it: 'I might hear that I'm no good.' When the supervisor asked him what stood in the way of inviting feedback from clients, he got in touch with his own anxiety and also began to see more clearly his own blindspot: 'I need to feel secure enough about me to run the risk of asking them. Otherwise I'm depriving them of the opportunity to recognize the progress they're making or to tell me if it's not helping, so that we can try to do something about it.'

The supervisee's words can be usefully transposed to the supervision encounter and they provide a fitting rationale for the inclusion of the review stage in the supervision model. Review emphasizes the collaborative nature of the enterprise and the mutuality of purpose; improving the quality and value of the work, which is being undertaken as a partnership. For many this provokes a very basic and real fear that can too easily get in the way of the supervisor actively encouraging feedback: the risk that 'I might hear that I'm no good'. The challenge for each of us as supervisors is to overcome that fear and demonstrate our commitment to our own continued learning through seeking feedback, which is no more than we expect our supervisees to do.

Grounding: Step 5-A

We are using this term to describe the process that takes place at the interface between the end of the bridging stage and the beginning of the process of review. Grounding is best described as a process of disengagement from the exploratory and planning work undertaken in the previous two stages and involves both supervisor and supervisee winding down before they look back over the immediate experience. In this sense it provides a counter-balance to the focusing stage: it has a de-focusing function as attention shifts from the supervision work itself to an appraisal of it. At this point we could say that the participants shift ground and move one foot back into the 'real world' whilst retaining the other foothold, for a while longer, in the 'artificial world' of the supervision encounter. Alternatively we can think of it as the process of 'earthing' the emotional and psychological 'charge' that can be generated in an intense supervisory discussion, dissipating some of that charge to create the best conditions for a more dispassionate discussion about the supervision experience to take place.

The grounding stage often comprises a quiet moment of reflection, or of simply 'being with' one another as both supervisor and supervisee withdraw and settle back in order to achieve the necessary level of objectivity required to evaluate the work. In our usage it is frequently marked by the supervisor saying something like 'Have we finished that part?' or, 'Have we done enough?' Often it is a place where amusement or humour enter into the discussion; classic ways of discharging energy. For example, both might share a sense of relief in emerging from work that has been difficult, if productive, perhaps by the supervisee exclaiming, 'I am glad to have got that off my chest', or words to that effect.

The grounding stage is also about supervisor and supervisee playing with 'what is around the edges' of the work. Moving back from the main focus provides both with the opportunity to alter or enlarge their immediate perspective, so that, for example, connections or patterns become more apparent. It might be that the supervisor here spots and highlights a habitual occurrence in the supervisee's work: 'It's interesting that this is the third time running we've explored dependency issues for your clients. It might be worth considering if that's significant in any way.' Or the supervisee might spot something there for themselves: 'I've just realized that we talked about dependency in my clients the last two times we met as well. It might be because it's quite an issue for me in my own therapy at the moment too.' Alternatively, a difference or the breaking out of a previously identified pattern might be recognized at this point. For instance where the supervisor notices 'We managed to get both your clients in this time without it seeming rushed, as it often is', and the supervisee responds 'I think I was clearer about what I wanted help with this time and that stopped me from going all over the place and then running out of time'. Having got their breath back, so to speak, the supervisor and supervisee can more easily move into some evaluation of the supervision experience.

Feedback: Step 5-B

Feedback in supervision covers both a process and the skills needed to engage in that process. By feedback we mean the giving and receiving of responses and reactions that have the purpose of improving the quality or the usefulness of the supervision. Karpenko and Gidycz (2012) discuss the importance of feedback being two-way, reminding us that 'it is important for the supervisor to be open to constructive feedback from the supervisees' (p. 148). Feedback that is only given by a supervisor to a supervisee, whether it is positive or negative, is a misuse of power and a perversion of the process in that it denies the supervisee the right or the opportunity to share his or her experience in a way that impinges on the other party. Feedback that only entails the supervisee sharing reactions, for example appreciation of how the supervisor helped with a difficult issue, may leave the supervisee wondering what the supervisor is thinking and feeling about them and their work, perhaps causing unnecessary anxiety or discomfort.

Miller *et al.* (2008) have presented a compelling case, based on their review of studies of therapist effectiveness, for there being a strong correlation between regularly seeking and acting upon feedback on their own performance and therapist excellence. Therefore, it is good practice to encourage all our supervisees to seek feedback from their clients as a routine activity, which we can best achieve by modelling this practice in our supervision. Feedback can focus on a number of aspects of the supervision, including: the dynamics of the relationship; specific skills and interventions (both the supervisee's with their clients and the supervisor's with the supervisee); the way the process is being managed (for example, timing or structure); styles and approaches used by both parties; and awareness of developments (for instance, in the client work or the supervisee's competence). It can occur at any point in the supervision, but is discussed here as it has, primarily, a reviewing function. A reciprocal process of systematic and honest feedback can enormously enhance the supervision task and relationship in the following ways:

- highlighting and reinforcing strengths and good practice;
- indicating areas for development and weaknesses to be addressed;
- challenging what appears not to have been seen, heard or felt;
- cementing and developing the supervision relationship;
- encouraging mutuality and collaboration;
- releasing pent-up feelings;
- clearing away confusions and misunderstandings;
- providing support and affirmation.

The ability to give and receive constructive feedback depends on a number of skills and qualities in both parties (Millar 2009; Poertner and Miller 1996; Wosket 2006). In considering how to give feedback to supervisees it is important for the supervisor to be aware, as pointed out by Gilbert and Sills (1999:181), that 'most people have emerged from such a shame based educational process that any feedback which is in any way critical seems to "devastate" the person'. One danger associated with this experience is that the supervisor may hold back from giving feedback that will help the supervisee learn and grow from fear of upsetting or undermining him or her. More seriously, the withholding of constructive feedback may mean that bad habits and poor practice go unchallenged and appear to be condoned by the supervisor's silence on the subject. Supervisors therefore have a duty to provide feedback to their supervisees in the service of enhancing therapeutic competence and safeguarding client welfare. How the feedback is given is the key to its effectiveness, and paramount above all else is the supervisor's ability to offer feedback that provides an equal balance of support and challenge.

Competence in offering feedback is enhanced where the qualities of empathy, openness, honesty and consistency are present in the giver. Feedback is made more acceptable to the recipient when it is balanced (positive with negative), managed with good timing and given regularly. It requires the communication skills of assertiveness, clarity and concreteness. The factors likely to undermine good feedback include generalization, defensiveness, vagueness, inconsistency, over-personalization, blaming and indecisiveness. Of equal importance is the ability to receive feedback and allow it, when appropriate, to make a difference. Perhaps paramount here are the willingness to listen and the ability to consider feedback before responding.

Feedback by the supervisor that is comprehensive, constructive, honest, balanced and freely and regularly given effectively takes the sting out of any evaluation and assessment that may be required and provides a powerful spur to the supervisee's development. Inman and Ladany (2008:502), summarizing research outcomes on this topic, state that 'findings from the various studies indicate that a stronger working alliance is related to goal-setting and feedback'. In the same way that personal growth and change are powerfully related to feedback from significant others in an individual's life, so too the development of the counsellor's professional persona is closely influenced by the supervisor's selective responses.

Evaluation: Step 5-C

The step of evaluation in supervision provides the opportunity for supervisor and supervisee to determine the value of the supervision experience and consider any implications for change. The focus here is mutual evaluation of the co-operative enterprise, not assessment of the supervisee, which is dealt with in the next step of the model. It is important to include the space for some evaluation of the work just undertaken in each supervision session. It is also valuable to stand back from the session-to-session work, on occasion, and evaluate the ongoing process.

Evaluation need not be a formal or formidable exercise, although questionnaires and checklists do exist (Arvidsson *et al.* 2008; Ellis *et al.* 2008; Wheeler *et al.* 2011; Zarbock *et al.* 2009) for the more quantitative analysis of the process, tasks and relationship. The model offered in this book itself provides a comprehensive and adaptable framework for monitoring the work. If both participants are familiar with the different steps and stages, they can go through them together as a way of checking whether sufficient attention is being given, in the best way, to each of the elements. This might throw up, for example, considerations about whether initial expectations are being met, whether improvements could be made to achieve a better match of styles and approaches, whether the supervisee is feeling sufficiently challenged and affirmed in the supervision, whether objectives are sufficiently clear and whether more attention needs to be paid to applying insights from supervision to work with clients.

Since first introduced by Kagan (Kagan 1984; Kagan *et al.* 1963) Interpersonal Process Recall (IPR) has remained a powerful tool for the immediate processing and evaluating of the supervision experience, and continues to be used in practice and as a research instrument (Crews *et al.* 2005; Frankel and Levitt 2009; O'Hara and Schofield 2008). IPR involves the supervisor and supervisee recording (preferably on video, although audio-only can also be helpful) a supervision session and then reviewing it together, stopping the recording at intervals to describe covert processes (thoughts, feelings, bodily sensations, fantasies and aspirations) associated with particular moments in the interview. The recording acts as a stimulus and provides cues for the participants to help them retrieve memories and perceptions that would otherwise be only fleetingly experienced and quickly forgotten. When IPR was first introduced it was considered very important to review the recording as quickly as possible after the actual session, so that kinesthetic or felt-experience memory remained accessible to the supervisee.

More recent exponents of the use of video and audio recordings for supervision and training purposes (e.g. Diener *et al.* 2007; Haggerty and Hilsenroth 2011; Huhra *et al.* 2008; Jencius *et al.* 2010) seem less concerned about timing, and report using recording in a range of ways to review client–therapist interaction. In a meta-analysis of the relationship between the therapist facilitating emotional expression in psychodynamic psychotherapy and beneficial outcome of therapy for the patient, Diener and colleagues (2007:939) found that 'use of audio- or videotaping for supervision demonstrated a moderate effect size, which suggests the importance of observing actual therapist techniques in order to maximize these dynamic treatment effects'. By this we understand the researchers to mean that recording for supervision had a significant positive impact upon the outcome of therapy for patients. Understandably some therapists are very concerned about the possible negative impact of using recording equipment in the consulting room. However, Marshall and colleagues (2001) found that clients adjust to their sessions being recorded within two sessions and that therapists are likely to overestimate the negative and underestimate the positive effects of session recording.

Session-by-session evaluation can be woven into the fabric of the discussion in a way that enhances and often throws new light on the exploratory work undertaken. We have found it of value in our supervision practice to give a specific amount of time, normally about ten minutes, at the end of each session, over to reviewing the work of that particular session. Here, such considerations as usefulness of the discussion and interventions used, whether goals were met, how the time was managed and the quality of the relationship can be addressed. Any implications for future work can be discussed as a result of this immediate appraisal.

This process can happen in a relaxed and spontaneous way by supervisor and supervisee taking the opportunity to share 'what was around that wasn't said'. Here are a supervisee's comments on her experience of using this end-of-session reviewing technique:

> The processing time at the end of supervision adds another valuable dimen-
> sion for me, as a supervisee, and has significantly enhanced our supervision
> relationship. It's about having permission to meet each other in that time on
> a more human, personal level, one which allows me to appreciate and
> understand both my supervisor and the process we have experienced together
> more fully. It gives a space for me to say what was going on for me during the

supervision, which would otherwise be left unsaid. I would feel cheated now without that space.

The willingness to engage in this process of self-disclosure clearly depends on the strength of the relationship and the level of trust established.

Reviewing the supervisory experience can provide powerful catalysis for development of the relationship by encouraging mutuality and the sharing of aspects of supervisee and supervisor vulnerability and humanity. As supervisors, we might share here, for instance, occasions where we have doubted our ability to be helpful, or felt we made a mistake, or where we had wanted to make an intervention but had held back through embarrassment or concern about how the supervisee would then perceive us. Openness about such fallibility discourages the supervisee from idealizing the supervisor and from thereby setting a dangerous precedent that could be passed on as a parallel process in the supervisee's therapeutic work. If this were to occur the client may then not experience their therapist as a complete person because the supervisee has set themselves up, like their supervisor, to appear infallible. Furthermore, this 'mini-evaluation' process can throw important light on the supervision material itself and often serves to highlight a parallel process that was occurring but not being acknowledged. Here are two brief examples of where such a phenomenon occurred in our own supervision work.

In the reviewing space at the end of a session the supervisor shared her appreciation of how carefully her supervisee had prepared for the supervision by bringing a list of issues to discuss. However, she also stated, in the following words, that this had given her a dilemma:

SUPERVISOR: Sometimes I felt I wanted to intervene and say 'Hold on a minute, there's more to that' when you were clearly wanting to move on to the next issue. It was hard for me because I felt I didn't want to take control of the session, yet there were things I wanted to say and couldn't. It was also difficult because I wanted you to get from the supervision what you had said you wanted at the beginning – which was to get through all those issues on your list.

SUPERVISEE: That's split my mind in two, because yes, how *do* we manage that? I agree, it's OK for you to say 'Just hold on a second' and I'd like you to do that. But it also throws light on my client. That's exactly my dilemma with her. She goes off on her own track and follows her own agenda even when I introduce something in response to what she's said. I'm realizing now that she's avoiding, as well as being in control. It's like I don't want to lose the moment and she skates off on something else.

The second example concerns a point in the supervision where the supervisee had requested some suggestions for ways to help his client increase her self-confidence. Rather than giving these suggestions, the supervisor had asked 'What are some of the ways you have helped other clients to become more self-confident?' The supervisee's response had been to laugh and say 'Well, it happens indirectly – through the relationship'. During the review stage of the session the supervisee returned to this incident to give some feedback to the supervisor.

SUPERVISEE: I'm glad now you didn't start suggesting how I could use techniques to increase my client's self-confidence, even though I thought that was what I wanted.

SUPERVISOR: Yes, it didn't seem right because I know you can do that. And if necessary you can go away and read up on assertiveness techniques, or whatever, without me needing to tell you.

SUPERVISEE: And I realize now that what I did to you is what my client does to me. He asks *me* 'how?' and I feel under pressure to come up with suggestions and take responsibility for him.

Such occurrences in supervision, as illustrated by these examples, serve to remind us that the supervision encounter can be a many-layered process. Immediate evaluation can be valuable in helping to peel away the various layers in order to understand more clearly what lies underneath in terms of the meaning and the message of the client's experience.

Assessment: Step 5-D

We have included assessment as a discrete step in the reviewing process in order to give consideration to any formal assessment function the supervisor may hold in relation to supervisees and their work. Whereas trainee supervision is the norm in the United States, and hence the supervisor usually has a clear assessing role, in Britain a large part of the supervision undertaken is practitioner supervision, where formal assessment is not usually part of the contract. In this section we will consider formative and summative assessment as they apply to the counsellor and psychotherapist in training.

As we stated in Chapter 4 when considering accountability within the Contract, any formal assessment responsibility that the supervisor holds needs to be made explicit to the supervisee at the start of the supervision relationship. Christie and colleagues (2004), writing from a clinical psychology perspective, are similarly unequivocal: 'it is also essential to make explicit the supervisor's role as evaluator – as well as clinical supervisor – and clarify their responsibility in making decisions about whether placements are passed or failed' (p. 22). The trainee practitioner is in a vulnerable position in having to suffer the subjective evaluation of the supervisor, and uncertainty and anxiety are increased for both parties where the issue is dodged or glossed over. The supervisor has a responsibility to make clear to the supervisee how he or she will be assessing their work, and the explicit criteria upon which the assessment will be based (Bernard and Goodyear 2009; Falender and Shafranske 2004; Hess *et al.* 2008).

In discussing this issue from an American perspective, where assessment is inherent in the supervision role, Welfare (2010:348) summarizes some key considerations:

> evaluation requires deliberate planning and careful execution. Evaluation is not a unidirectional, punitive process; rather it is a supportive, facilitative experience that is a catalyst for supervisee growth. Supervisees should be informed of evaluation procedures and consequences of underperformance before supervision begins. General counselor competencies and individualized goals shape the foci of ongoing supervision and provide structure to formative and summative evaluations.

Formative assessment

By formative assessment we are referring to estimations of the supervisee's work and development as he or she proceeds over the course of the supervision. Formative assessment is a process of continuous feedback, intended to support the supervisee to develop their practice in the best ways possible. Formative assessment should be provided by regular, constructive and encouraging feedback that is adjusted to match the trainee's level of development and expected competence at that level. Ideally, as Bernard and Goodyear (2009:21) point out, 'Formative evaluation . . . does not necessarily feel like evaluation because it stresses the process and progress of professional competence, rather than outcome'. Ongoing feedback is an enabling process that allows trainee counsellors and psychotherapists to know that they are moving in the right direction or gives the opportunity for corrective action if they appear to be faltering. Supervisees who receive regular feedback know where they stand and are spared a great deal of unnecessary anxiety. Conversely, as Bernard and Goodyear (2009:15) have remarked, 'when supervisors say nothing, supervisees may decide that their performance was exemplary or too awful to discuss'.

Good formative assessment should comprise feedback on those elements of professional competence that, when assimilated by the supervisee, will enable him or her to develop their own personal criteria for self-evaluation. There needs to be a balance of positive and constructive for, as Welfare (2010:345) suggests, 'frequent critical feedback may be discouraging to the supervisee and excessive positive feedback is unlikely to stimulate growth'. Welfare goes on to underline the importance of making judicious choices about what to give feedback upon, as, 'supervisors usually recognize more potential foci for feedback than the supervisee can effectively comprehend and integrate during a supervision session' (2010:345).

One of the central purposes of supervision is to improve client outcomes. Therefore impact upon the client is one of the key formative assessment criteria a supervisor should use in evaluating interventions and approaches used by the supervisee. While it has been demonstrated (Freitas 2002; Watkins 2011) that this is a difficult area to research effectively, Inman and Ladany (2008:507) suggest that there is some evidence that 'focusing on a particular skill or content area in supervision may not only help the trainee alter the skill or address the issue in counseling . . . but also lead the client to view the session more positively'. In our view this supports the supervisory practice of giving concrete and detailed formative feedback to supervisees about their interventions and the manner in which they address issues with their clients. More generally, keeping the criterion of positive client impact clearly in view can enable the supervisor to be less subjective in evaluating the supervisee and allow him or her to give practitioners greater permission to develop their own style and approach. So the question one is asking oneself here, as a supervisor, may well be: 'Even though my supervisee chose to do it differently to the way I would have approached it, did the client benefit?'

Summative assessment

In the words of Bernard and Goodyear (2009), summative assessment or evaluation means 'the moment of truth when the supervisor steps back, takes stock, and decides how the supervisee measures up' (p. 22). Some supervisors may feel very reluctant to make this judgement. Nevertheless it is a clear responsibility (Izzard 2001) for supervisors of trainees to do so, on behalf of current and future clients and the integrity of the profession. If the process of formative assessment has been well managed this will effectively take the sting out of any final assessment of the supervisee. The trainee counsellor or psychotherapist will have become aware, through supportive feedback, of areas of limitation and weakness, or even of the danger of failure, so that any negative appraisal does not take them by surprise. Trainees should also have received due credit for areas of strength and particular expertise so that they are spared the unhelpful experience of going along thinking their work was merely adequate, only to be suddenly surprised to learn that in some respects it has been outstanding.

Some agencies and training institutions require the supervisor to write a confidential statement of competence or report on the supervisee, which is composed by the supervisor alone. Our view on summative assessment in supervision is that it is best accomplished through a reciprocal process that mirrors the collaborative alliance that, ideally, has underscored the previous supervisory work. To this end we favour the use of a negotiated 'Joint Learning Statement' that is compiled by both supervisor and supervisee and based upon ongoing feedback, discussions and reflections that have taken place throughout the course of the supervision. Typically both supervisor and supervisee write separate sections, after discussion, setting out what each would like to see included. Both parties then read and confirm one another's statements or, if necessary, amend these after further discussion and negotiation. The agreed statement is then signed and dated by both the supervisor and the supervisee. Any outstanding areas of disagreement can be noted in writing by either party if resolution proves impossible. In our experience this contingency is rarely necessary if the preceding steps have been worked through with sensitivity and in a true spirit of collaboration, if regular feedback has been integral to the foregoing work and if the supervision relationship has been well developed and fostered. The main focus of the statement is the supervisee's current level of development, and the content of the document is likely to cover the following aspects of therapeutic practice and supervision:

- range and approximate number of clients seen;
- variety of client issues and problems dealt with, together with an indication of any special areas of interest;
- main themes and issues covered in the supervision;
- developments made in terms of growing awareness, skills and competencies;
- ability of the student to translate learning into practice;
- ability of the student to reflect upon, monitor and evaluate own practice (use of internal supervisor);
- particular strengths and areas of expertise shown;
- limitations, weaknesses and areas for further development;
- nature and development of the supervisory relationship;
- evaluation of the supervision experience from both the supervisor's and the supervisee's perspective;
- the student's short- and longer-term objectives for future development, consolidation of learning and further training;
- a statement by the supervisor indicating their opinion of the supervisee's fitness to practice at this stage of their training and development, outlining any reservations.

A thorny issue for the supervisor in assessing the supervisee's fitness to practice is that of the evaluation of what Welfare (2010:343) describes as 'interpersonal attributes'. Welfare suggests that these include 'ability to express emotions, personal maturity, perspective taking, ability to receive and integrate feedback, ability to manage conflict, motivation, respectfulness, and sense of responsibility' (2010:343). The supervisor has a responsibility to ensure, as far as possible, that fitness to practice includes a level of personal awareness and development that, at minimum, means that clients will not be exploited because of the supervisee's unresolved personal needs or problems. Therefore some appraisal of the personal qualities of the therapist, as well as of their skills and knowledge, is unavoidable. Evaluation of individual attributes will inevitably, on occasion, lead to the supervisee feeling judged as a person. This can be minimized by linking the articulation of any reservations about personal characteristics to specific examples from the supervisee's practice. Again, this highlights the importance of specific, sensitive, balanced and regular feedback that is based on a close appraisal of the work – for instance by listening to recordings and studying transcripts, rather than relying merely on supervisee self-reports. The following example will serve to make this clearer.

During the first year of supervision with a student on a two-year diploma course, the supervisor became increasingly concerned about the trainee counsellor's ability and willingness to tolerate strong feelings in his clients. The supervisor asked the counsellor to provide her with recordings of counselling sessions and through listening to these she noticed that the counsellor frequently introduced material from his own agenda – questions, suggestions and opinion – whenever a client began to exhibit distress. The supervisor was able to address this issue with the counsellor in a non-punitive manner using specific examples from the recorded material. In particular she asked the counsellor to consider in each instance what effect his interventions appeared to make on the client. They then discussed possible alternative interventions. Though initially resistant to considering the dysfunctional effect of this pattern of responses, the counsellor gradually began to accept that he might be deterring clients from doing work that they needed to do. He began in small ways to allow his clients to experience and express more of a range of emotions, although he continued to find this difficult. The counsellor himself had an aversion to owning and talking about feelings, a personality factor that appeared to be entrenched. In the end-of-year Joint Learning Statement the supervisor outlined her reservations, based on tangible evidence provided by the recordings, and gained the counsellor's agreement that these should be included in the following way. The counsellor's difficulty was mentioned as an area for further work and development. The supervisor included a written recommendation that he should undertake a period of counselling, where this issue could be explored on a personal level. In addition she stated that if he stayed at his current level of development she could not recommend that he worked with clients who needed to do cathartic work. These comments were balanced by others within the statement, which mentioned the counsellor's strengths, for instance his challenging-skills and ability to establish clear contracts and boundaries with clients.

A Joint Learning Statement, by its very nature, should encourage reciprocity and give the supervisee an opportunity to comment on the quality and usefulness of the supervision they have received. Although to do so requires courage where a vulnerable trainee wishes to make negative comments about a powerful supervisor, as trainers we are aware that this can and does happen. Supervisees have, for example, commented on difficulties in making regular appointments with busy supervisors who are hard to contact or pin down. More frequently, students have at times recorded having uncertainties or anxieties about what was expected of them in the initial stages of supervision, particularly where it seemed that the supervisor was either unaware of, or took no steps to allay, their difficulties.

Re-contracting: Step 5-E

This step, when it is necessary, follows naturally from the previous work on evaluation and assessment. It is the part of the model where the supervisor and supervisee review and renew their original contract, consider how to make changes arising from the review, or set new objectives for future sessions. The process of regular re-contracting ensures that both parties are continually making necessary readjustments to the work in order to enhance its effectiveness and smooth running. The supervision thereby evolves as a dynamic process, rather than remaining static or set in a particular mould. Re-contracting takes account of changes in the development of both the supervisor and the supervisee. It enables them, for instance, to move to the consideration of higher-order skills and competencies when the supervisee develops these over a course of training, as the following example illustrates.

> During the first year of a two-year diploma course in counselling, a trainee counsellor had concentrated in her supervision on the development and appropriate use of specific micro skills within the counselling process. She did this through presenting her supervisor with sections of audio recordings that provided the impetus for discussion and consideration of alternative strategies and interventions. In the second year of the course the counsellor re-contracted with her supervisor to give more attention to exploring the dynamics of counselling relationships and to the therapeutic use of self within her counselling work, particularly through the use of the advanced skill of immediacy. Though she continued, occasionally, to ask her supervisor to listen to sections of recordings, she also contracted to use verbal reporting and, on occasion, free association, as these methods of presentation proved more amenable to the exploration of relationship issues.

If agreement to re-contract as and when the need arises has been built into the original contracting at the start of the supervision, this gives permission for either party to suggest alternatives and improvements to the process and the relationship. It allows for the option of 'trying things out', rather than settling on the 'one right way' of doing things and then having to stick with that. Mistakes or 'near misses' can then be viewed as learning opportunities and necessary changes made without either party feeling they have lost credibility or failed in some way. It may be, for example, that the timing and frequency of meetings need to be re-scheduled if original arrangements are not proving satisfactory for either individual. Although the supervisee may, initially, have requested a mainly supportive relationship they may later decide that greater challenging on the part of the supervisor would be welcomed. If boundaries have slipped, perhaps with the supervisor being late for meetings on several occasions, this can be brought up by the supervisee if it has been agreed beforehand that such matters are important to review from time to time. Again it is clear that this process of mutual negotiation and review provides important modelling for supervisees in how to be with their clients.

Concluding the stages of the Cyclical Model

The Review stage of the model helps to maintain, develop and evaluate those elements that complement and underpin the exploratory work of the supervision. This stage provides both the counter-point to, and a way back into, the first stage of the model. Like the original Contract, the Review stage contains, supports and enhances the work undertaken in the central stage, Space. The last step in the Review stage, re-contracting, takes us back to the beginning of the model, where contracting is seen as an initial stage. It demonstrates both the flexibility and the circular nature of the model, which can be recycled at the service of the developing work and relationship.

In the chapters that follow we will lessen the intensity of our focus on the Cyclical Model in order to consider some important additional aspects of supervision that are likely to determine whether any model or theory of supervision is used to good effect.

Chapter 9

Supervising in groups

So far our focus, in line with the majority of the literature on supervision, has been on individual supervision, where one supervisee meets with one supervisor. Yet very many therapists are supervised within groups, and in terms of numbers participating this is probably the more common form of supervision in the field (Bernard 2006; Holloway and Johnston 1985; Prieto 1996). In particular, trainees often take part in group supervision as one of the elements of their course (De Stefano *et al.* 2007) and this form of supervision is also prevalent in many organizations offering counselling in the voluntary sector. Proctor (2000:26) has suggested that 'it is probably true to say that for most trainees and volunteers, their first experience of supervision will be in a group'.

The Cyclical Model has been recommended as a useful structure for group supervision (Harris and Brockbank 2011; van Ooijen 2003) and in this chapter we shall explore how it can be adapted as a guiding framework for this purpose. 'Group supervision' in general terms refers to supervision where there is more than one supervisee participating, each presenting different clients.

Why supervise in groups?

A number of writers on the subject (Bernard and Goodyear 2009; Borders and Brown 2005; Driscoll 2007; Hawkins and Shohet 2012; Kuechler 2007; Ögren and Jonsson 2004; Proctor 2008; Rowell 2010; Scaife 2010; Smith *et al.* 2007) have considered both the benefits and disadvantages of group supervision. The main themes and issues addressed in this literature are summarized and expanded on below.

Advantages of group supervision

1 Economies of time, money and expertise.
2 Minimization of supervisee dependency on supervisor.
3 Less hierarchical (encourages more input from supervisees and not just the supervisor).

4   Opportunities to learn from others, including those who work in different settings.

5   Exposure to a broader range of clients (with whom other therapists in the group are working).

6   Can lessen feelings of isolation and inadequacy as group members share their fears and mistakes.

7   Provides opportunities for supervisees to check out their emotional and intuitive reactions to clients by seeing if other group members share similar responses.

8   Access to a wider range of practice issues and experience (for instance ethical dilemmas).

9   Greater quantity and diversity of feedback from others (which in turn may heighten awareness of difference in peers and clients).

10   Providing opportunities for group members with personal and/or professional experience of particular aspects of difference to step in as 'consultants' to the group when appropriate (though as Ryde (2011a) has pointed out there is a need to remain alert to the danger of one person being put in the position of representing an entire cultural group).

11   A different quality of feedback to the supervisee than that gained in one-to-one supervision (for instance peers may adopt simpler language to explain processes in therapy and may be more attuned to peers' levels of experience than the (usually) more experienced supervisor leading the group).

12   Offers companionship in a profession where the work is predominantly private and undisclosed.

13   Provides a forum for receiving live and honest feedback (for example on the way a person may come across to clients based on how group members experience that person's quality of presence and way of communicating).

14   The variety of individual experience, backgrounds and perspectives in the group lessens the likelihood of group members having enduring blindspots (for example someone is more likely to come in from another angle or speak up from a different perspective on the work presented).

15   A more comprehensive and layered picture of the supervisee in relationship with her client may emerge (for instance there is more opportunity for group members to experience and transparently express parallel processes).

16   Greater opportunity exists for the use of creative and action techniques such as group sculpts, role play and psychodrama.

17   Feelings of incompetence, anxiety or hopelessness are decreased and normalized through validation, support and the sharing of similar experiences with others.

18   The supervisory process widens perspective on events and dilemmas (for example what may be experienced as an impasse with the client can be reframed as an opportunity through the sharing of different viewpoints).

19   Offers an open system that is adaptive and flexible to client need and supports creative development and the evolution of the profession.

20 For therapists who work with groups, group supervision can provide effective modelling and opportunities to learn good practice.
21 Provides members with opportunities to learn and practise supervision skills.

Limitations and disadvantages of group supervision

1 Not recommended as the sole form of supervision for trainees and inexperienced therapists, who may need the individual attention and containment provided by one-to-one supervision.
2 Can feel more exposing and risky to share one's personal and professional vulnerabilities in a group.
3 Possibility of insufficient supervision time for the size of each person's caseload or to deal with issues in depth.
4 Disparate levels of skills and experience may mean members struggle to get their needs met.
5 Group dynamics may undermine the task and focus of the group (for instance where needy or overpowering members take over).
6 Confidentiality and boundaries may be more difficult to manage (for example where supervisees belong to the same professional network or geographical area).
7 Sensitivity to individual differences may become lost and mean that 'minority' supervisees feel excluded or disadvantaged (for example where people forget to speak up for a hearing-impaired member or fail to actively encourage the participation of a group member who comes from a culture where deference to authority or minimal self-disclosure is the norm).
8 As most group supervision is of individual (not group) counselling, the group format may diffuse or fail to pick up parallel processes that more easily become mirrored in one-to-one supervision .
9 If not checked (by the group facilitator or by group members speaking out) the group may devote excessive time to issues of limited relevance or interest to some group members.
10 Individuals may experience a pressure to conform to a particular way of thinking about or viewing issues.
11 Unchecked destructive processes (for example scapegoating, defensiveness and competitiveness) may interfere with safe exploration and learning.

This summary captures a number of the pros and cons of group supervision and thereby implies that it is not helpful to think of group and individual supervision in opposition to each other. Rather they are different ways of developing awareness, skills and a sense of practitioner identity so important for all therapists. Research by Ray and Altekruse (2000) studied the effectiveness of group supervision compared with combined group and individual supervision as experienced by 64 masters-level supervisees and found both to be equally successful in increasing counsellor effectiveness. Participants in the study showed a preference for individual supervision over group supervision and this finding illustrates the value of giving supervisees a choice, wherever possible.

Types of group supervision

There are many forms of group supervision, both in the structure of the group itself and in how those involved in the group set about their collective task (Proctor 2008). We will start by briefly defining four different types of structure, whilst recognizing that these can be blended to create a considerable range of variations. As is often the case when classifying any form of group-work, the defining characteristic we are using is the presence and approach of leadership within the group.

Individual supervision in a group

As the heading suggests, this form of supervision is essentially one-to-one supervision that happens to take place in a group. The supervisor engages one participant at a time in supervision on aspects of their therapeutic work, whilst other participants silently observe. This is the most limited form of group supervision because of the restricted involvement, although a certain amount of learning is possible by observation.

Supervisor-led group

This category incorporates those forms of group where there is a clearly defined supervisor who takes a central position both in leading the group and in the supervision process itself. Participants can involve themselves within the discussion relating to supervisee material being presented by other group members, but there remains an implicit, or explicit, hierarchy of skills, experience and responsibility, with the supervisor typically taking up, or being elevated to, the position of expert.

Facilitated group

In this format an identified facilitator guides a supervision group. Someone acknowledged as the most experienced within the group may hold this role, or it may be an arrangement amongst a group of peers. In the latter situation one person may consistently hold this role, or it may be shared out amongst group members. The task of facilitation is distinct from that of supervision and is one of intentional group management. This includes setting up and managing structures and ways of functioning as a group that encourage effective group development. This is a set of skills that has to be learnt, and will not be possessed by all therapists or supervisors. It is a mistake too often made for practitioners experienced in one-to-one work to be thrust into a group facilitation role without the necessary skills, training and experience.

Peer group

This is a supervision group where there is an acknowledged level of equality and the tasks of both facilitation and supervision are shared amongst the members. These roles may rotate, being allocated to particular individuals at particular times, or they may move fluidly around the group, being picked up, or not, as necessity dictates. Whilst peer-group supervision is without a leader, it nevertheless still 'involves clear recognition of certain ground rules and authority' (Gomersall 1997:109). Thus it is not simply an unstructured discussion, but rather operates within agreed structures of time, purpose and role. When any member acts as facilitator, and other members are co-supervisors, they are invested with some degree of authority on behalf of the group. The challenge to any peer group is to find ways of using the consequent tension between equality and authority in a creative and successful manner.

Choosing a model of group supervision

In practice many supervision groups operate with a blend of different proportions of a number of these apparently distinct models. There is often movement from one model to another and it is easy to see a natural developmental graduation from the first model towards the fourth. Each has strengths and weaknesses that make them more or less appropriate to supervisees at particular stages of development.

Within a supervision group each supervisee has the potential to undertake three distinct roles. The first is as a supervisee, bringing material to present and receive supervision upon. The second is as a group member playing a part in the creation of a healthy group culture. The third is as a co-supervisor of the material presented by other supervisees within the group. For supervisees ready to undertake all three roles intentionally, and with some understanding, it is useful that they have the opportunity to do so.

In relation to Rønnestad and Skovholt's (2013) stages of practitioner development, those who are ready to move beyond, or have already passed, the stage of 'imitation of experts' can be expected to benefit from a peer group or one in which facilitation moves between peers. In contrast it is, in our view, unhelpful for therapists at a very early stage of their professional development to be expected to operate effectively in such groups. The complexities of the task of acting as co-supervisors to one another and the opportunities this provides for unwitting projection of shadow material (Page 1999a), which may result in destructive dynamics such as rivalry, envy, scapegoating and sabotage, may well get in the way of the priority task of developing as a counsellor or psychotherapist. For this reason we are not in favour of peer-supervision groups for novice practitioners as there is likely to be insufficient experience within the group members to manage the responsibilities involved in running such a group effectively (Lockett 2001). Where peer-facilitated supervision groups are used on training courses they need to be introduced carefully and gradually, perhaps starting as tutor-facilitated groups with the facilitator stepping back to allow some peer-group sessions as the group becomes more established.

It is important to recognize the complexity present within any supervision group. To take a very simplistic mathematical approach to this, consider the number of relationships (both actual and fantasy) possible within a given supervisory situation. In a basic one-to-one supervision relationship matrix there are three relationships: between supervisor and supervisee; between supervisee and client; and (presumably at a fantasy level because they would not normally meet) between supervisor and client. In contrast, in a typical supervision group of four supervisees with a supervisor/facilitator, we calculate there to be 56 different possible combinations of two or more people when also including a single client in the field. Whilst many of these combinations may never arise in any substantial way, this simple calculation nevertheless reflects the exponentially growing order of dynamic complexity as more people become involved in a supervision process.

The remainder of this chapter is written with the facilitated-group model in mind, in which an identified person occupies the role of facilitator and all group members participate in the supervisory tasks and functions of the group.

Setting up a supervision group

In writing about therapeutic groups, Whitaker emphasizes the importance of the person who is to be the 'conductor' (probably best thought of as a cross between leader and facilitator) of the group 'being involved in the planning from the start' (1985:5). This is to ensure that the leader/facilitator has thought through the aims of the group and the needs of those for whom it is intended. At this early stage it is also useful to be clear as to what is predetermined and what is negotiable. For example, who will be eligible to join the group; will the group be a closed one or open to new members; what will be the group size; will it be open-ended or meet for a fixed period?

Once the predetermined elements have been established potential supervisees can then be involved in further planning. This might include any negotiable aspects of the structure or functioning of the group, such as those discussed in the contracting section below.

The size of supervision groups

A group is more than two individuals and an important decision to be made when planning a group is how large it should be. In this there is a balance to be sought. As a group grows in size, so does the variety of experience and perspectives that it contains. However, so too does the complexity of dynamics along with the potential for individual members to become marginalized, or for supervisees to feel short-changed in the amount of time they are given to focus on their work.

When a group is first set up there is likely to be little conscious awareness of the impact of size on how the group functions and feels, except by those involved who have other experiences with which to compare. Nevertheless, size does play a significant part in the quality of a group. Typically supervision groups of three or four supervisees and one supervisor/facilitator provide the optimal size, balancing the desire for variety of perspective with a reasonable degree of simplicity in how they function.

Setting the 'contract'

In a supervision group the contractual issues can be grouped into two main areas: how supervision will be undertaken; and how the group will function. When the group meets for the first time, there will be a considerable degree of 'sizing each other up' taking place. There may be the need for consideration of prior and concurrent overlapping relationships between group members and/or the facilitator. It is helpful to declare these relationships within the group at the outset so that discussion of how they will be managed becomes part of the initial contracting.

It is important, as the group becomes a reality for participants, that there is an opportunity for everyone involved to 'buy into' being part of the group. Buy-in is important because as Proctor (2008:12) has stated, 'potentially the group *is* the supervisor', and therefore positive ownership of the agreed task and function by all participants is crucial to the success of the group. Buy-in also increases the sense of equality of power between those involved and can assist in the relationship-building aspect of the contracting stage of the supervision group's life. This can be quite a difficult time and if a supervision group is to be effective in fulfiling its purpose, it is important that 'good enough' working relationships based upon equality, mutual trust and respect for difference are established from the outset. Bernard and Goodyear (2009:257) put it like this: 'When a supervision group is working well there are no stars (including the supervisor) and no dunces. Rather, each supervisee is known for his or her particular talents, idiosyncratic ways of viewing clients, and personal supervision goals.'

The task of agreeing a clear contract is important in itself and can also provide a useful mechanism for containing early anxieties whilst group members become familiar with each other. As in any supervision contract, careful consideration needs to be given to ground rules, boundaries, accountability and expectations, as well as to working relationships. Within each of these areas there are aspects that are particular to groups and worth reflecting upon briefly.

Ground rules

In most groups establishment of ground rules will be the task of the group, though it is the facilitator's responsibility to ensure that this happens. In peer-group supervision the responsibility is shared equally between members. Setting the ground rules involves discussion about how the group will operate. This discussion is likely to cover:

- timing, duration and frequency of group meetings;
- financial arrangements;
- what model of group it is to be (including style of facilitation, tasks and purpose of the group);
- how sessions will start and how they will end;
- discussion of differences in theoretical, personal, cultural and professional backgrounds – how these might be welcomed and accommodated, and what they might be;
- what group members need in order to feel safe and to take risks;
- how time will be apportioned to supervisees;
- how group-process issues will be addressed;
- how people will behave towards one another (expectations about 'group etiquette' within a basic culture of empathy, respect and genuineness);
- how and when the effectiveness of the group will be reviewed;
- how supervisees might give feedback to one another during supervision time (this is likely to evolve as the group develops and will be largely determined by the preferences of the person presenting their work).

As part of contracting the ground rules it can be helpful for the facilitator to ask 'When I observe a difficulty in the group how would you like me to deal with this?' A question such as this invites a collaborative approach to the resolution of difficulties, and encourages group members to see the occurrence of these as both probable and legitimate aspects of the group process. As with individual supervision, some of the considerations listed above are likely to be discussed at the outset of the group while others will emerge for discussion as the group evolves. A good opening question for the facilitator to ask is 'What do we need to cover to make a good start to this group?'

One of the areas it is particularly useful to clarify is how supervisees are to give feedback to one another during supervision time. When a participant is presenting a client there are a number of different aspects that individual members of the group can pick up on. One may focus on the relationship between therapist and client, another on some aspect of the client's story, another on an ethical concern and another on the therapeutic goals. Each is valid and important, but there is a limit on time and, more crucially, on the volume and variety of feedback that the presenting supervisee can usefully absorb. There is a danger that the supervisee will become lost in the clamour of group members all wishing to push forward their own perspective on the case in question. Therefore there has to be some mechanism of negotiation as to which aspects will be taken up and followed through. The supervisee will typically decide this, with the understanding that if someone else in the group has a strong sense that another aspect of the situation is being avoided, this choice can be challenged. It is generally for the facilitator to mediate such challenges to ensure that the time spent on supervision is not eroded through a disproportionate amount of debate about how to proceed.

Boundaries

Particular attention needs to be paid to defining the boundaries of confidentiality, and it is worthwhile being explicit in agreeing this in order to reduce the likelihood of different understandings between members. It may seem clear that members may not talk about the client material or personal issues of other participants outside of the group. But what of group-process issues or what is learnt from the discussion? Can some things be talked about between participants outside of the group but not talked about to others who are not members of the group? Is it acceptable to identify who are members of the group to others or is this confidential information? By discussing such matters some guidelines can be agreed, and over time these guidelines may be refined by relating them to specific instances, such as a supervisee requesting permission to share a particular insight with a colleague who is not a member of the group.

It is also important to address matters of overlapping boundaries. For example, in any supervision group there is the possibility that one supervisee will know another's client(s). It can be useful to discuss such an eventuality in principle before it arises so that a shared understanding of how this will be managed can be reached. Another boundary issue for consideration is how to manage therapy and training issues if they arise for group members. This is one of the issues where there is likely to be a need for discussion as and when it arises, rather than a predetermined protocol.

It is also useful to reflect upon what relationships participants have with each other outside of the group. When a supervision group starts all members may be strangers to each other, but that will change over time. If two or more participants strike up friendships with one another outside of the group this will affect the dynamics within the group, setting up 'pairing' as described by Bion (1961). It is important that this is understood from the outset and that all involved are encouraged to be responsible in dealing with any such relationships that do develop outside of the group. It is also important to acknowledge what external relationships, if any, exist between members when a group starts and to recognize that this may also have an impact upon the group. If the group starts with some stronger bonds and with others feeling isolated or marginalized, then efforts need to be made to counteract the potentially harmful imbalance this can create.

Accountability

There is a degree of mutual interdependence within any supervision group. If one supervisee acts in a manner that others consider to be unprofessional in some way then everyone in the group can feel implicated by association, particularly if the membership of the group is well known within the local counselling community. Alternatively, powerful feelings of loyalty can result in a member of the group not being challenged about what they are doing when this needs to happen to safeguard themselves and others. Support and loyalty amongst group members need to be balanced with the willingness to challenge and confront poor practice.

Such matters are wrapped up in the complex area of mutual professional accountability within a supervision group. In the extreme, supervisors may be required by professional codes to take action if they are aware that their supervisees' practice is likely to put clients at risk of harm (BACP 2013a). Similarly there is a requirement that practitioners challenge their peers and/or take action where they consider that a peer's clients may be at risk (BACP 2013a). At best, rigorous and ongoing examination of good standards of practice, enhanced by congruent peer feedback, is woven into the fabric of the group process and becomes the norm for all members so that such extreme courses of action are rarely, if ever, called for.

It is not possible to define mutual accountability absolutely, but discussion can lead to some degree of shared understanding and agreements about practice. For example, it may be agreed that supervisees have a responsibility to bring to the immediate attention of the group any work they are undertaking with clients that could be considered unorthodox or contentious, or to involve professional risk of some form. This is not to suggest that counselling and psychotherapy practice should aim to be risk free, as that is unlikely to always serve the best interests of clients (Wosket 1999). It is incumbent upon group supervisees to recognize that other members of the group will be affected by any professional risk they decide to take and that they should therefore exercise responsibility in so doing.

Expectations

Again, it is useful to take the time to draw out of participants what each expects of one another, of the supervisor/facilitator and of the group itself. To explore expectations there are a number of questions that it can be useful to ask:

- What kind of group do we want this to be?
- What do we expect of each other?
- What kind of balance of support and challenge do we want?
- Do we want to work to an agreed formula or try a range of different approaches?
- Do we want to ensure fairness by giving all participants equal time, or decide how to apportion time in the light of the particular needs of individuals as they arise?
- What is expected of someone presenting an issue for supervision?
- What is expected of the facilitator/supervisor?
- What is expected of other supervisees when not presenting?

The answers to some or all of these questions may change over time and the questions themselves may usefully form part of the process of review.

Identifying the focus and presenting material for supervision

Two aspects are likely to be particularly relevant here: a 'how?' and a 'what?' The first concerns how time will be divided between people and the choosing of 'protagonists' (i.e. who will present, who will respond and in what way, who will observe and comment). The second is what the presenter decides to focus on in their presentation (which may include background/context, issues to highlight, what response they would like from the group). Our experience suggests that one of the advantages of routinely having an initial discussion and negotiation that covers who is bringing what issue for supervision, how much time they would like and what they are seeking from supervision is that this seems to have the effect of encouraging participants to be very clear about their focus.

To get the most from receiving supervision within a group it is important to involve other members of the group in discussion as early on as is feasible. This requires a certain discipline on the part of supervisees, namely presenting in a succinct and summarized format and giving only as much background as is needed for the issue to have a meaningful context. As a guideline, it might be suggested that presentations take no more than 20 per cent of the total time available for the piece of supervision, and less if possible. Further information can be fed in during the discussion if it proves to be pertinent, but prolonged presentation will inevitably result in a significant amount of information being given which has no immediate relevance to the discussion that subsequently takes place.

Working within the supervision 'space'

As a supervisee starts to present a particular piece of client work, or a therapy issue, so a felt response develops within the group. A supervision group has great potential for working creatively to harness the group energy arising from these felt responses as work is presented. As Shohet (2011a:202) points out, there are no 'wrong' responses and group members should be encouraged not to filter or censor these. All are grist to the mill, and feelings of withdrawal and boredom are as valuable to express and consider as feelings such as fear, anger, joy or relief. Responses may range from intense emotional reactions and heated debate through to polite, if incongruent, efforts to pay attention that belie the boredom felt. It is possible to plough on with the task regardless of these feelings, but it is precisely in responses such as these that one of the most important potential benefits of supervising in a group comes to the fore. The challenge is to find ways to work creatively with these responses in order to inform and support the supervision process.

The facilitator's role here is to watch out for 'group atmosphere'. If a group reaction seems to be emerging (e.g. restlessness, gigglyness, a surge or drop in energy) it is useful to ask:

- Is this is a common feeling in this group?
- What stimulated it? When did it start?
- Who doesn't feel it? What do they feel instead?

Identifying the source of responses

As already identified in Chapter 6, the felt responses within the 'space' can come from a range of sources, including counter-transference and parallel-process re-enactments. While it is not always possible to pin down the source of group and individual responses, it is important for the group, both through the facilitator and its members, to be aware of the unconscious or dissociated processes that may be at work. Furthermore the group supervisor should be equipped, in particular, to recognize and work with parallel-process phenomena, which, according to Benson (2010:246) are both 'ubiquitous and inevitable' whilst also providing a 'rich source of communication and information' about the group dynamics and the case-work presented.

Take the example of a supervisee presenting their work with a particular client where, within a few minutes, everyone in the group is struggling to pay attention, feeling tired, bored or otherwise lacking in energy and interest. There are a number of questions that may help shed light on what is taking place. Firstly, it is useful to ask if this is a shared feeling in this group, either in relation to this particular supervisee or more generally pervading the group. If either proves to be the case this needs to be addressed as it suggests that some underlying group dynamic is interfering with the group operating effectively, a phenomenon that Kutter (1993:179) has termed in group supervision 'reversed mirroring', with a focus either upon a specific member of the group or across the whole group.

This may be a form of scapegoating, well examined by Douglas (1995), where one member of the group is targeted as the imagined reason for all that is wrong with the group. This is a powerful and destructive dynamic, which can lead to the scapegoated member feeling abused and driven out. Typically, when this occurs without the dynamic being fully recognized and the projections identified by every group member, another member of the group will promptly find themselves in the vacated position of scapegoat. One of the other possible reasons for such a mood within a group is that something has gone wrong (for example session structure or time management has become sloppy) and has not been effectively dealt with, or for some other reason a general state of depression has set in.

If it is not the case that this is a common feeling permeating the group then the next question to address is whether this is reflecting some aspect of what is taking place between therapist and client in the case presented and which the therapist is unable to articulate or experience in a more direct way. For example, if the therapist is having a similar experience of feeling 'cut off' when with their client, then it makes sense to pursue what might be causing this, temporarily assuming that the group is reflecting back the supervisee's experience. If this is not the case, or if such exploration bears little fruit, then it may be worth applying the half-life test (Page 1999a). This can be achieved by agreeing to temporarily suspend the piece of supervision and move on to another supervisee, noting how quickly the feelings dissipate. Whilst this is rather messy it is pragmatically sensible. If the feelings dissipate quickly then this indicates the likelihood of a reflection of something (i.e. a parallel process) in the therapeutic work just presented. If they do not dissipate quickly then it suggests that the difficulties lie within the group itself and that this is where attention needs to be directed.

Monitoring patterns of energy

In the above example the energy level within the group became very low and this provided a key to something needing attention. When working in a group, it is important to pay close attention to this rather nebulous, but critical, notion of energy level. In a healthy functioning group the energy level is typically reasonably high, with people enjoying one another's company and the task of supervision. As a session gets under way and a member of the group presents an issue for supervision, a good quality of attention can be expected, and as participants get involved in discussion the energy level will often increase further. At this stage it is helpful for participants to offer their responses and reflections. This may be done in a thoughtful and reflective manner or, in contrast, it can have a more brisk quality, with different thoughts, feelings and images all being offered in rapid succession without being analysed. It is important that such a period of 'bombardment' does not continue for too long as this can lead to the supervisee feeling overwhelmed.

As suggested earlier in our consideration of ground rules, it is useful to have a mechanism in place for managing such a situation, probably through the supervisee identifying which avenues they want to explore further. It is an important part of the role of a facilitator to be aware of, and if necessary to intervene to manage, these energy levels. There is a delicate balance to be sought between encouraging and allowing as much creative input as possible whilst maintaining relevance to the supervisory task and keeping within the agreed schedule in order that all supervisees get the time they need.

If agreed as part of the contract, the facilitator may also come in and add to the content and discussion. Otherwise she needs to 'bite her lip' and hold back. One danger is that the facilitator gets too drawn into the content of the discussion and the supervision process, and thereby also gets caught up in group dynamics, rather than sitting back in order to observe and comment on them.

Creative ways of working within the supervision space

A number of creative ways of working that draw on the backgrounds and interests of group members can be used to explore issues within the supervision space. These include drawing, sculpting, psychodrama, role play, chair work, etc. Best practice is always to harness the creative energy, ideas and resources that exist within the group.

Creative ideas can emerge spontaneously – 'I've just had an idea – can we try this . . .?' They may also be planned, for example during a review the group members agree they would like to try some different ways of working. Creative approaches can enable the group to become more playful and spontaneous and get to know each other in different ways. We have included below a few ideas for working creatively within a supervision group.

1 Different members of the group take on the roles of different people or 'parts' in the client's story and then feed back 'as if' they are that person or part. The supervisee presenting may ask certain people to take on specific roles, or group members may volunteer to do so.

Example: The supervisee presenting says that she wants help with her difficulty in enabling her client to express and resolve an early experience of loss. She explains that the client's father died suddenly when he was six and he thinks he has 'never got over this', although he can't remember his father clearly and says he doesn't have any feelings about the event because he was so young.

The supervisee talks about her difficulty with this client while three different group members listen 'as if' one is the adult client, the second is the father who died and the third is the client at age six. They then feed back to the supervisee their thoughts, feelings, bodily sensations, fantasies and imaginings for her to reflect on and make use of any that are helpful.

2 Several people sit out and listen to the supervisee's presentation 'as if' they are the client and then feed back their 'gut' feelings to the supervisee.

Example: The supervisee talks about both his compassion and his frustration towards his client, who seems determined to persevere in seeing herself as 'bad and not worth bothering about'. After some discussion involving the rest of the group the facilitator pauses the process and invites the people sitting out to speak 'as if' they are the client and have been 'a fly on the wall' while the discussion took place. They may feed back anything they have been experiencing while the supervisee considers and reflects on these responses.

3 The supervisee presents her supervision issue and talks about her different responses and reactions in her work with her client. When she finishes, group members take on and amplify aloud all the different reactions the supervisee has mentioned while she listens and imagines herself to be the client.

Example: The supervisee has talked about feelings ranging from irritation to great warmth for her client, who keeps her at arm's length and is frequently despairing and hopeless. One group member tells the 'client' (i.e. the supervisee) about her feelings of irritation as fully as she can; another tells the 'client' about his warmth for her as fully as he can, and so on. The supervisee listens and is then given space to respond (firstly as her 'client' and then as herself if she wishes), and to reflect on what people have offered.

4 The group can be used to separate out and to highlight different sensory channels so that subtle and intuitive information can be picked up and fed back to the supervisee.

Example: The supervisee presents an issue about his work with his client. Three group members each take on different functions as follows. One concentrates on **looking** at the supervisee and prepares to feed back only what they *see* as he presents his client. The second person concentrates only on **listening** to the supervisee (it helps if they sit in a position where they can't see the supervisee) and feeds back only what they have *heard* (tones, themes and nuances, rather than verbatim content). The third person concentrates on **sensing** and **intuiting** (allows themself to have free-floating feelings, fantasies, hunches, daydreams and to go into dissociative states) and then offers back only what they have *sensed* and *intuited*. Each person then feeds back in turn what they have experienced to the supervisee, who is given time to reflect and make sense of this after each person has spoken.

It is very important that anyone who has taken a role in creative work is given the time and help they need to de-role afterwards as the experience can be very powerful. It is the facilitator's responsibility to ensure that this happens. For instance, protagonists can be invited to get up and walk around, and to say out loud their own name and the current date and place they are in. In all of the examples given above, group members who are not protagonists can do various things. They can be invited to offer feedback and observations after the creative work has taken place. They may help by acting as facilitators and timekeepers, or they may sit out and observe the process and then offer back their own learning from what they have witnessed.

Creating the 'bridge'

In group supervision, as in individual supervision, it is important to ensure that time is given to thinking through how new understanding and awareness arising from exploration of client work can be applied to the therapy situation. Some different ways of doing this are:

•   allowing this to emerge naturally out of the discussion;
•   moving on to the next supervisee whilst the person who just presented takes some time out to reflect on what has been said. This person is then given a space later to bring their reflections back to the group;

- explicitly inviting the presenting supervisee to 'gather up' and articulate any learning that she might wish to apply in her client work before moving on to the next presentation;
- allowing allocated time at the end for group members to individually feed back what has been meaningful to them and may be relevant to their counselling or psychotherapy practice. This is particularly useful where there has been an emotional component to the presentation as it allows 'recovery time' for the supervisee.

The facilitator may come in at this stage of the process to sum up or contribute (if this is part of the group contract). For example, they may pick up on a theme (such as the supervisee's goals for therapy appearing to be different to the client's) and ask the supervisee presenting if she has any thoughts about this. Here the facilitator acts as a 'bridge person'.

Reviewing the group

Review of a supervision group needs to take account of three main elements:

- the effectiveness with which the task is being performed;
- how well the group itself is functioning;
- how far individual needs are being met.

It is helpful if some time is given to reviewing at the end of every meeting, so that outstanding concerns or difficulties are picked up quickly, and also so that there is a conscious monitoring of the group's development by all involved. Less frequently, there may also be a need for a more thorough review, perhaps every six months, or at some natural points in the annual cycle of the group. Issues to be reviewed can include:

- practical aspects of the contract;
- how the group is developing;
- the extent to which needs and expectations are being met;
- the safety versus risk taking balance in the group's life;
- how group interactions and dynamics are helping/hindering the supervision work;
- patterns of operating: whether innovative ways of exploring material need to be introduced;
- whether it is time for the group to end or membership to change.

Session structure

At least in the early stages of a supervision group's life it is preferable for each session to have some structure (Wilbur *et al.* 1994). There needs to be some way of beginning, of people connecting with each other, of the group forming and in subsequent sessions re-forming. There are a number of ways that this can be done using one of the many exercises that have been devised for groups (Benson 2010; Bond 1986; Brandes and Norris 1998; Burley-Allen 1982; Proctor 2008; Remocker and Sherwood 1999). The basic purpose of any such exercise is essentially the same. Partly it is to assist everyone to bring their attention into the present, to put aside thoughts about what they have been doing prior to the group or are going on to do after the group, and to focus on the task in hand and the people they are with. There is also a secondary function of 'giving everyone a voice', ensuring that each member of the group speaks at least a few words.

The work of Stockton and Morran (1982) supports the view that in the early stages of supervision groups structure is important to establish an effective pattern of interpersonal behaviour. Structure helps to counteract the reluctance supervisees have been shown to have (Webb 2000) to talk about some matters, particularly in a group setting. So whether it is by describing what kind of animal I feel like at this moment, telling everyone the best thing to have happened since we last met or offloading what is distracting me from being fully present, the way of beginning needs to help the group warm and loosen up.

Unless the group has a predetermined way of dividing up the time, there needs next to be some negotiation about how the supervision time will be allocated between supervisees. It is generally advisable to allow a proportion of slippage time, perhaps five minutes per hour, so that there is a degree of flexibility to allow for the unexpected. Then the supervision itself takes place, and this should comprise the greater part of the total time of the session. The work of application, or 'bridge', can either be included in each person's time allocation or combined towards the end. As a rough guide there might usefully be about five minutes of application time within a half-hour supervisee presentation and discussion. Finally it is important to ensure that some time remains to review the session and do any re-contracting or planning that needs to take place before bringing the session to a close.

Typically there will be a certain amount of time pressure experienced and the person who acts as timekeeper, usually the facilitator, will need to be firm in keeping to the agreed schedule. At times this may feel arbitrary and inflexible, but it is important to recognize that once a group gets into poor timekeeping habits it is very hard to break this pattern, and the quality of time within the group will generally deteriorate as frustrations start to build. If it is consistently very hard to keep to agreed time it may be necessary to review whether the time allocation, or indeed the total session time, is sufficient for what the group has set out to achieve.

Group dynamics

Research evidence (Ögren *et al.* 2002) reveals that supervisees' 'undigested' (p. 166) experience of dynamics within supervision groups can be intensive and that it stays with them longer – at least two years – than other aspects of the experience (for instance discussion of client work or a sense of one's own development), which are likely to have been integrated some time before. A further significant study from Sweden (Ögren and Sundin 2009) revealed that supervisees in groups desire more of a focus on group interactions and dynamics than is generally recognized by group supervisors. Significantly, supervisors in this study reported having worked extensively with group interactions while their supervisees reported a much lower level of attention to group dynamics. This was also found to be the case in an earlier study by the same authors, where supervisors experienced there having been more of a focus on group dynamics than did their supervisees (Ögren and Sundin 2007).

As Ögren and Sundin's 2009 study considered a broad range of psychotherapy supervision groups (150 in total) over six years (2000 to 2006), these findings are not insignificant. Ögren and Sundin found that the group supervisor's ability to tolerate 'opposition and dissidence', particularly in the early stages of a group's life, appeared to enhance group members' 'tolerance and flexibility' as the group developed (2009:133). They identified that a key task for the group supervisor is to allow supervisees to develop their skills in unique and individual ways, and observed that:

> while the supervisor's role is not to encourage conflict within the group, our findings suggest that tensions between the trainees should be allowed to develop, and instead of trying to reduce or solve them, different views, values and interests held by the trainees should be allowed and examined thoroughly.
> (Ögren and Sundin 2009:137)

In a comparable study Boalt Boëthius and colleagues (2004) also found that toleration of turbulent group dynamics is advisable and that 'a certain amount of opposition and conflict in a group might contribute to a more flexible group interaction, and to the development and change in the group members' (p. 116).

One of the great advantages of having a well-defined structure, a clear way of being and working together, is that disruption of that structure is one indicator of some underlying dynamic process taking place, or of 'chaos' creeping in (Wosket and Page 2001). In the early stages of the development of a group, the structure provides an effective container for this potential chaos. Early difficulties in the life of a group can result from those primitive, and often unconscious, anxieties that most of us feel when entering an unknown situation with other people. We can easily feel threatened and react accordingly. Typical of those anxieties felt by individuals within the early stages of a supervision group are shame evoked by fear of 'getting it wrong' or a sense of incompetence or competitiveness – each of which may be powerful re-enactments of parental or family dynamics (Benson 2010). These powerful dynamic processes have been recognized for a long time (Bion 1961, 1970; Cartwright and Zander 1968; Schutz 1979) and an understanding of them remains important for anyone involved in setting up and facilitating a supervision group.

These predictable anxieties and disruptions need to be sensitively addressed by the group supervisor while remembering that the purpose of the group remains firmly that of supervision and not therapy. A mistake the group supervisor can make is to take on the responsibility for smoothing over disruptions and solving conflict – particularly where its origins may lie outside the group experience. Benson (2010:251) provides the following salutary advice to group supervisors:

> Remember that you do not need to resolve any cultural, ethnic or gender conflict. You are not responsible for past injustices or current vulnerabilities. You are responsible for the smooth operating of the supervision group and as such it is your obligation to engage members in any examination of their interaction and process that threatens to disrupt the group. It is a simple matter for you to point out how interactions that induce shame and resentment cripple the supervision group and must be dealt with sensitively and without blame.

We have made implicit reference already to the developmental process through which any supervision group, like any other small group, will move. Various models have been proposed to describe the main stages of group development, for example those of Tuckman and Jensen (1977), Schutz (1979) and Yalom (1985). These can be summarized as follows:

- *Coming together* – in which members seek to 'sniff each other out' and find a safe place for themselves within the group.
- *Testing* – during which there is a certain amount of testing boundaries, limits and authority. This can be a rather conflict-ridden period, although this may not be made explicit.
- *Cohesion* – finding a way to be sufficiently harmonious and developing a sense of group identity.
- *Functioning* – whilst the task will have been undertaken in the early stages, this becomes more effective and the group more creative, working on increasingly intimate issues, as the group reaches this level of development.
- *Closure* – as the group moves towards ending, whether ending completely or going through a transformation as members leave or join.

The behaviour of the facilitator needs to be tailored to some extent to the developmental stage of the group (Benson 2010; Corey 1990; Hayes 1989). In the early meetings of a supervision group, it is likely that there will be considerable caution in the material presented, and in the depth of exploration and challenge. Far from being avoidance this is quite appropriate, as group members undertake the task of supervising in a manner that provides a vehicle for group development.

Benson (2010:241) has suggested that the initial task of the group supervisor is to 'create a predictable and consistent space and promote a learning culture in which supervision can take place'. Effective supervision within a group context relies on a good degree of self-disclosure and risk taking by group members.

Research conducted by Smith *et al.* (2007) into supervisees' experiences of difficult situations in group supervision reveals that this capacity for risk taking is 'highly dependent on the kind of emotional climate that the supervisor is able to establish early on in the process' (p. 46). In this regard the Cyclical Model provides a useful framework during the early period of a group's life, helping to contain anxieties and to make the group's task and function explicit as all become used to working together. As the group progresses, more intimate disclosure, deeper exploration and more challenging responses can be expected in the supervisory space – as long as the supervisor is both a competent group facilitator *and* a skilled clinical supervisor.

Chapter 10

Ethical and professional issues

Supervisors have a responsibility to equip themselves adequately to deal with the ethical and professional dilemmas that their supervisees bring to them for help and support. Real dangers exist for themselves, their supervisees and their clients where they fail to do this (Cikanek *et al.* 2004). Yet facing the prospect of responding to ethical and legal issues can be a daunting prospect for the supervisor. In this chapter, we hope to provide some theoretical grounding, practical guidelines and concrete examples to help supervisors reflect on and develop their capacity to think through ethical concerns in collaborative, challenging and supportive ways with their supervisees.

Ethical principles

Many will be familiar with published ethical frameworks and principles governing the conduct of therapeutic practice. The theory that underpins these principles and frameworks has its roots in moral philosophy (Singer 1993). The purpose of such principles is, in general terms, to assist in determining how to act; how to decide what is 'good' and what is 'bad'.

Publication of the first edition of the British Association for Counselling and Psychotherapy (BACP) *Ethical Framework* (2001) coincided with publication of the second edition of this book, also in 2001. Both publications reflected a shift from strict codes of practice that had begun to be seen as somewhat rigid, outdated, censorial and culturally limited, to a more thoughtful stance of ethical mindfulness. The ethical principles included in the current BACP ethical framework (Bond 2010; BACP 2013a) are briefly summarized below as they apply to counselling, psychotherapy *and* supervision.

Ethical principles in counselling, psychotherapy and supervision

Autonomy

Respect for the client's and supervisee's right to be self-governing. This is fundamentally about freedom of choice and covers ethical issues such as informed consent, explicit contracting, the protection of privacy, and confidentiality.

Being trustworthy (fidelity)

Honouring the trust placed in the practitioner or being faithful to promises made, and this includes both explicit and implicit promises. Supervisors and supervisees who adopt this principle act in accordance with the trust placed in them and regard confidentiality as an obligation arising from that trust.

Justice

The fair and impartial treatment of clients and supervisees, and the provision of adequate services. This principle is fundamentally concerned with respecting human rights and dignity, and has particular implications for the supervisor in balancing the needs of supervisees and clients. It involves a commitment by the practitioner to avoid discrimination and to provide a fair and equal distribution of services.

Beneficence

A commitment to promoting the client's and supervisee's wellbeing. Acting in accordance with this principle requires the practitioner to work strictly within their limits of competence, and with adequate training and experience. It includes a requirement for observing rigorous procedures for assessment, review and closure, and for the close monitoring of these by supervisor and supervisee. Also included is an obligation to receive regular and sufficient supervision, and to engage in continuing professional development.

Non-maleficence

A commitment to avoiding harm to clients and supervisees. This principle involves avoiding the exploitation of clients and supervisees financially, sexually, emotionally or in any other way. It is fundamentally concerned with avoiding incompetence or malpractice, and this includes a responsibility to challenge the incompetence or malpractice of others within the profession.

Self-respect

Fostering the practitioner's self-knowledge and self-care. This principle includes a commitment by the practitioner to seek therapy as needed for ongoing personal development together with supervision and training to further both personal and professional development. It places a requirement on practitioners to engage in life-enhancing activities that ensure that they do not rely on relationships with clients or supervisees to meet their own emotional and other needs.

There is no fixed hierarchy of importance amongst these six ethical principles, although, generally speaking, non-maleficence, not doing harm to others, has prece-dence over the other five. Ethical decision making is greatly aided by identifying the perspective provided by consideration of each principle and seeking to find a path that takes account of them all.

At points throughout this chapter we will revisit the six ethical principles and give examples of the consideration of each by the supervisor. A key aim of the chapter is to link ethical thinking to collaborative practice. To this end we will also consider the notion of relational ethics (Gabriel and Casemore 2009) as it applies to the supervisory process. To begin with we will attempt to tease out a number of ethical considerations in supervision as they relate to the principles outlined above and give a few examples to show how they might apply in practice.

Managing boundaries

Boundary between therapy and supervision

We will first consider ethical issues raised by the boundary between therapy and supervision. We have already explored the nature of this boundary in some detail in Chapter 4 and it is given further consideration in Chapter 12 in relation to the supervision of experienced practitioners. Here we will confine ourselves to ethical implications.

In a study conducted by Henry and colleagues (2004) both supervisors (n = 78) and supervisees (n = 112) rated the personal issues of supervisees as one of the two topics most often identified as taken to supervision (the other being skills and techniques). These findings attest to the frequent occurrence and arguably, therefore, the legitimacy of supervisees being allowed to bring their own therapeutic issues to supervision. Furthermore as Neufeldt and Nelson (1999:134) have observed, supervisors do tend to take up these personal issues with their supervisees: 'emotional events in the life of the supervisee can be so intense that it is impossible not to respond to their disclosure'.

As it appears to be common for supervisees to bring their therapy issues to supervision and for supervisors to respond to these, the principle of autonomy requires that there be a reasonable degree of understanding between supervisee and supervisor as to how the interface between therapy and supervision is to be managed. As a rule of thumb we suggest it is legitimate for time to be spent on a supervisee's personal issues if they are impacting on client work or the supervisory relationship. Frawley-O'Dea and Sarnat (2001:140) sum this up rather neatly when they advise that 'the "treat" aspect of supervision remains indentured to the overarching goal of facilitating the supervisee's growth as a clinician'.

Research undertaken by Grant and Schofield (2007) identified a positive association between the amount of supervision a therapist receives and the amount of personal therapy undertaken. This Australian study of 316 professionally affiliated counsellors and psychotherapists revealed that 'those who receive more supervision also receive more personal therapy', and it is suggested that one reason for this may be 'that the reflective processes, which are an integral part of supervision, may identify more personal issues to be taken to therapy' (Grant and

Schofield 2007:9). These findings confirm that supervision often identifies personal issues for supervisees. When this happens the supervisor has an ethical responsibility to support supervisees in accessing therapy, should they appear to need this, and not to take on the job of therapist in what may then constitute an unhelpful dual role.

Confidentiality boundary

The other boundary issue we will explore here is that of confidentiality. As Bond (2000:150) has stated: 'Confidentiality is probably the single issue that raises the greatest number of difficulties for counsellors'. Because it can be such a perplexing and anxiety-provoking issue in therapy, it is inevitably a significant concern for the supervisor. The first aspect of confidentiality to establish is what position is being taken, both by the supervisee and the supervisor, in relation to this.

There is, in our view an idealized, position that the therapeutic boundary should be sacrosanct. It then follows that any breach of this is considered a violation that will be detrimental to the therapeutic process and must be minimized: 'The secure frame is the only means through which a healthy therapeutic symbiosis can be effected between the patient and the therapist' (Langs 1982:327). This can sound appealing because of the apparently unequivocal nature of the position. However, in practice, the therapeutic boundary is required to be sufficiently flexible to stretch out and include the supervisor, and this means that it cannot be the idealized, womb-like container the stated position seems to offer.

In addition, taking an idealistic approach can have serious consequences for the supervisee if carried through to its ultimate conclusion, since it could conceivably result in the therapist being subject to legal prosecution. This would be the likely consequence of refusing to give information when required to do so by a court of law (Bond 2010; Mitchels and Bond 2010, 2011), and as Boden (2005:159) has asserted, 'you cannot use your therapeutic approach as a legal defence'. This can result in a form of reluctant pragmatism – wishing to be absolute about confidentiality but in practice feeling bound by these legal constraints. There is an alternative position, which we both adopt, which is that therapy occurs within a context and that there may be occasions when material from the therapy or the supervision needs to be made available to others in that context. This should never be done lightly, or without clear contracting and understanding of the potential consequences.

The principle of informed consent requires that the practitioner, whether supervisor or therapist, makes explicit the exceptions to absolute confidentiality and whether or not permission would be sought before passing information on. One of us has the following wording in their written contract given to clients:

Confidentiality Contract
Normally discussions between us will remain confidential. However there are times when it may be necessary for me to involve other people. These are as follows:

For ethical reasons all therapists are required to receive regular supervision from another professional practitioner known as a supervisor. Your sessions may be discussed but I will take care to ensure your identity is protected.

If you disclose information that leads me to believe that you or someone else is at risk, then I will need to talk to you about ways of reducing this risk. It may be necessary to contact your GP, a social worker or another person. Wherever possible this will be discussed with you first and will only happen with your permission. However in an emergency I may need to act promptly to ensure your safety or that of someone else even without your express permission. Normally I would consult with an experienced colleague or supervisor before taking such action.

In exceptional circumstances I am required by law to communicate certain information to the relevant authorities (e.g. acts of terrorism, or if being subpoenaed by a court of law).

The supervisor needs to be equally clear as to the exceptional circumstances in which they would breach supervisory confidentiality. There are generally two sets of circumstances in which this might occur. The first of these is in the event that the supervisee is not prepared to act on information she has received where she, her client, or a third party may be in serious danger of harm. In such circumstances the supervisor may decide they have to act, presumably having asked the supervisee to do so in the first instance. The supervisor may also decide to break confidentiality if the supervisee is deemed to be acting in a way that is viewed as harmful to the client (or possibly a third party). We apply these general exceptions, which are a consequence of the principle of non-maleficence, to all supervisory relationships.

Having established in supervision the position that each participant holds with regard to confidentiality, both supervisor and supervisee need to satisfy themselves that they are comfortable with any differences revealed. For instance, neither of us would be prepared to supervise a counsellor or psychotherapist who took an absolute position about confidentiality. Conversely, the supervisor may find him or herself working with a supervisee who holds a somewhat slack approach to managing confidentiality. Baker and Patterson (1990) explored this topic and discovered evidence to suggest that 'therapists sharing clients' confidential information with family or friends is a serious ethical problem' (p. 295). Supervision on this matter may also mean assisting the supervisee in applying their theoretical understanding of boundaries to actual situations, many of which are fraught with ambiguities and uncertainties. This can result in the supervisor being faced with potentially quite dramatic situations.

Let us consider the not infrequent situation where the supervisee may bring to supervision concerns about what they should do in relation to a client who may be, or clearly is, suicidal. There is no legal requirement in England for the therapist to report suicidal risk (Bond and Michels 2008), and the supervisory task is usually, therefore, to help the therapist consider the details of this particular client's situation and then decide how to proceed. It can be tempting, in the anxiety of the moment, to take up unequivocal positions such as 'people should be entitled to take their own lives' or 'we must protect people from their self-destructive tendencies'.

The supervisor here needs to help the supervisee step aside from any such polarized position and explore the issues in relation to this particular client, while also taking into account any organizational policies or guidelines if relevant. This might, for instance, involve determining whether the client is making a rational choice of suicide (Snipe 1988), perhaps in the face of a deteriorating medical condition. This is very different to the case of the person who is suicidal as a consequence of a short-term depressive episode. There may be legal implications to be considered (Boden 2005; Swenson 1987), although if there is no statutory obligation to care for the client these are unlikely to be sufficiently significant to determine action. If it is decided to take some action, then what will be done has still to be determined and the supervisor's assistance with this can be crucial. In essence here the principle of fidelity and the implications for confidentiality will need to be balanced against actual or potential dangers to the client or a third party, where the principle of non-maleficence may apply.

Managing relationships fairly

In every supervisory situation there exists a minimum of three relationships: two actual relationships and one fantasy or indirect relationship (see Figure 10.1). Within and at the extremes of each relationship there are possibilities of abuse on the one hand and collusion on the other. The ethical principle of justice requires that fairness be maintained within and between each pair of relationships. Applying this principle specifically to the supervisor, it requires that she endeavour to be equitable in balancing her responsibilities towards the supervisee and the client. In psychodynamic terms it might be thought of as the parent being fair in dealings with her two children.

From this perspective the novel aspect in supervision is that one 'child' (the supervisee) is in an actual relationship with the parental figure whilst the other

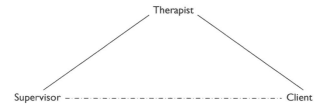

Figure 10.1 The supervisory relationship triangle.

relationship (with the client) is only a fantasy relationship, mediated by the first. As a consequence the 'parent' has to manage the principle of justice for herself – she cannot rely on being directly challenged should she favour one 'child' unduly.

To illustrate this let us consider two examples. In the first example the therapist is pressuring their unwilling client to leave an abusive partner. If in that situation the supervisor had allowed the supervisee to proceed with pushing the client then this would have been unjust: the supervisor would be favouring the supervisee at the expense of the client.

The second example is of a volunteer counsellor who has a client who has cancelled a number of sessions at the last moment. The supervisor focuses solely on the reasons why the client is cancelling, without offering the supervisee an opportunity to ventilate his own feelings of irritation and frustration towards the client. By acting in this way, the supervisor is setting aside the counsellor's feelings of resentment about being treated badly by the client and in so doing is being unjust, favouring the client at a cost to the counsellor. The application of the principle of justice requires that a way be found which respects the experience of the supervisee and assists the therapeutic process to move forward.

Supervising trainees

When a counsellor or psychotherapist is in training then a fourth party enters the network of relationships. This is the training institute or college, which for simplicity will be referred to as 'the course'. In Figure 10.2 we have endeavoured to indicate diagrammatically the nature of the set of relationships involved in this situation. The degree of solidity of each line indicates the extent to which it is a direct or indirect relationship. In two of these relationships ethical difficulties can arise. The first is relatively easy to deal with: the relationship between the client and the course. This is not a direct relationship, in any but the most unusual circumstance, but is an indirect relationship that is mediated by the trainee. It is

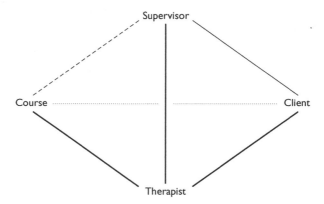

Figure 10.2 The relationship structure in trainee supervision.

important that the degree of confidentiality being afforded the client is explicit and agreed. This means that the client must know and give informed consent to the extent to which material from their sessions will be presented to others at the course and the measures, if any, which are being taken to protect their anonymity.

The second is more complex: the relationship between the course and the supervisor. In our experience there are a number of different types of contract between the supervisor and the course being used. At one end of the range the supervisor may be an employee of the training institute, who provides supervision as one of a number of aspects of their role. The issues that this raises include those of overlapping roles; for example, the supervisor might also be a trainer, therapist or manager within the training institute. If these roles overlap in relation to individual students then this can have potentially perilous ramifications, and options for avoiding or minimizing dual relationships are best considered (Copeland 2005; Gabriel 2005; Gabriel and Casemore 2009, 2010). For instance, while it is not uncommon in training organizations for tutors to provide some supervision it is advisable that students also have an external supervisor who does not hold an assessment role (Copeland 2005). Trainees on placement may be required to have an in-house supervisor. Best practice in this case is for the student to also have an external supervisor in order to minimize contextual 'interferences', such as role ambiguity and conflict (Itzhaky 2001). In comparing the experiences of clinical social workers who were supervised externally (n = 80) with those who received in-house supervision (n = 129), Itzhaky (2001:81) discovered that 'external supervisors were found to provide more constructive criticism to supervisees than internal ones, to carry out more confrontation when necessary and appropriate and to possess more expert-based authority (based on knowledge and skills) and less formal authority'.

At the other end of the spectrum the trainee may simply be told to go out and find their own supervision, and there is no direct relationship between the course and the supervisor. This is fraught with dangers: the supervision may be inappropriate, the supervisor may not be competent, there is no feedback mechanism in case of difficulty and there is no attempt to standardize the supervision experience. In our view the training institute has a responsibility to oversee the choice of supervisor, ensuring at the very least that the supervisor is competent and knows how to contact the course if they have serious concerns about the trainee's practice. It is to be hoped that the course does more than that, creating an effective line of communication within a clearly defined contract in which all parties know what information will be passed to whom, by whom and under what circumstances (Morrissey 2005). For this is the central issue: the appropriate movement of information within the network.

Let us consider the extreme situation in which the supervisor has substantial concern that the trainee is acting in a manner that is unethical and it has not been possible to rectify the situation through the supervisory process. We believe that the supervisor has a responsibility to communicate this concern to the course in some way. Not to do so risks the trainee being awarded a practitioner qualification, which could be tantamount to a licence to practice in an unethical manner. The supervisor has a responsibility to ensure that their concern is addressed by the trainee and the course, and that the trainee receives their qualification only if they are able to deal with the problematic area of their practice. This extreme situation can be formulated in terms of the supervisor and course sharing a mutual responsibility to the potential future clients of the trainee therapist. It is to be hoped that any training course includes a well-defined mechanism for just this extreme situation in their contract with the supervisors of their course members.

Thankfully the extreme is rare; however, there remains the question of what, if any, feedback mechanism should exist between supervisor and course. The course has an obligation to evaluate the trainee and on the basis of that evaluation to determine whether or not they should be awarded the qualification the course carries. The supervisor receives information, through the supervisory process, about the trainee's practice that is potentially very valuable to this evaluation process. However, any reporting mechanism is a potential threat to the supervisee's sense of trust in the safety of supervision, generating what Liddle (1986:119) describes as 'evaluation anxiety'. One way around this is to agree that the supervisor will not pass on any information to the course except in the event of serious concern about the trainee's practice. This deals with the issue from the supervisor's point of view but deprives the course of a valuable perspective. As a consequence the assessment of students may be distorted, for example, with greater emphasis on written work or self-presentation whilst skirting around assessing their ability to form and maintain therapeutic relationships.

It would seem preferable therefore to have some reporting mechanism. The difficulty is to do this in a way that does not implicitly encourage the supervisee to censor the more problematic areas of their practice, presenting only the more satisfactory aspects in supervision. This would undermine the ability of the supervisor to perform their function effectively. It is therefore important that any feedback mechanism assists the supervision process rather than threatens it. Provided that any reporting back builds upon, or at least has no negative effect upon, the trust between supervisee and supervisor, then it can work well for all concerned. Some methods employed to this end include: self-assessment by supervisees; mutual evaluation, where the supervisee and supervisor both provide each other and the course with written feedback, or the use of feedback statements agreed by both supervisor and supervisee.

Whatever mechanisms are in place must be transparent, clearly contracted and understood by trainee, supervisor and training institution. All this will be helped if the supervisor is able to convince the trainee that bringing their difficulties to supervision is a mark of good practice, not of failure, and that the supervisee's task is not to attempt to be perfect but rather to endeavour to learn. This is helped along by the quality of the working alliance that supervisors are able to construct with their supervisees. In this regard Jordan's (2007) research into trainees' (n = 98) perceptions of key supervisor variables reveals that the attributes that trainees value most in their supervisors, and which help them to develop and take risks, are the relational qualities of care and concern, partnered with clinical and supervisory experience. Further aspects of accountability in supervision are discussed below, when we turn our attention to the matter of clinical responsibility.

Minimizing harm

We have already made a number of references to the application of the principle of non-maleficence: ensuring that harm is not done to anyone. The specific issue we would like to address here arising out of this principle is that of competence. For the supervisor this means that they have a responsibility to ensure that they are competent to fulfil the supervisory role they are undertaking. This cannot be taken as a given. Goodyear and colleagues (2006) reviewed five years of supervision-related psychology journal articles from 1999 and made the sobering discovery that 'the largest category of article topics concerned supervision that was in someway harmful to the supervisee' (p. 143). Ellis (2001) meanwhile has argued that harmful supervision is a taboo subject that has been under-investigated, and he calls this 'the dark side of supervision' (p. 403).

In addition to having the necessary skills, knowledge and experience, being competent as a supervisor means being in a sufficiently emotionally stable state so that one's own emotional difficulties do not substantially intrude. It becomes particularly important for the supervisor to assess this honestly at times of emotional stress – for example, if experiencing a loss or a personal crisis. In a similar way issues of competence apply to the work of a therapist (whether trainee or qualified), who should take reasonable steps to ensure that they are maintaining and developing their own level of competence through continued professional and personal development, including personal therapy where advisable. This is also likely to involve attending workshops and training events, and keeping abreast of developments and new research in the areas in which they practise. The supervisor can play a useful role by encouraging the supervisee to attend courses and conferences, by recommending reading, suggesting a suitable therapist or offering information about relevant new developments of which the supervisor becomes aware.

Ethical decision making

At this point we will move to considering the application of supervisory ethics in practice. Gabriel (2005) and Gabriel and Casemore (2010) have published detailed step-by-step guidelines for ethical decision making. While these guidelines are valuable in describing a thorough and systematic process, they do require a good amount of time for reflection and consideration in order to work issues through in the manner recommended. This may indeed be exactly what is required. We would also like here to propose a more succinct process for working through ethical and professional issues that can easily be integrated into any supervision session. This decision-making model incorporates the ethical principles enshrined in the BACP

Ethical Framework and also uses the structure of the Cyclical Model of supervision. It is here described as a peer-group exercise in the form in which we use it on supervisor training courses. It can easily be adapted to one-to-one supervision as the sequence of steps remains the same.

Supervisees in the group start by deciding how to divide the time so that each person who wishes to receive supervision on an ethical issue is given an equal portion of time (*Contract*). A time-keeper is appointed and the following steps are used to work through each person's ethical dilemma:

1 One person brings a current ethical concern or dilemma from their own therapy or supervision practice (*Focus*).
2 Peer supervisors help the supervisee clarify and explore the issue (*Space*). They should beware of giving advice or seeking solutions too early in the process. The group is encouraged to: (i) note and share the feelings that come up for each person during this exploration; (ii) identify which of the six ethical principles given in the BACP framework (as summarized on pages 156–8) might come into play in relation to the issue being discussed.
3 Peer supervisors help the presenting supervisee consider possible courses of action (*Bridge*) and what might be the benefits, costs and consequences of each of these. The supervisee is then given space to say where they are now with the issue and what they can take forward from the discussion.
4 The group takes a few moments to debrief (*Review*). It can be helpful here to identify the learning or therapeutic potential emerging from exploration of the ethical issue – namely what have people in the group learned that might be of benefit to their work as therapists or supervisors?
5 The next supervisee in the group presents their ethical issue, repeating the process as outlined above.

As this sequence of steps seeks to make clear, ethical decision making in therapy and supervision needs to value and take account of personal, intuitive feelings and reactions as well as the kind of rigorous thinking that is buttressed by reference to ethical codes and frameworks (Ellis 2010). Often, an initial reaction that something just 'feels wrong' should be valued and pursued by the supervisor (or peer consultant in the exercise above) even where its connection to a moral or ethical prerogative is not immediately apparent and may need to be teased out. Along with 'courage' and 'rigorous thinking', Henderson (2009b:122) has highlighted 'intuition' as one of the three key personal qualities required by the supervisor to exercise their ethical responsibilities. Here is an example that may help to illustrate this point.

A supervisee, Errol, who had finished a successful piece of work with a client, Suzi (a student), mentioned in supervision that he had offered to be a point of contact, via email, for her during her year abroad at a European university. The supervisor felt immediate unease at this revelation although the supervisee talked only in positive terms about how Suzi was now ready to embark on a long-cherished goal to study abroad. Although initially unsure about the cause of her unease, the supervisor disclosed this feeling and asked her supervisee if he could slow down to give some space for thinking about this.

Through paying greater attention to her feeling of disquiet, the supervisor realized that this connected to concerns about autonomy, beneficence and dependence. Let us consider first the issue of autonomy as it applies here. In this case the principle of autonomy is double edged as it applies both to the client's and to the supervisee's right to be self-governing. Autonomy, in the sense of promoting the maximum degree of choice for all involved, has great significance in moral philosophy (Schneewind 1993). It encapsulates the *raison d'être* for much therapeutic work, is a major therapeutic goal and should be safeguarded as a priority.

This said, the task for the supervisor is to apply this ethical principle of autonomy both to the therapeutic work that is being supervised *and* to the practice of their supervision. Sometimes this will create a dilemma for the supervisor as the autonomy of the two participants, the supervisee and their client, may suggest two different courses of action – in which case two or more ethical principles may clash. The example given here is a case in point. In the interests of supervisee autonomy it could be argued that the therapist, Errol, should be left to make his own decision and face the consequences of this. However, in this case there is also the question of whether the client's autonomy might be undermined by the supervisee's actions if they were to encourage dependency. The principle of beneficence also comes into play in respect of whether the therapist's ongoing contact arrangements with his former client might potentially cause harm (nonmaleficence) or ultimately be of benefit to her.

In bringing to the fore the issue of dependency, this case illustration highlights one of the central issues relating to the principle of autonomy. The supervisor has a key task to ensure that the supervisee encourages clients to overcome entrenched dependency on their therapist (periods of temporary dependency may be therapeutically and developmentally desirable). In so doing the supervisor needs to be aware of the seductive quality for the supervisee of having a number of clients who 'look up to him, and value him as perhaps the only human being in whom they have felt able fully to confide' (Storr 1990:63).

It can be equally gratifying for the supervisor to have a number of supervisees looking up to them, perhaps in awe of their experience and apparent greater knowledge. As in therapy, there may be a period in the early stages of supervision when the supervisee needs, to a certain extent, to feel dependent on their supervisor. This may well be the case for trainees who may find themselves struggling in their new role. They may need to be able to phone their supervisor between sessions, ask for and receive advice and encouragement and, when faltering during the therapy sessions, ask themselves 'what would my supervisor do in this situation?' Where this occurs it is for the supervisor to point out that, in truth, it is the supervisee's own wisdom they are calling upon at such a moment, through the guise of imagining that they are appealing to the supervisor, and thereby start the process of building the therapist's sense of their own autonomy.

To return to our case illustration, the questions that began to form in the supervisor's mind took the following form: Would continuing contact between Errol and Suzi mean entering into a dual (in this case sequential) relationship where the counsellor became more like a long-distance friend or confidante to his ex-client? Had the ending of the therapeutic work been sufficiently clear and rigorous or had a boundary (between counselling and a subsequent social/supportive relationship) been fudged? Was there a danger of Errol unintentionally encouraging dependency between himself and his client? Would an ongoing attachment to her ex-counsellor be of benefit to Suzi or might it hold her back from seeking more appropriate support and friendship during her year abroad? What if Suzi experienced difficulties while she was away and wished to talk about these with her ex-counsellor – could there be a danger of Errol falling into doing uncontracted and uncontained therapy with her?

The supervisor raised these questions with Errol, and as they considered them together, Errol began to realize that what he had intended to offer as a kind of supportive 'check in' for his ex-client might turn into something more complicated and difficult to manage. Following this discussion he decided to set some clearer boundaries and limits for himself in managing his ongoing relationship with Suzi. Errol resolved to keep his responses to any emails from her brief, and limited to a warm acknowledgement of her message and to encouraging her to make her own autonomous decisions regarding any plans or dilemmas. He realized he would need to watch that he did not get drawn into doing informal, 'long distance' therapy and would advise Suzi to seek counselling locally if she seemed in need of this. Errol decided that on her return to the United Kingdom he would offer Suzi a review session in which he would make the ending of their work and relationship explicit. He realized that in this meeting, as well as sharing many appreciations of their work together, he might also need to say 'and it is now right that we won't be meeting again or keeping in touch'.

This example illustrates the point that ethical issues brought to supervision are often done so out of awareness of the supervisee (Bramley 1996; Frawley-O'Dea and Sarnat 2001). In this respect Henderson (2009b:116) notes that ethical dilemmas tend to fall into two categories: 'those that the supervisee has identified but does not know how to manage, and those that the supervisor identifies which the supervisee had not'. The vignette above may be thought of as an example of the latter. Whether brought intentionally or accidentally, ultimately it is the quality of the supervisory relationship that creates a safe enough container for any ethical issues to emerge (Morrissey 2005; Rye 2009; Wosket 2009).

Responsibility for the work of the therapist

Bordin (1983:38) reminds us that 'supervisors are part of a professional gate-keeping apparatus designed to protect the public and the profession'. However, as we have begun to see, the supervisor's responsibility to monitor the work of the supervisee may be complex to define in theory and also to accomplish in practice (Ellis 2010). Consideration of gatekeeping responsibilities in supervision cannot be divorced from the issue of who holds clinical responsibility for the client work.

It is generally accepted that clinical responsibility rests with the therapist where he or she is qualified and works independently (Bond 2000; Dunkley 2006). Where the practitioner is a trainee and works for an agency, on the other hand, clinical responsibility normally resides with the agency (Coate 2010). In this context BACP also advises that 'the involvement of training providers and supervisors external to the agency needs to be clarified, to avoid confusion over where accountability lies, particularly if things go wrong' (Coate 2010:3). Bond (2010) endorses BACP's view on clinical responsibility regarding the work of trainees and advises that supervisors of trainees 'ensure that the counselling agency and the training course take primary responsibilities in backing up the work of the trainee where a client is considered to be at risk' (p. 189).

BACP considers that best practice is for a specified person within an agency to hold clinical responsibility for the service (this includes both work undertaken by trainees and qualified practitioners) and that this person 'must be accountable for clinical decisions, particularly in relation to service contracts, boundaries, breaches of confidentiality and holding of at-risk clients' (BACP FAQs, February 2009 cited in Nutt 2011:52). In our view it is particularly important that a named person holds this responsibility wherever an organization has inexperienced and/or newly qualified therapists working as well as more experienced practitioners, as is often the case within voluntary organizations. In her article Nutt includes a helpful example of the wording of one counselling service's guidelines on clinical responsibility that follow BACP's best-practice recommendations (2011:53).

In discussing the role of the supervisor in holding clinical responsibility Morrissey (2005) makes a distinction between the situation in the United Kingdom and that in the United States, where supervisors have been held legally accountable for the work of their supervisees. She points out that in the United Kingdom, 'there is no line of responsibility between the client and the supervisor, although case law remains to be tested' (Morrissey 2005:308). The lack of case law does not mean that supervisors can abdicate clinical responsibility, for, as Morrissey argues, 'professionally and ethically they have a responsibility to anticipate (within reason) and minimise the possibility of negligence to the client and the supervisee' (2005:308). Indeed, in Morrissey's view, a supervisor 'could to some degree be held responsible for any harm caused to a client' where the supervisor was aware of a 'potential problem between the supervisee and client and failed to act promptly and appropriately' (2005:308). This view is echoed by Mitchels and Bond (2010), who advise that a supervisor has an ethical responsibility to attend to a client's welfare in supervision and to oversee the supervisee's work in such a way that benefit to the client is ensured.

A supervisor's access to the therapeutic work is normally mediated through the supervisee and by the material he or she chooses to bring to supervision (Wosket

2009). From this perspective alone, supervisors are not in a position to assume full clinical responsibility for a supervisee's practice. Neither would this seem desirable, for, as Bond (2000:191) has argued, practitioners need to learn that 'primary ethical obligations rest with the counsellor'. The supervisor's role is to support her supervisee in how he exercises ethical responsibility, rather than protect him from this. In a later edition of his book on counselling ethics, Bond (2010:188) emphasizes the importance of this supportive function and asserts that 'supervisors do not normally assume a direct responsibility to a client. They work to enhance the counselling work and the benefits for a client through the supervisee'.

From this discussion, we can see that direct supervisor access to client work remains only ever partial. This remains the case even where a selection of recorded client work is re-played in supervision sessions. The exception to this is where direct trainer/supervisor observation of all the counsellor's work may happen. This typically occurs only as part of an intensive training structure (Jencius *et al.* 2010) although recently Roth (2013) has argued for the extension of direct observation of a supervisee's work 'to all modalities of psychological therapy' (p. 137), either through reviewing recorded material or through co-working, in order to enhance ethical practice and protect the public from harmful practice.

It seems clear to us then that a supervisor has a duty of care to safeguard the interests of the clients of their supervisees whenever the supervisor considers those interests to be at risk in some way. In discussing this point Mitchels and Bond (2010:18) consider that, within supervision, 'the supervisor has responsibility for monitoring and evaluating the quality of the counselling practice of the supervisee' and give examples such as watching out for burnout in a supervisee, monitoring workloads, and assessing competency and stress levels where supervisees work with difficult or demanding clients. Greer (2003) provides a chilling account of a worst-case scenario where inadequate and insufficient supervision, despite the best efforts of the trainee to obtain this while on placement, contributed to the death of a client.

A further example may serve to illustrate our discussion here. One of us had a supervisee, one of whose clients had committed suicide. Although the supervisee was able to attend to her responses to this experience in supervision, it became apparent that she was being overprotective of other clients whom she deemed to be at possible suicide risk. This led to the therapist acting in a manner the supervisor considered to be inappropriate, namely contacting one of her clients by phone between sessions to check that she intended to keep the next appointment and asking another client to phone her to keep her informed of his state of mind. The supervisor initiated exploration of this issue and it transpired that the suicide of the client had re-triggered a sense of guilt in the supervisee about a relative who had died some time previously. The relative had not committed suicide but the supervisee had always carried a sense of responsibility for the death. Having identified this the supervisor and supervisee agreed that the latter had to find a way to contain her anxiety about her clients or stop working with clients who were a suicide risk until she had resolved her personal difficulties in this area. This was necessary to protect the autonomy of the current clients of this therapist.

Together with the issue of responsibility comes the question of the supervisor's potential legal liability for the actions of their supervisees. In England and Wales this appears to remain an untested area although given the structure of the law and the emphasis on the consultative nature of the supervisory relationship, it seems improbable that a supervisor would be found legally liable for the actions of their supervisee (Mitchels and Bond 2010). As Mitchels and Bond (2010:40) assert, a legal claim of this nature 'would be difficult to bring because it would depend on proof of a chain of legal causation linking the supervisor's advice with any subsequent actions by the supervisee, and again linking those actions directly with any resulting damage to the client'. Legal liability aside, it seems clear to us that the supervisor's best protection lies in their supervisee being prepared to use supervision honestly and to take heed of their supervisor's recommendations.

Relational ethics in supervision

The preceding discussion suggests that a supervisor's responsibility to monitor the work of the supervisee is not normally achieved by means of exhaustive scrutiny, nor indeed would such scrutiny be desirable. Usually it happens through the goodwill of the supervisee, who is relied upon to bring to the supervisor's attention that which needs to be addressed. Thus the quality of the supervisory relationship and in particular the degree of trust and understanding between participants determines the effectiveness of this monitoring (Frawley-O'Dea and Sarnat 2001; Wosket 2009). This brings us to a consideration of the part played by the quality of the supervisory relationship in mediating the management of ethical issues.

The notion of relational ethics in counselling and supervision has gained influence in recent years (Gabriel and Casemore 2009). This is an approach to ethics defined as:

> a co-constructed ethical and moral encounter, with associated relationship experiences and processes, that both influences and in turn is influenced by the complex multidimensional context in which the relationship occurs. The term relational ethics represents the complex medium through which decisions and interactions associated with the processes and progress of a relationship are mindfully and ethically engaged with.
>
> (Gabriel and Casemore 2009:1)

Weld (2012:33) has asserted that a capacity for 'professional disclosure' lies at the heart of effective supervision and nowhere is this more the case than when it comes to supervision of ethical issues. Research (Gray *et al.* 2001; Hess *et al.* 2008; Mehr *et al.* 2010) appears to confirm that the supervisee's capacity for disclosing sensitive and ethical issues in supervision (intentionally or unintentionally) is largely governed by the quality of the supervisory relationship. For instance, in their study exploring the reasons for trainee nondisclosure in supervision Mehr and colleagues (2010) found evidence to support the hypothesis that a strong supervisory alliance was related to a higher willingness to disclose.

Writing as a supervisee, Neath (2009) gives a personal insight into the connection between self-disclosure and relational ethics in supervision. While training as a counsellor, Neath states that he took every client regularly to supervision, putting the onus on his supervisor to check out that he was working ethically. He goes on to say: 'However, as our relational ethics develop I learn to understand that in fact it is the transparency of myself which offers her greatest scope on my practice' (p. 80). This comment emphasizes that the monitoring of ethical practice in supervision hinges to a great extent on the degree of openness and trust that supervisor and supervisee are able to forge in their relationship together.

Alongside a trusting relationship it is advisable for supervisors to ensure that their supervisees are conversant with the kinds of issues that need to be brought to the supervisor's attention for ethical reasons and that agreement on this is sought as part of developing a collaborative working alliance (Dow *et al.* 2009). By way of illustration Tune's (2001, 2005) research into the ethical use of touch in therapy revealed that therapists rarely brought issues of touch that they had initiated with clients to supervision for fear of their supervisors' censure. Others (Syme 2006; Uphoff, 2008) have observed that many therapists engage in touch with clients yet feel as if they need to withhold this part of their practice from their supervisors. As most supervisors would agree that it is important for supervisees to reflect on their use of touch with their clients, Tune's research raises the question of whether supervisors need to do more to encourage their supervisees to bring sensitive issues such as the use of touch to their supervisors' attention.

Supervisees' awareness of and willingness to bring ethical issues to supervision may only emerge over time and as the relationship develops. For example, one of us had a supervisee who had a couple of experiences of mismanaging boundary issues with his clients. He brought these to his supervisor's attention only after they had occurred and only when it became evident that something needed untangling. As a result of these incidents, his supervisor made this explicit request: 'In future I would like us to discuss together the pros and cons of you extending your boundaries with any clients before you decide to do this'. The supervisee agreed to this and the supervisor reminded him that she would always be willing to arrange additional supervision between sessions if he felt he needed to make an urgent decision about boundary management and was unsure what to do.

The directiveness apparent in a supervisor's request such as the one given above needs to be tempered by careful phrasing that emphasizes a collaborative approach to the management of ethical issues. If the supervisor has worked to establish a collaborative working alliance with the supervisee prior to the emergence of ethical issues the stage is already set to accommodate this kind of challenging and immediate dialogue (Chen and Bernstein 2000). Note that the supervisor's request given above invites the supervisee into an open discussion of boundary management, rather than delivering a prescriptive prohibition on any boundary crossing.

This is essentially the difference between *taking authority*, which the supervisor clearly does here, and *being authoritarian* in the sense of controlling or disempowering the supervisee. Henderson (2009b) notes that a key challenge for new supervisors is to learn and practice this vital difference.

Campbell (2000:98) makes a distinction between 'consultation in the expert mode and consultation in a shared-power mode' that is relevant here. In a collaborative, shared-power mode 'the focus of consultation shifts from problems solved by the expert to problems solved by the supervisee' (Campbell 2000:98). This is particularly important when it comes to working on ethical issues in supervision. Because ethical concerns can be the most anxiety-provoking and demanding of all the dilemmas that therapists encounter in their work and bring to supervision, a supervisee can easily defer to their (usually) more experienced supervisor, and look to him or her to provide advice and direction. It is tempting for supervisors to fall into this trap as it affords seductive opportunities to feel 'puffed up' and admired while showing how wise and resourceful they are. Packwood (2008:38) refers to this 'shadow' component of supervision as the 'narcissistic buzz' that can lead a supervisor to offer smart advice rather than the space needed by the supervisee to think their own way through issues and dilemmas. There is an allied danger here, identified by Hawkins and Shohet (2012:140), of the supervisor encouraging action 'out of reactivity' rather than providing a space to slow down so that supervisor and supervisee can think collaboratively together about a way through an ethical dilemma.

Although we have strongly advised against taking the stance of ethical inquisitor (see Chapter 2) it can be helpful for the supervisor to keep in mind the notion of running a 'supervisee health check' when exercising their duty of care towards supervisees and their clients. We have likened this (Wosket 2009) to the notion of the advisability of regular dental checkups intended to minimize the need for emergency treatment and extractions. To conclude the chapter we offer this idea of a supervisory health check through a list of the aspects of professional practice the supervisor might wish to ensure a supervisee has attended to in order not to leave themselves vulnerable to failures of judgement or, at worst, client complaints.

Running a supervisee health check

Context and setting: Where and how is the supervisee practising? If working privately, is the space where they see clients as professional, protected, quiet, safe, private and neutral as possible? If the supervisee is working for an organization are there any 'murky' practices that might make the supervisee vulnerable to complaints or unwitting poor practice? For instance, are organizational policies and procedures relating to the therapy provision written down and adhered to or is it 'assumed' that everyone is working to the same guidelines?

Boundaries: How does the supervisee approach boundary management? Are they firm and clear yet able to be flexible when therapeutically advisable? Do they have a tendency to be 'sloppy' with their boundaries (e.g. poor time keeping or overdisclosure) or to be overly rigid (e.g. refusing to speak to a client who attempts to make conversation on the way to or from the therapy room)?

Contracting: Is the supervisee's contracting with clients thorough and clear? Do they follow best-practice guidelines (Bond and Mitchels 2008; Mitchels and Bond 2011) in using written agreements to avoid ambiguity and misunderstandings? Does the contract include information on: data protection; the client's rights of access to their notes and records; their right to complain; the therapist's professional body; and the complaints procedure to which she or he adheres?

Administration and record keeping: Is the supervisee familiar with best-practice guidelines (Bond 2010; Bond and Mitchels 2008; Mitchels and Bond 2010) and do they adhere to these? For example, is their note-taking sufficiently detailed that specific issues relating to any misunderstanding or complaint could be tracked back in case-notes? Does the supervisee indicate in their notes where difficulties and dilemmas are taken to supervision and the outcome of this? Has the supervisee made a counselling 'will' (Mitchels and Bond 2010) whereby a trusted professional colleague will attend to their clients and records if the therapist dies or is unexpectedly incapacitated?

Self-care: How does the supervisee attend to self-care and monitor their energy and stress levels? Do they bring fitness-to-practice issues to supervision as and when these arise?

Chapter 11

Difference and diversity in supervision

There has been an increasing expectation in recent years (BACP 2013a), that counselling, psychotherapy and supervision practice are attuned to difference and diversity. In parallel, a growing number of writers and researchers have developed models, guidelines and training programmes for supervision practice that incorporate issues of difference and diversity as a core component (see, for instance, Bernard and Goodyear 2009; Faubert and Locke 2003; Henderson 2009a; Kim and Lyons 2003; Lago and Smith 2010; Power 2009; Rapp 2000; Ryde 2000; Wheeler 2006).

We take the view that, as supervisors, we have considerable responsibility for developing our own sensitivity to areas of difference and diversity, and for encouraging, enabling and sometimes challenging our supervisees to do the same. Difference and diversity are central dimensions of supervisory work and will inevitably require a political or cultural perspective to be part of our understanding of the experience of our supervisees and their clients, and to inform our supervisory approach.

To clarify terms, we understand 'discrimination' to refer to the unequal treatment of an individual or group, which may include restricting access to activities and resources, and reduced power and rights, whilst 'oppression' describes the hardship, injustice and cruelty that an individual or group may experience. We will draw upon writings on 'transcultural' and 'multicultural' therapy and supervision, whilst recognizing that these terms are sometimes used to describe a broad range of areas of cultural difference and at other times in a more circumscribed way, usually focusing on race and ethnicity. Typically, as Kagee (2007:343) has stated, 'multicultural emphasises the plurality of factors that form part of a multicultural exchange'. To illustrate our discussion we shall include examples from a number of strands of difference and diversity, as these terms are understood in the context of human equality. That said, we can only hope to cover some broad principles and the reader is referred to more specialized texts, for example Lago and Smith (2010) and Wheeler (2006), for a more detailed exploration of therapeutic work where specific aspects of difference are considered to be highly significant.

In the fields of counselling, psychotherapy and supervision we are always working with aspects of diversity and, as Rapp (2000) has observed, culturally competent supervision can be seen as a template for all good supervision. One danger that arises in broaching the subject of equality in supervision within a limited space is that of lumping together a large number of issues that deserve careful and separate consideration. As Bernard and Goodyear (2009) have shown through their extensive coverage of a whole spectrum of multi-cultural issues in supervision, responding to diversity requires a readiness on the part of supervisor and supervisee to acquire a broad range of culture-specific knowledge, competence and sensitivity. We are not suggesting that supervisors should adopt particular ways of working with particular groups; on the contrary, one of the key lessons from multicultural approaches is that every encounter is unique.

Equality Act 2010

We shall briefly consider the current equality legislation in the United Kingdom, as this is an important part of the professional context for all UK-based supervisors. In 2010 the Equality Act (UK Gov 2010) became law. This parliamentary bill superseded a number of previous bills, covering Race Relations (originally passed in 1965), Equal Pay (1970), Sex Discrimination (1975) and Disability Discrimination (1995). It sets out to create a streamlined framework for equality, which can evolve and develop as understanding of equality continues so to do. It covers equality in five broad areas:

- employment;
- education;
- the provision of goods, facilities and services;
- the management of premises;
- the exercise of public functions.

The Equality Act defines a set of 'protected characteristics', making it unlawful to discriminate on the basis of those characteristics. There is a limited exception where there is a genuine occupational requirement to select applicants for a post on the basis of a protected characteristic, for example only selecting female applicants for a support-worker role in a women's refuge. However, it is not generally lawful to restrict applicants on grounds of sex or ethnicity in order to ensure representation or balance in a team, although it may be lawful to engage in positive action to seek to increase the proportion of applicants with the less-represented sex or ethnicity through an advertising strategy.

At the time of writing, the protected characteristics are:

- age;
- disability;
- gender re-assignment;
- marriage and civil partnership;
- pregnancy and maternity;

- race;
- religion and belief;
- sex;
- sexual orientation.

These characteristics may well be amended and added to in the future, as other disadvantaged groups are identified. An example is when, in April 2013, the protected characteristic of race was expanded to include caste, following pressure by those concerned that this remained an area where discrimination was evident yet was not covered in the original legislation. There are a number of sources of further information about the definition and scope of these protected characteristics, most notably from the Equality and Human Rights Commission (EHRC 2010).

Alongside the Equality Act, there is an Equality Duty (superseding and building upon the previous equality duties for race, disability and gender) applying to public-sector bodies. This Equality Duty (EHRC 2012) has three general aims:

1 to eliminate unlawful discrimination, harassment and victimization, and other conduct prohibited by the Act;
2 to advance equality of opportunity between people who share a protected characteristic and those who do not;
3 to foster good relations between people who share a protected characteristic and those who do not.

The Act goes on to explain that having due regard for advancing equality involves:

- removing or minimizing disadvantages suffered by people due to their protected characteristics;
- taking steps to meet the needs of people from protected groups where these are different from the needs of other people;
- encouraging people from protected groups to participate in public life or in other activities where their participation is disproportionately low.

This pro-active approach requires a public body to publish progress against the equality objectives it has defined for itself and to have in place effective mechanisms for consulting people with protected characteristics about areas where they experience difficulty.

Beyond legal requirements

For supervisors in the United Kingdom the Equality Act is part of the context of our work and compliance with its requirements is an important consideration. We are all likely to be classed as providers of services and for those working in the public bodies or undertaking work on behalf of them, for example providing therapeutic services on behalf of the health service or a local authority, the Equality Duty will also apply. Whilst it is important to recognize our compliance obligations, this is only a minimal requirement: compliance mindedness is generally defensive, whilst a commitment to equality requires a more positive and active approach. For instance, UK legislation does not include people who are socially or economically disadvantaged (ONS 2013) as a protected characteristic, yet in the field of counselling and psychotherapy we need to be very mindful of the potential difference in social and economic background between ourselves and our clients or supervisees. At its simplest this might mean being aware of our charging policies and how they may restrict access to the services we provide. However, the potential for difference has many other, perhaps less apparent, layers, including the language we use, the assumptions we make, examples we may draw upon, values and principles we adopt, and so forth.

Knowledge and understanding of difference

Ancis and Ladany (2010) suggest that in order to be culturally competent supervisors we need to address our cultural knowledge and cultural self-awareness, which together provide the platform upon which to build our cultural skills. Knowledge of difference, in its widest meaning, encompasses our understanding of the full range of cultural and personal differences that can impact upon ourselves and others. We can enhance our understanding through reading, research and attending training programmes, and can identify key sources of information to refer to when we need to refresh our knowledge. In this regard Banks (1999) found evidence that reading and training improved knowledge and awareness of difference for white counsellors working with black clients. When supervising counsellors and psychotherapists working with bereaved clients we can, for instance, identify information resources about the different practices and beliefs relating to death in the main world religions (Parkes *et al.* 1997), and, where and when appropriate, offer these to our supervisees.

Awareness of our own characteristics and culture

We need to be conscious of our own values and beliefs (Garrett *et al.* 2001), have an appreciation of our personal and cultural identity, and understand how these influence the way we behave as supervisors, recognizing that this in turn is how we model therapeutic relationships with our supervisees. There is a general aspect to this, which will tend to influence all our relationships together with a specific cultural component of individual relationships. In some ways this parallels family position: the fact of being a second child of three will influence my basic relationship patterns and be one component in how I relate to everyone, but any specific relationship is constructed through a complex interlocking system of various aspects of shared history, who we each are and the context and nature of our relationships. Social identity includes a multiplicity of variables and it is therefore not a simple or singular task to reflect upon our own. Ancis and Ladany

(2010:63) offer a straightforward starting point for considering our identity from an equality perspective when they say:

> We believe that for any given demographic variable, people can belong to one of two societally based groups: (1) a socially oppressed group (SOG; female, person of color, gay/lesbian/bisexual, disabled, working class), or (2) a socially privileged group (SPG; male, white, heterosexual, European, American, physically abled, middle to upper class).

It can be an illuminating exercise to go through the protected characteristics defined within the Equality Act and categorize oneself as belonging to the socially oppressed or socially privileged group for each. This exercise can be extended by reflecting upon other aspects of personal identity not covered by the protected characteristics, where unwelcome, prejudicial or oppressive behaviour may be experienced – for example height, weight, build, hair colour, whether left-handed, wears glasses, etc.

Cultural self-awareness may be focused upon one characteristic, and being self-aware in relation to that one characteristic will not necessarily generalize into other areas of difference. An individual who is sensitized with respect to one characteristic may appreciate the difficulties being encountered by someone with a different characteristic, but equally they may not. Typically, awareness of being in the socially oppressed group emerges before recognition of privilege amongst those in the dominant group. History offers many examples of the oppressed rising up against the oppressors and far fewer in which the oppressors decided spontaneously to change their behaviour towards those they were oppressing. Carter (1995) is one of those who has referred to the time it took for racial categories in the United States to be extended to include 'White American', as an example of how the oppressed group tends to be defined against a 'norm', typically where that norm is the majority within that group or society.

As practitioners whose work has at its core a commitment to positive change and such principles as autonomy, justice and beneficence, it can be deeply challenging on a personal level to accept that our social identity and ways of behaving may unknowingly discriminate and oppress. Nevertheless, accepting that this may be the case, that our personal and professional shadow (Page 1999a) may contain unrecognized prejudice and intolerance, is essential if we are to improve our cultural awareness.

Ancis and Ladany (2010) offer a four-stage model for what they term 'Means of Interpersonal Functioning' or MIF. 'These stages', they argue, 'represent a progression from complacency and limited awareness regarding cultural differences and oppression to increased awareness of multicultural issues, cognitive complexity and commitment to cultural competence' (2010:64). Ancis and Ladany offer examples of thoughts, feelings and behaviours associated with each stage. We have paraphrased aspects of each stage below, using the example of the variable of gender from a male perspective.

Stage 1: adaptation

At this stage Ancis and Ladany suggest that the individual male is rationalizing traditional views of gender difference, linking social and psychological differences to biological differences. The male at this stage is unlikely to recognize ways in which women are treated less favourably than men as being unfair.

Stage 2: incongruence

The male will hold views that are inconsistent. For example, they might say 'It's great having Sally in the team as she has a really interesting way of looking at things, but on balance it is probably best that women stay at home to look after the children', thus minimizing the issue and rationalizing why the traditional status quo should be maintained.

Stage 3: exploration

As the discomfort of the incongruent position starts to emerge into his consciousness, the male is likely to feel guilty and start noticing examples where women are disadvantaged, exploited or oppressed.

Stage 4: integration

The male is now identifying opportunities to challenge behaviours and assumptions that disadvantage or oppress women, is sensitized to the issues and advocates for the rights of women. The primary feelings are of sadness about current inequality and optimism that changes can occur.

In principle this framework, in conjunction with the set of protected characteristics, offers a matrix within which we can consider our current level of awareness of difference. In practice, recognizing and circumventing our own defences is not an easy task and we are all likely to need the assistance of a therapist or supervisor of supervision, particularly in any areas where we are in the adaptation or incongruence stages.

Creating a conducive supervisory environment

The first skill that we need to practise and refine is that of creating appropriately open, respectful and mutual relationships with our supervisees. Mutuality within the relationship is crucial to the success of supervision work as it constitutes the cornerstone upon which all else is built. Given the power imbalances inherent within supervision, particularly in the early stages of a supervisory relationship, it is largely the supervisor's responsibility to create and maintain a supervisory relationship and environment in which areas of difference are openly addressed.

In a study by Taylor and colleagues (2006) of the perspectives of supervisors from black and minority ethnic backgrounds, nine of the ten participants 'thought it was important to take the initiative in addressing issues of multiple identities and culture, a markedly different practice than they experienced as supervisees' (p. 9). However, the researchers went on to say that 'the participants varied in the timing, content and style of those supervisory interventions' (Taylor *et al.* 2006:9). This is in accord with our own view that there are no universal answers to the questions of when it is best to raise issues of difference between ourselves and our supervisees. It is of note that in the same study, whilst 'ethnicity and gender were discussed as integral parts of the case by all participants, sexual orientation and spirituality were addressed by only half of the sample, and only when the supervisee's client brought them up first' (Taylor *et al.* 2006:9). This underlines that we do not, and arguably should not, treat all areas of difference in the same way and that each of us is likely to be more comfortable with some areas of difference than others.

As well as building supervisory relationships in which issues of difference can be openly discussed, we also need to acknowledge that supervisees have a right to hold safe within themselves aspects of their identity and experience that are not relevant to supervision. This view is reinforced by the perspective of one of our supervisees when we asked if she would be prepared to give her written views on this issue as a contribution to this chapter. The supervisee describes herself as 'an assertive amputee' and these are her words:

> Were you to bring up the subject of my disability during supervision without my prompting, I would at the very least be surprised. On a deeper level I think several things would happen. Initially I would feel offended but go with you on it out of politeness, all the while turning things over in my head which had little or nothing to do with my client. I would 'humour' you. Afterwards, my reflections would once again have little to do with my clients and during the weeks between supervision sessions I would gradually become angry and we would have to deal with this.
>
> The vital missing ingredients would be my clients.
>
> I *will* talk about my disability with you when it gets in the way, either on a practical level or when it is an issue within my client work. As you know, both these situations are rare. Otherwise, I simply accept that you see me as a whole person and don't treat me any differently to any of your other supervisees. Were this not the case I would feel that my clients were being overlooked in favour of my disability, and that I was being discriminated against.

The supervisee's words indicate that even an assertive supervisee might, initially, defer to her supervisor's directive, though finding this offensive. Her view reinforces how important it is that the supervisor does not act on assumptions based on possibly misinformed notions of what constitutes an appropriate approach for ensuring anti-discriminatory practice – put simplistically, the erroneous belief that issues of difference should always be up front and that it is the supervisor's responsibility to raise them. Rather than ameliorating power differentials, holding a fixed stance such as this will, in some instances, constitute a misuse of power.

The priority for the supervisor is to create the appropriate conditions that make it as easy as possible for the supervisee to raise issues of difference, when they wish to do so. The additional dimension in supervision is that of the work being supervised, so on rare occasions we may feel that we need to name an issue of difference between ourselves and a supervisee if it appears to be interfering with effective supervision. For example, when supervising a therapist who was struggling with what she described as the chauvinistic attitudes of her client towards his partner, the male supervisor was distracted by wondering what his supervisee imagined about his (the supervisor's) relationship, knowing that it was quite possible that his supervisee had heard his wife with their young children in other parts of the house, during supervision. The supervisor acknowledged that he was distracted by his thoughts, explained what they were, and went on to suggest that there may be unacknowledged elements of parallel process if he and the supervisee were containing their fantasies about each other in the same way that the therapist was containing her views about her client's attitude to his partner. This intervention eased some of the tension in the room and a lively discussion ensued about how to deal with having, or believing that we have, very different approaches to aspects of life from our clients. In reviewing the supervision session, the supervisee said that she was really pleased her supervisor had said what he did, as she now felt freed up to be more outspoken with him.

As a general rule we believe that supervisors should be guided by the preferences of their supervisees in how difference is acknowledged and addressed between them within the supervision space. An example where one of us worked with a mixed-race supervisee may serve to illustrate our thinking. During initial contracting and over a period of several months, where the work was regularly reviewed together, the supervisee did not draw attention to the supervisee's origin. It first became a subject for discussion when the supervisee chose in one session to discuss his responses to a West Indian client who had talked in a therapy session of his experiences of racism and said: 'You're black, like me, so you'll understand what I mean'. The supervisee brought his feelings of surprise and discomfort to explore in supervision, where he said, 'I don't think of myself as black and I was surprised when my client identified so closely with me'. To contrast with this account, we also know of the experience of a mixed-race supervisee who felt that her first supervisor exhibited racism in not drawing attention to the difference in colour between them. For her, this increased her sense of the imbalance of power between the two of them where she, as a trainee, already felt substantially less powerful than her white supervisor.

These two examples illustrate that, as supervisors, it is important that we don't assume we know the degree to which our supervisees wish their experience of difference to be discussed in supervision. This thinking has been reinforced by our experience of working with supervisees of different sexuality. For instance, when we supervise lesbian, gay or bisexual therapists it is evident that some wish their sexuality to be openly acknowledged and affirmed as part of their professional identity. Others have seen their sexuality as a private and personal matter that rarely becomes a topic for discussion in supervision, and only where it appears to have an immediate impact on client work.

Both supervisor and supervisee share a responsibility to acknowledge and consider difference. The supervisor has the responsibility to open up the potential space for discussion where there appear to be pertinent differences between supervisor and supervisee, or between the supervisee and their client(s) where it seems there are 'live' issues of difference that are not being addressed. The supervisee has a responsibility to be alert to issues of difference and diversity in their therapeutic practice and to bring these to supervision as appropriate. They also have a responsibility to let their supervisor know how they wish their own experience of difference to be acknowledged and explored within the supervision space.

Bernard and Goodyear (2009:147) make an important point when they state, 'It is not difference that matters. It is the power and privilege assigned to that difference.' From this it follows that it is the supervisor's responsibility, as the person who has the most power in the supervisory relationship, to establish the kind of atmosphere in which issues of difference can be openly and safely addressed by either party. A useful approach to developing sensitivity to aspects of difference and diversity in supervision is one that emphasizes goodwill on the part of the supervisor towards supervisees. Rapp (2000) points out that few people working in the field of counselling and supervision want, intentionally, to maintain their prejudices. Furthermore, Rapp asserts that 'in supervision we invite trust, we encourage people to show their limitations, and therefore we must not shame one another for sharing our weak spots, our blinkers and our prejudices' (2000: 96). Instead, she advocates a 'compassionate' approach to developing culturally sensitive practice that relies on encouragement of one another 'to let go of our insensitivities, preconceptions, prejudices and our irrational fear of difference' (2000:96).

Attitude of learner

Rapp (2000:99) has suggested that at the heart of good counselling and supervision lies the wisdom 'to assume as little as possible about another individual's very personal understandings of themselves and their world'. Gonzalez (1997) reflected this view in writing about the various roles he adopts as a supervisor working within a multicultural framework. He suggests that the most important role that the supervisor can take is that of 'supervisor-as-partial-learner' (1997:367). By this Gonzalez means that the supervisor owns and appropriately uses his or her acquired clinical wisdom, whilst also retaining an attitude of openness to learning from others whose experience may be different. In this sense, he identified a characteristic that supervisors would do well to acquire and one that has been described by Kaberry (2000:55) as the flexibility to move between 'didactic and dialectic modes according to the supervisee's needs and stages of development'. Gonzalez asserts that the advantage of taking on the role of supervisor-as-partial-learner is that in so doing he can 'genuinely learn from [his] supervisees without pretending that power differentials do not exist' or denying his own expertise (1997:368). He further recommends that the supervisor holds 'informed uncertainty as a frame of reference' (1997:367). In using the term 'informed uncertainty', Gonzalez suggests that the supervisor adopt a collaborative stance that 'allows for a full-hearted exchange of possibilities . . . between mutual experts' (1997:368), where supervisor, supervisee and client are equally valued as experts of their own experience.

> Supervisor-as-partial-learner has the potential to create an atmosphere where all involved can participate as fully engaged partners. Nobody (a) has to be the sole expert, (b) has to masquerade as being in a one-down position, or (c) has to pretend to buy into a socially constructed clinical reality that contradicts their personally constructed clinical reality.
>
> (Gonzalez 1997:370)

In advocating that supervisors adopt such a position, Gonzalez has proposed a stance towards multicultural supervision that aims to balance the acquired wisdom the supervisor is likely to bring to their role with an attitude of respectful enquiry that acknowledges that the supervisor will also be learning about the culture and background of their supervisee.

Acknowledging power and diversity

We have commented a number of times already on the inherent power imbalance between supervisor and supervisee. Usually the supervisee is junior to the more senior supervisor in terms of experience and status. Sometimes, within an organizational hierarchy where assessment takes place, the supervisor judges and the supervisee is judged, or more generally, the work of the supervisee is scrutinized and the supervisor does the scrutinizing. Overlaying these structural differences built into the roles of supervisee and supervisor (or perhaps more appropriately, underlaying, if remaining unconscious) are whatever psychological responses the supervisee brings with them about relating to people with some authority or power, or the supervisor has about having such authority or power.

When we consider the power balance in the supervisory relationship from the perspective of difference, we may find that the inherent imbalance is amplified if the supervisor is from a socially privileged group while the supervisee is from a socially oppressed group. Conversely, if the supervisor is from a socially oppressed group whilst the supervisee is from a more socially privileged group they may experience the tension resulting from a cultural power imbalance opposing the inherent power imbalance of the supervisory relationship. When considering the example of a black therapist working with a white client, Power

(2009) talks about pre-transference, referring to the 'fantasies which the white person holds about the black therapist long before they meet' (p. 165) and she goes on to say that 'A similar "pre-transference" would occur with any visible difference such as a disability or difference in body size' (p. 165). A similar unconscious process can occur in supervision with the potential for a further layer of parallel process from unrecognized dynamics of difference within the therapeutic relationship being brought to supervision. In some instances there will be a complex mix of supervisor and supervisee both being from a mix of socially privileged and socially oppressed groups. Whatever combination of dimensions is present, some of which may be known and recognized whilst others may be hidden, we can be certain there is an inevitable power dynamic in every supervisory relationship.

All these elements – inherent power and authority, and power dynamics resulting from difference and pre-transference – are aspects of what Frawley O'Dea and Sarnat (2001) describe as the 'asymmetry' of the supervisory relationship. A number of writers taking a feminist perspective (Fine and Turner 2002; Green and Dekkers 2010; Murphy and Wright 2005; Porter 2010; Prouty 2001) emphasize the importance of making explicit this asymmetry between supervisor and supervisee. They go on to advocate mutuality in specific aspects of the relationship, including asking questions, self-disclosure and addressing conflict. Some writers (Green and Dekkers 2010; Murphy and Wright 2005) advocate that a direct conversation about power in the supervisory relationship should take place in the early stages of supervision and as part of the initial contracting process. However, it may be that the supervisee needs time to develop trust in the supervisor before they feel able to have a more detailed discussion about how they experience power in the relationship.

It has also been argued (Prouty 2001) that diversity should be addressed early in the supervision relationship. There is evidence to suggest that addressing power and diversity in supervision is directly related to improved supervisee satisfaction with supervision (Gatmon *et al.* 2001; Inman 2006; Murphy and Wright 2005) and that this is further improved when the supervisee perceives their supervisor to be competent in discussing issues of diversity. Furthermore, Green and Dekkers (2010) found a direct correlation between the perception of supervisees that their supervisors were attending to power and diversity in the supervisory relationship and their satisfaction with supervision and attainment of learning outcomes (the 42 supervisees involved in this research were trainees). In the same study the supervisors (n = 22) rated their success in attending to issues of power and diversity in supervision significantly higher than their supervisees rated their perception that their supervisor attended to these issues. This supports the view that as supervisors we need to seek feedback from our supervisees about how effectively we communicate our openness to addressing issues of power and diversity.

Monitoring our awareness of culture and difference

A number of writers have considered ways of addressing multicultural issues in supervision. Garrett and colleagues (2001) introduced the VISION model, which provides a framework for considering the multicultural dimension for both supervisor and supervisee. We have summarized this as follows:

V – defining and reviewing the Values and beliefs of supervisor and supervisee;
I   – supervisees' Interpretation of their multicultural experiences (as a therapist and in supervision);
S – the supervisor planning the Structure of supervision is mindful of the cultural characteristics and needs of the supervisee;
I   – attending to the Interactional preferences of supervisee and supervisor;
O – the Operational strategies supervisor and supervisee are using to achieve supervisory goals, which may include culturally focused goals;
N – the Needs, of supervisee and supervisor, as these relate to what they are seeking to achieve.

There also exist multicultural supervision rating scales (Guanipa 2003; Szymanski 2003). The Feminist Supervision Scale (Szymanski 2003) measures four distinct areas: collaborative relationships; power analysis; diversity and social context; and feminist advocacy and activism. This scale was initially developed to be applied to the supervisor. Subsequently, Green and Dekkers (2010) have used the original scale for supervisors and devised an amended version for use by supervisees to report on their perception of their supervisors along the same dimensions.

One of the most effective ways a supervisor can evaluate their current level of cultural awareness is to record a supervision session (Huhra *et al.* 2008) where there is a cultural difference between themselves and the supervisee and then to review sections of the session in detail with their own supervisor of supervision. We have considered the use of recordings in Chapter 8 and will focus on supervision of supervision in some detail in Chapter 14.

There seems little doubt that rich learning can occur when we are immersed in multicultural situations (Coleman 2006). Frank, a middle-aged, white, heterosexual man had been supervising Julie, a white trainee counsellor in her mid-twenties, for a few months. Julie was on placement in a community-based counselling service. She brought the case of Moses to supervision, describing him as in his early twenties, in the United Kingdom from his home in central Africa, studying the second year of a three-year computing degree programme at the nearby university. Moses presented as depressed and anxious, saying that he was struggling to make friends. He said he had spent some time socially with two men from his course, but had told Julie that he was a bit uncomfortable with them as he thought they might be a gay couple. Julie explained to Frank that she had pursued this a little and asked Moses about his sexuality, at which point he appeared to become very uncomfortable and for the remainder of that session had, as Julie put it, shut down.

Already Frank's mind was racing with possibilities and he began to feel extremely uncomfortable. Frank knew that part of his discomfort was his awareness, gained from their initial contracting discussion about differences between them, that Julie was in what she described as a long-term lesbian relationship. He was concerned that Julie might be jumping to the conclusion that Moses was gay because of her own sexual orientation, and yet he feared that he might offend her if he raised this possibility. What Frank did say was 'Thinking about you, me and Moses I am feeling overwhelmed by all the multicultural aspects between the three of us. I wonder if it would be useful for us to just name all these different aspects of this situation.' That started a discussion in which he and Julie identified a number of areas of difference between client, counsellor and supervisor and acknowledged some unanswered questions. Frank admitted that he was uncertain, but thought homosexual activity might be illegal in Moses' home country and offered to find out and let Julie know. Julie concluded that she needed to find other areas to discuss with Moses to re-build the relationship between them, which felt ruptured by her question.

After this supervision session Frank was troubled by the way he had handled the situation and arranged to have a discussion with his supervisor of supervision. We shall return to this example later in the chapter.

Toporek and colleagues (2004) undertook a study into critical incidents in multicultural supervision, in which they invited 11 supervisors and 17 supervisees to recall one or more critical incidents involving multicultural issues in a supervisory context. Participants were asked to record what happened and also to rate the incident as positive, negative, helpful, challenging, supportive, offensive, harmful or threatening. Toporek *et al.* (2004:79) summarize their findings as follows:

> The results of this study suggest that multicultural incidents in supervision influence the supervision process and the multicultural competence of supervisors and supervisees. This influence may be positive or negative, depending on the supervisory relationship and the manner in which the cultural issues are addressed.

This is an important reminder that situations such as the one in which Julie and Frank found themselves can require great sensitivity and are not guaranteed to turn out well.

Facilitating supervisee cultural sensitivity

Sommer and colleagues (2009) have suggested that 'supervisors must create a safe space in which anxiety can be experienced in a way that challenges supervisees to stretch and grow' (2009:215). This is not easily achieved in the area of difference and diversity, in which beliefs can be strongly held and feelings profound. Attempting to address our own historic insensitivities honestly and with compassion towards ourselves, rather than simply burying those insensitivities beneath layers of undigested 'shoulds' and 'oughts' takes perseverance and courage. This is the task we may need to help our supervisees undertake as they come to meet clients who are different in ways they have not previously encountered. In part we achieve this by demonstrating our sensitivity and awareness to them as a person with their own culture, background and personal characteristics, which may be different to ours.

We also facilitate the development of supervisee cultural sensitivity by regularly considering in supervision the cultural context of the client, particularly ways in which they may be disadvantaged or socially oppressed. Some supervisees will work in settings where they see clients from a wide range of backgrounds and presenting varied issues of difference. For instance one of us worked for a number of years in a university counselling service, serving a student population that was roughly 20 per cent international and included representatives from over a hundred countries. Ten per cent of all the students had declared disabilities and a number were open about being lesbian, gay or bisexual. When new counselling staff and trainees first started in the service they often felt overwhelmed (and excited) by the wide variety of cultures and the issues of difference they were facing with their clients. With supervisees such as these the material is all there in their client work. Addressing multicultural experiences with clients is likely to lead to the development of sensitivity as therapists develop strategies for working in a variety of client-responsive ways.

Other supervisees may work for an agency with a client group that has a particular characteristic: women who have been sexually abused or subject to domestic violence, those with mental health difficulties, refugees or asylum seekers. If new to this work their priority will most probably be developing a depth of understanding about the specialist field in which they are working. Supervision can be a safe place where this development is encouraged, and if the supervisor is not themself a specialist in the same area, supervisor and supervisee can learn together. However, once the supervisee is feeling relatively comfortable with that client group it may be appropriate to introduce other areas of difference, inviting the supervisee to consider how they might develop their understanding of culture and difference more widely.

Some supervisees may find that most of their clients are relatively homogeneous on most or all variables of culture and difference. If the supervisee working in this setting comes from a similar background to their clients then they are at risk of not developing beyond their current level of awareness and competence relating to culture and difference. With these supervisees, and at the appropriate stage with those working in a specialist agency, it may be useful to suggest putting the area of difference on the supervision agenda, so they feel more prepared for future clients. Care is needed to avoid turning supervision into a mini training session, but there is a place for a limited amount of supervision time being spent considering the practice issues that may arise for the supervisee in the future. Difference is one example, alongside others such as working with a particular presenting issue that a supervisee feels could be challenging, the appropriate use of a new technique they have recently learned about or an ethical dilemma about which they have anticipatory concerns, even if they have yet to face this in their client work.

For those supervisees whose current client work is exposing them to a restricted range of multicultural dimensions, therapy dilemmas from the literature provide one source of stimulation for exploration. In the United Kingdom, the journal of the British Association for Counselling and Psychotherapy, *Therapy Today*, regularly includes professional dilemmas with suggestions about how these might be addressed in supervision. Alternatively, questionnaires addressing attitudes and experience in various areas of difference, for example Guanipa (2003), Szymanski (2003), or the *Self and Other* exercise described by Chang and Flowers (2010), can offer a starting point for discussion.

As Christiansen and her colleagues observe, 'regardless of how diversity is addressed through curricula, it appears that the supervision setting is an ideal place to address the cultural sensitivity of therapists and to reinforce what is learned during courses' (Christiansen *et al.* 2011:110).

Keeping the client central

Twin dangers exist in considering aspects of difference and diversity in supervision. The first is where issues of difference are either laboured to the point that other legitimate or more pressing supervision issues are missed; the second is that they are not given the attention they merit or are ignored completely. Chang and colleagues (2003) reviewed research on multicultural supervision from the perspective of cross-racial supervision (in the context of the United States). In summary they found that 'although cross-racial supervision is desirable it may be potentially problematic and can lead to unintentional racism, miscommunication, undiscussed racial and ethnic issues, over-emphasis on cultural explanations for psychological difficulties and overdependence on supervisor's knowledge' (2003:126). Thus when acknowledging and working with difference, the supervisor will need to navigate a course between two extreme positions. The first is that of assuming that all the difficulties and dilemmas that supervisees bring are significantly mediated by their experience of difference, or that all material from a particular case is related to areas of difference between the supervisee and client. This can lead to the experience of difference becoming exaggerated out of proportion to its relevance to the supervision issue and obscuring rather than illuminating that which requires attention. The second extreme position occurs where the supervisor adopts the stance of minimizing difference to the extent that it is treated as invisible and largely or wholly irrelevant to the supervision or therapeutic process.

We have noted parallels between the needs and experience of the counselling or psychotherapy client and the supervisee when considering issues of difference. However, it is important to be mindful that whilst we have a legitimate expectation that our supervisees are committed to developing their cultural knowledge, aware-ness and skills as part of their professional practice, it would be quite inappropriate to apply the same expectation to the client whose case is being brought to supervision. In this respect our responsibilities towards our supervisee and their client diverge. The client has their own reasons for engaging with counselling or psychotherapy and it would be another form of misuse of power to seek to impose a cultural agenda upon them. Bearing in mind the principle that parallel process moves in both directions, any significant or persistent over-emphasis of cultural issues or aspects of difference by a supervisor may have the effect of putting that on the client's agenda through the supervisee, so careful balance is required. This said, there are examples quoted (Adams 2010; Christiansen *et al.* 2011) of hostile racism and homophobia being expressed by clients, and in such instances a therapist should not have to tolerate personal attacks of a form or intensity that is experienced as offensive or even outlawed within the country in which they are working.

The risk of over-emphasizing difference in an unhelpful way is perhaps less commonly signalled in the literature than under-emphasis, but nevertheless requires attention. When discussing visible and hidden aspects of the client, Jacobs (2000b:211) made the point that 'although counsellors have to be open to the possible relevance of issues of difference, they may not be so for the client. To refer to the person's age, colour or ethnicity out of the blue may be intrusive and insensitive.' Collins (2000:211) has asserted that 'clients in counselling have every right to be secretive, defensive, or protective about "hidden" aspects of their identity' and has suggested that the counsellor's role is not to expose these hidden aspects 'but to support and facilitate an environment in which the client may begin to feel safe to explore these issues'. In discussing how to attend to visible and hidden aspects of the client, Gabriel (2000:212) has suggested that the therapist 'should regard the client's sexuality, origin or hidden disability as dimensions of their story that should be allowed to unfold over the process of the counselling work and relationship'.

With this in mind, we will pick up our earlier example. Frank discussed his anxiety about offending Julie with his supervisor and decided that he would acknowledge how he had felt when next with her. Julie and Moses had focused mainly on Moses' experience of social behaviour amongst students at university in comparison with what he was used to at home. Building on that, Julie and Moses had agreed a number of strategies that Moses could test out for meeting and engaging with people whilst in the United Kingdom. Moses was making some progress with these and on clinical measures his depression had lifted somewhat, although his anxiety remained high.

When Frank and Julie next met four weeks later, Frank asked to spend some time following up on Moses and sharing their reflections on their previous discussion. He explained that he had wondered if Julie was overreacting to the issue of sexual orientation with Moses but had been worried about offending her if he said that. Frank went on to admit that he didn't feel very confident speaking about sexual orientation as he had limited experience of doing so. Julie acknowledged that based on the subsequent work with Moses on social differences, she now felt she had become overfocused on Moses' sexual orientation. She had discussed this with a fellow trainee and realized that it was probably because she wanted to help people struggling with their sexuality, as others had helped her some years earlier.

Moses did not say anything further about his own sexual orientation, however towards the end of counselling did talk about his concerns for a friend at home who was at risk of persecution because he was gay. Meanwhile Julie's and Frank's supervisory relationship appeared to strengthen following this exchange rather than be damaged by it.

Target interventions

The discussion of how supervisors may help their supervisees develop their sensitivity to difference and culture indicates that a supportive and respectful stance is required. A simplistic attitude towards issues of difference in supervision might assume that discriminatory attitudes can be rooted out by a vigilant supervisor requiring their supervisees to make the necessary politically correct shifts in thinking and behaviour. Yet the true essence of sensitive supervision and therapy lies more in an ongoing commitment to remain open to challenge from others whose experience of the world may not sit comfortably with one's own, than in holding a fixed political stance.

The principle of appreciative enquiry focusing on strengths and competencies, as put forward by Gray and Smith (2009), is helpful in this regard. They have developed a framework of 'reflective conversations and questions' aimed at 'helping supervisees to become more critical, intentional, reflexive and socially just in their work' (2009:155). Drawing on solution-focused and narrative approaches, Gray and Smith (2009) emphasize:

- the importance of building upon strengths and resources the supervisee already possesses;
- identifying the 'exceptions' where the supervisee has been successful (and may not have noticed) in a situation with some similarities to the one being focused upon;
- 'coping' questions that elicit from the supervisee what is working with the client;
- constructing a positive image for the future of the supervisee's work with her client;
- using scaling questions (for example, 'On a scale of 1–10 how well do you feel you responded to your client's concerns about their sexual identity?') to encourage a sense of progress made;
- choosing to focus the discussion on progress as the supervisee develops rather than what is still not working to their satisfaction.

Any such strategic approach to interventions is likely to successfully support the development of a collaborative relationship and create a safe place where supervisees are willing to be open about their uncertainties. We are not suggesting that supervisors should develop special questions to pull out of a bottom drawer when an issue of cultural difference emerges, rather that our interventions need to be intentional and appropriate to both the issue under discussion and the current developmental stage of the supervisee. This may mean that we expand or adapt our current range of interventions to incorporate the cultural dimension, or that we need to develop new parts to our repertoire.

While giving due regard to difference and diversity in supervision inevitably requires a political or cultural perspective, it can also be useful to have a psychotherapeutic understanding of why such issues can generate strong feelings and result in people taking up inflexible positions. Adams (2010), an African American woman with a philosophy of supervision that is 'primarily psycho-analytic and is influenced by postmodern, feminist, and multicultural theory' (p. 43), throws light on this:

> For a variety of reasons, acknowledging cultural differences invokes intense and often unconscious emotional reactions . . . Analytic therapists hypothe-size that there is a pull toward similarity and the denial of difference that stems from the awareness that if someone is different from you, he or she is separate from you and not under your control. This anxiety is thought to stem from the infant's first awareness that the mother is separate and not under his or her control. To control the anxiety induced by this awareness, the source of difference has to be denigrated, annihilated or made similar; that is it must be denied. Indeed race and cross-cultural, multicultural dialogues may be the new royal road to the unconscious.
>
> (Adams 2010:46)

Such an interpretation is not an excuse for oppressive behavior, but having an understanding of the intra-psychic dynamics involved in such behavior can at times be helpful.

Invite open appraisal

If the place to initiate discussion of difference is in the contract stage of the Cyclical Model, then the review stage of the model provides a place to check that differences between supervisor and supervisee are being appropriately acknow-ledged and taken into consideration. For example, if supervisor and supervisee have agreed to review their work together six months after starting, it may be useful within any sort of mixed pair for the supervisor, at this point, to say something like: 'Over the few months we have been meeting I have become aware of how different your background and life experience appear to be in comparison with mine. I'm not sure if I have acknowledged this well enough and I wonder about how it affects our working relationship and whether this is something we need to talk more about.' This kind of opener may lead to more detailed exploration of how the different life experiences, values and beliefs of the supervisor and supervisee influence, say, their goals for therapy and their expectations of supervision. It may only be after the supervisor and supervisee have experienced a number of sessions working together that they are able to identify and name some of the different views and perspectives on supervision and therapy that appear to exist between them and have sufficient confidence in each other to be open about their experience of supervision.

Chapter 12

Supervising experienced practitioners

In the previous chapter we suggested that supervisors need to develop an ability to be supervisee-directed in response to their management of issues of difference and equality in supervision. This chapter explores a further aspect of supervisee responsiveness in considering the supervision needs of two particular groups of counsellors and psychotherapists: those who are experienced practitioners; and, within that group, those who work with extremes of client experience.

In researching the needs and preferences of supervisees both Ladany (2004) and Gazzola and Theriault (2007) have warned supervisors to beware of the 'cookie-cutter' approach to supervision by which all supervisees are treated as similar. Both of these publications highlight the importance of supervisors tailoring their approach to the unique needs of their supervisees. This is particularly important when it comes to supervising experienced practitioners who may well have specialist clinical interests and therefore particular supervision requirements. In this respect Creaner (2011:150) has stressed the importance of seeing each supervisee as unique and whole and as both 'a knower as well as a learner'. It is likely that experienced practitioners will have areas of expertise that are greater than those of their supervisors and a challenge here is for the supervisor to forge a collegial relationship with the supervisee where both can be knowers and learners together.

We have included this chapter because while the majority of the supervision literature is aimed at the supervision of trainees and newly qualified therapists, we remain convinced that seasoned practitioners are equally in need of the 'professional watering hole' (Grant and Schofield 2007:11) that supervision provides. Supervision research, in particular, has largely neglected the needs and wants of experienced therapists (Bailey 2012; Feltham 2000). Their requirements are, at times, sufficiently different to those of novice therapists to merit separate attention. Wosket (2006) considered a number of the benefits of ongoing supervision as identified by a group of experienced clinical psychologists. These included: (i) enhancing development of the 'internal supervisor'; (ii) offering a balance of challenge and support that can help to re-invigorate practice; (iii) providing a safe forum for the working through of ethical dilemmas; (iv) providing a place where transcultural issues and other aspects of working with difference can be raised and talked through; (v) promoting accountability – for example by providing evidence of having sought professional consultancy to deal with high-risk situations; and (vi) providing consultative support for any supervision work undertaken by the practitioner.

In our experience the difference with supervising experienced therapists often comes down to the need to work more closely at the interface between supervision and therapy in the service of enhancing the personal and professional development of the therapist. The supervision issues of mature practitioners are frequently also their life issues. In this regard Rønnestad and Skovholt's (2013) research into 'The Developing Practitioner' has confirmed that a supervision priority for more experienced therapists is 'to explore how personal issues are expressed in their therapeutic work' (p. 199).

Supervision and ongoing professional development

The personal and professional selves of many therapists become increasingly intertwined as they gain experience. To the extent that therapists come to draw on aspects of themselves in their therapeutic work, they need to bring to supervision those parts of the self that are affected by their clients (Wosket 2000b). Research suggests that this is not always easy to do and that many practitioners 'attempt to manage counter-transference reactions themselves' (Knight 2012:15). On the other hand, Aponte (1982) has written about how the personal issues that are aroused for therapists in their relationships with clients can impact on the therapy in productive ways when therapists find 'creative ways of handling these difficulties' (p. 46).

One of the few studies to have thrown light on the supervision needs of experienced practitioners was carried out by Winter and Holloway (1991). Findings from their study of 56 counsellors, ranging from novice to very experienced, indicated that the less experienced supervisees preferred to focus on their clients in supervision while the more experienced therapists preferred the focus of supervision to be on themselves, in particular 'on their own concerns related to personal growth issues, such as counter-transference, self-efficacy, and self-awareness' (Winter and Holloway 1991:98). More recently Rønnestad and Skovholt's (2013) research into the professional development of therapists over the career lifespan found that more experienced therapists wanted to explore not only personal issues in supervision but also how to make use of their own emotional reactions as therapeutic interventions with clients.

These findings support the view that more of an emphasis on the self of the therapist may be needed in the supervision of experienced practitioners. This is not to suggest that supervision for experienced therapists should constitute self-indulgent introspection – quite the reverse. Focus on the therapist's self in supervision can provide a broader or more in-depth perspective on the client, as the following example illustrates.

The supervisee, Aimee, a very experienced therapist, reported to her supervisor that she felt bored with her client, Estelle, in sessions. She didn't look forward to seeing her and felt unfocused and distracted when with her. Other feelings Aimee experienced towards her client were frustration and lack of empathy, and she lamented that she felt she wasn't doing 'proper' counselling. She was honest enough to admit that she didn't find working with Estelle as rewarding as her other more 'exciting' clients and often wondered why the client continued to come.

In the dialogue between them the supervisor's responses included the following questions:

'How is the connection between you and your client?'
'In what ways might you be contributing to this dynamic?'
'How congruent are you being with the client?'
'Are you owning your own part in how this relationship is evolving?'
'Are you expecting the client to interest and engage you?'

Although these were challenging questions, a trusting and open relationship between supervisor and supervisee was well established and Aimee welcomed these prompts and probes. As she reflected on her supervisor's questions Aimee realized that she had a tendency to disconnect from Estelle in sessions and then did not make the effort to re-connect. She recognized that she had 'almost given up on' Estelle and found herself merely 'going through the motions'. Because of Aimee's level of experience she did not need her supervisor's help in formulating strategies for re-engaging with the client. Aimee could do this for herself – what she *had* needed were the supervisor's questions to help her focus on her own emotional reactions to Estelle.

In the following supervision session Aimee reported that she had been able to go back to her client and, at a timely moment, say to her: 'I find myself wandering off when you tell me another story and I don't want to keep doing this. I want to be able to focus more on you and our relationship. I don't feel I am helping our session come alive in the here and now and I would like to be able to do this better with you.' When she said this, Estelle, for the first time, cried and said how much it mattered to her to hear that her counsellor cared enough to want to be with her in this way. From that point on Aimee reported feeling much more connected to her client. She felt she had re-gained her empathy and told her supervisor that she now really looked forward to seeing Estelle and felt they were beginning to make real progress.

This vignette also illustrates the potency of modelling in supervision. In a later session Aimee (herself a supervisor) mentioned that she had done a piece of supervision work soon after the supervision session described above. On that occasion her supervisee had said similar things about his own client – that there was little sense of focus, that he felt bored and irritated with the client and that the work didn't seem to be going anywhere. Aimee disclosed to her supervisee that she had just had a supervision session on a similar issue and had found considering some questions about her own responses to the client helpful. She then asked her own supervisee some similar questions, for example 'How far are you blaming your client for the difficulty between you?' and 'What are you bringing to the interaction that contributes to this difficulty?' Aimee reported that her supervisee had a similar 'light bulb' moment and felt able to go back to his client with a very different perspective on their impasse.

Mearns and Cooper (2005) have argued that supervisors have a key role to play in assisting the ongoing personal as well as professional development of therapists. They suggest that therapists who have completed their training need supervisors who are able to reflect a 'potentiality model' rather than a 'deficiency model' of supervision (2005:156). By this they mean that supervision for experienced and qualified therapists has a primary developmental function that helps enhance their ability to work with clients at relational depth, rather than a monitoring function that focuses on deficits (e.g. lack of skill or knowledge).

Williams (1995:265) has suggested that supervision has a particularly vital part to play in the therapist's growth at the point where they come to leave their original training model behind and begin to develop a personally authentic therapeutic orientation. He describes supervision as a 'wisdom culture' (1995:265) in which the supervisee is encouraged to acquire clinical wisdom through a process of exploration, reflection and discovery in which the basic tenets of their initial training are questioned and tested against the realities of clinical practice. The supervisor's role here, as expressed by Williams, is to help supervisees 'pick their way deliberately among the therapeutic models in which they have been trained and assist them in resolving the contradictory ideas of the therapeutic world, as well as the paradoxes that they and their clients face' (1995:266). This is difficult work for any therapist to attempt on their own, where it may easily lead to confusion, despondency or impasse. When such issues are 'chewed over' with an interested, supportive and affirming supervisor, a way forward may be found to take the therapist further along the path to becoming an authentic and personally determined practitioner.

We believe that there remains an educative component to the supervision of experienced practitioners. Part of the task of supervision is to help the mature therapist translate theory into practice as they continue to assimilate knowledge from further training courses, research, reading, workshops and conferences. Allied to this, supervision has the capacity to address deficits in initial training and plug any gaps in skills and knowledge that become apparent. An unavoidable limitation of training is that no matter how comprehensive, no training experience can prepare therapists in advance to deal with all the exigencies of daily clinical practice. Supervision is a place where the many challenges and uncertainties of day-to-day encounters with clients can be thought about and processed.

Rønnestad and Skovholt (2013:209) have conceptualized supervision for experienced therapists as 'a learning process akin to a qualitative research process where both participants create a new, extended, and more in-depth understanding of therapy/counseling'. In this way they emphasize that the supervision of experienced practitioners is often mutually enriching for both participants. Furthermore, good supervision can help to re-invigorate aspects of the therapist's professional self that may have atrophied during their original training experience – for example, attributes such as the courage to do things differently, or the ability to trust one's own sense of how to hold and maintain boundaries. The role played by supervision in helping to develop the therapeutic use of self is dealt with more fully in another publication (Wosket 1999).

Shame in supervision

Supervisees who bring their more personal selves to supervision are likely at times to experience feelings of disquiet, embarrassment or even shame. Hahn (2001:272) has described the experience of shame in supervision as involving 'feelings of inadequacy and a vivid sense of being condemned for these inadequacies'. Farber (2006) has pointed out that one unique aspect of psychotherapeutic work that heightens the potential for shame is that the therapist's essential tool is the self. Farber goes as far as to assert that struggling with therapeutic work, 'often feels tantamount to admitting one is struggling to be the human being one wants to be and should be' (2006:182). If the supervisee can take these feelings and concerns to supervision and receive a response that is neither shaming nor critical, they may then feel encouraged to undertake further self-scrutiny including, particularly, of what they may consider to be their less desirable attributes as a person and as a therapist.

The process of deliberately seeking out aspects of the self that seem, at first sight, most antipathetic to the task of counselling or psychotherapy requires the supervisee to act with considerable courage and integrity. To find one's own capacity to be vicious, cruel, competitive, exploitative, abusive, devious, or to recognize one's ability to take pleasure in the suffering of others, is unsavoury in itself. For a therapist to face such elements of who they are and accept the potential impact of this upon their relationships with clients will inevitably be deeply alarming for any practitioner who is truly committed to what they are doing. To find a way to allow such aspects of themselves to inform their work with clients requires a very detailed scrutiny of their internal responses to those clients (Page 1999a).

This journey from recognizing aspects of personal shadow to learning how to use this discovery to inform and improve therapeutic interactions is one in which the therapist needs to experience the support and assistance of their supervisor. The supervisor will need to communicate their acceptance of those potentially shameful aspects of their supervisee that are being brought out into the open. As Hahn (2001:272) has asserted: 'Supervisors are responsible for creating an atmosphere within which the experience of shame – and the defenses commonly used to guard against shame – can be identified, acknowledged and understood.'

Of course, supervisors also need to be alongside their supervisees in ensuring that clients are not being harmed. Supervisees can be over-cautious or have unnecessarily rigid boundaries in place and may need to be encouraged to loosen the hold they have on themselves sufficiently to allow internal dialogue between parts of the self to take place.

Take the simple example of a counsellor who has a strong puritanical streak that he has habitually masked, to himself as well as those around him, with an overlay of liberal acceptance. His resultant counsellor persona will be much appreciated by clients, but as a consequence he is likely to shy away from any confrontation that contains the slightest hint of moral judgement. The challenge to this counsellor is to learn how to listen to what the puritanical critic within him might like to say to his clients. His supervisor will need to encourage him to do this in the relative safety of the supervisory session. Then the supervisor can help him to tease out how some of these responses to clients might be transformed into useful questions or challenges. In this way the counsellor will become more rounded in his range of interventions, and also more congruent in the way that he relates to clients.

Supervising counsellors who work with extremes of client experience

An aspect of the supervision of experienced practitioners that has received scant attention in the literature is that of the supervision needs of therapists who find themselves working with extremes of client experience. We should say here that in using the term 'extremes of client experience' we are referring to the client who has experienced deep and abiding trauma through encountering that which lies beyond the normal range of human experience. In particular we are thinking here of clients who are survivors of organized and ritual abuse, mind control and torture (Eckberg 2000; Epstein *et al.* 2011; Miller 2012; Van der Veer 1998; Wilson and Droždek 2004). It is noteworthy that ongoing, career-long supervision for therapists who work with these issues is recommended even in North America, where continuing supervision beyond training is not the norm (Knight 2004b; Turkus, 2013).

We have thought it important to include a discussion of this topic for two reasons. The first is because working with survivors of extreme trauma often falls to therapists who work in voluntary settings and in private practice. Statutory health care services have tight constraints on time and financial resources, and are often unable to offer long-term or open-ended in-depth therapy. Yet survivors of extreme trauma require skilled, consistent and reliable help over an extended period of time in order to heal (Sanderson 2012). Counsellors and psychotherapists working to provide this level of service, with or without organizational support and containment, require supervisors who have the requisite levels of training, experience, skills and stamina (Ryde 2011b).

The second reason for placing this topic here is to emphasize that therapists who take on such work should normally be experienced practitioners and *not* trainees.

This is a point worth stressing, not least because it is an aspect of supervision that relates to the monitoring of both client and therapist welfare. In reality, it sometimes happens that supervisors find themselves supporting inexperienced therapists, who, for whatever reason, find themselves out of their depth with issues brought by their clients. It may be, for instance, that intake and assessment procedures to filter appropriate clients through to trainees are inadequate within the counselling organization where the trainee has found a placement. Or it may be that a trainee's desperation to accumulate the required number of counselling practice hours for their course, or for registration or accreditation, has temporarily overridden their ability to assess realistically what they are competent and capable of taking on. Supervisors of trainee and inexperienced therapists need to be vigorously alert to catching such occurrences in the early stages and support their supervisees to hand back, or refer on, those clients whose difficulties are beyond their current capacity to manage. We would like to emphasize that here we are entering a discussion about the supervision of experienced therapists who are competent to work with extremes of client experience.

In a rare research study into the supervision issues and needs of therapists who work with adult trauma, West (2010) has identified a number of aspects that require consideration, as identified by his participants (a panel of seven supervisors experienced in trauma work). Because of the dearth of research data on this topic, and because we largely agree with his conclusions, we have summarized West's findings in some detail below.

1   It is important for the supervisor to assess, at the contracting stage, supervisees' experience in the field of trauma work. Consequent to this, to ensure that supervisees have undertaken specific trauma training.
2   Similarly it is essential for supervisors supervising trauma therapists to have 'substantial experience, knowledge and training in psychological trauma' (West 2010:422).
3   Both supervisors and supervisees need to demonstrate commitment to continuing professional development in this area. Knowledge about dissociation, physiological experiencing and arousal levels are considered to be key.
4   Supervisors should be alert to the dangers of supervisees focusing too early on traumatic experiences. This was ranked higher as a concern than the danger of supervisees avoiding traumatic material (although this was also considered important).
5   Supervisors agreed about the importance of supervisees developing resilience and the ability to manage their own fears (for instance holding clear boundaries and being able to witness clients' experience without being overwhelmed by it).
6   Supervisors considered it essential to be alert to counter-transference reactions in supervisees, typified by over- or under-involvement.
7   The supervisor's awareness of parallel process is important – this may, for instance, alert them to the danger of vicarious traumatization of the supervisee.

8 The need for supervisors to keep a keen eye on organizational factors, for example the level of understanding of trauma within the organization and what expectations are put upon therapists working with these issues. (Examples given included: restraints on time-limited work; levels of training and experience required of therapists; taking proper account of self-care issues, including providing supervision of a sufficient quality; and ensuring that supervisees are working within their limits of competency.)

9 Supervisors need to be alert to where supervisees' personal histories may impact upon or overlap with the trauma work they are undertaking.

10 Supervisors need to pay attention to issues of balance, for instance where the supervisee appears to require a great deal of restorative supervision, or educative input, at the expense of other supervisory tasks or of attention given to other clients within their case-load.

11 Some supervisors within the study thought that ethical issues arose more often in trauma work and demanded a capacity for quick thinking.

12 A number of participants felt that supervisors might need specific skills of crisis intervention and debriefing.

While this list is extremely useful in identifying key topics that may need a focus in the supervision of trauma work it is also helpful, by inference, in highlighting the qualities and skills required of trauma therapists and their supervisors.

Impact of trauma work on the therapist

Therapists whose work brings them into contact with extremes of client experience will undoubtedly be extremely shaken by what they hear and witness, as this may be harrowing in the extreme. Ben-Shahar (2012:12) has written about the 'highly contagious' aspects of trauma that can affect the 'highly attuned and affectively-resonant therapist'. Supervision plays a key role here in providing a safe, secure and contained place in which therapists can debrief and even heal from this experience. It has an essential role to play in preventing or minimizing risks to the practitioner of vicarious traumatization and burnout (Barrington and Shakespeare-Finch 2013; Ellis 2010; Forester 2007; Knight 2004b; Tehrani 2007). Ryde (2011b:138) has articulated clearly the vital function supervision plays in trauma therapy when she writes: 'If hopelessness is to be borne and unbearable feeling held, then we cannot provide that for ourselves as a narcissistically heroic act.'

In reflecting on the importance of supportive supervision for his work with a client who had been ritually abused, Svensson (Sinason and Svensson 1994) identified the key elements provided by supervision as security and the need not to feel defensive. He gives this image to describe his experience of supervision:

It was like being a deep-sea diver but feeling secure that the person on the surface boat [his supervisor] would stay there supporting me with oxygen. I also knew that the woman in the boat would study with interest anything I brought up from such depths as well as be concerned for my physical and mental well-being.

(Sinason and Svensson 1994:20)

This image gives a picture of what supervision should ideally provide for supervisees involved in such work. Unfortunately, the reality is sometimes very different as there are a number of pitfalls that supervisor and supervisee may encounter.

One particular danger that arises where supervisors work with therapists who deal with extremes of client experience is that of avoidance. It is, of course, hard for both supervisor and supervisee to contemplate that which is beyond the normal range of the experience of a human being – even when contemplation is once (the therapist) or twice (the supervisor) removed and the experience itself belongs to the client. Add to this the fact that the more extreme the experience, the more likely it is that the client may need to re-visit, rather than merely report, what has happened to them in order to work through and integrate the experience. No wonder then that supervisor and supervisee may wish to protect themselves and each other from the raw pain of reviving such experience, even whilst they are also intent on helping the client.

Attempts at protecting the self and others, particularly when not fully in awareness, may translate into supervisor and supervisee getting hung up on questions such as: 'Is the client telling the truth?', or 'What do we do about this?' Questions such as these access a thinking rather than a feeling mode. As such they can take supervisor and supervisee away from the acute pain and terror of the client's original experience, and the impact on the therapist of hearing about this, and thus provide some refuge in intellectual discussion (Beckerman 2003). Although this might give temporary relief it is also a distancing strategy that may mirror the client's terror of staying with feelings and memories, perhaps expressed by questions to their therapist like 'What I'm remembering can't be true – can it?', or 'Do you think I'm mad?'

Carroll (2011:20) has stressed the importance of beginning with feelings in supervision and reaching understanding through emotion: 'Acknowledging the emotional impact first of all, allowing it to be felt and exist in safe supervision, begins the journey of understanding what is happening'. This is particularly important in supervision of trauma work, as there is a parallel here. The survivor of extreme trauma is likely to gain cognitive understanding of their experience only through and after the processing of raw emotional and bodily sensations that may first emerge as trauma flashbacks.

The therapist's capacity to 'hurt [the client's] pain' (Ben-Shahar 2012:16) may become the bridge through which the client is able to re-connect at an emotional level with his or her own trauma and thereby begin to heal. In supervision, the therapist may then need their own healing relationship, provided by the supervisor and the safe space that supervision provides. Here is an example to illustrate this point. One of us had the experience on several occasions in supervision of becoming ice-cold when talking about a particular client who had suffered ritual abuse, even to the degree of noticeably shivering, though the room was very warm. Gradually, as the client's dissociated experience of extreme trauma began to unfold and to be understood, the supervisor and supervisee were able to grasp why telling her 'chilling' story had such a physical effect on the therapist.

Ryde (2011b) has underscored the importance, in trauma work, of having a supervisor who understands and respects the supervisee and their work, and who can therefore 'remain thoughtful and non-reactive in the face of the extent of the difficulties inherent in the work' (p. 130). In a similar vein Forester (2007:126) has emphasized that the process of supervision of trauma work requires 'the ability to refrain from action, to remain curious, and to dwell with and endure experience rather than reacting'. Part of enduring the experience is likely to include understanding and considering the therapist's counter-transference to the client's material, which may well take a somatic form.

Somatic counter-transference is a common experience for the therapist in trauma work and has been defined as 'the effect on the therapist's body of the patient and the patient's material' (Forester 2007:129). The supervisee is likely to require their supervisor's help in maintaining a reflective capacity when experiencing their own disturbing counter-transference reactions. In relation to the 'chilling' example just given it was reassuring and grounding for the therapist to have her supervisor say: 'The temperature in the room has not changed but I think you are letting me know how frightening this is for your client and what it feels like for you to carry the weight of what she is disclosing.'

It is now well understood that survivors of extreme trauma may experience a range of dissociative phenomena that make piecing together a coherent account of their trauma history exceedingly difficult (Hunter 2004; Miller 2012; Rothschild 2000; Sinason 2002; Van der Hart et al. 2006). The therapist may experience a parallel dissociative process. Thus in discussing the supervision needs of trauma therapists, Richardson (2009:31) has observed that 'trauma is deskilling in nature because it can put parts of our brain out of action and so reduce our reflective capacity'. Supervision is key in helping to re-activate the trauma therapist's capacity to reflect on their experience of the work with the client.

In respect of this capacity to reflect on experience, Noelle (2003) has pointed out the benefits of the discipline of self-reporting (as opposed to playing recordings or reading from prepared notes) in supervision. She observes that 'creating a narrative in supervision helps me to synthesize and hold the interchange, both within the session and as part of a continuity from one therapy session to the next' (p. 131). A capacity for forming a coherent narrative from dissociative fragments (as experienced by the client and/or therapist) is paramount in the supervision of trauma work. Noelle also discusses the dynamic informational value of the observed experience of both supervisor and supervisee (of their own and each other's reactions) as the self-reporting takes place. This is illustrated in the example given above, where supervisor and supervisee were able together to connect the therapist's 'chilling' somatic counter-transference to the client's experience.

We discuss these phenomena further in Chapter 13, where we focus on relational and embodied supervision.

One particular form of parallel process that can occur for the therapist trying to make sense of their experience of a client's trauma narrative is to become incoherent or to feel struck dumb in supervision (Etherington 2009; Richardson 2009). The supervisee may find him or herself saying 'There is so much and I don't know where to start', or 'This feels huge and I don't know how to talk about it', or even 'I keep getting lost and losing my thread'. When this occurs it is important for the supervisor to trust the supervisee's process as a reflection of their work with the client and not to intervene as if the supervisee is unprepared, inarticulate or avoidant. Even where it is difficult for the supervisee to hold a focus, the supervisor can help to provide this, for instance by asking 'What do you need from me right now?'

In writing about the supportive supervision of workers who are involved with clients who have suffered ritual abuse, Youngson (1994:300) has emphasized that the supervisor who is too intent on finding solutions to help the worker 'feel better' will not provide the quality of listening needed by the worker in order for them to feel heard and helped:

> My own experience of both receiving and giving support is that the simple but by no means easy task of the supporter is to listen; to encourage the worker to talk more; to share more of his/her feelings; to empathically enter the world of the worker, as the worker has empathically entered the world of the client. This 'mirroring' is profoundly supportive, and the end result is a worker who has gained an integrated sense of self, and has been freed to see again, with clarity, the professional and personal tasks.

Knight (2004b) also emphasizes the importance of the supervisor entering the emotional world of the supervisee in a way that mirrors the therapist's capacity to be with the client on a feelings level. She recommends that supervisors of trauma therapists routinely conduct an 'affective check in' (2004b:96) with their supervisees as a way of eliciting, normalizing and validating the range of feelings that this work is likely to evoke.

Therapists and their supervisors are particularly prone to listen poorly and to disbelieve, or question, the truth of disclosures that they find unpalatable where what is disclosed proves uncomfortably dissonant with their own personal world-view or theoretical constructs (Orr 1999). This often happens in relation to the extreme abuse of children. There have been times when, as therapists and supervisors, we haven't *wanted* to believe what we are hearing from clients and supervisees and have found ourselves thinking 'I don't want this to be true, it is too horrific', but this is very different from *not* believing. Perhaps those who have difficulty accepting that abominations happen to babies and children degrade this natural reflex action of not *wanting* to know to one of *not* knowing – and hence not believing. Casement (1994:25) makes the telling observation that 'colleagues are more likely to criticise the therapist than be willing to believe what they themselves have not yet encountered, or dare to consider with an equally open mind'.

Where disbelief runs rife in such circumstances it can have unsettling consequences for the supervisee, as one of us experienced on the following occasion:

> I was once in the extremely uncomfortable position of unreservedly believing a client's disclosures of extreme childhood abuse while my supervisor, her supervisor, the consultant psychiatrist and the community psychiatric nurse (i.e. all the significant professional others involved in the case) were expressing disbelief in the client's story.
>
> At the time I felt deeply distressed, not only by my sense that the client had in effect been 'abandoned by disbelief' at the point where he had finally summoned the courage to tell his story, but also by what I myself experienced as abandonment by my professional colleagues as I continued to fight for the client from what felt like a very frightening and isolated position. I do not think it is without relevance that one of these professionals said to me: 'This is the worst case of abuse I have ever heard of', shortly before questioning the client's truthfulness and that another, with growing awareness of her need to shield herself, eventually conceded that perhaps she had been protecting herself in not believing the client because, as a mother herself, she did not want to know that such things could be done to a child.

In discussing how therapists may respond to disclosures of extreme child abuse, Casement (1994:23–4) has observed that the courage to believe 'means facing such degrees of deception and corruption of young children that one would no longer know what to believe. It is much less disorienting to think that these accounts could not be true.' In a situation such as this, not only does the therapist need the courage to believe if he or she is to hope ever to release the client from the isolation and torment that such extreme abuse can create, but so too does the supervisor. The supervisee needs to be held securely in the knowledge that their supervisor can tolerate the horror of the client's story with them without deflecting it through doubt, disbelief or rationalization.

In our own experience we have sometimes found ourselves wanting to apologize for bringing such material to supervision, or even checking out whether our supervisor can bear to hear it. We have learnt to check these impulses to spare the supervisor, as we know that in so doing we are also sparing ourselves. There is a version of the old adage at work here: 'If I don't let myself think or talk about it, it might go away.' This may be precisely the *modus operandi* by which the client has been living up to the time they entered therapy – and of course the experience has not gone away for them.

Supervisees have a duty to the client and a duty to care for themselves in bringing such material to supervision. It is precisely because they have had to feel *with* their clients in order to relieve them of some of the impact of their primary trauma that therapists need to take their secondary trauma to supervision, where they may need their supervisor to feel the impact that the client's story has had on them. Supervision here will sometimes serve the purpose of providing a sanctuary for the therapist and, by extension, for the client too. It can even be useful for the client who is fearful of overloading or contaminating their therapist with their disclosures to know that the therapist has a supervisor to whom they can go, in confidence, to offload their feelings. In this respect Perry (2003:195) has described the containing function of supervision in trauma work using the image of 'a series of permeable concentric circles rippling out from the patient, and containing all participants'.

How does the supervisor deal with their supervisee's secondary trauma and what, in effect, may then become their own tertiary trauma? It can be very difficult for the supervisor to stay in touch with the client when they are so aware of the impact the work is having on the therapist. The supervisor's attention and concern will naturally switch to the distress they are witnessing in their supervisee. A key and demanding task for both at this juncture is to help the supervisee manage what Youngson (1994:299) has termed 'the continual tension and balance between professional response and emotional reaction'. It is essential that this balance be managed well so that the supervisee is helped, as Youngson states, 'to separate personal reaction from the requirements of objective, professional evaluation and action' (p. 300).

The Cyclical Model of supervision can be useful here as an orientating device that enables the supervisor to think about task and process as well as alleviation of the supervisee's discomfort. In supporting therapists who work with extremes of client experience the task for the supervisor is 'frequently concerned with enabling the counsellor to remain buoyant and clear thinking in the midst of much turbulence' (Wosket 1999:215). The Cyclical Model, and more particularly the Space stage, can become a container for the chaos and distress of the client's story (Wosket and Page 2001).

An important quality of containment that the supervisor can provide is described by Hughes and Pengelly (1997:178) as 'the capacity to apply understanding to anxiety-laden experiences, in order to give them shape and meaning'. This understanding can help to put words to a situation, dilemma or dynamic and help 'prevent the build up of "nameless dread"', which could either paralyse the supervisee or 'catapult him into action as a means of avoidance' (Hughes and Pengelly 1997:178). The ability of the supervisor to tolerate uncertainty, chaos and confusion while striving for understanding is of paramount importance in helping the supervisee:

> To take responsibility for seeking meaning may challenge the supervisee to face the anxiety of not knowing. It is often difficult for a supervisor to believe that the supervisee may be contained just by their capacity to name the problem and struggle alongside him to find meaning while acknowledging that she does not yet know.
>
> (Hughes and Pengelly 1997:178)

Richardson (2009) has defined supervision, using an attachment paradigm, as 'a professional careseeking and caregiving relationship' that 'aims to optimise professional care of the client' (pp. 28–9). In this way supervision can be thought of as seeking to provide a secure base for the therapist (Fitch *et al*. 2010; Foster *et al*. 2007; Renfro-Michel and Sheperis 2009; Riggs and Bretz 2006). Looked at from this perspective, the key to effective supervision lies in the ability of both supervisor and supervisee to bear the weight of the emotional impact of the client's experience together within a mutually warm and supportive relationship. On occasion this will mean that both supervisor and supervisee will be distressed and may even cry together. This is not necessarily the same thing as a lack of containment. In this instance the supervisor's vulnerability in also being moved by the client's story will provide affirmation for the supervisee (Wosket and Page 2001). Containment, debriefing and affirmation, as discussed in Chapter 6, are key aspects of working within the supervision space.

Holding on to the sense of space is always helpful when dealing with extremes of client experience. As we have argued, the concept of exploratory space is useful in enabling supervisor and supervisee to not get too hung up on the necessity of determining the truth or otherwise of the client's story, or to think about immediate solutions. The Space stage of the model is there to provide containment for creative uncertainty, to give room for considering possibilities – not necessarily to deliver clarity, direction or resolution, although these will sometimes emerge. Richardson (2009:29) captures the balance between the thinking and experiencing components necessary in the supervision of trauma work when she writes:

> A key issue for both supervisor and supervisee is how to be a partner in thought to unbearable states of mind and remain an emotionally responsive witness to that which the client may have had to disown, without loss of coherence, loss of empathy or getting caught up in re-enactments.

In the supervision space we can take an 'as if' perspective that releases us from the need to know. Instead of asking 'Do you believe the client?', the supervisor who takes an 'as if' perspective is more likely to make interventions such as: 'What is it like for you to hear the client's story?', or 'If we consider that your client may be telling you what really happened, what does she need from you right now?', or even, 'How can I help you to bear the weight of knowing that this may have happened to your client?'

Because interventions such as these derive from the supervisor's intention to help the supervisee work more effectively with the client, they are enabling, supportive and facilitating. While questions such as: 'Do you think your client is telling you the truth?' or 'Can this really have happened?' may occasionally need to be asked if there are compelling reasons to doubt the client's reality, they do not provide a way of loosening or exploring the experience in supervision. Even when the question begs to be asked, it is incumbent on the supervisor to consider a way of asking that does not undermine the supervisee or the work they are doing. It is more respectful and enabling for the supervisor to pose the question as an idea that may have occurred to the therapist. For instance: 'I'm wondering if you have ever doubted the client's story.' An intervention phrased in this way is more likely to promote reflection and consideration of alternative perspectives than a closed question that may merely stimulate the supervisee to respond from a defensive place of self- or client protection.

In providing what the supervisee needs from the client in order to have both the capacity and the courage to work with clients with extreme trauma histories, the supervisor may have to contain a number of their own responses. In addition to the tendency not to want to believe the unbelievable or unimaginable (Epstein *et al.* 2011; Miller 2012), the supervisor may also need to contain their anxiety about witnessing great distress (both the client's and the supervisee's) and not knowing where the process of therapy will lead. We know of several occasions where a supervisor has peremptorily terminated a supervision relationship and were deeply shocked to hear of one case where the supervisor walked out of the room mid-supervision session. We would understand this as a situation where the supervisor was unwilling, unable or insufficiently skilled to deal with the extreme client trauma brought to supervision by the supervisee.

This kind of reaction can be thought of as a failure of the secure careseeking/caregiving function of supervision and, according to Richardson (2009), can lead to defensive reactions and responses such as 'advice to overwrought supervisees to refer the client on when there is no other suitable therapist available' or 'the impulse to avoid or rescue rather than reflect' (p. 31). She suggests that managing fear is an unavoidable component of working with extreme trauma and can generate 'problematic counter-transference responses' (2009:31) such as prematurely terminating therapy that is judged too difficult to proceed with.

As well as remaining alert to the danger of acting out an abandonment dynamic as a result of their anxiety, the supervisor, conversely, may need to resist impulses to take over and become excessively directive with the supervisee. Better responses from the supervisor are: to demonstrate confidence and belief in their supervisee; to seek out specialist supervision of supervision for the case; to be willing to undertake further specific training and knowledge acquisition (Etherington 2009); or to make a considered referral to another supervisor when they feel the work is beyond their level of competence. The supervisor will need to balance their concern for the client's welfare with enough trust in the supervisee to allow that they are likely to know best how to work with the client. The therapist will then be able to draw strength and energy from a supportive and resilient supervisor with which to top up their own. This, in turn, will enable the therapist to extend their capacity to help the client in ways that they might not be able to manage on their own, for instance by stretching their own courage, compassion and commitment beyond normal limits.

A further important container for therapists who work with extremes of client experience is supervision for the supervisor. The importance of supervision of supervision is paramount wherever supervisor and supervisee are encountering this kind of work. Firstly, this is important, as Ryde (2011b) has pointed out, due to the complexities of parallel processes that may embroil both supervisee and supervisor and which can lead to the supervisor unwittingly colluding with the supervisee that, for instance, the client's predicament merits unusual or exceptional boundary management. Secondly, due to the horrifying nature of the client material, the shock waves of extreme trauma may need to reverberate through a number of holding structures, each of which partially diminishes the impact of the after shocks as they settle and die away. If each container is sufficiently strong and resilient it will absorb a good percentage of the shock so that less will need to be passed to the next person in the chain. The supervisor's supervisor becomes one such important bracing device that needs to be in place to act as a buffer for the impact that the client's material will have made on both therapist and supervisor. If the shock is not absorbed and contained, it will reverberate back along the chain to the client with the subsequent danger that the client is further traumatized – for instance by the supervisor's or the supervisee's disbelief. More about the supervision of supervision is said in later chapters.

Chapter 13

Deepening supervision practice

Throughout the preceding chapters we have emphasized that supervision is a collaborative, relational process that benefits from structures and frameworks to shape and guide the work. When a safe container for the supervision process is in place both supervisor and supervisee can risk using more of themselves and being open to working in immediate and creative ways with what is emerging. In this chapter we will link our discussion to some relatively new ways of working as depicted in recent supervision literature. In terms of the Cyclical Model the ideas and examples given here are particularly pertinent to working within the supervision space. We will move in and out of narrating our own experience – often telling this in the first person as seems congruent with our theme. We shall explore ways of working that can enliven, deepen and enrich the encounter between supervisor and supervisee so that it may become a transformative experience for both (Carroll 2009, 2010; Churchill 2013; Frawley-O'Dea and Sarnat 2001; Shohet 2011b; Weld 2012).

As Weld has identified, liberating the transformative potential of supervision involves something of a paradox in that it entails deliberate employment of unexpected interventions by the supervisor – something 'a bit left field' (2012:44).

> It is when as supervisors we offer or bring in an observation that is not expected but still relevant, that we can literally 'interrupt' a way of thinking or being for the supervisee and in this potentially spark a moment of transformative change.
>
> (Weld 2012:42)

Here is an example from our own practice to illustrate this point. Recently one of us carried out a review with a supervisee. A key part of her feedback was that something she particularly liked about the supervision was that she often felt 'on the edge of my seat' because, in her words, 'I never know what you're going to say next'. She found this stimulating and contrasted this with a previous experience of supervision where she always felt as if she knew what the supervisor would say next, even from very early on in their work together. This had made the supervision seem predictable and formulaic, and the supervisee commented that she felt that 'I could have been alone in the room supervising myself' because 'I knew what he would say before he said it'.

This supervisee said she had come to realize that she valued having a supervisor who was experienced in a number of therapeutic approaches and had an integrative model of supervision. She felt that her experience with her previous supervisor had been limited by the fact that he worked only from his core therapeutic approach as both a counsellor and supervisor. The supervisee commented: 'In our supervision I feel you always have a different way of looking at things. That sometimes takes me by surprise but it means we are avoiding the danger of imposing a narrow view on the client and making her fit our theory'. Through this supervisee's comments we begin to see the value of the unexpected in supervision – a theme we will turn to next.

Encountering the mysterious and the unexpected in supervision

> A while ago I was kicked by one of my supervisees. This was certainly unexpected and seemed entirely accidental at the time it happened. I had gone downstairs to collect him from the waiting room in the building where I was working and as I led the way back upstairs to my room he unintentionally kicked the back of my leg as he followed closely behind. 'It's a good job you are not a psychodynamic supervisor', he quipped, 'or God knows what you would have made of that!' He explained later that he had felt an urgent need to get to me to debrief what had been happening in his work setting since we last met. He saw the unintentional kick as expressing this impulse – as he put it: 'I could hardly wait to get up the stairs and let it all out.'

This illustrates the point that there is usually some meaning to the unexpected when it happens in supervision, even where the event itself appears random or co-incidental.

As well as arising from our encounters with our supervisees, our learning about the unexpected in supervision has also come from our involvement in training therapists to become supervisors. This training has an experiential emphasis – participants on our workshops and courses spend a good amount of time practising being supervisors and honing their skills and awareness in this role. At the end of one recent course students were asked to give feedback on their experience of the training. A number of these supervisors-in-the-making talked about how *they* had encountered the unexpected. A particular theme for these students was the unexpected impact that supervision training had had on their practice of *therapy*. Here are some of the things they said during the course review in response to the following prompt:

Something I experienced on the course that was unexpected was . . .

- I've learnt that it is OK to be affected at a deep and emotional level by my clients.
- I've gained a richer, more powerful way of working as a therapist.
- I now stay much more with a focus on the process of what is happening between me and my clients, rather than just getting stories.
- I've learnt it's OK to really care about my clients.
- It has been like a re-birth of myself as a therapist.
- I didn't expect to find myself going back into therapy.
- I don't have to feel constrained to being a certain kind of practitioner – I have the freedom to be creative, flexible and playful.
- This experience has given me back my faith in the profession of therapy.
- The emotional turmoil I experienced, which highlighted the need for me to look at self-care and my support systems.
- I've learnt to see supervision as a completion of the therapy circle. I've experienced the power, strength and energy in the whole field, which is greater and more dynamic than just the energy between the therapist and client.

Something of particular interest in these comments is their expansive nature. These participants are saying in different ways that learning about supervision generates freedom, passion and creativity, and impacts upon the therapist (not always in pain-free ways) as well as upon the therapy. The final comment in the list given above highlights the potential that supervision holds to affect the whole field of energy in which the therapy takes place, including transformative energy for the therapist.

The unexpected has a tendency to occur in supervision (and therapy) through synchronicity, a term first coined by Jung ([1960]1969) and used here to denote events that are meaningfully connected within this field of energy but not in any directly causal way. An example of synchronicity is the phenomenon familiar to many therapists where the client appears to 'pop up' unexpectedly (usually in some symbolic or indirect way – though occasionally in a more direct way) in the supervision session. This can happen through the supervisee making a 'me but not me' remark or gesture that is more characteristic of the client they are talking about than of themselves (Wosket 2009). Or it may be that the client on whom the supervisee is trying to focus keeps getting 'pushed out' by another client who repeatedly intrudes into the supervisee's (or supervisor's) awareness and seems to clamour for attention. The example of synchronicity that follows is one where the client popped up in a more literal way.

> One of us was working towards her death with a client who had a terminal illness. Our journey together was, at different times, sad, painful, terrifying, inspiring, hilarious, despairing, uplifting and everything else imaginable. The

central task for me as her therapist was to do my best to stay alongside her while she tried to work out how to die.

Perhaps not surprisingly there were elements of the mysterious and unexpected in the work with this client. On one occasion she unknowingly found a way of connecting with me in a startling and powerful way in supervision. One evening I was sitting with my supervisor and talking about my feelings for my client as she was moving towards her death. I was crying and saying to my supervisor 'I need to do this here. I can do some crying with my client when she can cry but this is really hard for her and it can't happen very much yet. I am scared she will withdraw as her death approaches and decide she has to do this final ending on her own. She never does endings and finds asking for, or expecting, support almost impossible.' Just then my mobile phone buzzed audibly. I apologized and switched it off.

After the supervision session I listened to the message that had been left on my mobile at that precise moment in supervision. It was the client I had just then been discussing, distressed and in tears, asking if I could phone her. What to me seemed unexpected and extraordinary about this was that, firstly, I *never* leave my phone on in supervision. It is the only time in over 25 years of going for supervision that I have accidentally done this. Secondly, my client had *never* left an emotional message for me before. Indeed in the several years we had been working together she had only left me a message once or twice when she had needed to change or cancel an appointment. Also this was a Monday evening – a day she knew I did not work as a therapist and at a time in the evening when she knew I would not normally have my work mobile phone switched on. She had never done this before and it never happened again. She would not have known that I was at supervision at that time and on that evening. Yet by some strange synchronicity she was crying and reaching out for support at the exact same moment that I, in tears myself, was telling my supervisor she found these two things almost impossible to do.

Interestingly at our next therapy session my client, unprompted, asked me if I had told my supervisor how ill she was and I said 'yes'. She then disclosed her fear that my supervisor would say to me that she was 'not worth bothering with now' and would tell me I should 'ditch' her. It is almost as if her telephone call was unwittingly timed to signal and hopefully avert this danger. As if the act of phoning and leaving the message at that precise moment expressed both her desire and her fear – 'I don't want to be abandoned and I need both of you to know how frightened and desperate I am' – something she could never say directly and yet which she conveyed very powerfully to me through her message, its timing and the context in which it occurred.

A partial explanation of this kind of phenomenon is proffered by Frawley-O'Dea and Sarnat (2001:69) when, in writing from a psychodynamic perspective, they describe the supervisory relationship as comprising 'a complicated matrix of mutually influential relational configurations'. They suggest that when supervision is viewed in this way as a mutual influence process, 'the interpersonal maneuvers and internalized relational worlds of the three participant observers [client, therapist and supervisor] intersect to define what is seen and heard, and said and done, by whom and about whom' (2001:69). Here is another occasion where one of us experienced this 'intersection' of the client 'speaking up' in supervision.

My supervisee, Tara, had been discussing with me a concern about her client, Rob, becoming dependent on her. Rob had been expressing affectionate and admiring feelings towards his therapist over a number of sessions and in their last meeting had asked for a hug at the end of the session. Tara had agreed to this, partly because she couldn't find a way of refusing without feeling this would be devastating for Rob.

I asked her how she had experienced the hug. Tara said that she felt quite ashamed to tell me that, while on the one hand it had felt 'OK' and the right thing to do at the time, on the other hand she had noticed her body tensing and had found herself thinking 'I hope I don't catch that sickness bug' [Rob had mentioned that his daughter was unwell and off school with a winter vomiting virus]. I suggested that rather than merely feeling ashamed about the thought we could explore it as a welcome signal of something that might need attention.

When I said this Tara suddenly remembered that in the previous session the client had hinted for the first time that his relationship with his mother during childhood had been inappropriately sexualized. My supervisee had forgotten to come back to this in her last session with Rob, just as she had forgotten it in the hour we had just spent together trying to understand what the client was conveying in declaring his feelings towards his counsellor and asking for the hug.

Tara was startled by this realization and in remembering the forgotten sexual material she made sense of why she had experienced the reluctance to hug her client (expressed by her fear of catching the bug). It helped her to understand how she may have been trying to hold the balance between being open to Rob's feelings and impulses while holding a boundary so that the relationship did not become sexualized in any way. The way my supervisee described what happened at this point in the supervision was: 'It was as if the client spoke up *here* and said "don't forget what I told you!"'.

By its very nature we cannot anticipate or consciously induce the appearance of the mysterious and unexpected in supervision. However, we *can* ready ourselves for its appearance by adopting a stance of openness and acceptance to whatever comes. Mysterious and unexpected happenings provide an opening to another dimension of learning and often convey an accurate sense of what requires attention. Supervision can then become the 'catalyst that transforms experience into useable learning' (De Stefano *et al.* 2007:43). This is all about therapist and supervisor listening and being receptive – not just with the ears and eyes, but with intuition and the body too.

Developing the use of self in supervision

Like a number of writers on this topic, we consider therapy and supervision to be reciprocal processes in which therapist and supervisor are changed by their encounters with their clients and supervisees as well as vice versa (Kottler and Carlson 2005; Wilmot 2011). If this is so, then it follows that therapists need space in supervision to be able to explore the impact of these changes on the self.

So while taking care not to become therapists to their supervisees, supervisors do need to give space, time, attention and care to the therapist's self – particularly to the vulnerable and wounded parts of self. These are precisely the parts to which our clients can become unconsciously attuned and astute at activating (Lambers 2006; Wosket 2009). If personal material, particularly that which is difficult for the supervisee, can be allowed to surface in supervision it can be named and given emotional expression. Through the reflective process of supervision therapists can become freer to stand back and consider how their own issues are interwoven with and yet can be separated out from the client's (Knight 2012). At best they learn how their own emotional hurts can be transformed into empathic responses that have the potential to enrich their relationships with clients (Wosket 1999).

While supervision is not therapy it can, on occasion, undoubtedly be therapeutic. Wilmot (2011:73) considers that the therapeutic potential of supervision is liberated through the 'deep listening' that constitutes the core of the art of supervising. Smith-Pickard (2009:30) agrees that it is the quality of listening between supervisor and supervisee that makes the experience transformative:

> In supervision . . . I began to meet myself as a therapist in ways that had not been possible previously . . . In this atmosphere of exploration, I was listening to myself speak and meeting myself at the same time, whilst observing my supervisor respond to my words in a sort of mutual reciprocity.

In what Smith-Pickard terms 'this mutual reciprocity of encounter' he suggests that 'we become something or someone we never could have become by ourselves' (2009:31). Here is an example from our own practice of this process happening for a supervisee.

> The supervisee, Amelie, was discussing in supervision her annoyance and exasperation at the high frequency of cancelled sessions and extended breaks between sessions requested by some clients. On the face of it there were

practical reasons for this: Christmas holidays had intervened; a number of clients were taking time out from their counselling for financial or work reasons. However, Amelie began to question why this seemed to happen to her on a regular basis and whether her contracting and case management needed thinking about. Helped by a few pertinent questions and prompts from her supervisor Amelie began to realize that her own past experience of susceptibility to illness was impacting unhelpfully on how she conducted her practice.

For a number of years previously Amelie had experienced an ongoing debilitating illness that could flair up unexpectedly and mean that she had to stop working at short notice and for varying periods. In discussing this in supervision she became aware that, though she was no longer ill, this experience continued to shape her practice of counselling in several ways. For instance, rather than booking in a number of sessions in advance with clients she booked sessions week by week. In supervision Amelie realized that this was because she still did not feel confident about her capacity to be available long term. As a result clients did not come to expect, or experience, counselling as providing a predictable and regular commitment over a number of weeks or months. This may have contributed to the idea, for some clients, that counselling was something to dip in and out of and to be re-negotiated on a weekly basis.

Amelie also began to realize that she tended to be over-placatory with clients when they cancelled sessions or opted to take time out from counselling. She was quick to assure them that it was fine to do so, while inwardly feeling disappointed or exasperated. She began to see that this was also linked to her previous experience of illness – if she was very understanding about her clients' non-attendance, perhaps it was more likely that they would be the same with her if she had to cancel sessions at short notice due to health issues. In exploring this in supervision it occurred to Amelie that she might make changes that signified to clients that she anticipated their full commitment to the process in the same way that she now felt able herself to offer complete commitment to them.

This was a supervision session in which the supervisee challenged herself and took the initiative and responsibility for scrutinizing her work in this way. The supervisor provided the relationship and the space in which the supervisee could do this for herself and needed to do little else.

On reviewing the session together, Amelie commented that her supervisor had said two things that were very helpful. The first was 'I do not think about you as an unwell person' and the second was 'I'm wondering if you can now take the risk of being well?' Amelie experienced these interventions as both challenging and supportive, and expressed her determination to reflect further on changes she could make for herself and her practice following the insights gained. Supervision has been described as 'an intimate act of creation' (Frizell 2012:293) and we might think of this session as a transformative one for the supervisee, in which she began, with the help of her supervisor, to create a new self-narrative that included being a well rather than a not-well person.

The act of exploring the various ways that client material may trigger or overlap with the therapist's own issues can release valuable energy for the therapeutic task. Here are some of the ways in which supervision can become a catalyst that helps to release this energy:

- Alerting the supervisee to aspects of self-care that may need attention (for instance where the supervisee realizes that her own stress levels are similar to those of the client and may need addressing).
- Enabling the clearing of blocks to the supervisee's awareness (for example where client issues that mirror his own have been too painful for the therapist to allow into conscious awareness until supervision provides a safe enough space for this to happen).
- Alerting the supervisee to an impulse originating in herself that may be interfering with the client work. (This might reveal itself, for example, through over-identification with the client or an urge to rescue.)
- Helping the supervisee learn about their shadow side (Page 1999a) – both its dysfunctional and functional aspects (for instance, where the client evokes a voyeuristic response in the therapist about which she feels ashamed. Through supervision the therapist becomes aware that the client provides her with 'juicy titbits' because she fears her therapist will lose interest in her).
- Alerting supervisor and supervisee to parallel processes and their origins (for example, where the supervisor picks up that the supervisee's congruence with the client is faltering. Offering this awareness back to the supervisee helps him to realize that his own need to be liked has been re-activated by the client's approval-seeking behaviours).
- Helping to highlight unresolved issues on which the supervisee may need to do further work (for instance, where the supervisee suddenly finds herself saying in supervision 'I always seem to have problems with these kinds of women don't I?').
- Providing a safe space where the supervisee can explore having had a similar experience to the client and, through this, fine-tuning their understanding of the client's experience and deepening their empathy. (An example is where the therapist has experienced bullying in the past and through exploring this in supervision can better understand why the client finds it difficult to stand up for himself in an abusive relationship.)
- Providing a healing or transformative experience for the supervisee as well as (hopefully) for the client. (An example here would be where a supervisee is working with the bereaved mother of a teenage daughter who has ended her life through reckless behaviour. In supervision the therapist weeps as he

acknowledges the pain he may have caused his own mother through his own irresponsible and selfish acts as a teenager.)

Supervision issues such as these rarely sit forward in a supervisee's conscious awareness. Often they require a relational encounter between supervisor and supervisee to bring them to light. To a large degree this is made possible through the supervisor's capacity to pay close attention to what is going on in themselves, including tracking what is happening in their body and using this awareness to the benefit of the supervision.

Embodied relational supervision

In what we have written so far in this volume it will have become apparent that working with and through the supervisory relationship, together with paying attention to all levels of experience in a supervisory session, is central to our approach. In this section we will look at a more conscious and intentional way of working with relational and embodied processes as a way of deepening the encounter between supervisor and supervisee (and through a parallel process between therapist and client). We will consider both of these aspects of working within the supervision space here because, as we shall see, they are closely linked. In this respect and as Shaw (2003:142) has observed 'the supervisory relationship, like all other therapeutic relationships, is embodied'. Frizell (2012:295), meanwhile, makes the obvious but frequently neglected point that 'the supervisory relationship comprises the meeting of bodies, as well as minds, in a room'.

A number of leading figures in the field have highlighted the importance of the relational component of supervision. In her (2006) review of conceptual and empirical studies of supervision from 1999 to 2004, Borders concluded that the 'absolute critical role of the supervisory relationship resonates throughout the literature' (p. 101), while Borders and Brown (2005:67) have voiced the opinion that 'the supervisory relationship is the heart and soul of the supervision experience'. Nelson *et al.* (2001:407) have commented on the 'critical importance' of the supervision relationship in the training and development of psychotherapists. Based on 30 years of experience in the field, the veteran supervision researcher, trainer and practitioner Michael Ellis (2010:106) has argued, that 'The notion that supervision is all about the right techniques and using the right theory is a myth. Good supervision is about the relationship, not the specific theory or techniques used in supervision.' After several decades of conducting supervision research, Ladany concluded that 'If nothing else . . . I recommend that supervisors attend to the development of a strong supervisory alliance using and generalizing their psychotherapy skills' (2004:5).

Turning to empirical research, we find that in their study of evaluation in supervision, Zarbock and colleagues (2009) discovered that the relationship dimension contributed most to overall satisfaction with supervision for both supervisees (n = 90) and supervisors (n = 37). Meanwhile Renfro-Michel and

Sheperis's (2009) research into the relationship between a supervisee's attachment style and their perceived bond with their supervisor established that the working alliance is as important for qualified and mature supervisees as it is for trainees. They conclude that supervisors need to work just as hard to establish a sound working alliance with experienced therapists as they do with novice supervisees.

We support the view that the quality of the supervision relationship is the key determinant of its effectiveness not least because it is often through the quality of their engagement, when there is sufficient trust and mutual regard, that supervisor and supervisee can gain access to material that is not in immediate awareness. In Chapter 6 we looked at how unconscious material may emerge through transference, counter-transference and parallel process. Here we will consider how the body of supervisor and/or supervisee may provide a conduit for material that is dissociated or out of conscious awareness.

Embodied awareness has been defined by Cinotti (2012:7) as 'the ability to pay attention to ourselves by registering physical sensations, emotions and movements at the moment in which they take place and without mediation of our narrative self'. In essence then, this is about tracking our moment-to-moment experiencing without trying to impose meaning on it. In thinking about embodied awareness in supervision, we are acknowledging the value of trusting the communication that happens through our bodies – our physical sensations and feelings – as well as our minds (Christopher 2010). The supervisor who values an embodied relational approach learns to use embodied awareness as a guide to enable her to work in a collaborative way with her supervisee to help the two of them to discover together new awareness and meaning. In supervision, as in therapy, the body can usually be trusted to reveal that which needs attention (Meekums 2007; Rothschild 2000).

Shaw (2003) has conducted research that reveals the potency of embodied experience in supervision. In his doctoral research interviews with experienced therapists about their bodily experiences in therapy, Shaw (2003:108) found that 'vivid somatic reactions' occurred even during those interviews. One therapist, for example, reported feeling sick as she recalled her work with one client. Shaw (2003:142) recommends that the informational value of the therapist's bodily responses should receive greater attention in supervision:

> If it is possible for therapists to evoke such strong responses in a research interview setting, I would suggest that in clinical supervision this information could be used to explore what these bodily feelings mean for the therapist and the client, thereby building up a picture of the body narrative within therapy.

In like manner, Heuer (2005:111) advocates bodywork as 'an important and reliable tool in supervision' for uncovering unknown aspects of the client's experience:

> Here also I am paying close attention to the feeling aspects of voice, facial expression, gestures and body posture of my supervisee, trusting that

consciously as well as unconsciously in a form of parallel process the body of the supervisee can be understood as the carrier of the emotional expressions of the patient we are discussing.

The capacity of supervisor and supervisee to work with embodied process is determined by the quality of their basic affective relationship (see Chapter 6). Feindler and Padrone (2009:283–4) have summarized the critical components of effective relational supervision as 'mutuality, authenticity, shared meaning, collaboration and trust'. Where these key relational principles are in place, it becomes possible for supervisor and supervisee to begin to enact and gradually make explicit hitherto unrevealed intra- and interpersonal dynamics that may be central to the client's life and experience. Such enactments are especially potent where they emerge as aspects of the client's experience that have been suppressed or dissociated, as examples given later in the chapter will illustrate.

How this works in practice is that the supervisor and supervisee together co-construct experience and meaning from material generated by the therapist as he or she brings their client work to supervision. Material may be brought intentionally or unintentionally, through cognitive, emotional and embodied experience. In contrast to more didactic forms of supervision, the supervisor who works in an embodied relational way does not consider herself to have any privileged opinion or perspective on the content or process of the work. The key tools of her trade are attunement to her own and her supervisee's experience rather than technical advice, theoretical knowledge or expertise – although these will also inform her way of working.

Indeed excessive use of supervisory techniques may be considered a defence against feeling or appearing inept. Bernard and Goodyear (2009) have observed that a capacity for ineptness in a supervisor is preferable to an attitude of fixed expertise. They put it this way: 'Supervision at its best is a healthy balance of authority and humility. Supervisors who opt for confusion over stagnation model the essence of professional growth for their supervisees' (2009:243). If supervisees develop an excessive reliance on theory, as can be the case where this is modelled by their supervisors, they may begin to employ this as a defensive manoeuvre whereby they come to 'focus attention on what they know, rather than on what they do not know' (Hahn 2001:276) as protection against feelings of shame and exposure. Paradoxically this may prevent supervisees using supervision effectively to enhance their learning and development while also triggering feelings of incompetence when, inevitably, they do come up against *not* knowing.

The relational embodied supervisor is skilled in dual awareness. She learns to hone her capacity to immerse herself and her bodily experience unselfconsciously in the moment-by-moment experiencing she shares with her supervisee. At the same time, and *almost simultaneously*, she learns to stand back from that immersion in order to reflect upon and begin to integrate her experience cognitively. Here she is developing the capacity, eloquently described by Patrick Casement in his writing on the internal supervisor (Casement 1985), both to participate spontaneously *and* step back in order to observe the process from what has been termed an 'island of contemplation' (p. 31)..

This process is more one of a repetitive series of small actions of immersion followed by reflection than a simultaneous experiencing of participation and observation. An analogy that perhaps fits this process is one of diving into a swimming pool – the supervisor repeatedly dives into her relational and embodied experience of being with her supervisee, immerses herself fully and deeply in this, and then re-surfaces to evaluate and reflect on that experience. This reflective process in supervision can be thought of as closely related to the process of 'mentalization' – a term actively employed in work with, amongst others, trauma clients (Van de Hart *et al*. 2006). As defined by Ogden and Steele (2008), mentalizing 'is the process by which we make sense of the contents of our own minds and the minds of others'. Mentalization involves the accurate perception and understanding of the motivations and intentions of others and of oneself, and the development of meta-cognition (the ability to think about thinking).

Transferred to the activity of supervision, mentalizing can be thought of as 'the capacity to reflect coherently upon experience – rather than being embedded in it or defensively dissociated from it' (Wallin 2007). Later in the chapter, through the example of working with Rajinder, we provide an example of the supervisor's mentalizing process. At this point we give an example of a mentalizing process as experienced by a supervisee:

> Darek worked in GP surgeries and brought to supervision his difficulty in working with young people who struggled to show energy and commitment within the counselling process. He would often experience a sense of distance and disconnection with these reluctant or ambivalent younger clients and could find himself feeling bored, critical, impatient, hopeless or stuck when with them. Darek found these feelings in himself hard to accept and worked with his supervisor to try to restore his empathy for these clients (for example trying to look beyond their behaviour to what this might signify). Although Darek had brought this issue to supervision on several occasions and his supervisor had gently enquired if it connected with his younger self in any way, its meaning and resolution continued to elude them.

> The turning point came when Darek was once again reflecting on this difficulty in relation to his work with a young man in his teens. On this occasion his supervisor encouraged him to move from reflection to experience by asking him what happened in his feelings when he sat with this young man. Darek associated to a strong,. uncomfortable feeling of despising the client. The supervisor encouraged him to stay with this feeling at which point he suddenly connected to his own experience as a teenager. He realized that he had been defending against identifying with his adolescent clients as it was hard for him to think back to aspects of his own teenage years that had at times been difficult and isolating. As we talked about this in supervision Darek

began to empathize with his own lost, despondent teenage self, instead of trying to keep that part of himself separated off and in the past. Making this connection significantly developed his capacity to connect better with younger clients who were struggling (as he himself was back then) with identity, meaning and motivation. Rather than being simply immersed in the difficulty he experienced, at this point Darek was able to stand aside from this difficulty and, with the help of his supervisor, reflect upon it in a new way (the mentalizing process).

As supervisors we can best apply mentalizing by shifting our focus from *content* to *process*. In so doing we become less concerned with *what* is on our supervisee's mind and more concerned with *how* they are experiencing showing us what is on their mind. Ogden and Steele (2008) describe this process and the quality of presence needed to activate it:

> Mentalizing requires the capacity to be present, to accurately read relational cues, and to be mindful and tolerant of one's own inner experiences . . . The process of mentalizing . . . is influenced by many factors, including the capacity to observe one's mental actions, as well as posture, sensation and movement of the body.

It follows that it is always helpful for the supervisor to orient their attention both to their own and to their supervisee's body states, including posture, breathing, movement, and pace and tone of voice, in the belief that these influence and convey the mentalizing process (Forester 2007). Gubi (2007:119) characterizes supervision as a place where supervisees tend to bring 'points of tension' rather than 'points of flow'. Attunement to body states is particularly useful in uncovering and elaborating these areas of tension. Hence if a supervisee is talking about a rupture in their relationship with their client we are as likely to say something like 'What happens in your body as you are telling me about this difficulty?', or 'Where do you experience this difficulty – is it in your mind, your feelings or your body?' as we are to ask questions about the *content* of the difficulty, such as 'What do you think is the cause of this difficulty with the client?' Some of the examples that are given later in the chapter will illustrate this more clearly. To assist the process of mentalizing in supervision it is helpful for the supervisor to:

- focus on mental and body states in the here and now (as opposed to reporting on past experience);
- invite the supervisee to notice their inner experience – thoughts, feelings, fantasies, sensations, etc.;
- pay attention to somatic components (embodied experience) – both their own and the supervisee's (for example 'A sudden chill has come over me as you talk about your client – I don't know if you feel that too').

Supervisees may need permission and encouragement to pay more attention to their own body states and sensations both in their client work and supervision. Supervisors can help by demonstrating this for their supervisees. For instance they can model, through self-disclosure, that the 'unacceptable' feelings, impulses, sensations and experiences that a therapist may encounter in themselves, such as sexual arousal and disgust, are permissible and containable, and can be spoken about and even welcomed for their therapeutic value (Wosket 1999). The danger exists that if the supervisor cannot tolerate and express this kind of material it becomes split off or suppressed by the supervisee, who then fails to bring it to supervision so that it is left to fester and become potentially toxic – to the super-visee and also to the detriment of her client work.

This process is helped along whenever the supervisor is willing to disclose their moment-to-moment experiencing with their supervisee – including taking the risk of divulging difficult or confusing experiences (Farber 2006; Feindler and Padrone 2009). Frawley-O'Dea and Sarnat (2001:190) liken this aspect of supervisor self-disclosure to sending a 'postcard from the edge' of the relational scene between therapist and client. The term they choose reminds us that a postcard often conveys a view (in words and/or pictures) that the recipient has not seen until the postcard is delivered. Thus in relational supervision the supervisor and supervisee can be thought of as (unwittingly) enacting a missing piece of the dynamic jigsaw that forms the relational pattern of the therapeutic dyad. It is through the supervisor's disclosure of what they are experiencing in the supervisory relationship (the sending of the postcard) that this missing piece is brought into view so that it can be examined and thought about.

In relational supervision, what Frawley-O'Dea and Sarnat (2001) describe as either 'regressive' or 'progressive' relational paradigms can be enacted and made explicit. A regressive relational paradigm can be understood as something happening between the supervisee and supervisor that mirrors a difficulty in the client's history of relationships. A progressive relational paradigm, on the other hand, means that supervisor and supervisee mirror something constructive that is beginning to emerge in the relationship between therapist and client. Here is an example of what may be thought of as the enactment of a regressive relational paradigm. It also illustrates a mentalizing process experienced by the supervisor:

> My supervisee, Rajinder, is talking in quite theoretical terms about her client, Joseph. She is thinking carefully and sensitively about how to encourage him to face up to some of the big themes in his life that he seems to be avoiding. I am finding it hard to stay with my supervisee and notice that I am starting to feel bored and fidgety. From this awareness of what is happening in my body I say to her: 'I am struggling to follow you closely here and I'm beginning to feel disconnected from you. Maybe I am experiencing something of the gap you experience with Joseph when you encourage him to look at this big issue and he seems reluctant. I feel in contact with your client's experience – like I can understand a bit how hard he finds this.'

I ask Rajinder how she experiences being with the client when he seems reluctant to engage. She says that Joseph goes into quite a childlike place, his voice becomes 'a bit whingey' and he starts to blame himself for being stupid. I ask her how she reacts to this and she begins to tell me what she says to the client. I stop her and instead invite her to stay with her embodied reactions and tell me what her *feelings* and *sensations* are like. Rajinder says that she experiences two different things simultaneously. She feels both caring towards Joseph and slightly irritated by him at the same time. Exploring this further she realizes that she often feels like this with him – like she both wants to reach out to him and has an impulse to withdraw at the same time. Suddenly this makes sense to her in terms of Joseph's insecure, ambivalent attachment experience as a child – that this may mirror the approach and avoidance dynamic he experienced with a mother who was inconsistently attentive and often looked to her son to meet her emotional needs. Rajinder now spots both the danger and the informational value of finding herself acting out this parental role through her mix of close and distancing feelings and behaviours towards her client.

It is when Rajinder is encouraged to stay with her embodied reactions and begins to trust the usefulness of her impulses and feelings that she becomes better attuned to her client's experience. When working from a more cognitive and theoretical framework her contact with her client felt disrupted in the same way that the supervisor's attunement to the supervisee in supervision slipped. The mentalizing process for the supervisor involved noticing in her body and trusting the dip in contact she felt with Rajinder, especially as this was unusual between them, and then to voice her reflections about this. 'What is the quality of my contact like with my supervisee?' is always a useful question for the supervisor to have in mind. Here are some additional questions that may help the supervisor to use him or herself more fully in a relational and embodied way.

Questions to encourage development of the supervisor's use of self

- What am I distracted by in this supervision session?
- What feels different or unusual?
- How are my energy levels – where are the peaks and dips?
- What are my feelings towards my supervisee at this point?
- What are my feelings towards my supervisee's client?
- What image or metaphor helps me picture my supervisee with his/her client?
- What fantasies am I having about my supervisee/their client?
- How congruent am I being with my supervisee?
- How competitive am I being with my supervisee?
- Who is talking most and what is the pace and tone of voice?
- What is the power like between us?

- What is happening in my body as I work with my supervisee?
- What sensations and feelings am I experiencing?
- What is the 'unacceptable' thought/feeling/sensation/impulse I am having?
- How connected do I feel with my supervisee?
- How connected do I feel with my supervisee's client?
- Am I inviting any collusion, or being invited to collude, with my supervisee?
- Am I playing any game with my supervisee?

In contrast to the above example of a possible enactment of a regressive relational paradigm, given below is an example of what may be thought of as an enactment of a progressive relational paradigm – that is, something positive happening between supervisee and supervisor which opened up the potential for something new and healing in the client's relational experience. Hopefully what the following vignette illustrates is that working with supervisees' embodied experience can be so powerful because it is a way to liberate and bring into awareness what the supervisee *knows but doesn't know that they know*.

> In supervision my supervisee, Nadia, is telling me about her difficulty in feeling connected to her client, Eliot, who begins each session by giving a report about his current psychological understanding of himself, supported by references from the counselling literature he is reading. This usually goes on for some time and can leave Nadia feeling intellectually inferior to her client.

> I ask Nadia what is happening in her body as she experiences this. She says that inside she feels irritated, distracted, hopeless, stuck, paralysed and as if she is not doing her job properly. She feels that she doesn't know what Eliot wants from her. As we explore these feelings and sensations, Nadia begins to realize that her embodied experience is telling her a great deal about the client's need to feel valued, recognized and validated – none of which he received as a child. This realization comes from her sense of feeling compelled to listen and approve of the effort he has clearly put into preparing all this material. She feels she wants to try hard to remain interested and to hear what Eliot is telling her despite how uncomfortable this feels.

> This realization helps Nadia to get back in touch with her strengths of listening, observing and gathering information. She talks about these as qualities she developed from her role in her own family and she tells me a little about the difficult dynamics she experienced as a child within that family. She remembers how often she sat on the stairs as a child, listening to her parents arguing, trying to work out what was going on and how best to protect her younger brothers from this.

> Nadia begins to understand that this personal experience has given her the capacity to give her client exactly what he needs – careful, focused, warm

attention. She is relieved to find that she has an ability to sense what is going on for Eliot and what he needs even when he can't, or doesn't know how to, ask for this directly. She had come to supervision thinking she needed to find a way of challenging and interrupting the client's opening monologue. She leaves supervision thinking that she needs to let him know that the way he opens the sessions is working – he gains her attention, interest and recognition.

This example illustrates two aspects of the concept of mentalizing discussed above. Firstly, through supervision, the supervisee is developing her capacity to 'think about her thinking' about her client. Rather than merely feeling embedded in her experience of the client Nadia is able to hold this experience in mind and reflect coherently on it. Secondly, she is holding the client in mind in such a way that she can now think about feeding back to him her experience of him in their relationship. This is likely to be in contrast to the rigid mentalizing Eliot may well have developed as a result of his early, impaired attachment experience. Put more simply, the client may have come to therapy expecting to be disregarded and invalidated, as he was as a child. Instead he finds himself heard, understood and validated in the way that his therapist can let him know that she thinks about him and what he might need.

Concluding reflections

In her book on a homeopathic approach to supervision, Ryan (2004:21) states that 'clinical supervision is the art of appreciative or compassionate enquiry'. In this chapter we have discussed an approach to supervision that relies less on a set of skills and competencies and more on compassionate enquiry into the supervisee's experience of being with their client. Ryan proceeds to write about how in homeopathy, as in therapy, 'the quality of a healing relationship is characterized by *getting alongside* and by *minimum intervention*' (2004:22). Transferring these qualities to the practice of supervision she suggests that a key question for the supervisor to hold in mind is 'What is the minimum intervention that "gets alongside" the practitioner in supervision to restore them to autonomy and relatedness?' (2004:22). If we begin, as Ryan does, to consider supervision as the art of minimum intervention, this takes us closer again to the notion of *being* rather than of *doing*.

Ryan (2004:11) states one key principal of homeopathic practice as 'a minimum, vital and similar stimulus only is required to restore well being'. This is a useful principle to apply to supervision whenever it appears that being, more than doing, may be what is needed. Here is a final example from our supervision practice that may serve to illustrate this point:

> My supervisee, Zack, is the manager of a counselling service as well as a therapist within that service. Not surprisingly he sometimes experiences

cross-contamination between these two roles and is experiencing just this when he comes to supervision. Zack starts by talking about three of his clients with whom he feels similarly stuck, deskilled and overwhelmed. He feels caught in a strong impulse to fix things for them, which is adding to his difficulties. His managerial role is very much about fixing things and he knows this is creeping into his work as a therapist. He initially wants help from me to work more effectively with these clients.

I am struck by how congested he seems to feel in his work, both as a manager and a therapist. I say this to him and then add 'When I feel overwhelmed in sessions I sometimes take time to look out of the window at the trees.' We are sitting at that same window and Zack says 'I do that here too. It's good. I don't do it at work. I never take the time to slow down and look around me.' We then spend a quiet moment or two together looking out of the window.

This is really all I needed to say in that supervision session (although I did say a few other things too). Zack then uses the rest of the session to develop his own ideas for creating more space in his professional life and in his therapy sessions. He decides to start taking a proper lunch hour out of the office instead of eating a quick sandwich at his desk, where he is, as a consequence, always available to others. He decides to start cycling to work again instead of driving, a journey of some 35 minutes that takes him along a cycle path where he can look at the trees. We explore together a few options for giving himself space when he needs to think or settle himself in sessions with clients. Finally he hits on the idea of going on a mindfulness workshop as part of his continuing professional development and of asking his organization to fund this.

The minimum intervention, on this occasion, might be thought of as the supervisor's few words about looking out of the window followed by both supervisor and supervisee doing this quietly together. If there was a healing and transformative moment where both came together in relationship and alongside each other in the supervision session, then that was it. On this occasion, that shared moment of looking out proved far more potent than a busy looking in on the supervisee's client work. Perhaps in supervision, as in life, we sometimes need to look away to see what is really under our noses.

Chapter 14

Training and development of the supervisor

The practice of supervision has moved forward considerably over the past few decades and has reached a stage where anyone serious about becoming a supervisor might reasonably be expected to undertake one of the many supervisor training programmes available. That said, Henderson holds the considered opinion that 'the majority of supervisors are neither accredited nor trained on an assessed course' (2009a:xxii). Whilst many of those who have been supervising for the greatest number of years will have started doing so when there were few if any comprehensive training programmes available and therefore had to learn through a mixture of attending workshops, reading and being guided by wise mentors (or trained by their supervisees), this is no longer the case. The professionalization of supervision has continued to grow apace and this is reflected in training now on offer in the United Kingdom. For instance, there is at least one supervision course available (at the time of publication), at the University of Strathclyde, that is tailored to requirements for British Association for Counselling and Psychotherapy (BACP) supervisor accreditation, is closely linked to competency frameworks for supervision (Roth and Pilling 2008; Turpin and Wheeler 2011) and is endorsed by BACP under their continuing professional development programme.

In the first part of this chapter we will explore some elements of the content, process and benefits of training, whilst in the second we will consider how supervisors can continue to develop their practice, seeking to ensure that they are both up-to-date in their understanding and fresh in their approach.

Training

As with any multidimensional interpersonal task, supervisors require solid foundational training in order to fulfil their role with competence, confidence and credibility. There is a developing literature about the content and process of training (see for example: Borders 2010; Falender and Shafranske 2012; Gonsalvez and Milne 2010; Henderson 2009a; Holloway and Carroll 1999; Roth and Pilling 2008; Turpin and Wheeler 2011; Watkins 2012b) and currently, as Borders puts it, 'the need for supervisor training is widely accepted' (2010:130).

The amount and kind of training preferred or required by those practising or intending to practise as supervisors will differ depending on variables such as therapeutic training and experience, prior knowledge and experience of supervision, and the developmental levels and orientations of those they will supervise. Supervisors who have been practising for a number of years and feel relatively comfortable with their own approach and style will still gain much from attending workshops, conferences or training days designed to sharpen up and provide feedback on skills and keep them abreast of new developments. They would also be well advised not to dismiss the possibility of attending an extended foundation training that will offer them a depth of space in which to reflect upon and consolidate their supervision approach.

Practitioners new to the role will benefit from extended initial training designed to provide a basic level of skills, theory and practice. In addition, one of the key areas for development is what Henderson (2009c) describes as a sense of inner authority; that genuine personal authority which at best can be used to nurture and protect both supervisee and client. Echoing this theme, an experienced trainer of supervisors, when asked about the biggest challenges facing trainee supervisors, suggested that 'most people come to supervision training not quite realizing what a responsibility it can be' (Jill Burns 2013: personal communication). This begs the question then, of how we engage with trainee supervisors in a collaborative process of understanding these responsibilities and developing their authority to undertake them appropriately.

Comprehensive supervisor training programmes

Comprehensive supervisor training programmes come in a number of shapes and sizes. Some are based on a traditional learning programme model where a group of students enrol and follow the programme through, typically with set contact hours, often in the evenings or at weekends to allow students to study without disrupting their working week. Others operate in blocks or modules, sometimes with student peer groups or facilitated supervision- or skills-development groups meeting on a more regular basis. Alongside these quite traditional approaches to teaching and learning, at the time of writing there is at least one university-based online programme in clinical supervision available in the United Kingdom (Townend and Wood 2009). There may be others offering a blended learning approach with online learning alongside face-to-face components of the programme. Fully or partially online programmes are clearly of particular help to those who will usually supervise online, although they may lack the face-to-face groupwork components that many trainees seem to value highly.

Each programme will have its strengths and weakenesses, and it is to be hoped that those seeking training will explore the options available to them and consider carefully what format, structure and delivery method will best enable them to prepare effectively to take on the challenges of becoming a supervisor. We each have our preferred ways of learning (Honey and Mumford 2006) and the different types of courses will fit our style to varying degrees. Whilst it is often useful to go a little way outside our comfort zone to challenge ourselves to take on new approaches, it is advisable to choose a programme that will give us the learning experiences we need in order to make best use of the opportunities the programme offers. It is also wise to consider the current requirements for supervisor accreditation by the professional bodies, if that is a future aspiration, in order to understand how different training programmes will prepare supervisors for meeting those requirements.

Portfolio learning

The second route of supervisor education involves creating a personalized portfolio of learning experiences that may, for example, comprise a range of workshops, short courses or conferences and perhaps a peer-support or seminar group, alongside receiving supervision of supervision work. Hellman (1999:216) has described a portfolio as a 'purposeful collection of a learner's work that tells the story of their efforts, progress and achievements'. Hellman has outlined what she considers to be the five major components of a supervision portfolio as: 'self-reflection, self-evaluation, learning progression, individual active learning, and peer collaboration' (1999:216). Drawing on her work, we have summarized these as follows:

1   *Self-reflection*: observation and analysis of one's actions and responses in order to integrate new learning into existing knowledge and expertise.
2   *Self-evaluation*: realistic self-appraisal based on feedback from peers, supervisees, supervisors, clients, trainers, etc.
3   *Learning progression*: a formative record of the development of skills and competencies over time. It involves monitoring progress through an evaluation of levels of skills, awareness and experience as they develop and as learning goals are set and achieved.
4   *Active learning*: the ability to present evidence-based competence to others, through the compilation of a portfolio that demonstrates a broad range of knowledge and expertise in supervision. (This may include audio or video-recorded material of supervision practice.)
5   *Peer collaboration*: a portfolio that includes peer feedback and evaluation will demonstrate a collaborative and dynamic relationship with fellow practitioners similarly engaged in professional development.

The advantages provided by the portfolio route include that it is tailor-made for and by the individual, and knowledge and experience can be accrued over a long period of time and in manageable amounts. A greater breadth of approaches and styles may be available through exposure to a variety of supervision perspectives provided by a range of practitioners and trainers. Disadvantages of training in this more *ad hoc* way are that it is an easy matter for the would-be supervisor to be seduced into concentrating their energy and attention on those aspects of supervision that they find most attractive. This could lead to serious gaps in their knowledge or awareness which may not be identified – for example, the more sober elements of ethics and accountability may be ignored in favour of the more tantalizing aspects of dynamics and parallel process.

Apprenticeship model

There is a third training route, which can supplement the previous two and is particularly relevant to learning how to act as supervisor/facilitator of group supervision. We are referring to the apprenticeship model, learning 'on the job' by working alongside an experienced group supervisor. Provided the arrangements are made carefully, and the role of the inexperienced group supervisor made explicit in the contracting stage, this can be a legitimate and potentially invaluable training experience. It is appropriate both for someone inexperienced in supervising, or for an experienced one-to-one supervisor looking to supervise in groups. This is quite a different experience to that of acting as a group supervisor on a training programme, where the other course members act as supervisees. Both are legitimate, and probably at least one is essential, for, as Proctor (2008:189) puts it, 'One thing is certain, a group is the only forum which can offer the opportunity for trying out the group supervisor role'.

Training aims for an integrative supervisor

In Chapter 1, we made the distinction between approach-oriented supervisors, who work exclusively within a specific therapeutic orientation, and integrative or eclectic supervisors, who are able to supervise the client work of practitioners from a range of approaches. We will focus on the training requirement for an integrative supervisor, which the reader can adapt if interested to a more approach-specific perspective. Given this, we suggest that whichever route is taken, the training process for a supervisor should fulfil five aims. We will look at these in turn and consider how each may be accomplished.

Gain an understanding of the various theories, models and approaches relating to supervision of counsellors and psychotherapists in order to develop a knowledge base for supervisory practice

This requires the trainee supervisor to study those approaches to supervision with which they are not already familiar. On a comprehensive training course it might be reasonably expected that students will be introduced to the main extant models and theories of counsellor supervision, such as psychodynamic, cognitive-behavioural, client-centred, developmental, integrative and relational (see Chapter 1). In addition they need, as we emphasized in Chapter 2, a conceptual understanding or framework for supervision. The model we have presented in this book has been designed for such a purpose: providing supervisors with an integrating framework within which to review and practise these approaches. There needs to be an opportunity to consider in some detail significant concepts derived from individual approaches or theories. Most central here are the concepts of the internal supervisor (Casement 1985; Henderson and Bailey 2009) and the phenomenon of the parallel process, without the consideration of which, supervision students would be sadly deprived.

It is quite possible to gather a range of theoretical inputs and opportunities to consider specific issues on supervision workshops or at conferences, augmented by personal study. We would suggest that the opportunity to reflect and consider these approaches in relation to one's own practice is also necessary for a thorough understanding to be achieved. For those using the portfolio route this can perhaps be best provided by a mixture of a seminar group or peer-learning group, perhaps of supervisors at a similar stage of development, alongside being supervised on one's own supervision work. It seems particularly important that this supervision is undertaken with an experienced supervisor who will be able to make the necessary connections between theory and practice.

Those who intend to supervise in groups need to ensure that their training provides them with a good working model of groups and how they function. This is not a luxury but an essential. As Lammers (1999:106) puts it, 'For effective work in this area [supervising teams and groups] supervisors need specific competence in the complex processes which are part of groups and organisations.' This requires the ability to contain and manage group processes such that they do not interfere with supervision and, ideally, to help the supervisor develop the facilitation skills needed to make best use of the group as a resource to enhance supervision.

Develop and practise a range of intervention and feedback skills relevant to the function of supervision

In our view it is vital that a training process provides an opportunity to try out different skills and strategies within the relative safety of a peer group. This provides an opportunity to experiment, where there is explicit permission to make mistakes, with others who also want to learn in this way. One of us had the experience of meeting regularly with a group of peers to try out the techniques and methods of a new approach which was, at that time, unfamiliar to us all. The group provided a powerful learning experience as a consequence of the depth of feedback offered alongside the direct experience of being on both the 'giving' and 'receiving' ends of the supervision practice. This creates a sense of common purpose and should reduce any sense of competition or need to 'get it right'.

The training group is a place where students can practise and receive peer and tutor feedback on their developing supervision-intervention skills. In a group of four, for instance, students are able to alternate between the roles of supervisor, supervisee, observer and technician (wherever possible with the use of video recording and playback facilities). Students are best advised to use real supervision issues arising from their work with clients, rather than role play, when acting as the supervisee, so that the emotional content is genuine. This gives the trainee supervisor an opportunity to take some risks and try new ideas and ways of working with supervisees who are also supervisors in training and robust enough to take some experimentation.

One student gave her account of a training group on a supervision course:

> I suppose the training group for me was a place to do these things: to test out my style as a becoming supervisor; to provide an opportunity to translate the ongoing theoretical input into practice; and to take risks and experiment in my way of being as a supervisor. The group had to feel safe enough for me to do this – and was. I don't know whether this was something only our group achieved, but certainly it happened, largely due to our being very open at our first meeting about where we were coming from and our valuing of each other's experiences, both personally and professionally.

> I remember very hesitatingly sharing a pressing need to know how I was perceived there as a supervisor, having recently had some sense that all was not well in my relating to some clients, which I found undermining and upsetting. This group had become the one place where I felt I could share that kind of thing. By that stage I could trust the other members to be honest and supportive, which they were. In these ways this group, like one's own first family, modelled for me what life (in this sense as a supervisor) is supposed to be about.

Group supervision training can similarly make use of the peer-training-group structure, offering different members the opportunity to try out the role of supervisor/facilitator and receive feedback from other members. By working in a group that maintains its membership over a number of weeks or months, the opportunity arises to experience and reflect upon the development of the group and the implications of this for the role and interventions of the supervisor.

Increase awareness of personal and professional strengths and areas for development

It can be expected that awareness of personal and professional strengths and areas for development will come out of the skills practice already considered, but we would like to mention two other training devices that can be used in order to meet this aim. The first is that of supervision of the supervision work of the trainee supervisor. This can be in an individual or group setting and we recommend that this supervision should be provided by an experienced supervisor: peer supervision is insufficient at this stage of the development of the supervisor.

The following vignette chronicles an occasion within a supervision-of-supervision group where the interaction of the group members played out the dynamics of a supervision issue, and also provided the answers to the supervision dilemma brought by the presenter: the (male) supervisor presented a session with a supervisee in which the female supervisee had recounted a difficult first session with a male client. The client was a drug user with a history of psychiatric treatment and a tendency to violent behaviour. The counsellor had felt intimidated and frightened by the client, who had, during the course of the session, recounted to her several sexual fantasies, which involved violence towards women. The counsellor felt that she didn't want to work further with the client and had brought this to supervision. The supervisor's issue was to ask the group for help with how he could enable the counsellor to get over her feelings of reluctance in working with the client.

There were various responses to this presentation. One male group member said, thoughtfully, that maybe the issue was more about how to help the counsellor stop labelling the client as 'difficult to work with' because of his psychiatric history. A female participant thought that the important issue of whether the counsellor had been abused by the client, in being expected to listen to the violent fantasies, had been glossed over. This comment was not taken up by the rest of the group and the discussion proceeded to consider if the counsellor might do better to refer the client to a specialist drug-counselling agency. The female group member became increasingly agitated during this discussion and finally broke in, saying, 'I think this is important. If the counsellor was being abused by the client, that needs addressing first.'

She was supported by another, male, participant who revealed that he was also feeling that the supervisor's main concern should be to safeguard his supervisee from the risk of abuse. He also shared his surprise that the supervisor was talking about what seemed to be a disturbing issue in a very calm and unemotional manner. The female member then suggested that perhaps they could use the dynamics within the group to throw light on the issue. She turned to the presenting supervisor and said, 'I'm feeling really frightened and uncomfortable now and if I was your supervisee I'd be wanting you to say to me [raising her voice]: "No! You *don't* have to work with this person. He has been abusing you and you don't have to take that. It is OK for you not to finish a session if a client is doing that to you and you feel abused. You can terminate the interview and refuse to see him again".' The male participant who had supported her came in: 'Yes, and I would want you to say that with some passion. I would want to know that you felt the feelings of outrage first – so that I knew you were on my side before we talked about the possibility of a referral to another agency.'

The presenting supervisor then began to realize that this kind of response might have been what his supervisee needed, rather than the very calm and considered interventions that he had made at the time. Although his characteristic composure and restraint with supervisees was normally appropriate, in this case it had been incongruent. He now revealed to the group that during the supervision he had felt at times both agitated and sexually aroused, and that embarrassment had prevented him from using his awareness of these reactions to throw light on the issue. Instead he had thought that appearing calm and unruffled would be most helpful for his supervisee.

It is fascinating to note that the sequence of responses of the three group members mentioned – pensive, agitated and passionate – were parallels of the reactions experienced, but not all owned, by the presenting supervisor. The feelings in the group, when aired and explored as if they might have some bearing on the issue under discussion, had told the story of what had been missed and what the supervisee needed. The first male participant, who had overlooked the sexual element in favour of a more cerebral consideration of issues (as the supervisor had done with his supervisee), had played an important role, as his lack of affective response had fuelled the agitation experienced by the other group members at not being heard. This had allowed the dynamics to develop and play out the story more forcefully. A training course where supervision-of-supervision groups are established and meet frequently provides excellent opportunities for supervisors to learn to recognize and work with parallel processes such as these.

The second training structure is that of keeping a learning journal or learning log (Moon 2006). This is often required on training courses, but it is equally possible for an individual to choose to do this for themself. The main purpose of keeping a journal is that doing so promotes the discipline of regular reflection and the setting of learning objectives. Additionally such a log, compiled over time, creates a record that illustrates the learning which has been accomplished.

Enable supervisors to develop their own informed style and approach to supervision, integrating both theory and practice

Developing one's own style is a process that, it is hoped, will continue throughout the supervisor's career (Rønnestad and Skovholt 2013). However, it is particularly important that the supervisor who is intending to operate with a degree of eclecticism creates coherence within their practice. We would anticipate this process happening naturally as part of the training process. It does seem important, however, that the supervisor is able to begin to articulate their own approach to supervision at an early stage. This can be achieved on a training programme by requiring participants to present an essay that defines their own supervision approach and the theoretical elements which inform it, and to link this to their practice. This has the effect of encouraging trainees to think through how they would address all aspects of the supervision process as well as providing a marker by which the individual can assess the distance they have travelled during the time of the course.

Develop awareness of equality, ethical and professional issues in order to enhance the professional identity of the supervisor and instil good standards of practice

This awareness comes from a number of the structures already described. It is helpful to study the equality and ethical principles involved in the practice of supervision, as outlined in Chapters 9 and 11. This can be done by personal study and reflection, or by attending presentations and discussions on a course, or at conferences. In addition it is important to be familiar with current thinking within the profession, which is again best achieved via conference participation and through reading professional journals. The understanding of equality, ethical and professional issues and their application in practice will come through the experience of being supervised on one's supervision work. In this respect being part of a supervision group is clearly advantageous over individual supervision, as the supervisor is exposed to a greater range of issues and dilemmas through the presentations of other group members.

Such issues can also be usefully addressed on training programmes using a Problem-Based Learning approach (Barell 2007; Savin-Baden 2003), in which a problem is identified, either by the tutors, the students or in collaboration. The students then research, explore and experiment with possible solutions or ways forward, generally in small peer groups. There is a modification of this approach known as Inquiry- (or Enquiry-) Based Learning, where the starting point is more broadly an issue of interest, rather than a problem (Scaife 2010).

This section will conclude with the retrospective reflections of a supervisor, 12 months after completing a one-year supervision training programme:

> I suppose the two main things on my mind when starting the course were: 'Am I good enough to be a supervisor?' and 'What is the significance of the third dimension when the counselling dyad becomes the supervision triad of counsellor, client and supervisor?' The course itself exposed me to different models of supervision, gave me the opportunity to receive feedback on my supervision and to take some risks in a safe environment, and challenged me to ask the question 'How much of myself do I reveal as a supervisor?'
>
> The result was that I 'passed the course', which means, I hope, that I have reached a certain standard, and I certainly have more confidence in my supervision. I have referred back to the course many times and have thought of the people that I worked with and wondered what they might say of me if they were observing this piece of supervision. What might they have done that was different? This obviously diminishes as time goes by but I have often wished to return to the training groups where we shared our supervision practice to re-experience some of that valuable feedback.
>
> The nature of the course was also important to me in that everyone was as much themselves as possible in the training situation. I have tried to continue

this in my work with supervisees and when I meet with my own supervisor. I think this has made my supervision relationships closer and more creative but not, I hope, in a sloppy or unprofessional way. I have also noticed that supervisees challenge me more these days!

On a more personal note, in an age where machines seem to dictate how we live our lives, I have tried to hold on to the humanity of counselling and counselling supervision. In order for this to be reinforced it is necessary, at least for me, to experience from time to time the humanity of a safe, friendly and challenging training situation. Without such training I think it might be possible for the supervisor to be the supervisor-adviser.

Supervisor development

One of the characteristics of a professional is active and serious engagement in a process of continuous learning and development. As the leaders of their profession supervisors are expected to demonstrate this commitment, and this is largely about retaining a passion for the work.

> Passionate supervision is about the humanity of the practitioner. Clients can engender difficult feelings. Staying open and not shutting down and becoming detached, cynical or bored requires a lively and safe forum in which to address our countertransference.
>
> (Hewson 2008:37)

In order to offer this opportunity for passionate supervision we have to stay energized and awake as we supervise. To do so it seems clear that we must be learning and developing, otherwise we risk stagnation. So, what are the mechanisms available to help us achieve that?

Supervision of supervision

The first learning and development strategy for supervisors that we will consider is taking their supervision work to supervision. To circumvent the otherwise inevitable confusion over titles, we will follow the convention adopted by others (Henderson 2009b; Power 2013) and refer to the supervisor providing supervision of supervision as the 'consultative supervisor', leaving the word 'supervisor' to be used to describe the person who is receiving supervision upon their supervision. In Britain, supervision of supervision is seen by many as a necessary requirement for supervisor development (Henderson 2004; Mander 2002; Power 2013; Wheeler and King 2000) and is mandated by BACP (BACP 2013a). It can take place within a group, or one-to-one, each bringing advantages and disadvantages.

Individual supervision is focused time with space for reflection and also offers another model for supervision. We would generally recommend it as the option of choice for a supervisor in the early stages of their practice. Individual supervision offers dedicated time for supervisors to unpack aspects of their experience of supervising, to identify strengths and priorities for development, to tease out the impact of different types of interventions and to explore some of what Borders describes as the 'subtle and nuanced' (2009:200) elements of supervisory style.

However, individual consultative supervision neither affords the range of different perspectives nor provides the fertile soil from which the kind of paralleling phenomena, as described above, can spring and flourish. Yet a group may be more at the mercy of the vicissitudes of wayward dynamics. Competitiveness or rivalry may be present; a powerful or needy member may claim more of a share of time and attention than a less assertive member. The fear of exposure or ridicule may prevent participants openly airing doubts and difficulties that go to the heart of their supervision work. It may be easier to share the real 'horrors' with a supportive individual consultative supervisor than within a group.

In Chapter 3 we postulated that a therapist can experience supervision as more exposing than being a client in their own therapy. Taking this to the next layer it follows that supervisors may experience consultative supervision as even more exposing than supervision of their therapeutic work, depending on their capacity to tolerate exposing their own vulnerabilities, uncertainties and possibly mistakes. It can be helpful to remind ourselves that the anxieties we may experience as we prepare for consultative supervision, whether individual or group, are probably similar to the anxieties that at least some of our supervisees experience as they prepare to come for supervision. Therefore we might consider what might help relieve our anxieties and what that tells us about what our supervisees might want from us.

Being in a supervision-of-supervision group can enable the supervisor to develop an awareness of the helping potential of ignorance, confusion and uncertainty and can encourage tolerance of such feelings. Where a sufficient level of trust and courage exists, group members can allow bafflement, bewilderment, frustration or unease to come to the fore in the faith that clarity and understanding will eventually emerge from the murkiness or chaos. The following is a description of such a process operating in a supervision-of-supervision group.

The supervisor presented the following dilemma. Her supervisee was counselling a client who had been physically and emotionally abused. The supervisee, in turn, felt that he was in danger of being abused by the client, who constantly tried to overstep time boundaries and 'deluged' him with an avalanche of material, which he found difficult to contain within the therapy hour. The supervisee's response was to feel overwhelmed, deskilled and 'like giving up'.

The supervisor shared with the supervision group that she, too, felt drowned by the number of issues that the supervisee brought to supervision. She found it impossible to get her supervisee to stay with a focus and had difficulty with separating his client issues from organizational issues, which were also contributing to his difficulties. The supervisor started to outline the number of issues brought by the counsellor to supervision and the group responded by asking questions in an attempt to obtain clarity.

Suddenly one group member broke in, saying in an exasperated tone, 'Hang on, I'm getting lost and I feel that I can't take in any more of this.' Other members of the group ventured that they too were feeling swamped by the detail and amount of information the supervisor was giving out. One participant then said to the supervisor, 'What would help me to get a handle on all this is to be clear about your focus – what is it you want from the group?' Another member then commented, 'That makes me want to ask you "What is it your supervisee wants from *you*?"' The supervisor thought about this for a moment and then said, 'I think he wants me to give him some space. If I can create a space for him, perhaps he can feel less harassed. If that happens he might be able to offer his client some space instead of trying to deal with everything at once. Because I think that's what the client really needs – some space where it's safe to be herself, because that's what she's not had – not someone to try to solve all of her problems.'

Experiences such as this, where internal feelings and reactions are used to throw light on the supervision material, can help supervisors to develop their own internal consultant. This raises the question of how, if at all, the internal consultant of the supervisor is different from the internal supervisor of the therapist. It is, perhaps, in this area of dealing with covert processes, thoughts and emotions that the main difference is apparent. The internal supervisor of the wise therapist may recommend caution within a therapy session: 'Don't burden your client too readily with your stuckness' or 'Hold on to that feeling – keep it in awareness and see what happens to it.' The internal consultant of the supervisor is more likely to urge in-session divulgence of fantasies, feelings and hunches: 'Go ahead, risk it – this supervision session is a one-off.' It is normally advantageous for the supervisor to make their internal struggles and sensations explicit and to ask for the supervisee's help in understanding the relevance of these. As one of us has observed on another occasion:

> I have learned that my internal responses when with a supervisee usually provide the best clue to what is going on for the counsellor, the client, or both. It is as if I am in some way "standing in for the client" and listening out for what the counsellor might have missed, or what the client is trying to get the counsellor to hear, but is unable to say directly.
>
> (Wosket 1999:222)

For instance, a supervisor who suddenly feels frightened when the supervisee talks about wanting to encourage their client to move to a deeper level of disclosure is wise to share this feeling with the supervisee. They can then, together, consider whether it provides a clue to the issue. Perhaps further disclosure would be frightening for the client, or uncomfortable for the supervisee, or the supervisor's reaction may signal that the client is not yet ready to engage in deeper exploration. In a therapy session, on the other hand, it would be judicious for the therapist who suddenly feels afraid, and is not sure why, to hold the feeling in awareness for a while rather than blurt it out. To do so might alarm or startle the client, or give out a message to the client that the therapist cannot tolerate strong or disturbing feelings. Should the feeling persist the therapist may well choose to share something of their internal process, but will by then have taken the time to consider for themselves how to disclose this and what it may be about, for example by saying, 'I felt apprehensive for a minute there when you mentioned about having had a difficult time last year. I wonder if it would be quite hard for you to talk about that here?'

Supervisor therapy

Consideration of the internal processes of the supervisor leads us to raise the issue of therapy for the supervisor. The supervisor needs to have dealt with their own personal issues, and to keep dealing with them as they arise, in order to maintain a reasonable level of internal equilibrium and objectivity. If this is not happening the supervisor may well misread, ignore or suppress covert reactions to the supervisee's material. If lack of experience as a client means that the supervisor is apprehensive about their own self-disclosure they are likely, in the example above, either to suppress awareness of their frightened feelings or attribute them to their own personal material getting in the way.

We feel strongly that it is imperative for supervisors to have had experience of being a client, and to continue to have access to personal therapy as they develop as a supervisor. As we explained in Stage 4 (Bridge) of the model, it is important for both supervisor and supervisee to consider the client's perspective on any change or difference that might be instigated with the client following the supervision session. The supervisor, standing one back from the therapeutic encounter, may be in a position to see this more clearly than the supervisee, but only if she has had sufficient understanding of what it is like to be a client. If the supervisor has had her own experience of hiding things from her therapist, hoping he will guess what she has only the courage to hint at; if she has felt disappointment at the apparent lack of progress of her therapy; if she has felt needy and dependent or distrusted her therapist; or if she has felt furious, despairing or sexual with him, she is far more likely to pick up on what her supervisee's client may be feeling at various moments.

It has been proposed that the principles of attachment can be appropriately applied to the supervisory relationship (Neswald-McCalip 2001; White and Queener 2003), on the basis that supervisees will at times seek security and comfort from their supervisor. Riggs and Bretz (2006) undertook a study into the attachment processes of supervisees (n = 87) through exploring their own attachment style, their perceptions of the attachment styles of their supervisors and of the supervisory bond. Their results indicated that supervisee self-reported early experiences of parental indifference predicted compulsive self-reliance in the supervisee, which in turn predicted that the supervisee would perceive their supervisor to have an insecure attachment style, which went on to have a direct negative impact on the supervisee perception of the quality of the supervisory bond and the success of supervision tasks. Our reason for including this study is that it points to a direct correlation between the attachment style of both supervisor and supervisee and the quality of the supervisory relationship. Given that 'attachment processes are so fundamental and mostly unconscious' (Riggs and Bretz 2006: 559) the authors conclude:

> From the perspective of attachment theory, supervision that directly considers the impact of trainees' and supervisors' interpersonal styles in therapy and/or supervision, and also encourages self-exploration or personal psychotherapy, may uncover maladaptive attachment strategies and promote opportunities for individuals to override an insecure attachment style in the service of effectively treating clients and supervising future trainees.
>
> (2006:564)

Finally, there is a question of basic credibility; in our view it is reasonable to expect that every senior member of a profession offering services as ubiquitous as counselling and psychotherapy will have engaged with the services that profession offers. It is encouraging therefore to have discovered examples of supervisor-training programmes that make experience of having been a client a requirement for applicants.

Additional continuous professional development

There are a variety of additional activities that can help to keep our interest in supervision alive and our practice fresh. These include reading books, articles and blogs about supervision and attending supervision conferences and workshops. It can also help to focus thoughts by writing an article about supervision or to research an aspect of our supervision work and write that up for publication. Similarly, preparing to lead a workshop or a seminar on a supervision topic will require careful thinking and research into what else has been produced on the subject. The supervision 'community' is perhaps less visible than the equivalent counselling and psychotherapy 'communities'; nevertheless, it exists, and each of these activities helps develop dialogue within that community.[1]

Note

1   In Yorkshire we have an association known as the Yorkshire Supervisors Forum, which puts on workshops 3–4 times per year and acts as a focal point for many supervisors in this region.

Chapter 15

Beyond supervising the counsellor and psychotherapist

To this point, our principle focus has been on supervising the work of counsellors and psychotherapists, allowing that this embraces a broad spectrum of those who undertake therapeutic practice. We are well aware that supervision is routinely used in a wide range of other professions (Bachkirova *et al.* 2011; Bond and Holland 2010; Owen and Shohet 2012) and, since first publishing *Supervising the Counsellor*, we have been asked to provide supervision to a number of people working in fields other than our own. In this chapter we will explore some of the differences and similarities that can emerge when undertaking supervision with those in roles other than that of counsellor or psychotherapist, with examples from three diverse areas. We will then consider overlaps and distinctions between the roles of coach, mentor and supervisor before considering specifically supervision of coaches and mentors. Finally, we return to supervision of supervision, from the perspective of the providing supervisor.

Supervising practitioners working in other fields

For us the progression to supervising those working in fields other than counselling and psychotherapy has evolved naturally, as will no doubt be the case for others with a good reputation for their clinical supervision of counsellors and therapists. A supervisor might be approached to supervise the manager of a counselling service who wants to reflect upon their managerial work, or to supervise the work of a complementary medicine practitioner who wants to increase their understanding of the psychological dynamics at play in their interactions with clients. The supervisor may wish to step out of familiar and perhaps comfortable territory and actively seek opportunities to work with supervisees outside counselling and psychotherapy as a next step in developing their career. While some potential supervisees have sought us out, others have been encouraged by managers who want to offer supervision as a source of support and professional development. In either case the supervisor may need to find accessible language to describe supervision in the broadest terms to those for whom it is an unfamiliar concept or one that has connotations of direction and evaluation.

Typically, we describe supervision as a space where it is possible for someone to stand back from the task to reflect on aspects of the work, consider any areas where there is stuckness or difficulty and also look at positive and negative impacts the work has upon them. The value of reflection in a wide variety of work settings has been well recognized with attention drawn to it particularly by Schön (1983), who introduced the term 'reflection-in-action' to describe the capacity to reflect on what is occurring as it is happening, as distinct from 'reflection-on-action', which describes reflection on what has already taken place. He explored its application in fields as diverse as design, psychotherapy, town planning and management. In so doing Schön (1983) was intending to challenge the primacy of what he termed 'technical rationality', in which, 'there is an objectively knowable world, independent of the practitioner's values and views' (p. 163). He explored how the reflection-in-action process enabled the practitioner to develop new understandings and perspectives that create possibilities to take forward an aspect of their work in which they have felt stuck.

The ideas that Schön introduced, sometimes encompassed by the phrase 'reflective practitioner', built upon more recently by authors such as Johns (2009) and Scaife (2010), offer a useful starting place in discussions with someone who is unfamiliar with the term 'supervision' as it is understood in counselling and psychotherapy. In our experience there may need to be a period of 'pre-supervision' where common ground and understanding are teased out so that the potential supervisee can decide whether they wish to proceed. Others arrive ready to 'give it a try' so that an initial contract can be agreed and work can begin on a trial basis.

For the supervisor, there are some general ways in which working with a supervisee from outside of the fields of counselling and psychotherapy may be different from working with a supervisee from within those fields:

- The contracting frame of reference may be quite different. In some instances this form of supervision is entirely voluntary and is sought out by the supervisee. On occasions it may be suggested by a manager or mentor but may not be a requirement of the supervisee's professional body. In other situations the supervision may be part of a package being contracted with an organization, with terms and expectations that have a significant impact upon the supervisory relationship, process and desired outcomes.
- The foci the supervisee brings may not be familiar to the supervisor. The material might include individual client work using unfamiliar modalities such as complementary medical practices, pastoral care with children or vulnerable adults, coaching frameworks or it might include organizational issues with which the supervisor is not directly familiar, such as working with matters of governance and strategy or undertaking impact evaluation of a mentoring programme.
- This may lead into investigation (in the Space stage) of systemic issues or organizational culture (Carroll 2006; Hawkins and Smith 2006) or developing

means to achieve objectives rather than seeking greater psychological understanding. The supervisor may need to suspend their well-developed therapeutic
understandings when considering boundaries and relationships with their
supervisee and be comfortable addressing complex organizational dynamics.

• Goal setting and action planning in the Bridge stage will need to be undertaken mindful of the supervisee's role and function, whilst paying attention to
any external performance measures that are being applied to their work.
Considering the 'client's perspective' may have to include consideration of
the needs and expectations of a range of stakeholders.

• In the Review stage, assessment and evaluation may have to address externally agreed frameworks and measures, and may require agreement over
feedback being given to third parties external to the supervision; all of which
may have some parallels with the review process with trainee therapists,
although in a significantly different context.

Emphasizing these differences raises two questions:

1   Is it helpful for supervisors within the field of counselling and psychotherapy
to undertake supervision with those in other fields?
2   What additional resources does a supervisor from a counselling and psychotherapy background need in order to supervise practitioners in other fields?

To enable us to consider these questions in a concrete way we shall explore three
examples from practice.

When Akira requested supervision his manager was surprised: Akira was
employed to provide dyslexia support to university students. He was very clear
in requesting supervision from an experienced supervisor in the university
counselling team, specifically to increase his understanding of the interpersonal
dynamics he experienced with some of the students he supported, which left
him uncomfortable in some cases and bemused in others. Akira's manager
agreed to his request for supervision, initially on a trial basis. For the first few
sessions the supervisor felt that the work was going well. Akira brought
examples of students with whom he worked and his supervisor, through
introducing the basic transactional analysis ego states (Stewart 2007) and the
principles of transference and counter-transference, was able to offer concepts
that enabled Akira to make more sense of some of his tutorial experiences.

During these discussions, the supervisor noticed a common pattern emerging
of students seeming to rely on Akira to see their final drafts of essays before
they would submit their work for marking, thereby putting pressure on him to
offer appointments at short notice, as deadlines loomed. His supervisor
became a little frustrated with Akira's seeming willingness to squeeze in the
extra sessions this required and wanted him to challenge this tendency in those
students. Akira was reluctant to do so, explaining that from his perspective he

did not have the right to start challenging the students he saw. As he succinctly put it, 'I am paid to provide dyslexia support, not therapy.'

Akira and his supervisor recognized that they needed to find a way of exploring this pattern in a way that was congruent with Akira's role, as he understood it. The supervisor asked Akira to explain to him in more detail the nature of his contract with the students. From this request it emerged that students with dyslexia were provided with a great deal of information and encouragement to use the support available to them, but that the nature of the support they could expect and in particular the limits of that support were not clearly defined. Encouraged by their discussions, Akira formulated a more precise and explicit contract about what he did and did not offer to students. Holding to the boundaries of that contract implicitly challenged those students who sought to set up a more dependency-based relationship. At times Akira found it hard to maintain the boundaries of his new contract, but gradually settled into doing so, coming to appreciate that it was an improvement to his practice.

With Akira it was the supervisor's frustration that guided her to unpick the nature of the contract with the students: with hindsight the supervisor realized that she had assumed that as clear a contract existed between the tutor and students as she was used to having with counselling supervisees. Having identified that the student contract needed improvement, it was for Akira to do this work, although the supervisor was happy to comment on a draft from her experience of working agreements with clients and supervisees. The supervisor's feelings of frustration did not lead to an exploration of Akira's feelings, but rather to a piece of practical work. We might interpret Akira's statement that he was not there to provide therapy as a signal that he did not want to explore his feelings; perhaps the supervisor was influenced by that comment.

To some extent the supervisor was in the familiar territory of clarifying the nature of the contract between supervisee and client, but it took a while to recognize this, probably because dyslexia support itself was unfamiliar to her. It was in the Bridge stage that a new strategy was developed, initially by writing the more precise contract. It was only when putting this into practice that Akira came to appreciate that he was no longer walking such a fine line between appropriate tutorial assistance with skills development and giving some students preferential assistance with work for which they received marks. Within the embryonic profession of dyslexia support[1] of that time, this was a well-recognized dilemma and Akira was pleased to have found a means, through his new contract, to manage this dilemma in his work. It was probably this most of all that fuelled his commitment to his new way of working.

Returning to the two questions posed above, it was helpful for a counselling supervisor to supervise Akira because she had both the understanding of contracts and also sufficient sensitivity to the dynamics of boundary erosion to be willing to challenge him about allowing that to continue. The supervisor was sufficiently resourced for this particular aspect of their supervision while also being happy to ask Akira to lend her books to learn more about the details of dyslexia support. Arguably supervision (or mentoring) by an experienced dyslexia support provider may have been more efficient in identifying the contracting issue, but the important work of exploring the psychological dynamics between Akira and his students was also a high priority, and the supervisor had the right background and experience for that aspect of their work together.

The second example comes from supervising Luke, a chaplain working for a hospital trust. The issue we will focus upon emerged quite early in the supervisory relationship, when Luke talked about his experience of visiting a teenage patient, who was an in-patient on a children's ward.

> Luke was told that the patient was in hospital because she had damaged tendons and some infection in self-inflicted wounds to her arm. In describing his brief ward visit to see the patient, Luke spoke with considerable feeling about some of the comments made, either directly to him or in his hearing, by two members of the ward staff. These were openly critical of the patient's behaviour, showed little compassion towards possible underlying reasons for her self-harm or any understanding of the way that some people use self-harming to manage intense feelings (Martin 2013; Strong 2000). Luke was troubled by their apparent lack of understanding and compassion towards the patient and angry that the hospital did not appear to be helping the ward staff to play a more constructive part in her support and treatment.

> When the supervisor felt Luke had fully expressed his feelings and concerns he broached the question of whether it was appropriate for Luke to take any action about what he had witnessed. Together Luke and his supervisor explored the various possible actions he could take, from talking to a senior nurse or a consultant on the ward to raising concerns through the hospital management structure. During the discussion they were very mindful of how Luke understood his role, which was to offer spiritual support to patients, their relatives and staff in the hospital through pastoral engagement and leading services (such as baptisms, weddings and anointing of the sick) when asked to do so. After careful consideration Luke concluded that he would not take any action at that stage, but would be alert when he visited that ward and, as he had done on the first day he had visited this patient, continue to gently challenge comments made directly to him by ward staff, if he felt they were misguided. Key factors that influenced Luke in reaching his conclusion included his recognition of the privilege inherent in his role of chaplain in having considerable freedom to visit patients, relatives and staff in the hospital as he chose (and as asked to do so) and the priorities of his role, which balanced support of patients, relatives and staff. He concluded that although he could see an argument for making a more formal challenge regarding what was effectively part of the medical care of the patient this would risk

undermining goodwill towards chaplains, which was widespread amongst staff and essential to the chaplains, who relied on ward staff for a high proportion of their referrals.

Although he did not say so at the time, Luke's supervisor initially found it hard to support Luke's decision to take no formal action, as his own instinct was that the potentially anti-therapeutic behaviour by ward staff needed to be challenged. However, when exploring this in his own supervision he quickly realized that his instinct was not based upon anything he knew about Luke's work, but rather it came from his own perspective. In a therapeutic context Luke's supervisor might well challenge actions by others, or encourage supervisees to challenge actions by others, when he felt that those actions were undermining the therapy being undertaken. This was a useful step for the supervisor in teasing out for himself the sometimes subtle differences between a pastoral and therapeutic role.

In this example the supervisor had a range of useful understandings and experience to draw upon when supervising Luke. While his therapeutic supervisory instincts caused him an internal conflict, this could have been unhelpful if voiced immediately, and his experience was sufficient to guide him to contain his own views. Luke had originally sought him out for supervision because he was undertaking a therapeutically oriented training programme. Thus at that stage of his development he wanted a supervisor with a therapeutic background. Whether he would benefit from moving to supervision by another chaplain became an important question to return to in reviews, although availability of suitable alternative supervisors would remain a restricting factor.

The third of our examples is Catharine, the head teacher of a large, inner-city primary school, who approached one of us for what she described as some supervision of her work.

An initial exploratory session took place in which Catharine focused mainly on her concerns with some of the racial dynamics in her school, a school with a predominantly white staff team and a pupil cohort mainly from Asian backgrounds. It transpired that Catharine had been discussing her concerns with an adviser from the education authority and with the school's governing body. It was one of her governors, with a counselling background, who suggested she seek supervision. Following the initial session, a contract for six further sessions was agreed, during which Catharine's goals, various relationships and multicultural dynamics within the school were explored. The key issues that quickly emerged were Catharine's frustration with some in her team and her disappointment with failed attempts to involve parents more fully in the life of the school.

The work with Catharine was clearly very different to counselling supervision, but it did involve facilitated reflection on aspects of her work. In the second session Catharine spoke with considerable distress about two incidents in her early weeks at the school when she had felt attacked and criticized by the parents involved. She readily recognized how these experiences had undermined her usual self-confidence and left her fearful that any overtures she made might be misunderstood. Catharine was sufficiently liberated by this cathartic discussion to develop a strategy to approach local Asian community leaders, through members of her staff team (an administrator, a teacher and a member of maintenance staff) within that same community.

The sequence of steps in this stage of the work with Catharine can be summarized as follows:

1   identifying the focus upon a specific aspect of her work;
2   examining the effect upon her of that aspect of her work;
3   allowing the emergence of difficult incidents that undermined her self-confidence;
4   taking time to explore and give attention to the associated feelings;
5   shifting into a problem-solving approach to develop a new strategy to tackle the issues.

This is likely to be a familiar sequence for supervisors and indeed to those working therapeutically. It is commonly the case that offering a safe space in which an individual is able to express strong emotions about a difficult situation will result in that person being able to see the situation in a different way. Catharine's supervisor had no knowledge or experience of working in a school or in community development. In the early stages of the process this was not of great relevance: the supervisor was able to take up a position of attentive enquirer, paying full attention to the supervisee and the stages of the supervisory process, and used their lack of knowledge to ask questions from a perspective of naïve interest. Once difficult events emerged, it was straightforward to facilitate a cathartic release of the associated feelings.

The unfamiliar territory for the supervisor emerged when, applying the Cyclical Model, they moved into the Bridge stage. Catharine needed a practical strategy to take back to the school and initially had no ideas. The supervisor, equally bereft of solutions, started by asking what they hoped would be a facilitative question – 'What are you trying to achieve?' – to which Catharine responded that she wanted to increase the involvement of parents from the local Asian community in the life of the school. The supervisor, aware that Catherine lacked confidence to take the initiative herself, went on to ask, 'Are there people in your team who can help you with this?' That was sufficient for Catharine to start to develop the idea of inviting staff who she knew were actively involved in the local Asian community to help her, and from there, map out her plan.

Of note here is how, during supervision, Catharine became able to devise and later put into operation a constructive strategy with minimal assistance. She had previously not been able to do this despite discussing the issue with the educational adviser and her governing body. When reviewing their work together, both Catharine and supervisor concluded that it was the supervisor's capacity to allow Catharine to attend to her distress that freed her up to consider the situation with renewed clarity and creativity.

The work with Catharine made best use of her having a supervisor from a therapeutic background. However, the limitations of the supervisor did emerge when they moved to action planning. Ideally, a supervisor with more experience and understanding of developing school–community relationships could have been more helpful at that stage. More generally, if working with the head teacher of a school, a supervisor needs to have a basic understanding of, for example, the balance of responsibilities between a head teacher, the local education authority and the governing body in order to be able to address any governance or systemic issues that emerge.

The work with Catharine was called 'supervision' because that was what she asked for, but should a six-session contract to find a solution to a specific area of difficulty in an aspect of her work more appropriately be called 'coaching'?

Coaching, mentoring and supervision

The Greek mythological figure called Mentor was a friend to Odysseus, and guide and teacher to his son, Telemachus (Tripp 1988). Modern usage of the term 'mentor' is often that of an experienced practitioner who acts as guide and teacher to a junior colleague. A mentoring relationship is primarily for the benefit of the mentee, and Downey (2003) suggests that mentoring is more concerned with long-term and career goals, rather than short-term performance issues. Thus it may have a defined outcome in mind, although often it is developmental; a new member of staff in an organization will sometimes be allocated a mentor to guide them through their acclimatization period. Hill emphasizes that 'the skill of the mentor comes from past experiences and is broadbased . . . the mentor usually is someone more senior, has experience in the field and a degree of success in the context of the work' (2004:11).

Mentoring has been a formally recognized role within the nursing profession in the UK since the 1970s (Gopee 2008; Kinnell and Hughes 2010), with well-structured training and development programmes for mentors. Whilst on a placement trainee nurses and midwives will have an identified mentor whose role is to facilitate and oversee the trainee's learning experiences, providing guidance and enabling reflection while helping to prepare the trainee for more autonomous practice as a qualified nurse or midwife. However, this is a profession-bound approach; what of mentoring between those with different backgrounds, trainings and roles?

For a number of years one of us was a mentor in a Yorkshire-based mentoring scheme[2] in which a number of public-sector organizations, along with some from the private sector, exchanged mentoring so that each mentee had a mentor from a different organization within the scheme, typically for a 12-month period. Thus someone working in the Fire Service might mentor someone working in an insurance company while someone working in the city council might mentor someone working in a college or university. There was a matching process which sought to find some areas of common ground or experience, but it was a given that the mentor would always work in a different organization and often in a very different field to the mentee and generally participants indicated that they appreciated this aspect of the scheme.

Moving on to coaching, Whitmore (2009) offers the following definition: **'Coaching is unlocking people's potential to maximize their own performance**. It is helping them to learn rather than teaching them' (p. 10, original emphasis). Thus coaching is perhaps slightly further toward the facilitative end of the facilitation–teaching continuum, while mentoring is closer to the teaching end.

Hay makes the point that the European Mentoring and Coaching Council (of which she had been President) 'made a policy decision to refer to **coaching/ mentoring** as a single term' (original emphasis) (2007:4). She explained their reasoning as follows: 'At least, in that way, we felt that people would be prompted to spell out their definitions rather than realizing too late that they had been discussing different things' (Hay 2007:4). Rather like the terms counselling and psychotherapy, the terms coaching and mentoring share much common ground, whilst each has distinct aspects, as understood by different people in different contexts. In relation to coaching, mentoring and organizational consultancy, Hawkins and Smith (2006:xiii) seek to distinguish supervision as follows:

> Although supervision uses many of the skills of coaching, mentoring and consultancy, its main difference is that it both creates shift in the relationship and shows up the process by which the shift occurs. In this way the supervisee can not only experience the process, but also see how to replicate it in their craft practice.

This helpfully emphasizes the double-level nature of supervision, although it seems likely that this distinction will not always be so clear in operation as coachees and mentees will sometimes wish to observe the process through which their coach or mentor facilitates shifts, with the intention of facilitating similar processes with colleagues they lead or manage. In our view it remains the case that supervision is undertaken with supervisees who are themselves working with others in some structured way and that the development of work with their 'clients' is the primary focus of supervision. On this basis the work undertaken with Catharine, as described in the previous section, would be better described as coaching.

What we can say with confidence is that coaching, mentoring and supervision share many characteristics and that in every contract to provide coaching/ mentoring/supervision, the coach/mentor/supervisor needs the necessary skills, knowledge and experience for the work they will undertake, and if significant gaps or deficits emerge it is important that these are recognized and addressed.

Supervising coaches and mentors

The last decade has seen a rapid rise in the number of practitioners offering coaching and mentoring, and as coaching has grown and sought to form itself into a recognizable and respected profession, increasing numbers of coaches have sought out supervision of their practice. It appears that many have sought out supervisors from the counselling and psychotherapy field, although a number of authors (Bachkirova *et al.* 2011; Carroll 2006; Hawkins and Smith 2006) make clear their view that supervising coaches requires a set of skills, understanding and, preferably, experiences additional or different from those required to be an effective supervisor of therapeutic work. It could be that coaches have sought supervisors from the world of counselling and psychotherapy simply because that is where there are currently a significant number of experienced supervisors across the United Kingdom. However, there are also some indications that the picture may be more complex.

In response to her survey about the relevance of unconscious dynamics to executive coaching, Turner (2010) found that 88.9 per cent of her 279 respondents said that the unconscious is relevant to coaching, with only 1.1 per cent saying it was not and 10 per cent unsure. In summarizing her findings Turner (2010:24) goes on to say:

> it is clear from both the survey responses and the interviews that the unconscious is widely accepted as central to coaching for a large number of coaches. What appears to vary is the ease with which coaches feel they are able to deal with unconscious processes.

This chimes with the view of Bluckert, that 'Psychological mindedness alongside business knowledge and awareness combined with coaching skills are increasingly seen as top level competency areas for executive coaches' (2005:173).

A simple example may help to make this more concrete.

> Georgina, a relatively inexperienced coach, brought her work with a male client to supervision. The client travelled a long way for the sessions and was very eager to learn as much as he could in the time available. Georgina felt under pressure to prepare a lot of material for the client to work with during their sessions. The supervisor was uncomfortable; he felt Georgina was being a bit mistreated and that she was allowing that to happen. He asked Georgina to remind him what the coachee said he wanted from coaching, which was that he wanted to understand how his behaviour contributed to him feeling that he gave a lot but colleagues did not appreciate him. The supervisor then asked Georgina if she felt well appreciated by her client and she said that she did; he particularly liked being able to work with all the materials she provided. The supervisor asked again how well she felt appreciated for who she was and the skills, insight and warmth she offered during the sessions, rather than the materials she produced. At this challenge Georgina paused and smiled, having seen the parallel between what she was doing in coaching and what her client was doing at work.

That moment marked a deepening of the focus between Georgina and her coachee as she started to put their relationship more into the foreground, alongside the tasks they worked on together. Georgina needed a supervisor who could help her to shift to the relationship level in her work with her client, and in this instance a supervisor from a counselling background was well able to provide what she needed. This was very familiar territory to the supervisor, fitting with his experience of supervising therapists. Thus it could be that some coaches are seeking out supervisors with a background in counselling, psychotherapy or psychology because they are looking for a supervisor who will help them develop their psychological mindedness or understanding of unconscious processes.

The coaching/mentoring profession is going through a transition period and at present some coaches/mentors are seeking out and can benefit from undertaking supervision with a supervisor from a counselling and psychotherapy background, whilst some may need what can only be provided by a supervisor who is themselves an experienced coach/mentor. In her study of the experience of a small sample of experienced business coaches, Maxwell (2009) found that they all felt that they worked some of the time in the boundary area between coaching and therapy, and it is possible to see how a good fit between a supervisor and a coach could enhance the coach's work at that boundary. A supervisor with a therapeutic background might be particularly well able to work with a coach from a business background in this territory.

It is also important for the supervisor to recognize that coaches and mentors are different from counsellors and therapists: different in their training, their contract with clients and their approach. Passmore and his colleagues (2010) undertook a study to explore whether therapists and coaches are also different in personality. For this purpose they used the Myers Briggs Type Inventory with a sample of coaches and counsellors. This is a personality instrument used to measures four pairings of personality preferences, based on Jung's ([1921]1971) work on psychological types:

- introvert–extrovert, which describes whether you gather energy for your inner world or the external world;
- sensing–intuiting, which describes how you take in information – through your senses or at a big-picture level, recognizing associations and patterns;
- thinking–feeling, which is concerned with the way you make decisions, with thinkers taking a rational, logical approach and those with a feeling preference putting weight on needs and values;
- judging–perceiving, which describes how we live; those with a judging preference being more planned and organized, those with a perceiving preference being more spontaneous and flexible.

Passmore and his colleagues (2010) found, when averaging preferences across each group, that both coaches and counsellors had a strong intuitive preference relative to the general population. While the coaches had a significantly stronger thinking preference, counsellors had a stronger feeling preference. This would suggest that supervisors from a therapeutic background, who may also be likely to have a strong feeling preference, may need to adapt their approach when supervising coaches and mentors with a more thinking preference.

Supervision of practising supervisors

In earlier chapters we commented on the value of having access to supervision of supervision from the perspective of the practising supervisor who receives supervision of their supervisory work. In this final section we want to consider this from the perspective of the providing supervisor. To circumvent the otherwise inevitable confusion over titles, we shall continue to follow the convention adopted by others (Henderson 2009b; Power 2013) and refer to the supervisor providing supervision of supervision as the 'consultative supervisor', leaving the word 'supervisor' to be used to describe the person who is receiving supervision of their supervision.

Wheeler and King's (2000) research into the practice of consultative supervision of supervision revealed that 'supervisors of counsellors appear to regard supervision of supervision as important, helpful and necessary' (p. 287). They also noted that over half their sample had the same supervisor for their counselling and supervision work. Henderson (2009b) confirmed that this practice of having one supervisor for counselling and supervision remained the case in 2008, with many having 'informal arrangements, if any, about the proportion of time spent reviewing their supervisory work. Most are happy about this, trusting to their own internal supervisor to identify when to bring issues for another's perspective' (p. 221).

Respondents in Wheeler and King's (2000) research were asked to list five issues they had taken to supervision of their supervision in the previous year and similarly five issues that supervisors had brought to them for consultative supervision in the previous year. The two sets of data were in strikingly similar proportions, with both sets of responses placed into six categories: ethical issues; boundaries; competence of supervisees; training; contracts; supervisee/client relationship. They noted that only one respondent had mentioned multicultural issues being raised. Further research is needed to investigate whether developments in multicultural counselling and supervision are reflected in the supervisory issues supervisors now bring to consultative supervision, and whether these now include more attention to aspects of working with difference and diversity.

Writing from a psychodynamic perspective, Power (2013) offers a number of examples where consultative supervision has appeared to assist the supervisor. These include holding or containing the supervisor when they are the object of difficult projections, helping to tease out complex dynamics, particularly in group supervision, offering a balance of empathy and challenge when something is going wrong in the supervisory relationship, working with power differentials within the supervisory structure and exploring both conscious and unconscious concerns for supervisees who are trainee therapists.

Similarly coming from a psychoanalytic background, Mander (2002) offers a number of fascinating insights into the inner workings of the consultative supervisor as they strive to hold back their insight in favour of facilitating a deepening exploration in collaboration with the supervisee. She observes that

> The narcissistic pleasure of being the one in the know is difficult to curb, but in my experience it is ultimately less satisfying (because it is also guilt-inducing) than being present when the other person in the session makes a discovery, comes to an understanding or makes a connection.
>
> (2002:136)

We are in no doubt that the role of consultative supervisor requires a significant level of experience in the field, and have previously used the analogy of a grandparent to describe it. A grandparent will have been a parent and will likely have seen their child through to the stage of maturity when they may become a parent themselves. Through that process it is to be hoped that they have learned how to offer support where it is wanted, whilst avoiding any comments or behaviour that can be construed as criticism or attempts to take over.

Thus, in our view, a supervisor would be unwise to undertake the role of consultative supervisor until they are confident they are ready to be a 'grandparent' within the profession. Wheeler and King (2001:117), when considering what makes a good consultant supervisor, suggested that

> such a person should have as a primary responsibility their involvement in the important process of supporting and guiding the development of a competent, reflective and independent supervisor, who can provide a service to the profession and the public that is second to none.

We have found the Cyclical Model to be an effective structure for use in consultative supervision of supervisors. With trainee or inexperienced supervisors it models the application of an effective supervision structure and with more experienced supervisors it provides a means of ensuring that the management of the supervision process can be undertaken efficiently, maximizing the amount of time that can be spent on their work. We enjoy and continually learn from opportunities to work with other supervisors of all levels of experience.

Notes

1   This took place around 2001, when dyslexia support in UK Higher Education was still in its infancy, following the Special Educational Needs and Disability Act (SENDA) in 2001 and the introduction of a stream of national funding through the Disabled Students Allowance. Students with a confirmed diagnosis of dyslexia could apply for funding for specialist study-skills support.
2   The Yorkshire Accord Scheme. For further details see: www.yorkshireaccord.co.uk/.

References

Adams, D.M. (2010) 'Multicultural pedagogy in the supervision and education of psychotherapists', *Women & Therapy*, 33, 1–2: 42–54.

Adamson, F. (2011) 'The tapestry of my approach to transformational learning in supervision', in R. Shohet (ed.) *Supervision as Transformation: A Passion for Learning*, London: Jessica Kingsley.

Allen, G.J., Szollos, S.J. and Williams, B.E. (1986) 'Doctoral students' comparative evaluations of best and worst psychotherapy supervision', *Professional Psychology: Research and Practice*, 17, 2: 91–9.

Allphin, C. (1987) 'Perplexing or distressing episodes in supervision: how they can help in the teaching and learning of psychotherapy', *Clinical Social Work Journal*, 15, 3: 236–45.

Amundson, N.W. (1988) 'The use of metaphor and drawings in case conceptualisation', *Journal of Counseling and Development*, 66, 8: 391–3.

Ancis, J.R. and Ladany, N. (2010) 'A multicultural framework for counselor supervision', in N. Ladany and L.J. Bradley (eds) *Counselor Supervision*, 4th edn., New York, NY: Routledge.

Andersson, L., King, R. and Lalande, L. (2010) 'Dialogical mindfulness in supervision role-play', *Counselling and Psychotherapy Research*, 10, 4: 287–94.

Anthony, K. and Nagel, D.M. (2010) *Therapy Online: A Practical Guide*, London: Sage.

Aponte, H.J. (1982) 'The person of the therapist: the cornerstone of therapy', *Family Therapy Networker*, 6, 2: 19–21, 46.

Armstrong, P. and Schnieders, H.L. (2003) 'Video and telephone technology in supervision and supervision-in-training', in S. Goss and K. Anthony (eds) *Technology in Counselling and Psychotherapy: A Practitioner's Guide*, Basingstoke: Palgrave Macmillan.

Arviddson, B., Skärsäter, I., Baigi, A. and Fridland, B. (2008) 'The development of a questionnaire for evaluating process-oriented group supervision during nurse education', *Nurse Education in Practice*, 8, 2: 88–93.

Ashby, R.H. (1999) 'Counselor development and supervision: an exploratory study of the integrated developmental model', unpublished doctoral dissertation, University of Oklahoma.

Aveline, M. (1997) 'The use of audiotapes in supervision of psychotherapy', in G. Shipton (ed.) *Supervision of Psychotherapy and Counselling: Making a Place to Think*, Milton Keynes: Open University Press.

BAC see: British Association for Counselling

Bachkirova, T., Jackson, P. and Clutterbuck, D. (2011) *Coaching and Mentoring Supervision: Theory and Practice*, Maidenhead: Open University Press.

BACP see: British Association for Counselling and Psychotherapy

Bailey, C. (2012) 'Do we need supervision?', *Therapy Today*, 23, 10: 30–1.

Baker, L.C. and Patterson, J.E. (1990) 'The first to know: a systematic analysis of confidentiality and the therapist's family', *The American Journal of Family Therapy*, 18, 3: 295–300.

Bambling, M., King, R., Raue, P., Schweitzer, R. and Lambert, W. (2006) 'Clinical supervision: its influence on client rated working alliance and client symptom reduction in the brief treatment of major depression', *Psychotherapy Research*, 16, 3: 317–31.

Banks, N. (1999) *White Counsellors – Black Clients: Theory, Research and Practice*, Aldershot: Ashgate Publishing.

Barell, J. (2007) *Problem-based Learning: An Inquiry Approach*, 2nd edn., Thousand Oaks, CA: Corwin Press.

Barrington, A.J. and Shakespeare-Finch, L. (2013) 'Working with refugee survivors of torture and trauma: an opportunity for vicarious post-traumatic growth', *Counselling Psychology Quarterly*, 26, 1: 89–105.

Bartlett, W.E. (1983) 'A multidimensional framework for the analysis of supervision of counseling', *The Counseling Psychologist*, 11, 1: 9–17.

Beckerman, N.L. (2003) 'Sexual assault: a supervisor's perspective on countertransference', *The Clinical Supervisor*, 21, 2: 99–108.

Ben-Shahar, A.R. (2012) 'Do cry for me Argentina! The challenges trauma work poses for holistic psychotherapy', *Body, Movement and Dance in Psychotherapy: An International Journal for Theory, Research and Practice*, 7, 1: 7–21.

Benson, J.F. (2010) *Working More Creatively with Groups*, 3rd edn., Abingdon: Routledge.

Bernard, J. (2006) 'Tracing the development of clinical supervision', *The Clinical Supervisor*, 24, 1–2: 3–21.

Bernard, J.M. and Goodyear, R.K. (1992) *Fundamentals of Clinical Supervision*, Boston, MA: Allyn & Bacon.

—— (2009) *Fundamentals of Clinical Supervision*, 4th edn., Boston, MA: Allyn and Bacon.

Berne, E. (1961/1975) *Transactional Analysis in Psychotherapy* (first published 1961), London: Souvenir.

Bion, W.R. (1961) *Experiences in Group*, London: Tavistock.

—— (1970) *Attention and Interpretation,* London: Tavistock.

Blocher, D. (1983) 'Towards a cognitive developmental approach to counseling supervision', *The Counseling Psychologist*, 11, 1: 27–34.

Bluckert, P. (2005) *Psychological Dimensions of Executive Coaching*, Maidenhead: Open University Press.

Blumenfield, M. (ed.) (1982) *Applied Psychotherapy Supervision*, New York, NY: Grune & Stratton.

Boalt Boëthius, S., Ögren, M-L., Sjøvold, E. and Sundin, E.C. (2004) 'Experiences of group culture and patterns of interaction in psychotherapy supervision groups', *The Clinical Supervisor*, 23, 1: 101–20.

Boden, J. (2005) 'Suicide: professional and ethical considerations', in R. Tribe and J. Morrissey (eds) *Handbook of Professional and Ethical Practice for Psychologists, Counsellors and Psychotherapists*, Hove: Brunner-Routledge.

Bond, M. and Holland, S. (2010) *Skills of Clinical Supervision for Nurses: A Practical Guide for Supervisees, Clinical Supervisors and Managers*, Maidenhead: Open University Press.

Bond, T. (1986) *Games for Social and Life Skills*, London: Hutchinson.

—— (2000) *Standards and Ethics for Counselling in Action,* London: Sage.

—— (2010) *Standards and Ethics for Counselling in Action*, 3rd edn., London: Sage.

Bond, T. and Mitchels, B. (2008) *Confidentiality and Record Keeping in Counselling and Psychotherapy*, London: BACP/Sage.

Borders, L.D. (1989) 'A pragmatic agenda for developmental supervision research', *Counselor Education and Supervision*, 29, 1: 16–24.

—— (1992) 'Learning to think like a supervisor', *The Clinical Supervisor*, 10, 2: 135–48.

—— (2006) 'Snapshot of clinical supervision in counseling and counselor education: a five-year review', *The Clinical Supervisor*, 24, 1–2: 69–113.

—— (2009) 'Subtle messages in clinical supervision', *The Clinical Supervisor*, 28, 2: 200–9.

—— (2010) 'Principles of best practices for clinical supervision training programs' in J.R. Culbreth and L.L. Brown (eds) *State of the Art in Clinical Supervision*, New York: Routledge.

Borders, L.D. and Brown, L.L. (2005) *The New Handbook of Counseling Supervision*, New York: Lawrence Erlbaum.

Borders, L.D. and Leddick, G. (1987) *Handbook of Counselling Supervision*, Alexandria, VA: American Association for Counseling and Development.

Bordin, E.S. (1983) 'A working alliance based model of supervision', *The Counselling Psychologist*, 11, 1: 35–42.

Boyd, J. (1978) *Counselor Supervision: Approaches, Preparation, Practices*, Muncie, IN: Accelerated Development.

Bradley, L.J. (1989) *Counselor Supervision: Principles, Process and Practice*, 2nd edn., Muncie, IN: Accelerated Development.

Bradley, L.J. and Gould, L.J. (2001) 'Psychotherapy-based models of counsellor supervision', in L. Bradley and N. Ladany (eds) *Counselor Supervision, Principles, Process and Practice*, 3rd edn., Philadelphia, PA: Brunner-Routledge.

Bramley, W. (1996) *The Supervisory Couple in Broad-Spectrum Psychotherapy*, London: Free Association Books.

Brandes, D. and Norris, J. (1998) *The Gamesters' Handbook 3*, Cheltenham: Stanley Thornes.

Breene, C. (2011) 'Resistance is a natural path: an alternative perspective on transformation', in R. Shohet (ed.) *Supervision as Transformation: A Passion for Learning*, London: Jessica Kingsley.

British Association for Counselling (BAC) (1992) *Code of Ethics and Practice for Counsellors*, Rugby: BAC.

British Association for Counselling and Psychotherapy (BACP) (2001) *Ethical Framework for Good Practice in Counselling and Psychotherapy*, Rugby: BACP.

—— (2008) *Counselling and Psychotherapy Workloads* (BACP Information Sheet 4), Lutterworth: BACP.

—— (2009) *Accreditation of Training Courses*, 5th edn., Lutterworth: BACP.

—— (2010) *Ethical Framework for Good Practice in Counselling and Psychotherapy*, revised edn., Lutterworth: BACP.

—— (2012) *Supervisor Accreditation*: http://www.bacp.co.uk/accreditation/Accreditation%20(Supervisor)/index.php (accessed 8th January 2013).

—— (2013a) *Ethical Framework for Good Practice in Counselling and Psychotherapy*, revised edn., Lutterworth: BACP.

—— (2013b) *Guidelines for Accreditation as a Counsellor/Psychotherapist*: http://www.bacp.co.uk/admin/structure/files/pdf/11451_guide.pdf (accessed 25th October 2013).

Brockbank, A. and McGill, I. (2006) *Facilitating Reflective Learning Through Mentoring and Coaching*, London: Kogan Page.

—— (2007) *Facilitating Reflective Learning in Higher Education*, 2nd edn., Maidenhead: Open University Press.

Buckley, P., Conte, H.R., Plutchik, R., Karasu, T.B. and Wild, K.V. (1982) 'Learning dynamic psychotherapy: a longitudinal study', *American Journal of Psychiatry*, 139, 12: 1607–10.

Bucky, S.F., Marques, S., Daly, J., Alley, J. and Karp, A. (2010) 'Supervision characteristics related to the supervisory working alliance as rated by doctoral-level supervisees', *The Clinical Supervisor*, 29, 2: 149–63.

Budman, S.H. and Gurman A.S. (1988) *Theory and Practice of Brief Therapy*, New York, NY: Guilford.

Burley-Allen, M. (1982) *Listening: The Forgotten Skill*, New York: John Wiley & Sons.

Campbell, J.M. (2000) *Becoming an Effective Supervisor: A Workbook for Counselors and Psychotherapists*, Philadephia, PA: Accelerated Development.

Carroll, M. (1988) 'Counselling supervision: the British context', *Counselling Psychology Quarterly*, 1, 4: 387–96.

—— (1996) *Counselling Supervision: Theory, Skills and Practice*, London: Cassell.

—— (1999) 'Supervision in workplace settings', in M. Carroll and E. Holloway (eds) *Counselling Supervision in Context*, London: Sage.

—— (2006) 'Supervising executive coaches', *Therapy Today*, 17, 5: 47–9.

—— (2009) 'Supervision: critical reflection for transformational learning, part 1', *The Clinical Supervisor*, 28, 2: 210–20.

—— (2010) 'Supervision: critical reflection for transformational learning (part 2)', *The Clinical Supervisor*, 29, 1: 1–19.

—— (2011) 'Supervision: a journey of lifelong learning', in R. Shohet (ed.) *Supervision as Transformation: A Passion for Learning*, London: Jessica Kingsley.

Carroll, M. and Gilbert, M.C. (2005) *On Being a Supervisee: Creating Learning Partnerships*, London: Vukani Publishing.

Carter, R. (1995) *The Influence of Race and Racial Identity in Psychotherapy: Towards a Racially Inclusive Model*, New York, NY: John Wiley & Sons.

Cartwright, D. and Zander, A. (eds) (1968) *Group Dynamics: Research and Theory*, 3rd edn., London: Tavistock.

Casement, P. (1985) *On Learning from the Patient*, London: Routledge.

—— (1994) 'The wish not to know', in V.Sinanson (ed.) *Treating Survivors of Satanist Abuse*, London: Routledge.

Casemore, R. and Gallant, M. (2007) 'Supervision: viewed from a distance', *Therapy Today*, 18, 10: 44–5.

Cashwell, T.H. and Dooley, K. (2001) 'The impact of supervision on counselor self-efficacy', *The Clinical Supervisor*, 20, 1: 39–47.

Celenza, A (2007) *Sexual Boundary Violations: Therapeutic, Supervisory and Academic Contexts*, Lanham, MD: Jason Aronson.

Chang, C.Y and Flowers L.R. (2010) 'Multicultural supervision competence', in J.R. Culbreth and L.L. Brown (eds) *State of the Art in Clinical Supervision*, New York, NY: Routledge.

Chang, C.Y., Hays, D.G. and Shoffner, M.F. (2003) 'Cross-racial supervision: a developmental approach for white supervisors working with supervisees of color', *The Clinical Supervisor*, 22, 2: 121–38.

Chang, C.Y., Hays, D.G. and Milliken, T.F. (2009) 'Addressing social justice issues in supervision: a call for client and professional advocacy', *The Clinical Supervisor*, 28, 1: 20–35.

Chen, E.C. and Bernstein, B.L. (2000) 'Relations of complementarity and supervisory issues to supervisory working alliance', *Journal of Counseling Psychology*, 47, 4: 485–97.

Cheon, H.S., Blumer, M.L.C., Shih, A.N., Murphy, M.J. and Sato, M. (2009) 'The influence of supervisor and supervisee matching, role conflict, and supervisory relationship on supervisee satisfaction', *Contemporary Family Therapy*, 31: 52–67.

Christiansen, A.T., Thomas, V., Kafescioglu, N., Karakurt, G., Lowe, W., Smith, W. and Wittenborn, A. (2011) 'Multicultural supervision: lessons learned about an ongoing struggle', *Journal of Marital and Family Therapy*, 37, 1: 109–19.

Christie, D., Lee-Jones, R. and deSousa, S. (2004) 'Changing the perspectives on supervising the supervisors: what would be helpful?', *Clinical Psychology*, 43, 19–22.

Christopher, J.C. (2010) 'Integrating mindfulness as self-care into counselling and psychotherapy training', *Counselling and Psychotherapy Research*, 10, 2: 114–25.

Churchill, S. (2013) 'Transformational supervision', *Therapy Today*, 24, 6: 33–5.

Cikanek, K., Veach, P.M. and Braun, C. (2004) 'Advanced doctoral students' knowledge and understanding of clinical supervisor ethical responsibilities: a brief report', *The Clinical Supervisor*, 23, 1: 191–6.

Cinotti, N. (2012) 'The role of embodied awareness in mindfulness and bioenergetics', *International Journal of Psychotherapy*, 16, 3: 6–16.

Coate, M.A. (2010) *Guidance for Trainee Placements*, BACP Information Sheet T3, Lutterworth: BACP.

Coleman, M.N. (2006) 'Critical incidents in multicultural training: an examination of student experiences', *Journal of Multicultural Counseling and Development*, 34, 3: 168–82.

Collins, D. (2000) Commentary, in C. Jones (ed.) 'Visible, or hidden, aspects of the client', *Counselling*, 11, 4: 210–12.

Cooper, M. and McLeod, J. (2011) *Pluralistic Counselling and Psychotherapy*, London: Sage.

Copeland, S. (2005) *Counselling Supervision in Organisations: Professional and Ethical Dilemmas Explored*, London: Routledge.

Coren, A. (2001) *Short-Term Psychotherapy: A Psychodynamic Approach*, Basingstoke: Palgrave.

Corey, G. (1990) *Theory and Practice of Group Counseling*, 3rd edn., Pacific Grove, CA: Brooks/Cole.

Coursol, D., Lewis, J. and Seymour, J. (2010) 'The use of videoconferencing to enrich counselor training and supervision', in K. Anthony, D.M. Nagel and S. Goss (eds) *The Use of Technology in Mental Health: Applications, Ethics and Practice*, Springfield, IL: Thomas.

Creaner, M. (2011) 'Reflections on learning and transformation in supervision: a crucible of my experience', in R. Shohet (ed.) *Supervision as Transformation: A Passion for Learning*, London: Jessica Kingsley.

Crews, J., Smith M.R., Smaby, M.H., Maddux, C.D., Torres-Rivera, E., Casey, J.A. and Urbani, S. (2005) 'Self-monitoring and counseling skills: skills-based versus IPR training', *Journal of Counseling and Development*, 83, 1: 78–85.

Crocket, K., Pentecost, M., Cresswell, R., Paice, C., Tollestrup, D., De Vries, M. and Wolfe, R. (2009) 'Informing supervision practice through research: a narrative enquiry', *Counselling and Psychotherapy Research*, 9, 2: 101–7.

Crook Lyon, R. and Potkar, K. (2010) 'The supervisory relationship', in N. Ladany and L. Bradley (eds) *Counselor Supervision*, 4th edn., New York, NY: Routledge.

Culbreth, J.R. and Brown, L.L. (2010) (eds) *State of the Art in Clinical Supervision*, New York, NY: Routledge.

Cummings, P. (2002) 'Cybervision: virtual peer group counselling supervision – hindrance or help?', *Counselling and Psychotherapy Research*, 2, 4: 223–9.

Daniels, J. (2000) 'Whispers in the corridors and kangaroo courts: the supervisory role in mistakes and complaints', in B. Lawton and C. Feltham (eds) *Taking Supervision Forward: Enquiries and Trends in Counselling and Psychotherapy*, London: Sage.

Davis, A.H., Savicki, V., Cooley, E.J. and Firth, J.L. (1989) 'Burnout and counselor practitioner expectations of supervision', *Counselor Education and Supervision*, 28, 3: 234–41.

De Stefano, J., D'Iuso, N., Blake, E., Fitzpatrick, M., Drapeau, M. and Chamodraka, M. (2007) 'Trainees' experiences of impasses in counselling and the impact of group supervision on their resolution: a pilot study', *Counselling and Psychotherapy Research*, 7, 1: 42–7.

Deaver, S.P. and Shiflett, C. (2011) 'Art-based supervision techniques', *The Clinical Supervisor*, 30, 2: 257–76.

Delano, F. and Shah, J.C. (2006) 'Professionally packaging your power in the supervisory relationship', *Scottish Journal of Residential Child Care*, 5, 2: 34–44.

Diener, M.J., Hilsenroth, M.J. and Weinberger, J. (2007) 'Therapist affect focus and patient outcomes in psychodynamic psychotherapy: a meta-analysis', *American Journal of Psychiatry*, 164, 6: 936–41.

Doehrman, M.G. (1976) 'Parallel processes in supervision and psychotherapy', *Bulletin of the Menninger Clinic*, 40, 1: 9–104.

Douglas, T. (1995) *Scapegoats: Transferring Blame*, London: Routledge.

Dow, D.M., Hart, G.M. and Nance, D.W. (2009) 'Supervision styles and topics discussed in supervision', *The Clinical Supervisor*, 28, 1: 36–46.

Downey, M. (2003) *Effective Coaching*, London: Texere.

Driscoll, J. (2007) *Practising Clinical Supervision: A Reflective Approach for Healthcare Professionals*, 2nd edn., London: Elsevier.

Drisko, J.W. (2000) 'Play in clinical learning, supervision and field advising', *The Clinical Supervisor*, 19, 1: 153–65.

Driver, C. and Martin, E. (eds) (2002) *Supervising Psychotherapy: Psychoanalytic and Psychodynamic Perspectives*, London: Sage.

—— (eds) (2005) *Supervision and the Analytic Attitude*, London: Whurr.

Dryden, W. and Feltham, C. (1992) *Brief Counselling: A Practical Guide for Beginning Practitioners*, Buckingham: Open University Press.

Dunkley, C. (2006) 'Supervising in cases of suicide risk', *Therapy Today*, 17, 1: 31–3.

Eckberg, M. (2000) *Victims of Cruelty: Somatic Psychotherapy in the Treatment of Posttraumatic Stress Disorder*, Berkeley, CA: North Atlantic Books.

Eckler-Hart, A. (1987) 'True self and false self in the development of the psychotherapist', *Psychotherapy*, 24, 4: 683–92.

Edwards, J.K. (2012) *Strengths-based Supervision in Clinical Practice*, Thousand Oaks, CA: Sage.

Egan, G. (1986) *The Skilled Helper: A Systematic Approach to Effective Helping*, 3rd edn., Pacific Grove, CA: Brooks/Cole.

—— (2010) *The Skilled Helper: A Problem-Management and Opportunity-Development Approach to Helping*, 9th edn., Belmont, CA: Brooks/Cole.

—— (2013) *The Skilled Helper: A Problem-Management and Opportunity-Development Approach to Helping*, 10th edn., Belmont CA: Brooks/Cole.

EHRC (2010) 'Protected characteristics': http://www.equalityhumanrights.com/advice-and-guidance/new-equality-act-guidance/protected-characteristics-definitions/ (accessed 6th June 2013).

—— (2012) 'The essential guide to the public sector equality duty, revised 3rd edition': http://www.equalityhumanrights.com/advice-and-guidance/public-sector-equality-duty/guidance-on-the-equality-duty/ (accessed 10th June 2013).

Ekstein, R. and Wallerstein, R. (1972) *The Teaching and Learning of Psychotherapy*, 2nd edn., Madison, CT: International Universities Press.

Ellis, M.V. (1991) 'Research in clinical supervision: revitalising a scientific agenda', *Counselor Education and Supervision*, 30, 3: 238–51.

—— (2001) 'Harmful supervision, a cause for alarm: comment on Gray et al. (2001) and Nelson and Friedlander (2001)', *Journal of Counseling Psychology*, 48, 4: 401–6.

—— (2010) 'Bridging the science and practice of clinical supervision: some discoveries, some misconceptions', *The Clinical Supervisor*, 29, 1: 95–116.

Ellis, M.V. and Dell, D.M. (1986) 'Dimensionality of supervisor roles: supervisors' perceptions of supervision', *Journal of Counseling Psychology*, 33, 3: 282–91.

Ellis, M.V., D'Iuso, N. and Ladany, N. (2008) 'State of the art in assessment, measurement and evaluation of clinical supervision', in A.K. Hess, K.D. Hess and T.H. Hess (eds) *Psychotherapy Supervision, Theory Research and Practice*, 2nd edn., New York, NY: John Wiley & Sons.

Epstein, O.B., Schwartz, J. and Schwartz, R.W. (eds) (2011) *Ritual Abuse and Mind Control: The Manipulation of Attachment Needs*, London: Karnac.

Etherington, K. (2009) 'Supervising helpers who work with the trauma of sexual abuse', *British Journal of Guidance and Counselling*, 37, 2: 179–94.

Evans, J. (2009) *Online Counselling and Guidance Skills: A Practical Resource for Trainees and Practitioners*, London: Sage.

Falender, C. A. (2010) 'Relationship and accountability: tensions in feminist supervision', *Women & Therapy*, 33, 1–2: 22–41.

Falender, C. A. and Shafranske, E. P. (2004). *Clinical Supervision: A Competency-Based Approach*, Washington, DC: American Psychological Association.

—— (2012) 'The importance of competency-based clinical supervision and training in the twenty-first century: why bother?', *Journal of Contemporary Psychotherapy*, 42, 129–37.

Farber, B. (2006) *Self-Disclosure in Psychotherapy*, New York: Guilford Press.

Farber, B.A. and Heifetz, L.J. (1982) 'The process and dimensions of burnout in psychotherapists', *Professional Psychology*, 13, 2: 293–301.

Faubert, M. And Locke, D.C. (2003) 'Cultural considerations in counselor training and supervision', in G. Roysircar, D.S. Sandhu and V.E. Bibbins Sr. (eds) *Multicultural*

Competencies: A Guidebook of Practices, Alexandria, VA: Association of Multicultural Counseling and Development.

Feindler, E.L. and Padrone, J.J. (2009) 'Self-disclosure in clinical supervision', in A. Bloomgarden and R. Mennuti (eds) *Psychotherapist Revealed: Therapists Speak About Self-Disclosure in Psychotherapy*, New York, NY: Routledge.

Feltham, C. (1997) *Time Limited Counselling*, London: Sage.

—— (2000) 'Baselines, problems and possibilities', in B. Lawton and C. Feltham (eds) *Taking Supervision Forward: Enquiries and Trends in Counselling and Psychotherapy*, London: Sage.

—— (2002) 'A surveillance culture?', *Counselling and Psychotherapy Journal*, 13, 1: 26–7.

—— (2012) 'Brief/Time-limited therapy', in C. Feltham and I. Horton (eds) *The Sage Handbook of Counselling and Psychotherapy*, 3rd edn, London: Sage.

Feltham, C. and Dryden, W. (1994) *Developing Counsellor Supervision*, London: Sage.

Fenichel, M. (2003) 'The supervisory relationship online', in S. Goss and K. Anthony (eds) *Technology in Counselling and Psychotherapy: A Practitioner's Guide*, Basingstoke: Palgrave Macmillan.

Fine, M. and Turner, J. (2002) 'Collaborative supervision: minding the power', in T.C. Todd and C.L. Storm (eds) *The Complete Systemic Supervisor*, Boston, MA: Allyn and Bacon.

Fitch, J.C., Pistole, M.C. and Gunn, J.E. (2010) 'The bonds of development: an attachment-caregiving model of supervision', *The Clinical Supervisor*, 29, 1: 20–34.

Fleming, J. and Benedek, T.F. ([1966] 1983) *Psychoanalytic Supervision: A Method of Clinical Teaching*, New York: International Universities Press.

Forester, C. (2007) 'Your own body of wisdom: recognizing and working with somatic countertransference with dissociative and traumatized patients', *Body, Movement and Dance in Psychotherapy: An International Journal for Theory, Research and Practice*, 2, 2: 123–33.

Foster, J.T., Lichtenberg, J.W. and Peyton, V. (2007) 'The supervisory attachment relationship as a predictor of the professional development of the supervisee', *Psychotherapy Research*, 17, 3: 343–50.

Frankel, Z. and Levitt, H.M. (2009) 'Clients' experience of disengaged moments in psychotherapy: a grounded theory analysis', *Journal of Contemporary Psychotherapy*, 39: 171–86.

Frankland, A. (2001) 'A person-centered model of supervision', *Counseling Psychology Review*, 16, 4: 26–31.

Frawley-O'Dea, M. and Sarnat, J. (2001) *The Supervisory Relationship: A Contemporary Psychodynamic Approach*, New York: Guildford Press.

Freeman, E. (1985) 'The importance of feedback in clinical supervision: implications for direct practice', *The Clinical Supervisor*, 3, 1: 5–26.

Freitas, G.J. (2002) 'The impact of psychotherapy supervision on client outcome: a critical examination', *Psychotherapy: Theory, Research, Practice, Training*, 39, 4: 354–67.

Freud, S. ([1895] 1980) 'The psychotherapy of hysteria', in S. Freud and J. Breuer, *Studies on Hysteria*, Harmondsworth: Penguin.

—— ([1914] 1986) 'On the history of the psychoanalytic movement', in *Historical and Expository Works on Psychoanalysis*, Harmondsworth: Penguin.

Friedlander, M.L., Siegal, S.M. and Brenock, K. (1989) 'Parallel processes in counseling and supervision: a case study', *Journal of Counseling Psychology*, 36, 2: 149–57.

Frizell, C. (2012) 'Embodiment and the supervisory task: the supervision of dance movement psychotherapists in training', *Body, Movement and Dance in Psychotherapy: An International Journal for Theory, Research and Practice*, 7, 4: 293–304.

Gabbard, G.O. (2002) 'Post-termination sexual boundary violations', *Psychiatric Clinics of North America*, 25, 3: 593–603.

Gabriel, L. (2000) Commentary, in C. Jones (ed.) 'Visible, or hidden, aspects of the client', *Counselling*, 11, 4: 210–12.

—— (2005) *Speaking the Unspeakable: The Ethics of Dual Relationships in Counselling and Psychotherapy*, London: Routledge.

Gabriel, L. and Casemore, R. (eds) (2009) *Relational Ethics in Practice: Narratives from Counselling and Psychotherapy*, London: Routledge.

—— (2010) *Guidance for Ethical Decision Making: A Suggested Model for Practitioners*, BACP Information Sheet P4, Lutterworth: BACP.

Garbutt, L.M. (2009) 'Managing psychotherapeutic practice between external supervision sessions: understanding and using the concept of an internal supervisor', unpublished D.Psych. thesis, Middlesex University and Metanoia Institute.

Gard, D.E. and Lewis, J.M. (2008) 'Building the supervisory alliance with beginning therapists', *The Clinical Supervisor*, 27, 1: 39–60.

Garrett, M.T., Borders, L.D., Crutchfield, L.B., Torres-Riviera, E., Brotherton, D. and Curtis, R. (2001) 'Multicultural supervision: a paradigm of cultural responsiveness for supervisors', *Journal of Multicultural Counseling & Development*, 29, 2: 147–58.

Garrett, T. (2002) 'Inappropriate therapist-patient relationships', in R. Goodwin and D. Cramer (eds) *Inappropriate Relationships*, Mahwah, NJ: Lawrence Erlbaum.

Gatmon, D., Jackson, D., Koshkarian, L., Martos-Perry, N., Molina, A., Patel, N. and Rodolfa, E. (2001) 'Exploring ethnic, gender, and sexual orientation variables in supervision: do they really matter?', *Journal of Multicultural Counseling and Development*, 29, 2: 102–13.

Gazzola, N. and Theriault, A. (2007) 'Super- (and not-so-super-) vision of counsellors-in-training: supervisee perspectives on broadening and narrowing processes', *British Journal of Guidance and Counselling*, 35, 2: 189–204.

Gilbert, M. and Sills, C. (1999) 'Training for supervision evaluation', in E. Holloway and M.Carroll (eds) *Training Counselling Supervisors*, London: Sage.

Gilbert, M.C. and Evans, K. (2000) *Psychotherapy Supervision: An Integrative Relational Approach to Psychotherapy Supervision*, Buckingham: Open University Press.

Gill, S. (ed.) (2001) *The Supervisory Alliance: Facilitating the Psychotherapist's Learning and Experience*, Northvale, NJ: Jason Aronson.

Gnilka, P. B., Chang, C. Y and Dew, B. J. (2012) 'The relationship between supervisee stress, coping resources, the working alliance and the supervisory working alliance', *Journal of Counseling & Development*, 90, 1: 63–70.

Gold, J.H. (2006) 'Why psychotherapy supervision is essential for mental health professionals', in J.H. Gold (ed.) *Psychotherapy Supervision and Consultation in Clinical Practice*, Lanham, MD: Jason Aronson.

Gomersall, J. (1997) 'Peer group supervision', in G. Shipton (ed.) *Supervision of Psychotherapy and Counselling: Making a Place to Think*, Buckingham: Open University Press.

Gonsalvez, C.J. and Milne, D.L. (2010) 'Clinical supervisor training in Australia: a review of current problems and possible solutions', *Australian Psychologist*, 45, 4: 233–42.

Gonzalez, R.C. (1997) 'Postmodern supervision: a multicultural perspective', in D. Pope-Davis and H. Coleman (eds) *Multicultural Counseling Competencies: Assessment, Education and Training, and Supervision*, Thousand Oaks, CA: Sage.

Goodyear, R.K. and Bradley, F.O. (1983) 'Theories of counselor supervision: points of convergence and divergence', *The Counseling Psychologist*, 11, 1: 59–67.

Goodyear, R.K., Bunch, K. and Claiborn, C.D. (2006) 'Current supervision scholarship in psychology: a five year review', *The Clinical Supervisor*, 24, 1–2: 137–47.

Gopee, N. (2008) *Mentoring and Supervision in Healthcare*, London: Sage.

Goss, S., Anthony, K. and Nagel, D.M. (2012) 'Wider uses of technology in therapy', in C. Feltham and I. Horton (eds) *The Sage Handbook of Counselling and* Psychotherapy, 3rd edn., London: Sage.

Grant, J. and Schofield, M. (2007) 'Career-long supervision: patterns and perspectives', *Counselling and Psychotherapy Research*, 7, 1: 3–11.

Gray, L.A., Ladany, N., Walker, J.A. and Ancis, J.R. (2001) 'Psychotherapy trainees' experience of counterproductive events in supervision', *Journal of Counseling Psychology*, 48, 4: 371–83.

Gray, S.W. and Smith, M.S. (2009) 'The influence of diversity in clinical supervision: a framework for reflective conversations and questioning', *The Clinical Supervisor*, 28, 2: 155–79.

Green, M.S. and Dekkers, T.D. (2010) 'Attending to power and diversity in supervision: an exploration of supervisee learning outcomes and satisfaction with supervision', *Journal of Feminist Family Therapy*, 22, 4: 293–312.

Greer, J.A. (2003) 'Where to turn for help: responses to inadequate clinical supervision', *The Clinical Supervisor*, 21, 1: 135–43.

Groman, M. (2010) 'The use of telephone to enrich counselor training and supervision', in K. Anthony, D.M. Nagel and S. Goss (eds) *The Use of Technology in Mental Health: Applications, Ethics and Practice*, Springfield, IL: Thomas.

Guanipa, C. (2003) 'A preliminary instrument to evaluate multicultural issues in marriage and family therapy supervision', *The Clinical Supervisor*, 21, 1: 59–75.

Gubi, P.M. (2007) 'Exploring the supervision experience of some mainstream counsellors who integrate prayer in counselling', *Counselling and Psychotherapy Research*, 7, 2: 114–21.

Haggerty, G. and Hilsenroth, M.J. (2011) 'The use of video in psychotherapy supervision', *British Journal of Psychotherapy*, 27, 2: 193–210.

Hahn, W.K. (2001) 'The experience of shame in psychotherapy supervision', *Psychotherapy: Theory, Research, Practice, Training*, 38, 1: 272–82.

Harris, M. and Brockbank, A. (2011) *An Integrative Approach to Therapy and Supervision: A Practical Guide for Counsellors and Psychotherapists*, London: Jessica Kingsley.

Hart, G.M. (1982) *The Process of Clinical Supervision*, Baltimore, MD: University Park Press.

Hawkins, P. and Shohet, R. (1989) *Supervision in the Helping Professions*, Milton Keynes: Open University Press.

—— (2000) *Supervision in the Helping Professions*, 2nd edn., Buckingham: Open University Press.

—— (2006) *Supervision in the Helping Professions*, 3rd edn., Maidenhead: Open University Press.

—— (2012) *Supervision in the Helping Professions*, 4th edn., Milton Keynes: Open University Press.

Hawkins, P. And Smith, N. (2006) *Coaching, Mentoring and Organisational Consultancy: Supervision and Development*, Maidenhead: Open University Press.

Hawthorne, L. (1975) 'Games supervisors play', *Social Work*, 20, 3: 179–83.

Hay, J. (2007) *Reflective Practice and Supervision for Coaches*, Maidenhead: Open University Press.

Hayes, R.L. (1989) 'Group supervision', in L.J. Bradley, *Counselor Supervision: Principles, Process and Practice*, 2nd edn., Muncie, IN: Accelerated Development.

Heery, F. (2008) 'The supervisory relationship: a learning process', *Éisteach: A Quarterly Journal of Counselling and Psychotherapy*, 8, 2, 22–5.

Hellman, S. (1999) 'The portfolio: a method of reflective development, in E. Holloway and M. Carroll (eds) *Training Counselling Supervisors*, London: Sage.

Henderson, P. (2004) 'Supervision of supervision', *Counselling and Psychotherapy Journal*, 15, 5: 43–5.

—— (2007) 'Approaches to supervision theory', *Therapy Today*, 18, 8: 46–7.

—— (ed.) (2009a) *Supervisor Training: Issues and Approaches*, London: Karnac.

—— (2009b) *A Different Wisdom: Reflections on Supervision Practice*, London: Karnac.

—— (2009c) 'Developing authority from the inside out', in P. Henderson (ed.) *Supervisor Training, Issues and Approaches*, London: Karnac.

Henderson, P. and Bailey, C. (2009) 'The internal supervisor: developing the witness within', in P. Henderson (ed.) *Supervisor Training: Issues and Approaches*, London: Karnac.

Henry, P.J., Hart, G.M. and Nance, D.W. (2004) 'Supervision topics as perceived by supervisors and supervisees', *The Clinical Supervisor*, 23, 2: 139–52.

Heppner, P.P. and Roehlke, H.J. (1984) 'Differences among supervisees at different levels of training: implications for a developmental model of supervision', *Journal of Counseling Psychology*, 31, 1: 76–90.

Heron, J. (2001) *Helping the Client: A Creative Practical Guide*, 5th edn., London: Sage.

Herron, W.G. and Teitelbaum, S. (2001) 'Traditional and intersubjective supervision', *The Clinical Supervisor*, 20, 1: 145–59.

Hess A.K. (ed.) (1980) *Psychotherapy Supervision: Theory, Research and Practice*, New York, NY: John Wiley & Sons.

Hess, A.K, Hess, K.D. and Hess, T.H. (eds) (2008) *Psychotherapy Supervision: Theory, Research and Practice*, 2nd edn., Hoboken, NJ: Wiley.

Hess, S.A., Knox, S., Schultz, J.M., Hill, C.E., Sloan, L., Brandt, S., Kelley, F. and Hoffman, M.A. (2008) 'Predoctoral interns' nondisclosure in supervision', *Psychotherapy Research*, 18, 4: 400–11.

Heuer, G. (2005) '"In my flesh I shall see God": Jungian body psychotherapy', in N. Totton (ed.) *New Dimensions in Body Psychotherapy*, Maidenhead: Open University Press.

—— (2009) 'Spooky action at a distance: parallel processes in Jungian analysis and supervision', in D. Mathers (ed.) *Vision and Supervision: Jungian and Post-Jungian Perspectives*, Hove: Routledge.

Hewson, J. (1999) 'Training supervisors to contract in supervision', in E.L. Holloway and M. Carroll (eds) *Training Counselling Supervisors*, London: Sage.

—— (2008) 'Passionate supervision: a wider landscape', in R. Shohet, *Passionate Supervision*, London: Jessica Kingsley.

Hill, P. (2004) *Concepts of Coaching: A Guide for Managers*, London: Institute for Leadership and Management.

Hoffman, M.A., Hill, C.E., Holmes, S.E. and Freitas, G.F. (2005) 'Supervisor perspective on the process and outcome of giving easy, difficult, or no feedback to supervisees', *Journal of Counseling Psychology*, 52, 1: 3–13.

Hogan, R.A. (1964) 'Issues and approaches in supervision', *Psychotherapy: Theory, Research and Practice*, 1, 3: 139–41.

Holloway E.L. (1995) *Clinical Supervision: A Systems Approach*, Thousand Oaks, CA: Sage.

Holloway, E.L. and Johnston, R. (1985) 'Group supervision: widely practiced but poorly understood', *Counselor Education and Supervision*, 24, 4: 332–40.

Holloway, E.L. and Carroll. M. (eds) (1999) *Training Counselling Supervisors*, London: Sage.

Honey, P. and Mumford, A. (2006) *The Learning Styles Helper's Guide*, Maidenhead: Peter Honey Publications.

Horowitz, M.J. (1989) *Introduction to Psychodynamics: A New Synthesis*, London: Routledge.

Horton, I. and Varma, V. (eds) (1997) *The Needs of Counsellors and Psychotherapists*, London: Sage.

Houston, G. (2013) *Gestalt Counselling in a Nutshell*, London: Sage.

Hughes, L. and Pengelly, P. (1997) *Staff Supervision in a Turbulent Environment*, London: Jessica Kingsley.

Huhra, R.L., Yamokoski-Maynhart, C.A. and Prieto, L.R. (2008) 'Reviewing videotape in supervision: a developmental approach', *Journal of Counseling and Development*, 86, 4: 412–18.

Hume, G.B. (1977) *Searching For God*, London: Hodder & Stoughton.

Hunter, M. (2004) *Understanding Dissociative Disorders: A Guide for Family Physicians and Health Care Professionals*, Carmarthen: Crown House Publishing.

Inman, A.G. (2006) 'Supervisor multicultural competence and its relation to supervisory process and outcome', *Journal of Marital and Family Therapy*, 32, 1: 73–85.

Inman, A.G. and Ladany, N. (2008) 'Research: the status of the field', in A.K. Hess, K.D. Hess and T.H. Hess (eds) *Psychotherapy Supervision: Theory, Research and Practice*, 2nd edn., New York, NY: John Wiley & Sons.

Inskipp, F. (1999) 'Training supervisees to use supervision', in E.L. Holloway and M. Carroll (eds) *Training Counselling Supervisors*, London: Sage.

Inskipp, F. and Proctor, P. (1994) *Making the Most of Supervision*, Twickenham: Cascade.
—— (1995) *Becoming a Counsellor Supervisor*, Twickenham: Cascade.
—— (2002) *The Art, Craft and Tasks of Counselling Supervision*, 2nd edn., Twickenham: Cascade.

Ishiyama, F.I. (1988) 'A model of visual case processing using metaphors and drawings', *Counselor Education and Supervision*, 28, 2: 153–61.

Itzhaky, H. (2001) 'Factors relating to "interferences" in communication between supervisor and supervisee: differences between the external and internal supervisor', *The Clinical Supervisor*, 20, 1: 73–85.

Izzard, S. (2001) 'The responsibility of the supervisor supervising trainees', in S. Wheeler and D. King (eds) *Supervising Counsellors: Issues of Responsibility*, London: Sage.

Jacobs, D., David, P. and Meyer, J.M. (1995) *The Supervisory Encounter*, New Haven, CT: Yale University Press.

Jacobs, M. (1986) *The Presenting Past*, Milton Keynes: Open University Press.

——— (2000a) 'Supervision of supervision' ('Taking supervision forward: a roundtable of views'), in B. Lawton and C. Feltham (eds) *Taking Supervision Forward: Enquiries and Trends in Counselling and Psychotherapy*, London: Sage.

——— (2000b) Commentary, in C. Jones (ed.) 'Visible, or hidden, aspects of the client', *Counselling*, 11, 4: 210–12.

Jacobsen, C.H. (2007) 'A qualitative single case study of parallel processes', *Counselling and Psychotherapy Research*, 7, 1: 26–33.

Jacoby, M. (1984) *The Analytic Encounter: Transference and Human Relationship*, Toronto: Inner City Books.

Jeffery, B. (2008) 'All at sea', *Therapy Today*, 19, 2: 37–8.

Jencius, M., Baltimore, M.L. and Getz, H.G. (2010) 'Innovative uses of technology in clinical supervision', in J. Culbreth and L. Brown (eds) *State of the Art in Clinical Supervision*, New York: Routledge.

Johns, C. (2009) *Becoming a Reflective Practitioner*, 3rd edn., Chichester: John Wiley & Sons.

Johnson, R.A. (1991) *Owning Your Own Shadow*, San Francisco: Harper.

Jones, G. and Stokes, A. (2009) *Online Counselling: A Handbook for Practitioners*, London: Palgrave.

Jordan, K. (2007) 'Beginning supervisees' identity: the importance of relationship variables and experience versus gender matches in the supervisee/supervisor interplay', *The Clinical Supervisor*, 25, 1–2: 43–51.

Jung, C.G. ([1951]1968) *Aion, The Collected Works: Vol. 9, Part II*, 2nd edn., London: Routledge & Kegan Paul.

——— ([1960]1969) 'Synchronicity: an acausal connecting principle', in *The Structure and Dynamics of the Psyche, The Collected Works: Vol. 8*, 2nd edn., London: Routledge & Kegan Paul.

——— ([1921]1971) *Psychological Types, The Collected Works Vol. 6*, 2nd edn., London: Routledge.

Kaberry, S. (2000) 'Abuse in supervision', in B. Lawton and C. Feltham (eds) *Taking Supervision Forward: Enquiries and Trends in Counselling and Psychotherapy*, London: Sage.

Kadushin, A. (1985) *Supervision in Social Work*, 2nd edn., New York, NY: Columbia University Press.

Kagan N. (1980) 'Influencing human interaction – eighteen years with IPR', in A.K. Hess, *Psychotherapy Supervision: Theory Research and Practice*, New York, NY: Wiley.

——— (1984) 'Interpersonal process recall: basic methods and recent research', in D. Larsen (ed.) *Teaching Psychological Skills*, Monterey, CA: Brooks/Cole.

Kagan, N., Krathwohl, D. and Miller, R. (1963) 'Stimulated recall in therapy using videotape – a case study', *Journal of Counseling Psychology*, 10, 3: 237–43.

Kagee, A. (2007) 'Multicultural aspects of supervision: considerations for South African supervisors in the helping professions', *Social Work – Stellenbosch*, 43, 4: 343–9.

Karpenko, V. and Gidycz, C. A. (2012) 'The supervisory relationship and the process of evaluation: recommendations for supervisors', *The Clinical Supervisor*, 31, 2: 138–58.

Kauderer, S. and Herron, W.G. (1990) 'The supervisory relationship in psychotherapy over time', *Psychological Reports*, 67, 2: 471–80.

Kim, B.S.K. and Lyons, H.Z. (2003) 'Experiential activities and multicultural counselling competence training', *Journal of Counseling and Development*, 81, 4: 400–8.

King, D. (2001) 'Clinical responsibility and the supervision of counsellors', in S. Wheeler and D. King (eds.) *Supervising Counsellors: Issues of Responsibility*, London: Sage.

Kinnell, D. And Hughes, P. (2010) *Mentoring Nursing and Healthcare Students*, London: Sage.

Knight, C. (2004a) 'Integrating solution-focused principles and techniques into clinical practice and supervision', *The Clinical Supervisor*, 23, 2: 153–73.

—— (2004b) 'Working with survivors of childhood trauma: implications for clinical supervision', *The Clinical Supervisor*, 23, 2: 81–105.

—— (2012) 'Therapeutic use of self: theoretical and evidence-based considerations for clinical practice and supervision', *The Clinical Supervisor*, 31, 1: 1–24.

Knox, S., Burkard, A.W., Edwards, L.M., Smith, J.J. and Schlosser, L.Z. (2008) 'Supervisors' reports of the effects of supervisor self-disclosure on supervisees', *Psychotherapy Research*, 18, 5: 543–59.

Koltz, R.L. (2008): 'Integrating creativity into supervision using Bernard's discrimination model', *Journal of Creativity in Mental Health*, 3, 4: 416–27.

Koob, J.J. (2003) 'The effects of solution-focused supervision on the perceived self-efficacy of therapists in training', *The Clinical Supervisor*, 21, 2: 161–83.

Kopp, S. (1977) *Back to One: A Practical Guide for Psychotherapists*, Palo Alto, CA: Science and Behaviour Books.

Kottler, A. and Carlson, J. (2005) *The Client Who Changed Me*, New York, NY: Routledge.

Kron, T. and Yerushalmi, H. (2000) 'The intersubjective approach to supervision', *The Clinical Supervisor*, 19, 1: 99–121.

Kuechler, C.F. (2007) 'Practitioners' voices: group supervisors reflect on their practice', *The Clinical Supervisor*, 25, 1–2: 83–103.

Kutter, P. (1993) 'Direct and indirect ("reversed") mirror phenomena in group supervision', *Group Analysis*, 26, 2: 177–81.

Ladany, N. (2004) 'Psychotherapy supervision: what lies beneath', *Psychotherapy Research*, 14, 1: 1–19.

Ladany, N. and Lehrman-Waterman, D.E. (1999) 'The content and frequency of supervisor self-disclosures and their relationship to supervisor style and supervisory working alliance', *Counselor Education and Supervision*, 38, 3: 143–60.

Ladany, N. and Melincoff, D.S. (1999) 'The nature of counselor supervisor nondisclosure', *Counselor Education and Supervision*, 38, 3: 161–76.

Ladany, N. and Bradley, L. (eds) (2010) *Counselor Supervision*, 4th edn., Philadelphia, PA: Routledge.

Ladany, N., Walker, J.A. and Melincoff, D.S. (2001) 'Supervisory style: its relation to the supervisory working alliance and supervisor self-disclosure', *Counselor Education and Supervision*, 40, 4: 263–75.

Ladany, N., Friedlander, M.L. and Nelson, M.L. (2005) *Critical Events in Psychotherapy Supervision: An Interpersonal Approach*, Washington, DC: American Psychological Association.

Ladany, N., Constantine, M.G., Miller, K., Erickson, C.D. and Muse-Burke, J.L. (2000) 'Supervisor countertransference: a qualitative investigation into its identification and description', *Journal of Counseling Psychology*, 47, 1: 102–15.

Lago, C. and Smith, B. (eds) (2010) *Anti-Discriminatory Practice in Counselling and Psychotherapy*, 2nd edn., London: Sage.

Lahad, M. (2000) *Creative Supervision: The Use of Expressive Arts Methods in Supervision and Self-Supervision*, London: Jessica Kingsley Publishers.

Lambers, E. (2000) 'Supervision in person-centred therapy: facilitating congruence', in D. Mearns and B. Thorne (eds) *Person-Centred Therapy Today: New Frontiers in Theory and Practice*, London: Sage.

—— (2006) 'Supervising the humanity of the therapist', *Person-Centred and Experiential Psychotherapies*, 5, 4: 266—76.

Lammers, W. (1999) 'Training in group and team supervision', in E.L. Holloway and M. Carroll (eds) *Training Counselling Supervisors*, London: Sage.

Lampropoulos, G.K. (2003) 'A common factors view of counseling supervision process', *The Clinical Supervisor*, 21, 1: 77–95.

Langs, R. (1982) *Psychotherapy: A Basic Text*, New York, NY: Jason Aronson.

Lawton, B. (2000) 'A very exposing affair', in B. Lawton and C. Feltham (eds) *Taking Supervision Forward: Enquiries and Trends in Counselling and Psychotherapy*, London: Sage.

Leach, M.M., Stoltenberg, C.D., McNeill, B.W. and Eichenfield, G.A. (1997) 'Self-efficacy and counselor development: testing the Integrated Developmental Model', *Counselor Education and Supervision*, 37, 2: 115–24.

Leddick, G.R. and Bernard, J.M. (1980) 'The history of supervision: a critical review', *Counselor Education and Supervision*, 19: 186–96.

Leddick, G.R. and Dye, H.A. (1987) 'Effective supervision as portrayed by trainee expectations and preferences', *Counselor Education and Supervision*, 27, 2: 139–53.

Lehrman-Waterman, D. And Ladany, N. (2001) 'Development and validation of the evaluation process within supervision inventory', *Journal of Counseling Psychology*, 48, 2: 168–77.

Lenz, A.S and Smith, R.L. (2010) 'Integrating wellness concepts within a clinical supervision model', *The Clinical Supervisor*, 29, 2: 228–45.

Liddle, B.J. (1986) 'Resistance in supervision: a response to perceived threat', *Counselor Education and Supervision*, 26, 2: 117–27.

Lidmila, A. (1992) 'The way of supervision', *Counselling*, 3, 2: 97–100.

—— (1997) 'Shame, knowledge and modes of enquiry in supervision', in G. Shipton (ed.) *Supervision of Psychotherapy and Counselling: Making a Place to Think*, Buckingham: Open University Press.

Lietz, C.A. and Rounds, T. (2009) 'Strengths-based supervision: a child welfare supervision training project', *The Clinical Supervisor*, 28, 2: 124–40.

Lockett, M. (2001) 'The responsibilities of group supervisors', in S. Wheeler and D. King (eds) *Supervising Counsellors: Issues of Responsibility*, London: Sage.

Macnab, C. (2004) 'Supervision in time-limited settings', *Counselling and Psychotherapy Journal*, 15, 9: 40–2.

Magnuson, S., Wilcoxon, S.A. and Norem, K. (2000) 'A profile of lousy supervision: experienced counselors' perspectives', *Counselor Education and Supervision*, 39, 3: 189–202.

Mander, G. (1998) 'Supervising short-term psychodynamic work', *Counselling*, 9, 4: 301–5.

—— (2002) 'Supervision of supervision: specialism or new profession?', in C. Driver and E. Martin (eds) *Supervising Psychotherapy*, London: Sage.

Marshall, R.D., Spitzer, R.L.,Vaughan, S.C., Vaughan, R., Mellman, L. A., MacKinnon, R.A. and Roose, S.P. (2001) 'Assessing the subjective experience of being a participant in psychiatric research', *American Journal of Psychiatry*, 158, 2: 319–21.

Martin, L. (2013) 'Self-harm: the solution, not the problem?', *Therapy Today*, 24, 6: 23–5.

Mattinson, J. (1977) *The Reflection Process in Casework Supervision*, London: Institute of Marital Studies, Tavistock Institute of Human Relations.

Maxwell, A. (2009) 'How do business coaches experience the boundary between coaching and therapy/counselling?', *Coaching: An International Journal of Theory, Research and Practice*, 2, 2: 149–62.

McIntosh, N, Dirks, A., Fitzpatrick, J. And Shuman, C. (2006) 'Games in clinical genetic supervision', *Journal of Genetic Counseling*, 15, 4: 225–43.

Mearns, D. and Cooper, M. (2005) *Working at Relational Depth in Counselling and Psychotherapy*, London: Sage.

Mearns, D. with updates by Docchar, C. and Richards, K. (2008) *How Much Supervision should you have?*, Lutterworth: BACP.

Meekums, B. (2007) 'Spontaneous symbolism in clinical supervision: moving beyond logic', *Body, Movement and Dance in Psychotherapy: An International Journal for Theory, Research and Practice*, 2, 2: 95–107.

Mehr, K.E., Ladany, N. and Caskie, G.I. (2010) 'Trainee nondisclosure in supervision: what are they not telling you?', *Counselling and Psychotherapy Research*, 10, 2: 103–13.

Millar, A. (2009) 'Developing skills: practice, observation and feedback', in P. Henderson (ed.) *Supervisor Training: Issues and Approaches*, London: Karnac.

Miller, A. (2012) *Healing the Unimaginable: Treating Ritual Abuse and Mind Control*, London: Karnac.

Miller, S., Hubble, M. and Duncan, B. (2008) 'Supershrinks', *Therapy Today*, 19, 3: 4–9.

Milne, D. (2009) *Evidence-Based Clinical Supervision: Principles and Practice*, Chichester: BPS Blackwell.

Mitchels, B. and Bond, T. (2010) *Essential Law for Counsellors and Psychotherapists*, London: BACP/Sage.

—— (2011) *Legal Issues Across Counselling and Psychotherapy Settings*, London: BACP/Sage.

Moon, J. A. (2006) *Learning Journals: A Handbook for Reflective Practice and Professional Development*, 2nd edn., London: Routledge.

Morrissey, J. (2005) 'Training supervision: professional and ethical considerations', in R. Tribe and J. Morrissey (eds) *Handbook of Professional and Ethical Practice for Psychologists, Counsellors and Psychotherapists*, Hove: Brunner-Routledge.

Muratori, M. (2001) 'Examining supervisor impairment from the counselor trainee's perspective', *Counselor Education and Supervision*, 41, 1: 41–56.

Murphy, M.J. and Wright, D.W. (2005) 'Supervisees' perspectives of power use in supervision', *Journal of Marital and Family Therapy*, 31, 3: 283–95.

Najavits, L.M., Ghinassi, F., Van Horn, A., Weiss, R.D., Siqueland, L., Frank, A., Thase, M.E. and Luborsky, L. (2004) 'Therapist satisfaction with four manual-based treatments on a national multisite trial: an exploratory study', *Psychotherapy: Theory, Research, Practice, Training*, 41, 1: 26–37.

Neath, N. (2009) 'Relational ethics: a perspective after the essays and marking', in L. Gabriel and R. Casemore (eds) *Relational Ethics in Practice: Narratives from Counselling and Psychotherapy*, London: Brunner-Routledge.

Nelson, M.L. and Friedlander, M.L. (2001) 'A close look at conflictual supervisory relationships: the trainee's perspective', *Journal of Counseling Psychology*, 48, 4: 384–95.

Nelson, M.L., Gray, L.A., Friedlander, M.L., Ladany, N. and Walker, J.A. (2001) 'Towards relationship-centred supervision: reply to Veach (2001) and Ellis (2001)', *Journal of Counseling Psychology*, 48, 4: 407–9.

Neswald-McCalip, R. (2001) 'Development of the secure counselor: case examples supporting Pistole & Watkins' (1995) discussion of attachment theory in counseling supervision', *Counselor Education & Supervision*, 41, 1:18–27.

Neufeldt, S. (1997) 'A social constructivist approach to counseling supervision', in T. Sexton and B. Griffin (eds) *Constructivist Thinking in Counseling Practice, Research, and Training*, New York, NY: Teachers' College Press.

Neufeldt, S.A. and Nelson, M.L. (1999) 'When is counseling an appropriate and ethical supervision function?', *The Clinical Supervisor*, 18, 1: 125–35.

Noelle, M. (2003) 'Self-report in supervision: positive and negative slants', *The Clinical Supervisor*, 21, 1: 125–34.

Norris, D. M., Gutheil, T. G. and Strasburger, L. H. (2003) 'This couldn't happen to me: boundary problems and sexual misconduct in the psychotherapy relationship', *Psychiatric Services*, 54, 4: 517–22.

Nutt, C. (2011) 'Reflections on clinical responsibility', *Therapy Today*, 22, 7: 52–3.

O'Connell, B. (1998) *Solution-Focused Therapy*, London: Sage.

O'Connell, B. and Jones, C. (1997) 'Solution focused supervision', *Counselling*, 8, 4: 289–92.

O'Hara, D. and Schofield, M.J. (2008) 'Personal approaches to psychotherapy integration', *Counselling and Psychotherapy Research*, 8, 1: 53–62.

O'Shaughnessy, T., Mori, Y., Kaduvettoor, C.B. and Weatherford, R.D. (2010) 'Counseling and psychotherapy-based models of counselor supervision', in N. Ladany and L. Bradley (eds) *Counselor Supervision*, 4th edn., Philadelphia, PA: Routledge.

Ogden, P. and Steele, K. (2008) *Mentalization, Mindfulness and the Body in Chronic Traumatization*, International Society for the Study of Trauma and Dissociation: http://www.isst-d.org (accessed 3rd April 2009).

Ögren, M-L. and Jonsson, C-O. (2004) 'Psychotherapeutic skill following group supervision according to supervisees and supervisors', *The Clinical Supervisor*, 22, 1: 35–58.

Ögren, M-L. and Sundin, E.C. (2007) 'Experiences of the group format in psychotherapy supervision', *The Clinical Supervisor*, 25, 1–2, 65–82.

—— (2009) 'Group supervision in psychotherapy: main findings from a Swedish research project on psychotherapy supervision in a group format', *British Journal of Guidance & Counselling*, 37, 2: 129–39.

Ögren, M-L., Apelman, A. and Klawitter, M. (2002) 'The group in psychotherapy supervision', *The Clinical Supervisor*, 20, 2: 147–75.

Olson, M.M., Russell, C.S. and White, M.B. (2002) 'Technological implications for clinical supervision and practice', *The Clinical Supervisor*, 20, 2: 201–15.

ONS (2103) Definition of the NS-SEC classification, see: http://www.ons.gov.uk/ons/guide-method/classifications/current-standard-classifications/soc2010/soc2010-volume-3-ns-sec—rebased-on-soc2010—user-manual/index.html (accessed 25th June 2013).

Orr, M. (1999) 'Believing patients', in C. Feltham (ed.) *Controversies in Counselling and Psychotherapy*, London: Sage.

Overholser, J.C. (2004) 'The four pillars of psychotherapy supervision', *The Clinical Supervisor*, 23, 1: 1–13.

Owen, D. and Shohet, R. (2012) *Clinical Supervision in the Medical Profession: Structured Reflective Practice*, Maidenhead: Open University Press.

Owen-Pugh, V. and Symons, C. (2013) 'Roth and Pilling's competence framework for clinical supervision: how generalisable is it?', *Counselling and Psychotherapy Research*, 13, 2: 126–35.

Packwood, D. (2008) 'Gandalf's apprentice: the magic of supervision', *Therapy Today*, 19, 6: 36–8.

Page, S. (1999a) *The Shadow and the Counsellor*, London: Routledge.

—— (1999b) 'Make use of supervision', in I. Macwhinnie and S. Rigby, *NVQ/SVQ Level 3 Counselling*, London: Hodder & Stoughton, in conjunction with BAC.

Parkes, C.M., Laungani, P. and Young, B. (1997) *Death and Bereavement Across Cultures*, London: Routledge.

Passmore, J. Holloway, M. and Rawle-Cope, M. (2010) 'Using MBTI type to explore differences and the implications for practice for therapists and coaches: are executive coaches really like counsellors?', *Counselling Psychology Quarterly*, 23, 1: 1–16.

Pelling, N. (2008) 'The relationship of supervisory experience, counseling experience, and training in supervision to supervisory identity development', *International Journal for the Advancement of Counseling*, 30, 4: 235–48.

Perry, C. (2003) 'Into the labyrinth: A developing approach to supervision', in J. Weiner, R. Mizen and J. Duckham (eds) *Supervising and Being Supervised: A Practice in Search of a Theory*, Basingstoke: Palgrave.

Peyton, P.R. (2004) 'Bullying in supervision', *Counselling and Psychotherapy Journal*, 15, 6: 36–7.

Poertner, S. and Miller, K. M. (1996) *The Art of Giving and Receiving Feedback*, Urbandale: Provant Media Publishing.

Porter, N. (2010) 'Feminist and multicultural underpinnings to supervision', *Women and Therapy*, 33: 1–6.

Power, A. (2009) 'Supervision – A space where diversity can be thought about?', *Attachment: New Directions in Psychotherapy and Relational Psychoanalysis*, 3, 2: 157–75.

—— (2013) 'Supervision of supervision: how many mirrors do we need?', *British Journal of Psychotherapy*, 29, 3: 389–404.

Prieto, L.R. (1996) 'Group supervision: still widely practiced but poorly understood', *Counselor Education and Supervision*, 35, 4: 295–307.

Proctor, B. (1988) 'Supervision: a co-operative exercise in accountability', in M. Marken and M. Payne (eds) *Enabling and Ensuring*, Leicester: National Youth Bureau and Council for Education and Training in Youth and Community Work.

—— (2000) *Group Supervision: A Guide to Creative Practice*, London: Sage.

—— (2008) *Group Supervision: A Guide to Creative Practice*, 2nd edn., London: Sage.

Proctor, B. and Ditton, A. (1989) 'How counselling can add value to organisations', *Employee Counselling Today*, 1, 2: 3–6.

Prouty, A. (2001) 'Experiencing feminist family therapy supervision', *Journal of Feminist Family Therapy*, 12, 4: 171–203.

Quarto, C.J. (2003) 'Supervisors' and supervisees' perceptions of control and conflict in counseling supervision', *The Clinical Supervisor*, 21, 2: 21–37.

Rabinowitz, F.E., Heppner, P.P. and Roehlke, H.J. (1986) 'Descriptive study of process and outcome variables of supervision over time', *Journal of Counseling Psychology*, 33, 3: 292–300.

Rapp, H. (1996) *Integrative Supervision: Inter subjective Assessment in a Reflective Learning Space*, London (private publication).

—— (2000) 'Working with difference: culturally competent supervision', in B. Lawton and C. Feltham (eds) *Taking Supervision Forward: Enquiries and Trends in Counselling and Psychotherapy*, London: Sage.

Ray, D. and Altekruse, M. (2000) 'Effectiveness of group supervision versus combined group and individual supervision', *Counselor Education and Supervision*, 40, 1: 19–30.

Reising, G.N. and Daniels, M.H. (1983) 'A study of Hogan's model of counselor development and supervision', *Journal of Counseling Psychology*, 30, 2: 235–44.

Remocker, A.J. and Sherwood, E.T. (1999) *Actions Speak Louder: A Handbook of Structured Group Techniques*, 6th edn., Toronto: Churchill Livingstone.

Renfro-Michel, E.L. and Sheperis, C.J. (2009) 'The relationship between counseling supervisee attachment orientation and perceived bond with supervisor', *The Clinical Supervisor*, 28, 2: 141–54.

Rennie, D.L. (1994) 'Clients' accounts of resistance in counselling: a qualitative analysis', *Canadian Journal of Counselling*, 28, 1: 43–57.

Rice, L.N. (1980) 'A client-centred approach to the supervision of psychotherapy', in A.K. Hess (ed.) *Psychotherapy Supervision: Theory, Research and Practice*, New York, NY: John Wiley & Sons.

Richardson, S. (2009) 'Supervision of work with trauma and dissociation', *Interact*, 9, 2: 28–33.

Ricketts, T. and Donohoe, G. (2000) 'Clinical supervision in cognitive behavioural psychotherapy', in B. Lawton and C. Feltham (eds) *Taking Supervision Forward: Enquiries and Trends in Counselling and Psychotherapy*, London: Sage.

Riggs, S.A. and Bretz, K.M. (2006) 'Attachment processes in the supervisory relationship: an exploratory investigation', *Professional Psychology: Research and Practice*, 37, 5: 558–66.

Robson, M. and Whelan, L. (2006) 'Virtue out of necessity? Reflections on a telephone supervision relationship', *Counselling and Psychotherapy Research*, 6, 3: 202–8.

Rodgers, A. (2011) 'Supervision through conversation: being seen, being real', in R. Shohet (ed.) *Supervision as Transformation: A Passion for Learning*, London: Jessica Kingsley.

Rogers, C.R. (1951) *Client Centred Therapy: Its Current Practice, Implications and Theory*, London: Constable.

—— (1961) *On Becoming a Person: A Therapist's View of Psychotherapy*, London: Constable.

—— (1978) *On Personal Power*, London: Constable.

Rønnestad, M.H. and Skovholt, T.M. (2013) *The Developing Practitioner: Growth and Stagnation of Therapists and Counselors*, New York, NY: Routledge.

Rosenfield, M. (2012) 'Telephone counselling', in C. Feltham and I. Horton (eds) *The Sage Handbook of Counselling and* Psychotherapy, 3rd edn., London: Sage.

Roth, A. (2013) 'Commentary on Owen-Pugh and Symons', *Counselling and Psychotherapy Research*, 13, 2: 136–7.

Roth, A.D. and Pilling, S. (2008) 'A competence framework for the supervision of psychological therapies': http://www.ucl.ac.uk/clinical-psychology/CORE/supervision_framework.htm (accessed 2nd June 2013).

Rothschild, B. (2000) *The Body Remembers: The Psychophysiology of Trauma and Trauma Treatment*, New York, NY: Norton.

Rowell, P.C. (2010) 'Group supervision of individual counselling', in N. Ladany and L. Bradley (eds) *Counselor Supervision*, 4th edn., Philadelphia, PA: Routledge.

Russell, J. (1996) 'Sexual exploitation in counselling', in R. Bayne, I. Horton and J. Bimrose (eds) *New Directions in Counselling*, London: Routledge.

Ryan, S. (2004) *Vital Practice: Stories from the Healing Arts: The Homeopathic and Supervisory Way*, Portland, OR: Sea Change.

Ryde, J. (2000) 'Supervising across difference', *International Journal of Psychotherapy*, 5, 1: 37–48.

—— (2011a) 'Culturally sensitive supervision', in C. Lago (ed.) *The Handbook of Transcultural Counselling and Psychotherapy*, Maidenhead: Open University Press.

—— (2011b) 'Supervising psychotherapists who work with asylum seekers and refugees: a space to reflect where feelings are unbearable', in R. Shohet (ed.) *Supervision as Transformation: A Passion for Learning*, London: Jessica Kingsley.

Rye, J. (2009) 'The supervisor I want to be', *Therapy Today*, 20, 7: 28–30.

Safran, J.D. and Muran, J.C. (2001) 'A relational approach to training and supervision in cognitive psychotherapy', *Journal of Cognitive Psychotherapy* 15, 1: 3–15.

Sanders, P. (2007) *Using Counselling Skills on the Telephone and in Computer-Mediated Communication*, 3rd edn., Ross-on-Wye: PCCS Books.

Sanderson, C. (2012) 'Talking point: hear them and believe them', *Therapy Today*, 23, 9: 8.

Sarkar, S. P. (2004) 'Boundary violation and sexual exploitation in psychiatry and psychotherapy: a review', *Advances in Psychiatric Treatment*, 10: 312–20.

Sarnat, J. (1992) 'Supervision in relationship: resolving the teach-treat controversy in psychoanalytical supervision', *Psychoanalytic Psychology*, 9, 3: 387–403.

Savin-Baden, M. (2003) *Facilitating Problem-Based Learning: Illuminating Perspectives*, Maidenhead: Society for Research into Higher Education and Open University Press.

Scaife, J. (2008) *Supervision in Clinical Practice: A Practitioner's Guide*, 2nd edn., London: Routledge.

—— (2010) *Supervising the Reflective Practitioner: An Essential Guide to Theory and Practice*, London: Routledge.

Schneewind, J.B. (1993) 'Modern moral philosophy', in P. Singer (ed.) *A Companion to Ethics*, Oxford: Blackwell.

Schön, D. A. (1983) *The Reflective Practitioner: How Professionals Think in Action*, New York, NY: Basic Books.

Schutz, W. (1979) *Profound Simplicity*, London: Turnstone Books.

Searles, H.F. (1955) 'The informational value of the supervisor's emotional experience', *Collected Papers on Schizophrenia and Related Subjects*, London: Hogarth Press.

—— (1962) 'Problems of Psychoanalytic Supervision', in J. H. Masserman, *Psychoanalytic Education: Science and Psychoanalysis, vol. 5*, New York: Grune & Stratton.

Selekman, M. and Todd, T. (1995) 'Co-creating a context for change in the supervisory system: the solution-focused supervision model', *Journal of Systemic Therapies*, 14, 3: 21–33.

Shainberg, D. (1983) 'Teaching therapists how to be with their clients', in J. Welwood (ed.) *Awakening the Heart*, Boulder, CO: New Science Library.

Sharratt Wise, P., Lowery, S. and Silverglade, L. (1989) 'Personal counseling for counselors in training: guidelines for supervisors', *Counselor Education and Supervision*, 28, 4: 326–37.

Shaw, R. (2003) *The Embodied Psychotherapist: The Therapist's Body Story*, Hove: Brunner-Routledge.

Shohet, R. (ed.) (2008) *Passionate Supervision*, London: Jessica Kingsley.

—— (2011a) 'Another way of knowing: emptying our minds and undoing projections – a life skill', in R. Shohet (ed.) *Supervision as Transformation: A Passion for Learning*, London: Jessica Kingsley.

—— (ed.) (2011b) *Supervision as Transformation: A Passion for Learning*, London: Jessica Kingsley.

Shulman, L. (2006) 'The clinical supervisor-practitioner working alliance: a parallel process', *The Clinical Supervisor*, 24, 1–2: 23–47.

Sinason, V. (ed.) (2002) *Attachment, Trauma and Multiplicity: Working with Dissociative Identity Disorder*, Hove: Brunner-Routledge.

Sinason, V. and Svensson, A. (1994) 'Going through the fifth window: "other cases rest on Sundays. This one didn't"', in V. Sinanson (ed.) *Treating Survivors of Satanist Abuse*, London: Routledge.

Singer, P. (ed.) (1993) *A Companion to Ethics*, Oxford: Blackwell.

Sloan, G. (2005) 'Clinical supervision: beginning the supervisory relationship', *British Journal of Nursing*, 14, 17: 918–23.

Smith, A.J., Kleijn, W.C. and Hutschemaekers, G.J. (2007) 'Therapist reactions in self-experienced difficult situations: an exploration', *Counselling and Psychotherapy Research*, 7, 1: 34–41.

Smith-Adcock, S., Scholl, M.B, Wittman, S., Tucker, C. and Graham, M.A. (2010) 'Using expressive arts in counseling supervision', in J. Culbreth and L. Brown (eds) *State of the Art in Clinical Supervision*, New York, NY: Routledge.

Smith-Pickard, P. (2009) 'Sexuality in supervision', *Therapy Today*, 20, 2: 28–31.

Smythe, E.A., MacCulloch, T. and Charmley, R. (2009) 'Professional supervision: trusting the wisdom that comes', *British Journal of Guidance and Counselling*, 37, 1: 17–25.

Snipe, R.M. (1988) 'Ethical issues in the assessment and treatment of a rational suicidal client', *The Counseling Psychologist*, 16, 1: 128–38.

Sommer, C.A., Derrick, E.C., Bourgeois, M.D., Ingene, D.H., Yang, J.W. and Justice, C.A. (2009) 'Multicultural connections: using stories to transcend cultural boundaries in supervision, *Journal of Multicultural Counseling and Development*, 37, 4: 206–18.

Stafford, D.E. (2008) 'Supervision – the grown-up relationship?', *Therapy Today*, 19, 9: 38–40.

Stainsby, K. (2009) 'Playing at supervision', *Therapy Today*, 20, 5: 35–7.

Stark, M.D., Frels, R.K. and Garza, Y. (2011) 'The use of sandtray in solution-focused supervision', *The Clinical Supervisor*, 30, 2: 277–90.

Starr, F., Ciclitira, K., Marzano, L., Brunswick, N. and Costa, A. (2013) 'Comfort and challenge: a thematic analysis of female clinicians' experiences of supervision', *Psychology and Psychotherapy: Theory, Research and Practice*, 86: 334–51.

Sterba, R. (1934) 'The fate of the ego in analytic therapy', *International Journal of Psychoanalysis*, 15: 117–26.

Sterner, W. R. (2009) 'Influence of the supervisory working alliance on supervisee work satisfaction and work-related stress', *Journal of Mental Health Counseling*, 31, 1: 249–63.

Stewart, I. (2007) *Transactional Analysis Counselling in Action*, 3rd edn., London: Sage.

Stockton, R. and Morran, D.K. (1982) 'Review and perspective of critical dimensions in therapeutic small group research', in G.M. Gazda (ed.) *Basic Approaches to Group Psychotherapy and Group Counselling*, 3rd edn., Springfield, IL: Thomas.

Stokes, J. (2009) 'Boundaries: separateness, merger, mutuality', in D. Mathers *Vision and Supervision: Jungian and Post-Jungian Perspectives*, Hove: Routledge.

Stoltenberg, C. and Delworth, U. (1987) *Supervising Counsellors and Therapists: A Developmental Approach,* San Francisco, CA: Jossey-Bass.

Stoltenberg C.D. and McNeill, B.W. (2010) *IDM Supervision: An Integrative Developmental Model for Supervising Counselors and Therapists*, 3rd edn., New York, NY: Routledge.

Stoltenberg, C.D., McNeill, B.W. and Crethar, H.C. (1994) 'Changes in supervision as counselors and therapists gain experience: a review', *Professional Psychology: Research and Practice*, 25, 4: 416–49.

Stoltenberg, C.D., McNeill, B.W. and Delworth, U. (1998) *IDM Supervision: An Integrated Developmental Model for Supervising Counselors and Therapists*, San Francisco, CA: Jossey-Bass.

Storr, A. (1990) *The Art of Psychotherapy*, 2nd edn., Oxford: Butterworth Heinemann.

Strong, M. (2000) *A Bright Red Scream*, London: Virago.

Sturm, D.C., Presbury, J. and Echterling, L.G. (2012) 'The elements: a model of mindful supervision, *Journal of Creativity in Mental Health*, 7, 3: 222–32.

Swenson E.V. (1987) 'Legal liability for a patient's suicide', *The Journal of Psychiatry & Law*, 14, 3: 409–34.

Syme, G. (2006) 'Fetters or freedom: dual relationships in counselling', *International Journal for the Advancement of Counselling*, 28, 1: 57–69.

Szymanski , D.M. (2003) 'The feminist supervision scale: a rational/theoretical approach', *Psychology of Women Quarterly*, 27, 3: 221–32.

Tamborski, M., Brown, R.P. and Chowning, K. (2012) 'Self-serving bias or simply serving the self? Evidence for a dimensional approach to narcissism', *Personality and Individual Differences*, 52, 8: 942–6.

Taylor, B.A., Hernández, P., Deri, A., Rankin, P.R. and Siegel, A. (2006) 'Integrating diversity dimensions in supervision: perspectives of ethnic minority AAMFT approved supervisors', *The Clinical Supervisor*, 25, 1–2: 3–21.

Tehrani, N. (2007) 'The cost of caring – the impact of secondary trauma on assumptions, values and beliefs', *Counselling Psychology Quarterly*, 20, 4: 325–9.

Teyber, E. (2000) *Interpersonal Process in Psychotherapy: A Relational Approach*, Belmont, CA: Brooks/Cole Wadsworth.

Thomas, J.T. (2007) 'Informed consent through contracting for supervision: minimizing risks, enhancing benefits', *Professional Psychology: Research and Practice*, 38, 3: 221–31.

Ticho, E.A. (1972) 'Termination of psychoanalysis: treatment goals, life goals', *Psychoanalytic Quarterly*, 44: 315–33.

Toporek, R.L., Ortega-Villalobos, L. and Pope-Davis, D.B. (2004) 'Critical incidents in multicultural supervision: exploring supervisees' and supervisors' experiences', *Journal of Multicultural Counseling and Development*, 32, 2: 66–83.

Townend, M. and Wood, W. (2007) 'E-learning the art of supervision', *Therapy Today*, 18, 6: 42–4.

Townend, M. and Wood, W. (2009) 'Online learning and teaching of supervision of counselling and psychotherapy', in P. Henderson (ed.) *Supervisor Training: Issues and Approaches*, London: Karnac.

Tracey, T.J., Ellickson, J.L. and Sherry, P. (1989) 'Reactance in relation to different supervisory environments and counselor development', *Journal of Counseling Psychology*, 36, 3: 336–44.

Tripp, E. (1988) *Dictionary of Classical Mythology*, London: Collins.

Tuckman, B. and Jensen, M. (1977) 'Stages of small group development revisited', *Group and Organisational Studies*, 2, 4: 419–27.

Tudor, K. and Worrall, M. (eds) (2004) *Freedom to Practice: Person-Centred Approaches to Supervison*, London: PCCS Books.

—— (2007) *Freedom to Practice Volume II: Developing Person-Centred Approaches to Supervision*, London: PCCS Books.

Tune, D. (2001) 'Is touch a valid therapeutic intervention? Early returns from a qualitative study of therapists' views', *Counselling and Psychotherapy Research*, 1, 3: 167–71.

—— (2005) 'Dilemmas concerning the ethical use of touch in psychotherapy', in N. Totton (ed.) *New Dimensions in Body Psychotherapy*, Maidenhead: Open University Press.

Turkus, J.A. (2013) 'The shaping and integration of a trauma therapist', *Journal of Trauma and Dissociation*, 14, 1: 1–10.

Turner, E. (2010) 'Coaches' views on the relevance of unconscious dynamics to executive coaching', *Coaching: An International Journal of Theory, Research & Practice*, 3, 1: 12–29.

Turpin, G. and Wheeler, S. (2011) 'IAPT supervision guidance': http://www.iapt.nhs.uk/silo/files/iapt-supervision-guidance-revised-march-2011.pdf (accessed 2nd June 2013).

UK Gov (2010) 'Equality Act': http://www.legislation.gov.uk/ukpga/2010/15/contents (accessed 5th June 2013).

Uphoff, A. (2008) 'Touch and the therapeutic relationship: shifting a paradigm', in S. Haugh and S. Paul (eds) *The Therapeutic Relationship: Perspectives and Themes*, Ross-on-Wye: PCCS Books.

Vallance, K. (2005) 'Exploring counsellor perceptions of the impact of counselling supervision on clients', *Counselling and Psychotherapy Research*, 5, 2: 107–10.

Van der Hart, O., Nijenhuis, E. and Steele, K. (2006) *The Haunted Self: Structural Dissociation and the Treatment of Chronic Traumatization*, New York, NY: Norton.

Van der Veer, G. (1998) *Counselling and Therapy with Refugees and Victims of Trauma: Psychological Problems of Victims of War, Torture and Repression*, 2nd edn., Chichester: Wiley.

Van Ooijen, E. (2000) *Clinical Supervision: A Practical Guide*, Edinburgh: Churchill Livingstone.

—— (2003) *Clinical Supervision Made Easy*, Edinburgh: Churchill Livingstone.

Veach, P.M. (2001) 'Conflict and counterproductivity in supervision – when relationships are less than ideal: comment on Nelson and Friedlander (2001) and Grey et al. (2001)', *Journal of Counseling Psychology*, 48, 4: 396–400.

Villas-Boas Bowen, M. (1986) 'Personality difference and person-centred supervision', *Person Centred Review*, 1, 3: 291–309.

Wallin, D. (2007) *Attachment in Psychotherapy*, New York: Guildford Press.

Walsh, B.B., Gillespie, C.K., Greer, J.M. and Eanes, B.E. (2003) 'Influence of dyadic mutuality on counselor trainee willingness to self-disclose clinical mistakes to supervisors', *The Clinical Supervisor*, 21, 2: 83–98.

Watkins, C.E., Jr. (ed.) (1997) *Handbook of Psychotherapy Supervision*, New York, NY: Wiley.

Watkins, C.E., Jr. (1999) 'The beginning psychotherapy supervisor: how can we help?', *The Clinical Supervisor*, 18, 2: 63–72.

—— (2011) 'Does psychotherapy supervision contribute to patient outcomes? Considering thirty years of research', *The Clinical Supervisor*, 30, 2: 235–56.

—— (2012a) 'On demoralization, therapist identity development, and persuasion and healing in psychotherapy supervision', *Journal of Psychotherapy Integration*, 22, 3: 187–205.

—— (2012b) 'Educating psychotherapy supervisors', *American Journal of Psychotherapy*, 66, 3: 279–307.

—— (2013) 'On psychotherapy supervision competencies in an international perspective: a short report', *International Journal of Psychotherapy*, 17, 1: 78–83.

Weaks, D. (2002) 'Unlocking the secrets of "good supervision": a phenomenological exploration of experienced counsellors' perceptions of good supervision', *Counselling and Psychotherapy Research*, 2, 1: 33–9.

Webb, A. (2000) 'What makes it difficult for the supervisee to speak?', in B. Lawton and C. Feltham (eds) *Taking Supervision Forward: Enquiries and Trends in Counselling and Psychotherapy*, London: Sage.

Webb, A. and Wheeler, S. (1998) 'How honest do counsellors dare to be in the supervisory relationship? An exploratory study', *British Journal of Guidance and Counselling*, 26, 4: 509–24.

Weiner, J., Mizen, R. and Duckham, J. (eds) (2003) *Supervising and Being Supervised: A Practice in Search of a Theory*, Basingstoke: Palgrave.

Weld, N. (2012) *A Practical Guide to Transformative Supervision for the Helping Professions: Amplifying Insight*, London: Jessica Kingsley.

Welfare, L.E. (2010) 'Evaluation in supervision', in N. Ladany and L.J. Bradley (eds) *Counselor Supervision*, 4th edn., New York, NY: Routledge.

West, W. (2010) 'Supervising counsellors and psychotherapists who work with trauma: a Delphi study', *British Journal of Guidance and Counselling*, 3, 4: 409–30.

West, W. and Clark, V. (2004) 'Learnings from a qualitative study into counselling supervision: listening to supervisor and supervisee', *Counselling and Psychotherapy Research*, 4, 2: 20–6.

Wheeler, S. (ed.) (2006) *Difference and Diversity in Counselling: Contemporary Psychodynamic Perspectives*, Basingstoke: Palgrave Macmillan.

—— (2007) 'What shall we do with the wounded healer? The supervisor's dilemma', *Psychodynamic Practice: Individuals, Groups and Organizations*, 13, 3: 245–56.

Wheeler, S. and King, D. (2000) 'Do counselling supervisors want or need to have their supervision supervised? An exploratory study', *British Journal of Guidance and Counselling*, 28, 2, 279–90.

—— (2001) 'Supervision for supervisors: what are the implications for responsibility?', in S. Wheeler and D. King (eds) *Supervising Counsellors: Issues of Responsibility*, London: Sage.

Wheeler, S. and Richards, K. (2007) 'The impact of clinical supervision on counsellors and therapists, their practice and their clients: a systematic review of the literature', *Counselling and Psychotherapy Research*, 7, 1: 54–65.

Wheeler, S., Aveline, M. and Barkham, M. (2011) 'Practice-based supervision research: a network of researchers using a common toolkit', *Counselling and Psychotherapy Research*, 11, 2: 88–96.

Whiston, S.C. and Emerson, S. (1989) 'Ethical implications for supervisors in counseling of trainees', *Counselor Education and Supervision*, 28, 4: 318–25.

Whitaker, D.S. (1985) *Using Groups to Help People*, London: Routledge & Kegan Paul.

White, V. and Queener, J. (2003) 'Supervisor and supervisee attachments and social provisions related to the supervisory working alliance', *Counselor Education and Supervision*, 42, 3: 203–18.

Whitmore, J. (2009) *Coaching for Performance*, 4th edn., London: Nicholas Brealey Publishing.

Wilbur, M.P., Roberts-Wilbur, J., Hart, G.M., Morris, J.R. and Betz, R.L. (1994) 'Structured group supervision (SGS): a pilot study', *Counselor Education and Supervision*, 33, 4: 262–79.

Wiley, M.O. and Ray, P.B. (1986) 'Counseling supervision by developmental level', *Journal of Counseling Psychology*, 33, 4: 439–45.

Wilkins, P. (1997) *Personal and Professional Development for Counsellors*, London: Sage.

Williams, A. (1995) *Visual and Active Supervision: Roles, Focus, Technique*, New York, NY: Norton.

Wilmot, J. (2011) 'If you want to go faster, go alone. If you want to go further, go together: work as transformation through supervision', in R. Shohet (ed.) *Supervision as Transformation: A Passion for Learning*, London: Jessica Kingsley.

Wilmot, J. and Shohet, R. (1985) 'Paralleling in the supervision process', *Self and Society: European Journal of Humanistic Psychology*, 13, 2: 86–91.

Wilson, J.P. and Droždek, B. (eds) (2004) *Broken Spirits: The Treatment of Traumatized Asylum Seekers, Refugees, and War and Torture Victims*, New York: Brunner-Routledge.

Winter, M. and Holloway, E.L. (1991) 'Relation of trainee experience, conceptual level, and supervisor approach to selection of audiotaped counseling passages', *The Clinical Supervisor*, 9, 2: 87–103.

Worthen, V.E. and Lambert, M.J. (2007) 'Outcome oriented supervision: advantages of adding systematic client tracking to supportive consultations', *Counselling and Psychotherapy Research*, 7, 1: 48–53.

Worthington, E.L. (1987) 'Changes in supervision as counselors and supervisors gain experience: a review', *Professional Psychology: Research and Practice*, 18, 3: 189–208.

Wosket, V. (1999) *The Therapeutic Use of Self: Counselling Practice, Supervision and Research*, London: Routledge.

—— (2000a) 'Integration and eclecticism in supervision', in S. Palmer and R. Woolfe (eds) *Integrative and Eclectic Counselling and Psychotherapy*, London: Sage.

—— (2000b) 'The interface between supervision and therapy in the supervision of experienced practitioners' ('Taking supervision forward: a roundtable of views'), in B. Lawton and C. Feltham (eds) *Taking Supervision Forward: Enquiries and Trends in Counselling and Psychotherapy*, London: Sage.

—— (2006) *Egan's Skilled Helper Model: Developments and Applications in Counselling*, London: Routledge.

—— (2009) 'Relational ethics in supervision', in L. Gabriel and R. Casemore (eds) *Relational Ethics in Practice: Narratives from Counselling and Psychotherapy*, London: Brunner-Routledge.

Wosket, V. and Page, S. (2001) 'The Cyclical Model of counsellor supervision: a container for creativity and chaos', in M. Carroll and M. Tholstrup (eds) *Integrative Approaches to Supervision*, London: Jessica Kingsley.

Yalom, I. (1985) *The Theory and Practice of Group Psychotherapy*, 3rd edn., New York, NY: Basic Books.

Yardley-Matwiejczuk, K.M. (1997) *Role Play: Theory and Practice*, London: Sage.

Young, J.S. and Borders, L.D (1999) 'The intentional use of metaphor in counseling supervision', *The Clinical Supervisor*, 18, 1: 137–49.

Young, T.L., Lambie, G.W., Hutchinson, T. and Thurston-Dyer, J. (2011) 'The integration of reflectivity in developmental supervision: implications for clinical supervisors', *The Clinical Supervisor*, 30, 1: 1–18.

Youngson, S.C. (1994) 'Ritual abuse: the personal and professional cost for workers', in V. Sinanson (ed.) *Treating Survivors of Satanist Abuse*, London: Routledge.

Yourman, D.B. (2003) 'Trainee disclosure in psychotherapy supervision: the impact of shame', *Journal of Clinical Psychology*, 59, 5: 601–9.

Zarbock, G., Drews, M., Bodansky, A. and Dahme, B. (2009) 'The evaluation of supervision: construction of brief questionnaires for the supervisor and the supervisee', *Psychotherapy Research*, 19, 2: 194–204.

Index

Note: Page numbers followed by 'f' refer to figures, followed by 'n' refer to notes and followed by 't' refer to tables.

Robson, M. 10, 11
Rogers, C.R. 2, 24, 64
role: boundaries 57–8; play 113; play, in
    groups 149
Rønnestad, M.H. 2, 7–8, 12, 31, 86, 116,
    140, 195, 198, 235
Roth, A. 16, 170, 228
Ryan, S. 226
Ryde, J. 137, 175, 199, 201, 203, 209

S
safety 88
Sarnat, J. 1, 9, 27, 30, 93, 158, 168, 171,
    185, 210, 213, 223
satisfaction: research into 62, 80, 185, 218;
    supervisee 80, 81–2, 105–6, 185,
    218–19
Scaife, J. 8, 35, 42, 136, 236, 243
scapegoating 147
Schofield, M. 126, 158, 159, 194
Schön, D.A. 243
Self and Other 189
self-disclosure: in groups 154; providing a
    climate for 70–1; research into 62–3, 64,
    89, 110, 171–2; of sensitive material 55,
    56, 62–3, 171–2; of supervisees 89–90,
    171–2; of supervisors 50, 64, 90, 110,
    111–12, 128, 223, 234–5
self-doubt 69–70
self-efficacy research 13–14
self-respect 157–8
self, use of 195–6, 215–18, 224–6
sensitive material, disclosing of 55, 56,
    62–3, 171–2; research into 62–3
'seven-eyed' model 36–7, 38
sexual involvement 57
sexuality 182–3; case study 186–7, 190–1
'shadow' side of supervisee 179, 198;
    containing 104–5
Shah, J.C. 63
Shainberg, D. 102
shame in supervision 153, 198–9, 220
Shaw, R. 218, 219
Shohet, R. 8, 9, 31, 36, 38, 136, 146, 173,
    210, 242
Sinason, V. 201, 202, 203
Six Category Intervention Analysis 82–3
'Skilled Helper' model 114
skills: deficit 68; study of supervisory 27
Skovholt, T.M. 2, 7–8, 12, 31, 86, 116,
    140, 195, 198, 235
Smith, A.J. 155
Smith, M.S. 72, 191

Smith. N. 243, 250, 251
Smith-Pickard, P. 215
Smythe, E.A. 97, 98
social and economic background,
    differences in 178
social constructivist approaches to
    supervision 12
solution-focused approach 72, 82, 191
somatic: counter-transference 203;
    reactions in supervision 219
space stage 40f, 41–2, 86–106, 87f;
    affirmation 105–6; containment 103–5,
    206–9; in group supervision 146–50;
    supervising practitioners outside
    psychotherapy 243–4, 248
space stage: challenge 100–3; by
    confirmation 101–2; of impact of
    supervisee's behaviour on client 102–3;
    to supervisee's expectations of client
    103; to therapist to listen to indirect
    communication 102
space stage: collaboration 88–96, 91f;
    basic affective relationship 88, 89, 90–1,
    91f; components of supervisory
    relationship 88–9, 91f, 100; counter-
    transference 94; non-disclosure by
    supervisee 89–90; parallel processes
    94–6; recommended best practice for
    supervisors 89–90; reflective alliance
    91, 91f, 92; research into 88–90, 94;
    transference 93–4;
    unconscious/dissociated process 92–3;
    and 'what is not said' in supervision
    90
space stage: investigation 96–100;
    metaphor and imagery, playing with
    98–100; play in supervision 97–8;
    research into 98
Stainsby, K. 97
Starr, F. 62, 80, 81
starting to supervise 32–3
Steele, K. 221, 222
Stoltenberg, S.C. 4, 5–6t, 7, 36, 101, 110,
    116
stress 62, 69
styles, supervisory: developing 79–80,
    235; 'lousy' supervisor traits 80–1;
    research into 16, 80–2
success, acknowledging and consolidating
    71–2
suicide risk 51, 84–5, 160–1, 170–1
summative assessment 131–3
Sundin, E.C. 153

Lightning Source UK Ltd.
Milton Keynes UK